Great Relationships and Sex Education

Great Relationships and Sex Education is an innovative and accessible guide for educators who work with young people to create and deliver Relationships and Sex Education (RSE) programmes. Developed by two leading experts in the field, it contains hundreds of creative activities and session ideas that can be used both by experienced RSE educators and those new to RSE.

Drawing on best practice and up-to-date research from around the world, *Great RSE* provides fun, challenging and critical ways to address key contemporary issues and debates in RSE. Activity ideas are organised around key areas of learning in RSE: Relationships, Gender and Sexual Equality, Bodies, Sex and Sexual Health. There are activities on consent, pleasure, friendships, assertiveness, contraception, fertility and so much more. All activities are LGBT+ inclusive and designed to encourage critical thinking and consideration of how digital technologies play out in young people's relationships and sexual lives.

This book offers:

- Session ideas that can be adapted to support you to be creative and innovative in your approach and that allow you to respond to the needs of the young people that you work with.
- Learning aims, time needed for delivery, suggested age groups to work with and instructions on how to deliver each activity, as well as helpful tips and key points for educators to consider in each chapter.
- Activities to help create safe and inclusive spaces for delivering RSE and involve young people in curriculum design.
- A chapter on 'concluding the learning' with ideas on how to involve young people in evaluating and reflecting on the curriculum and assessing their learning.
- A list of recommended resources, websites, online training courses and links providing further information about RSE.

With over 200 activities to choose from, this book is an essential resource for teachers, school nurses, youth workers, sexual health practitioners and anyone delivering RSE to young people aged 11–25.

Alice Hoyle is an expert relationship and sex education teacher and youth worker, specialising in supporting practitioners via training, resources and online communities.

Ester McGeeney is a youth worker and researcher who specialises in conducting youth centred research on relationships and sexualities and in using research to create innovative training and education materials.

"Thanks to all the ideas in this book I'm really enjoying teaching RSE and I can see how much the young people are loving it too. The detailed notes and pointers are really helpful for me, especially when tackling tricky topics like gender. I'm advising every teacher I know to go get a copy!"

– **Bryden Joy,** Teacher

"*Great Relationships and Sex Education* has to be the go-to book for new and experienced practitioners who want to create an engaging, inclusive and empowering relationships and sexuality education curriculum. Every chapter carefully supports practitioners to develop awareness and confidence on a range of issues from consent to sexual identity with an impressive set of links to find out more about an area of learning or pedagogic technique. Packed with hundreds of interactive activities that can be adapted to any learning environment, this is one of the most comprehensive evidence-based resources from two of the most experienced leading scholar-practitioners in the field."

– **Emma Renold,** Professor of Childhood Studies, Cardiff University

Great Relationships and Sex Education

200+ Activities for Educators Working with Young People

Alice Hoyle and
Ester McGeeney

Routledge
Taylor & Francis Group

LONDON AND NEW YORK

First published 2020
by Routledge
2 Park Square, Milton Park, Abingdon, Oxon OX14 4RN

and by Routledge
52 Vanderbilt Avenue, New York, NY 10017

Routledge is an imprint of the Taylor & Francis Group, an informa business

British Library Cataloguing-in-Publication Data
A catalogue record for this book is available from the British Library

Library of Congress Cataloging-in-Publication Data
A catalog record has been requested for this book

ISBN: 978-0-8153-9361-0 (hbk)
ISBN: 978-0-8153-9363-4 (pbk)
ISBN: 978-1-351-18827-2 (ebk)

Typeset in Helvetica
by Newgen Publishing UK

Visit the eResources: www.routledge.com/9780815393634

Dedication

This book is dedicated to all the young people who want, need and deserve great Relationships and Sex Education. We hope this book makes a difference to the educators in your life and that the activities make a difference to you.

Contents

CHAPTER 1
Introduction

Who, what and why

This is a book of activity ideas for developing Relationships and Sex Education (RSE) programmes with and for young people. It is aimed at all educators who work with young people, including teachers, youth workers, school nurses, professional relationship and sex educators, and all the rest of us who work with young people as part of our roles to develop and deliver RSE programmes. There are ideas in this book for those who are new to RSE and for those who have been designing and delivering RSE programmes for years.

We are both educators, living and working in the UK. Alice is a qualified teacher with a MSc. In Sexual Health Education. She currently works as a youth worker and RSE specialist writing, delivering and training on a wide range of RSE programmes from early years to post 16 and parents. Ester is a trained youth worker and social researcher with a PhD entitled *Good Sex?: Young people, sexual pleasure and sexual health.* Ester researches young people's sexual and digital cultures and writes, trains and facilitates RSE programmes across the UK.

Over the past five years Alice and Ester have both worked with researchers at the University of Exeter on the *Sex and History* project to develop education resources that use historical objects as the starting point for conversations about sexuality, relationships, gender and the body. Alice has worked with Justin Hancock to develop the *DO...RSE* online resources which encourage educators to be reflective of their own practice and clarify their own values before starting to develop or deliver an RSE curriculum. Ester has spent many years delivering education and training around including pleasure in RSE programmes, including developing online training resources as part of the *Brook Learn* training modules. Ester has been working in Wales for the past two years, supporting Professor Emma Renold at Cardiff University in her work developing a new framework for RSE curriculum in Wales that is underpinned by rights, gender equity, inclusivity, creativity, empowerment and co-production. All of these projects are strongly reflected in this book, not just in the activities we use and resources that we recommend but in the ethos, approach and core values that underpin all the activities in the book.

In addition to those mentioned earlier, this book draws on our own experiences of working alongside some of the best educators in the field. It includes new ideas that we have developed through our own practice as well as activities created and used by fantastic individuals and organisations around the world. There are also some old favourites that have been around in the RSE community for a long time and for good reason. We wrote this book to bring together all the great RSE ideas and resources we know of and collate them in one easy and accessible guide. We hope that this saves educators time searching online and offers new and creative ideas for RSE that are grounded in research, experiences and a set of key principles.

This book is written with UK educators in mind, although those in other parts of the world may want to use, adapt and develop the activity ideas. At the time of writing in the UK there is an increased national focus on RSE as governments in England and Wales have made the landmark decision to make RSE compulsory in all secondary schools (with Relationship Education becoming compulsory in English Primary schools and Relationship *and* Sexuality Education becoming compulsory in Welsh Primary schools). Also at this time governments in England, Scotland and Wales have been engaged in revising and updating the guidance on RSE. These changes are most welcome since the research evidence suggests that the quality and quantity of RSE in the UK has historically not been good enough. It has been too little, too late and too focussed on biology, reproduction and the negative *outcomes* of relationships and sex such as unwanted pregnancy, sexually transmitted infections, violence and abuse. Whilst these are all important issues to cover in RSE, research tells us that this happens at the expense of tackling key issues such as gender and sexual equality, positive relationships and sexual pleasure. We also know that RSE programmes fail to meet the needs of LGBT+ young people. Current national policy developments in the UK therefore present new opportunities to improve the quality and quantity of RSE and to ensure that all provision is inclusive, affirmative and rights based.

The research also tells us that what is needed to tackle the current gaps in RSE programmes is high quality professional training. We could not agree more. Our book is no replacement for good quality professional training and we would recommend that anyone delivering RSE has regular training, development and support. Where this isn't possible, we recommend seeking out peer support online or in your local area so that you can share ideas, get support and reflect on your practice with other educators. As a starting point you may want to complete the self reflection tool produced by *DO…RSE for schools*[1] which will enable you to unpack your own attitudes, values, knowledge and skills in delivering this subject. Throughout the book we also provide as much guidance and support as we could squeeze in and signpost to fantastic resources and organisations that can support your delivery. Some of the links we have included may age but we hope that the organisations and individuals who produce them will continue to keep their high quality and inspirational content up to date.

A note on research

There is a wealth of international research on RSE. Much of this consists of small- scale qualitative studies of young people's experiences of RSE within different social and cultural contexts and small, medium and large-scale surveys of young people's views and experiences of RSE. This research is often child and young person centred and seeks to put the experiences of children and young people at the heart of education policy and practice. There are also a number of international evaluations of RSE programmes that seek to ascertain the impact of RSE for children, young people and wider populations. Here the focus is often on the public health benefits of RSE, rather than the wider benefits and outcomes of RSE. There is a focus in the literature on the views and experiences of secondary age young people (or of young adults' views on their secondary education) and on education about sex and sexual health, rather than relationships. Internationally there is also scarce research on professional training for RSE. In the UK there is a focus on the delivery of RSE in England, with far less research conducted in the devolved nations.

The most authoritative source of evidence on sexual behaviours and attitudes in Britain is The National Survey of Sexual Attitudes and Lifestyles (NATSAL) which is a representative survey of over 15,000 people aged 16-74 in Britain. The survey is conducted every ten years allowing for longitudinal comparisons.[2] There is no equivalent evidence on relationships or the wider aspects of sexuality beyond sexual behaviours, sexual health and sexual attitudes.

Useful resources that provide a summary of recent research and that are free and accessible to educators without research training include:

- Two articles by Pandora Pound and colleagues that synthesise qualitative research on RSE:
  - Pound, P, Denford, S, Shucksmith, J, Tanton, C, Johnson, A, Owen, J, Hutten, R, Mohan, L, Bonell, C, Abraham, C & Campbell, R, (2017) 'What is best practice in sex and relationship education? A synthesis of evidence, including stakeholders' views'. BMJ Open, vol 7. https://bmjopen.bmj.com/content/7/5/e014791
  - Pound, P, Langford, R & Campbell, R, (2016) 'What do young people think about their school-based sex and relationship education?: A qualitative synthesis of young people's views and experiences'. BMJ Open, vol 6. https://bmjopen.bmj.com/content/6/9/e011329
- UNESCO (2018) *International Technical Guidance on Sexuality Education: An Evidence-Informed Approach*. (Revised edition.) (See *Useful resources* at the end of this book.) A summary of international evidence underpinning RSE as well as an example curriculum with eight concepts and corresponding topics and learning objectives.
- Renold, E & McGeeney, E (2017) *Informing the Future of the Sex and Relationships Education Curriculum in Wales*. A summary of recent evidence relating to RSE. There is a focus on Wales but this is relevant to educators working in England and all the devolved nations.
- The Sex Education Forum's evidence page provides summaries and links to up to date relevant research, with a focus on England.[3]

Great RSE is...

There are very many different ways of designing and facilitating Relationships and Sex Education programmes, based on different theoretical and philosophical approaches. Our approach to RSE is based on the following six principles which draw on an international body of research evidence and our own experiences of developing and delivering RSE and training other educators to do the same. For a more detailed exploration of these (and other) principles and the underpinning research evidence we recommend you read the freely available report by Emma Renold and Ester McGeeney, *Informing the Future of the Sex and Relationships Education Curriculum in Wales* (2017 – see *Useful resources*).

Co-produced with young people

A key feature of high quality RSE programmes is that they are designed and developed with young people. At a minimum this means asking young people what they are already learning (and remembering that learning about relationships and sex happens in many informal and formal settings – not just in curriculum time!), what else they would like to learn about and what issues and topics are important to them. The first chapter in this book (Chapter 2: *Creating safer spaces*) has some simple and creative ideas for how to do this. It also means creating spaces for young people to reflect on and evaluate their learning, providing you with valuable feedback for future programming. The last chapter of this book (Chapter 8: *Concluding the learning*) contains some quick fire and more in-depth ideas for how to do this.

Co-production also means seeing the young people that you work with as your fellow enquirers. Many of the activities in this book can be extended into small-scale research projects in which young people are encouraged to investigate their online and offline worlds and think critically about what they observe and find out. Working in this mode means that you do not need to have all the answers when it comes to relationships and sex and are discouraged from delivering RSE in a didactic manner. Rather you are the facilitator tasked with creating a safe and engaging learning environment in which young people can ask questions and pursue lines of enquiry that are important to them.

We know from the research that there is often a gap between young people's lived experiences of relationships and sex (the issues they face, the questions they have) and the content of RSE curriculums. One way of closing this gap is to ensure that we create opportunities to listen to young people and work with them to create a curriculum. Adopting an approach to RSE that is creative and critical involves asking young people to create and imagine the experiences, issues and scenarios explored in the curriculum. This helps ensure that discussions are rooted in young people's everyday experiences and that all young people see themselves and each other in what they are learning. It also helps move beyond what young people know and need to know to explore the social and historical contexts within which messages about relationships and sexuality are created and circulated.

Inclusive and critical

It is essential that all RSE programmes are inclusive. We know from the research that too often RSE focuses only on heterosexual relationships; for example, by delivering programmes that assume relationships always happen between a man and woman (they don't!), or that all sex can lead potentially to pregnancy (it can't! This is only the case if you have penis-in-vagina sex and there are *so* many other ways of having sex). This privileging of heterosexuality in RSE programmes reflects and contributes to the privilege given to heterosexuality in all areas of western society. RSE programmes are a great space to explore and challenge this inequity.

Being inclusive means, therefore, not only ensuring that we use language, case studies and scenarios that are inclusive of LGBT+ people (the ideas and resources in this book will help with this) but that we create spaces to think critically about privilege, power and equality. There are activity ideas to address some of these big concepts in Chapter 4: *Gender and sexual equality*, but we have also embedded a critical pedagogy throughout the book. Many of the activities contain questions for you to explore with your co-enquirers that aim to develop critical thinking skills and to connect RSE topics such as contraception, online safety and consent with questions of social justice. This means asking young people to consider what is just, fair and ethical.

Being inclusive also means that all young people see themselves and others reflected in the curriculum. This is part of ensuring that the curriculum reflects the lived experiences of all young people. This means not only recognising diversity and difference across the domains of sex, gender, sexuality and relationships, but exploring how these forms of difference interlink and intersect with others such as religion, (dis)ability and ethnicity. If this sounds like a tall order then always start with co-production. Young people will take you to the case studies, scenarios, role models, folk devils and images that they relate to and that feel relevant to them and those in their communities.

Rights based

International research states that the most effective RSE programmes are those that adopt a rights- and gender-based approach. This means situating your RSE programme within the United Nations on the Convention of the Rights of the Child (UNCRC) and ensuring that your curricula explores and enables these rights: for example, a child or young person's right to protection from violence, abuse or neglect; the right to an education that enables them to fulfil their potential; the right to be raised by, or have a relationship with, their parents; and the right to express their opinions and be listened to.

Young people's sexual and relationship rights are part of an evolving set of human rights that contribute to the freedom, equality, dignity and wellbeing of all people. A rights-based curriculum is the foundation for a curriculum that can be empowering and transformative. It seeks not just to impart knowledge to young people and create opportunities for them to develop new skills but to connect relationships and sexuality with questions of social justice, power and privilege, diversity and difference, equality and equity. These are all concepts that we explicitly address in activities in Chapter 4: *Gender and sexual equality*, but which underpin all the activities in this book.

Safe and ethical

Educators' number one priority in RSE sessions must be keeping participants safe. Many of the activities included in this book ask participants and educators to address social inequalities, confront ethical dilemmas and to address topics that may be considered sensitive or taboo. This can feel risky and uncomfortable, particularly if we are not used to having these conversations in our everyday lives and particularly given the unequal power relations that play out in any group context. To make this work possible, therefore, educators and participants need to work together to create as safe a learning environment as possible. This book starts with a chapter called *Creating safer spaces* which is dedicated to activities which aim to help educators and young people establish a safe enough working environment to do this week. This includes activities for creating a group agreement, building group relationships, reflecting on what it means to take risks within a group and creating LGBT+ inclusive spaces. We also close with a chapter that aims to help you close sessions safely with ideas for activities that involve checking in and reviewing the curriculum and reflecting on the learning environment.

We know that social inequalities play out in RSE sessions. We know that girls don't always feel safe in RSE lessons and worry about being called a 'slag' for speaking up about sex. We also know that LGBT+ young people experience bullying and discrimination in schools and are ignored or silenced through RSE curriculums. The activities in this book aim to address these inequalities rather than deliver RSE in spite of them! Adopting the critical, inclusive and creative approach that we advocate here, that starts with young people's experiences and the issues affecting their lives, will help you to do this. Given these inequalities, however, there are limits to how safe you can make your RSE sessions. We also need supportive colleagues, managers and institutions and robust policies and procedures for promoting equality and addressing inequalities at our places of work. We also need clear guidance, good resources, status and authority within our subject and a space to be reflective. These are all things that many of us work without. If this is the case for you, seek out the support of colleagues in the RSE community who can help you to keep yourself safe and to work in ways that are safe and ethical for others.

Throughout the book we talk about ethical relationships and ethical decision making. Our work is influenced by those who have written about and developed 'ethical' RSE curriculums, in particular Jenny Walsh, Moira Carmody and Sharon Lamb. Here the focus is on supporting young people to think through the ethics of personal choices and reflect critically on the moralities of the cultures and environments around them. The aim of an ethical RSE curriculum is not to establish hard and fast rules for what is and is not acceptable but to enable young people to become ethical decision makers and critical thinkers. This is a curriculum that is much more than health education. It is interdisciplinary and broad, drawing history and philosophy among other disciplines, to address human rights, consent and human dignity.

Creative and curious

Great RSE uses creative approaches that are interactive and engaging, designed to inspire young people's curiosity and imagination. Such an approach moves away from more traditional pedagogies that are based on the transmission of knowledge from teacher to learner. We know that these approaches are limited as they do not create space for critical thinking, interactivity and discussion or for exploring what this knowledge means in different cultural and relationship contexts. For example, the knowledge transmission model might involve an educator giving young people information about the law in relation to sexual consent and students listening to this information without being able to explore the grey and ambiguous areas of consent that are not covered by the legislation or the gendered inequalities that shape dynamics of power and control within relationships. See Chapter 6: *Sex* for examples of activities that were developed with young people to enable you to explore these difficult areas of consent.

Many of the activities in this book encourage you and your learners to get creative. Where possible we encourage you to fork out for good quality resources and creative materials. Having decent pens, brightly coloured post-it notes and good quality craft materials changes the feel of a learning environment and changes what feels possible. Further, having high quality resources helps give value to the often undervalued subject of RSE. Lots of the activities in this book invite you to work with groups of young people to create objects, posters, poems, songs, films, crafts and social media campaigns. Where possible we urge you to treat these outputs and objects as high value items. Showcase them at high profile events, keep them safe, show what they can do with your energy and the energy of your group behind you.

A creative approach to RSE is much more than including a creative or arts-based activity, such as role play or craft-making, within an RSE session (although you will find plenty of these in this book!). It is about an approach to teaching and learning that sees creativity as the key strategy for enabling successful learning. In particular, for critical thinking, problem solving and for imagining new ideas and ways of being in the world. There are activities in the book for remaining gendered power relations through writing science fiction plots, creating genital galleries to rethink body norms and beauty ideals and storyboarding the fertilisation journey to learn about fertility whilst rethinking gendered norms about aggressive sperm and passive eggs.

Creative approaches also allow you to use hypothetical scenarios and characters to discuss difficult or sensitive issues without compromising young people's confidentiality. You can also explore some of the emotional, sensual and sensory aspects of relationships and sexualities that are often left out of traditional approaches to RSE, but that are crucial to children and young people's decision making and negotiation of relationships, risk and sexuality.

Holistic and interdisciplinary

Great RSE is holistic. We advocate shifting away from a curriculum based on single issues or topics (e.g. a lesson on 'pornography', 'contraception', 'healthy relationships') towards developing a curriculum that integrates the issues that are important to young people around key themes or areas of learning. In schools this is best done as part of a whole school approach, linking together the RSE curriculum with pastoral support and school policy (how to respond to homophobia and support LGBT+ pupils), extra-curricular activities (a focus on women in sport at your sports day, a school play exploring friendship) school displays and any themes that you focus on in assemblies and/or form time.

RSE is fundamentally an interdisciplinary subject. Drama, Music, Literature, Science, History, Media Studies, Physical Education and Art are all fantastic disciplines within which to explore relationships and sexuality. Further, as you will see from the activities in this book, approaches from each of these disciplines are essential for delivering safe, critical and creative RSE programmes. We have flagged in some places where it may be possible to deliver an 'RSE' activity in a history or drama lesson but we hope that our book inspires you to think of RSE as a cross-curricular subject that can be woven into other programmes of learning as well as having its own standalone curriculum.

Although this book is divided by topic (Relationships, Sex, Bodies, Gender and Sexual Equality, Sexual Health), the activities are overlapping. To deliver high quality holistic RSE you will need to build a project, lesson or scheme of work using activities from across the chapters. It isn't possible, for example, to facilitate meaningful learning about contraception without first exploring what the human body looks and feels like, what we mean by 'sex', how to communicate and negotiate in relationships and how gender and sexual stereotypes shape our contraceptive decision making and choices. A segregated disciplinary RSE programme might explore these issues separately; contraception in science, communication in drama and gender norms in PSHE or Health and Wellbeing, for example. An interdisciplinary approach would bring disciplines and topics together. For example, by engaging in a feminist analysis of how 'sex' is often depicted in science textbooks as always heterosexual, reproductive and penetrative – starting when a man has an erection and ending when he ejaculates. This analysis could lead to discussions about scientific 'objectivity' and how what we know about sex, relationships and gender is always shaped by the social and historical context.

RSE curricula have been justifiably criticised for focussing too heavily on the risks of relationships and sex, such as unwanted pregnancy, sexually transmitted infections and sexual violence. Whilst these are important issues for many young people, they are addressed at the expense of exploring the positive and pleasurable aspects of relationships and sexuality such as desire and intimacy. This can leave young people with a good idea of what a 'bad' relationship looks like but with no sense of what it looks or feels like to enjoy relationships and bonds with others, or with no idea about what their own values and priorities are when it comes to relationships. Similarly, how can we expect the young people we work with to know what 'bad sex' is if they don't also know what 'good sex' is and that they have a right to enjoy their sexuality without harm?

Many of the activities in this book invite young people to explore some of the difficulties and challenges associated with relationships and sex – relationship conflict, oppressive gender norms, homophobia, sexually transmitted infections, sexual coercion. But the activities also engage young people in imagining otherwise and envisioning positive changes in their lives and communities. They also invite young people to explore the joys and pleasures of their own bodies and their relationships and experiences with others. As part of a holistic approach to RSE we encourage you to abandon the frames of 'risk' and 'pleasure' and the risk/pleasure binary and to use the activities in this book to have conversations that are open to exploring a whole range of motivations, outcomes and feelings including risk, pleasure, ambivalence, boredom and indifference to sex and relationships. If this feels challenging, remember to start with where young people are at and encourage them to be critical and curious about the relationships, people and issues they encounter in their on- and offline communities.

How to use this book

In addition to the Introduction, this book has seven chapters. The first, *Creating safer spaces*, has activities to help you create safe learning environments and involve young people in designing and developing the curriculum. The last, *Concluding the learning*, includes activities to involve young people in evaluating and reflecting on the curriculum and assessing their learning. The remaining five chapters each cover different, overlapping areas of the RSE curriculum: *Relationships* (Chapter 3), *Gender and sexual equality* (Chapter 4), *Bodies* (Chapter 5), *Sex* (Chapter 6) and *Sexual health* (Chapter 7). Each chapter contains close to 30 activity ideas for you to explore, alongside tips and points for the educator to consider. Each activity has a summary for educators that outlines the activity aim and purpose, a list of resources needed, an indication of the time needed to facilitate the activity and a suggestion as to which age group the activity will work best with. The summary, resources, time and age are indicated in the text using the following symbols.

 Summary: A description of the activity that includes the activity aim and type of activity (e.g. creative activity, individual activity, small group activity etc).

 Time: The minimum time you need to allow for this activity.

 Resources: The resources you will need for this activity.

 Age: The age group that we think this activity will work best with.

This book is not meant to be read in a linear fashion. We encourage you to dip in and out of the different chapters when working with young people to design, develop and review your RSE curriculum. The activities are varied, to suit different ages, group sizes and styles of teaching and learning. Use and adapt the ideas and make them work with the young people and communities that you work in. Find out what the 'hook' is for the group of young people that you are working with. What are group members interested in? Music? Drama? Sports? Public speaking? Gaming? Film-making? Physics?

Educators often say that they are unsure about the content of an RSE curriculum. What should they cover and when? How do they know what is age appropriate? And what will the parents say? We have provided guidance around what age each activity in this book is suitable for but this is a blunt tool as the suitability of an activity will depend on the context in which you are working and the evolving capacities and capabilities of the young people you work with. Ensuring that you work with young people to develop your curriculum is the best way of ensuring that it is developmentally appropriate and meets their needs. And make sure you involve parents in this process too – find out what their ideas and concerns are, involve them in the curriculum development process and invite them into your place of work to see what work you are doing. In our experience very few parents ever object when you do this (although unfortunately they rarely get involved in positive ways either…but that's another book!)

Historically, UK governments have not provided any curriculum resources to support schools and youth workers to deliver Relationships and Sex education. This seems unlikely to change in England and Northern Ireland, although something may be developed in Wales. Recently the Scottish government launched a new curriculum resource for delivering *Relationships, Sexual Health and Parenthood Education* in Schools, although these are not mandatory to use. The absence of a state curriculum has created a gap for educators but it has also meant that there have been opportunities for educators to innovate and develop resources that are best suited to their schools and communities. Internationally there are some excellent resources to help educators to develop their curricula. UNESCO (see reference on p. 3) has recently published comprehensive guidance for developing an RSE curriculum, based on the available international evidence. The guide outlines eight key concepts, each of which is broken down into key topics. Each topic is broken down into learning objectives for each age group from 5–8 years old to 15–18+. The number of objectives may feel overwhelming but this is a great place to start. Choose one concept and work with young people, staff and parents in your place of work to explore what people already know, what they want to learn about and how these issues affect their everyday lives. It will help you plan and prioritise what to include in your curriculum. You can focus on another concept next term or next year – you can't do it all at once! See the ideas in Chapter 2 of this book to help you do this.

Once you have listened and consulted and sketched out the bare bones of your curriculum with some learning objectives in mind, you can turn to the activities in this book. They will help you develop your pedagogy and give you ideas about how to bring the learning objectives to life in ways that are engaging and relevant for young people. There is definitely not an activity for every learning objective in the UNESCO guidance! But there are a wide variety of learning techniques that can be adapted to explore a whole range of topics and key concepts. We encourage you to innovative and to enjoy being creative, critical and curious! Remember to start with creating a safe learning environment and to always make opportunities for feedback and reflection – for yourself as well as for the young people that you work with. Try to be reflective about your own comfort zones – stretch yourself but not too far so that you feel panicky, anxious or out of your depth. This can be difficult if you feel isolated at your place of work or have very little time for corridor conversation or reflective meetings. If this is the case join online educator groups where you can ask questions and share experiences or find out if there are any local forums that you can get time off to attend. Every relationship and sex educator needs a good community of peers for support, inspiration and reflection.

Acknowledgements

We would like to thank all the fantastic relationship and sex educators and organisations whose ideas have been included, with permission, in this book. It's a privilege to share a space with you all.

We would also like to thank all the relationship and sex educators who have read and commented on draft chapters and kept us going with their supportive feedback. We hope this book is useful and well used by you all. Particular thanks go to the Great RSE Facebook support group of fabulous RSE consultants and teachers, especially Andrew Pembrooke, Boo Spurgeon, Brian Reeve Hayes, Bryden Joy, Catherine Kirk, Caroline Stringer, Lisa Andrews, Lou Pope, Sam Beal and Sian Rowland. Also a huge thank you to Emma Renold for her ideas, support and critical eye, Vicky Edwards for her critical and supportive feedback on two of our chapters and to our hugely talented illustrator Chrissy Baxter. We could not have done it without you all!

We would also like to thank all those amazing educators we have worked alongside over the years and from whom we have learnt so much. It's impossible to untangle all the ways that you have shaped our thinking and the activities included in this book. Particular shout outs needed for Justin Hancock, Laura Hurley, Lisa Hallgarten, Gail McVicar, Malin Stenstrom, Elsie Whittington, Ali Hanbury, Susie Langdale and many other fantastic current and former colleagues at Brook, FPA, PSHE Association, RSE hub and the Sex Education Forum.

We would also like to thank all the young people we have worked with over the years whose ideas, questions and stories have challenged us both and shaped the way that we work. Particular thanks go to the incredible group of young people from Space LGBT+ group at Off the Record Bath and North East Somerset especially AR, JO, KT, MG, RB, PB, PE, EL and ESP whose insights have really strengthened some of the activities included in the book.

And finally we would like to thank our families for all the childcare and support required to make this book possible. Thank you Ben, Chris and Mandy and to Andy, Sue, Janet, Harry, Helen and Phil. And to Elsa, Iris, Ada and Erin – thanks for your patience.

Notes

1   www.dosreforschools.com/media/1175/reflective-preparation.pdf
2   www.natsal.ac.uk/home.aspx
3   www.sexeducationforum.org.uk/resources/evidence

CHAPTER 2
Creating safer spaces

This chapter is full of ideas for how to create and sustain positive and inclusive learning environments for RSE. It also has activities for how to involve young people in co-creating an RSE programme and reflect on their learning. Unlike other chapters it doesn't focus on a particular topic or area of learning. Rather it includes the essential activities that you need to embed within any RSE programme or session.

Many of the activities in this book ask participants and educators to confront ethical dilemmas and social inequalities and to address topics that may be considered sensitive or taboo. This can feel uncomfortable and challenging for both educators and young people, particularly if we are not used to talking about these topics or confronting these issues in our day to day lives. To make it possible for learning to take place it is therefore vital that educators and participants are able to work together to create a positive and safe space. This does not mean shying away from topics that may feel uncomfortable or 'unsafe' as there is value in moving out of our comfort zones and having our thoughts and values challenged. What it does mean is that educators need to support learners to create a learning environment in which they feel safe and included and to help them reflect on the process of learning. We recommend that every RSE programme starts by creating a group agreement and working with participants to create a safe working environment and then following this with activities that enable participants to share their thoughts and ideas on what and how they want to learn in RSE.

Creating and sustaining safer spaces in RSE is not, however, just about how you set up a session and facilitate participant engagement. It is also about closing the session safely. Please see the final chapter in this book, Chapter 8: *Concluding the learning*, for activities and ideas on how to close the session and enable participants to reflect on and evaluate their learning.

Chapter summary

Section 1: Establishing a safe space. Activities and ideas for building a group working agreement and creating a safe working environment. This includes activities on personal values and boundaries, as well as on what language to use to talk about sex and how to ensure that your space is LGBT+ inclusive.

Section 2: Icebreakers, energisers and warm up activities. This section includes three interactive and high energy icebreaker activities that encourage participants to have fun and interact with each other. This is followed by three warm up activities that encourage participants to think about what they do and do not feel safe to share about themselves within the group setting.

Section 3: Developing a curriculum with young people. This section provides activities to help educators co-create an RSE curriculum with young people that meets their interests and needs, ensuring that the learning is relevant to participants and reflects the realities of their everyday lives.

Points to consider

- Once you have recognised the need to create a safe learning environment for RSE you can't just call your working space 'safe'! This needs to be done consciously and deliberately. Always start by setting a group agreement and revisiting this at the start of every session.
- A safe space is never completely safe so it is sometimes helpful to talk about *safe enough spaces*. This is because any learning environment will be shaped by wider social differences and inequalities (such as racial or gender inequalities) and the power relationships that exist between participants and between participants and educators. This means that a space is rarely completely equal, which can lead to some participants feeling excluded or judged. The activities in this chapter (as well as those in Chapter 4: *Gender and sexual equality*) will help educators to address exclusions and inequalities directly, but we also need to make sure we call out incidents of sexism, homophobia, racism and other forms of exclusion. It's not all about the educator though – it's also important to have robust policies and procedures for promoting equality and addressing inequalities at your place of work.
- Think about the physical space you are using. How inclusive and safe is it for you and your participants? For example, do you have posters on the walls showing that this is an LGBT+ inclusive space? How private/public is the space you are using and how might this affect what participants are comfortable doing? How are the chairs set up? Sitting in a circle works much better for encouraging group discussion than rows of chairs and tables. Although some participants may find the circle too exposing particularly when working in larger groups. If this is the case group participants around tables in smaller circles/groups.
- Many of the activities in this book aim to encourage participants to talk with others about topics that we often find it difficult to talk about. This is important for supporting young people to develop confidence in communicating about these topics with others. Remember, however, that not all young people like group discussions and some find them very challenging to take part in. Vary the types of activities that you include so that all learners can participate.

- There are a variety of teaching techniques that can be utilised to help a space feel safer; for example, using anonymous question boxes, not picking on individuals to answer a question, allowing participants to pair and share or having small group discussions before sharing with the larger group. This chapter includes examples of these techniques to help you do this.
- There has always been debate about whether RSE is better delivered to single or mixed gender groups. The research is inconclusive and suggests that there are advantages and disadvantages to both approaches. In general we advocate delivering the activities in this book to mixed gender groups. However, there may be occasions when it is helpful to do a focussed piece of work with a single gender group. For example, work around positive relationships, masculinity, pleasure and the body. Make sure that you don't fall into the trap of only exploring masculinity with boys and femininity with girls. Remember that everyone needs to learn about different bodies and genders, as well as about menstruation, contraception, pleasure and desire.
- When doing single gender work allow trans and non-binary young people to choose which group they would feel most comfortable working in. Where possible and appropriate have a confidential check in ahead of the session to ensure the young person is clear about their right to choose.

Section 1: Establishing a safe space

Creating a group agreement

 To invite all participants to contribute to creating a group agreement about how to create and maintain a safe enough space for learning.

 5–15 minutes dependent on approach

 Flipchart/whiteboard and pens, post-it notes (optional).

 11+

Introduce the aims of the session or programme and explain that for some people these can be challenging or sensitive topics to talk about. Explain the importance of creating a learning environment in which everyone feels safe and respected and able to share their views and listen to others. Ask the group 'What do we need to do to make sure this is a safe space where everyone feels able to join in and share their views?' Or you may want to say, 'What ground rules do we want to set in this group to make sure this is a safe space for learning and discussion?'

Ask participants to call out ideas and suggestions and write them on the board/flipchart. You may need to give suggestions if participants are not forthcoming. This should take five minutes.

Alternatively, give each participant a post-it note and ask them to write one thing that they want everyone to do to create a learning environment in which they can participate. Ask participants to stick them on the board/flipchart/wall. As a group look at the responses and group similar ones together. Use this to agree and write down a working agreement. This should take about 10–15 minutes.

Ask everyone if they are happy to agree to the working agreement. Display your group agreement and keep it displayed for the duration of the programme. Briefly revisit the working agreement at the start of every session and refer to the ground rules whenever someone is not adhering to them. For example, when someone asks a personal question, or puts someone down. Eventually participants will start to remind one another.

Example group agreement

We will…

- Respect each other and listen when others are speaking.
- Ask questions that we have (either out loud or by putting something in the anonymous questions box).
- Make sure we don't ask personal questions of each other.
- Remember it's ok to pass if someone doesn't want to speak or take part.
- Keep the conversation in the room and respect each other's confidentiality.
- Remember the limits to confidentiality. Educators have to pass on information if they have concerns about our safety or the safety of others.
- Speak for ourselves and not for others.
- Try not to make assumptions and judgements about others.
- Be mindful not to put each other down.
- Challenge sexist, homophobic, transphobic, racist, disablist assumptions and comments and be sure to avoid making them ourselves.
- Remember it's ok to have fun and laugh with, but not at, others in the group.
- Seek help and talk to someone we trust if we need to.

Note: You will also need to agree as a group what language/terms you are going to use during a session or programme. For example, are slang and colloquial terms ok to use, or are you going to use agreed terms only? What words are offensive/off limits? What do we do when we don't like the language someone is using? Some educators recommend using 'correct terms' only in RSE programmes to avoid the use of offensive or discriminatory language. This can work in some contexts, but in others it can be a barrier to young people feeling comfortable to share their thoughts and ideas for fear of saying the 'wrong thing'. Use your judgement about what will work best and discuss these issues openly with participants. You can either include this as part of your discussion or if you have time we recommend you follow this activity with the 'Sex talk' activity on p. 25. If you do not have time you may find the questions in this activity useful when discussing whether or not a word or term is ok to use in your working environment.

Writing the rules

Based on an activity developed by Sharon Lamb and her graduate students as part of the *Sexual Ethics for a Caring Society Curriculum* (SECS-C). www.sexualethics.org/. Used with permission.

An alternative activity for creating ground rules or for revisiting ground rules that the group established previously. This is a more challenging activity that confronts inequality and difference and encourages greater critical thinking. It is based on the philosopher John Rawls' thought experiment commonly referred to as the 'Veil of Ignorance'.

20–30 minutes

Script and sentence starters for educator. Pens and paper.

12+

Imagine you are about to enter a new society. You don't know much about it. You know it will have people and families and politics, and an economy. You also know that it will have rules – like every society – to protect people and to ensure the economy works. The problem is you don't know what these rules are or how you fit into this new society.

Imagine you are waiting behind a curtain and when you step out you will be in this new society. You don't know if you will be Black, White, Asian or Arab in this new society, you don't know whether you will be an immigrant or born here, whether you are able-bodied or have a disability or a long term health condition that affects you day to day. You don't know if you are from a very religious family or an atheist family or whether you are wealthy, poor or just about managing.

You don't know if you are gay, or straight or bisexual, or whether you are transgender or questioning your gender. You also don't know whether you have had sex before or not, or whether you have been sexually abused in your past or have escaped this kind of trauma. You don't know if you have been bullied or not, or whether you are someone who has lots of friends, just a few or none at all.

Imagine not knowing each of these things about yourself. Now think about what rules you would want for your protection so that you know you will be safe when you arrive in this society whatever your identity.

Imagine you are going to start school in this new society – what rules do you want in your new classroom to ensure that you are safe and protected?

After a few moments ask participants to open their eyes. Ask participants to start to create a set of rules for this imagined classroom, by imagining themselves as having different identities. Use the following sentence starters to help you do this. When your rules start to sound alike for each situation, you can jump to the end and just come up with three general rules.

You may want to ask participants to do this task individually by asking them to complete the following sentences and then come up with three general rules together.

Sentence starters:

- If you had a disability, the rule you would want to have in the classroom that would protect you would be:
- If you were Black:
- If you were gay:
- If you were Christian:
- If you came from a strictly religious family:
- If you came from a family with no religious views:
- If you had been sexually abused in the past:
- If you were transgender:
- If you had been bullied:
- If you were Muslim:
- If you were questioning your sexuality:
- If you had been hurt recently by a partner:
- If you have low self-esteem:
- If you [INVENT YOUR OWN]:

To end the activity lead a discussion about safety within the classroom. If you are not in a school, ask participants to reflect on their experiences in classrooms past or present:

- What kinds of things have made you feel unsafe in a classroom? Participating? Handing in work? Talking about yourself? Expressing your views?
- What kinds of things have other people said that have made you feel unsafe? Think about teachers and peers.

Use your discussion to write a group working agreement, using the following questions. If you have previously created a working agreement, return to it and reflect on whether this activity has enabled participants to think differently about safe/unsafe spaces and the value of having rules to protect themselves and others:

- How do we make everyone in the session feel safe and able to contribute if they want to?
- How do we respond to people if they share something personal? How do we make sure no one feels forced to share more than they are comfortable with?
- How do we disagree?
- Who has the power in the room?
- What will we do if someone violates the agreement?
- What will we do if someone gets hurt?
- How do we be inclusive?

- How do we convey respect?
- What's the difference between disagreeing and disrespecting?
- Can we speak with emotion, disagree and still be respectful? How?

Where are my safe spaces?

Adapted from the *Sex and History Project* LGBT history resources.[1] Used with permission.

 An individual, reflective activity that helps participants think about what makes them feel safe and unsafe. This is an alternative way of generating a group agreement that is more personal and reflective (and takes longer). Good for smaller groups who will be working together over a period of time. This activity also works well as a way into talking about personal relationships and can be used as an alternative to the 'Personal universes' activity in Chapter 3: *Relationships*, p. 50.

 20–30 minutes

 Paper and pens. Arts materials (optional).

 Age 11+

Ask participants to individually brainstorm all the places they go and spaces they spend time in. Create a map of these on a piece of paper (this can be a mind map or drawing depending on time).

Ask participants to circle or mark all those spaces that they feel safe and comfortable in and consider the following questions:

- Do you feel like you can be yourself in these spaces?
- How do you feel when you are in a safe space where you can shine and be yourself?
- What makes this a safe space for you?
- Are there any where you don't feel safe? Or where you feel judged? Uncomfortable? Or like you can't be yourself? Why don't you feel safe in that space?
- Does your age, sex, gender, sexual orientation, race, disability, faith or other protected characteristics or factors such as appearance, clothing, style, height or size play a part in making some spaces feel safe and others feel unsafe?
- What can you do to create safer spaces for others?

Encourage participants to represent their thoughts on their maps, showing how they feel in different spaces. You may want to ask participants to share their responses but some may not feel safe enough to do so. Where appropriate you can ask participants to create a visual representation of their safe space and/or how they feel in their safe space and create a display for your school or classroom.

If you have not already established a group agreement, use this activity to help you do this. Encourage participants to use their reflections on what makes them feel safe/unsafe in different spaces to generate a list of what they want from their learning environment in order to make them feel safe enough. Some participants may find thinking about unsafe spaces upsetting so be mindful and supportive of this.

Values egg

This activity has been inspired by the *Values Bell* produced as part of the *Faith, Values and SRE* project from the *Sex Education Forum* managed by Simon Blake and Zarine Katrak.[2]

 To encourage participants to reflect on their personal values and how these may influence how they interact with the world, particularly around relationships and sex. 45 minutes

 List of values/set of values cards and a blank values egg for each participant. Pens. 13+

Explain that we are going to reflect on our personal values and consider how these may influence our decisions and choices, in particular around relationships and sexuality. There are five steps to this activity.

Give participants a list of core values (see 'Core values list' box) and ask them to choose their top three. Alternatively give each participant a set of values cards, with one value printed on each card. If using cards, participants need to sort the cards into piles of most important, somewhat important, less important and then use this to identify their three 'most important' values. Encourage participants to share their top three if they want to.

Core values list

Participants and educators are encouraged to add other values they feel resonate with them.

• Achievement	• Family	• Organisation
• Authority	• Freedom	• Pleasure
• Community	• Friendships	• Religion
• Compassion	• Fun	• Reputation
• Contribution	• Happiness	• Respect
• Creativity	• Humour	• Safety
• Curiosity	• Independence	• Success
• Determination	• Kindness	• Wealth
• Equality	• Love	• Wisdom
• Fairness	• Loyalty	
• Faith	• Openness	

Give each participant a blank values egg and ask them to complete the sentence starters with their three most important values in mind. Instruct participants to start in the middle (I value) and work their way outwards. For example, if they selected the values 'equality', 'freedom' and 'respect' they may write something like: *I value equality and believe that everyone has the right to be treated with respect. I believe that everyone should be treated equally. I feel upset and angry when I hear people making sexist comments and calling girls 'slags'. I think that people should be respectful towards others. I speak up when I hear people being disrespectful or if they are being sexist or racist.*

When participants have completed their values eggs, ask them to consider how the values that they hold influence their choices and decisions, particularly around relationships and sex. Responses can be written around the egg.

Offer participants opportunities to share and discuss their values eggs and how that might impact on what and how they share in sessions, in pairs or larger groups (use your judgement). Finish with a group discussion using the following questions OR by asking participants to write down their reflections.

Discussion/self-reflection questions

- What are values?
- Where do they come from?
- What are your own values? How do these influence your day to day life?
- How does your family influence your values and attitudes?
- How might your values (personal, faith, family) influence your decisions and choices around relationships and sex?
- How have your values influenced your participation in the RSE programme?
- *[Question to revisit at the end of a series of RSE sessions]* Have the RSE sessions and listening to the views of others helped clarify your values? Have your views changed in any way?

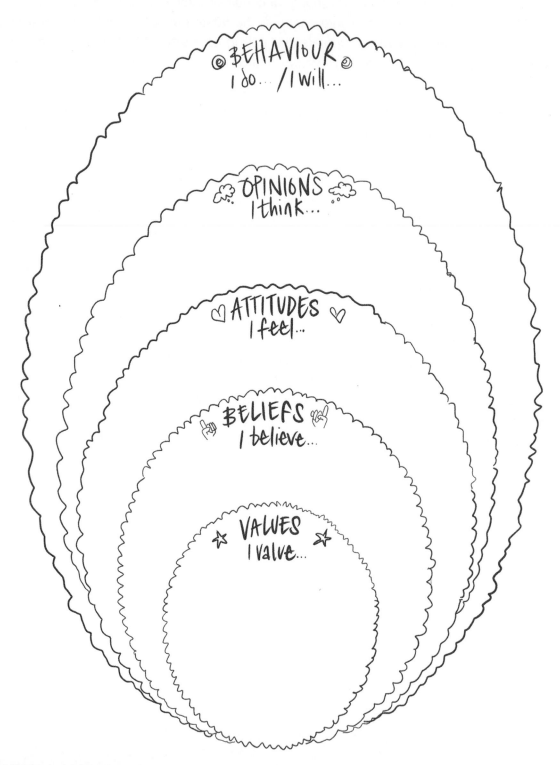

FIGURE 2.1 Values egg
Illustration by: Chrissy Baxter

Comfort, Stretch and Panic

Adapted from an activity created by educators at *Brook* as part of their *Great Expectations* education programme.[3] Shared with permission.

 Working in groups means working outside of our comfort zones and being open to new experiences and being challenged by others. This activity helps to explore how it feels to be in and out of your 'comfort zones' and why it is important to stretch beyond your comfort zones and try new experiences. 20–30 minutes

 Flipchart/whiteboard and pens. 11+

Draw the Comfort, Stretch, Panic model on a flipchart/whiteboard and explain the model to the group. As you explain the model ask the group to list the feelings and physical changes that someone would experience if they were in each zone.

- **The Comfort zone** includes everyday activities – doing familiar things, going to the same places and mixing with the same people. When most of your activities are in this zone life is, of course, 'comfortable' but you do not learn very much or develop yourself. Here you may feel relaxed, comfortable, bored, unchallenged, content.
- **The Stretch zone** is the area of novelty, exploration and adventure. Here are the things that are out of the ordinary, either things you haven't done for a long time or those that you have never done before. This zone is not really a comfortable place but it is a stimulating one. It is where we stretch and challenge ourselves mentally, emotionally or physically. Here you may feel excited, switched on, scared, nervous, uncomfortable, your heart might be racing and you may feel twitchy or fidgety.
- **The Panic zone** is the area of things-to-be-avoided, either because they are unacceptable to you or because they are currently a 'stretch' too far. This doesn't mean that they will always be a stretch too far. In this zone someone may feel fearful, panicky, hot, red in the face, pumped up, scared, excited, full of adrenaline.

Ask the group for some examples of activities and experiences that would be in each zone and write examples on the model. Young people may disagree about which activities go where. For example, what is a Stretch activity for one person can be a Comfort or Panic zone activity for someone else. It is helpful to highlight this as a way of showing that we all have different personal boundaries and limits. What is useful is to be able to identify your own boundaries/limits and be aware of how they change over time and depending on the situation. It is also important to recognise that others have their own limits that will be different from your own so just because you feel ok with something it doesn't mean that other people will too.

Introduce participants to the idea that learning new things about relationships and sexuality may take them out of their Comfort zone and into the Stretch zone. This may not always feel comfortable but it is important for challenging and stretching ourselves to think differently and imagine otherwise.

Sometimes the learning may take us into the Panic zone. This would never be the educator's intention because when someone is in the Panic zone then learning cannot take place and it doesn't feel like a good place to be. As a group agree a signal for participants to use if they feel the session is taking them into the Panic zone. This may need to be an agreed group safe word or some participants may prefer to have a private signal with the educator so that other participants are not made aware of the situation. In this situation the person in the Panic zone could then discreetly be allowed to run an errand or go to the toilet. Make sure you follow up with the participant at an appropriate time to explore how to make the session safer for them in future.

Follow this activity with 'Risk it' (see the following activity) or to explore this model further and use it to consider how participants feel in their relationships with others see Chapter 3, the 'Comfort, Stretch and Panic in relationships' activity on p. 51. Here the model is used to explore the difference between healthy and unhealthy relationships and to think about ways of supporting those who feel powerless, panicky or out of control within their relationships.

FIGURE 2.2 Comfort, stretch, panic model
Illustration by: Chrissy Baxter

Risk it

Adapted from an activity created by educators at *Brook* as part of their *Great Expectations* education programme.[4] Shared with permission.

 This activity follows on from the previous one. It aims to give young people opportunities to take risks and make decisions about risk-taking within a safe environment. It also aims to reframe risk as a normal and necessary part of young people's lives – something that they need support with and opportunities to practise doing safely.

 Set of 'risk it' cards, coins, a prize for the group.

 20 minutes

 13–16 (or adapt the game for all ages by making up developmentally appropriate and engaging tasks)

Note: This activity should only be used in small group settings as part of an ongoing programme of work.

Explain to the group that we are going to play a game called 'risk it' in which participants will be divided into two teams. Each team starts in a restricted, unsafe area and has to win 20 coins to pass into the safety zone. To get coins participants must complete individual tasks. The tasks are in three levels:

Comfortable tasks – one coin
Stretch task – two coins
Challenging task – three coins

To play the game, flip a coin to decide which team goes first. The educator begins by asking the first team to select a group member to do a task and say which level they want. The educator will then select a card from the pack and read the task out.

There is a list of tasks given in Table 2.1 but we have not assigned them as comfortable, stretch or challenging. Instead the educator should use their knowledge of the participant to best assess which task to assign (e.g. a young person who is very confident might be comfortable with some public speaking tasks which others might find really challenging but they might not be able to do something such as name three things they like about themselves).

Once the participant has completed the task the team will receive the relevant number of coins.

Switch between alternate teams until one team reaches 20. They are the winning team and should be given the prize of your choice.

Rules

- If a participant chooses not to do a task then they can nominate a team mate. In this instance the team will only win one coin.
- If the team chooses not to do a task then they will have to give one of the coins back. Each team can only pass on a maximum of three tasks.
- A team member cannot do the same task twice.
- Everyone must do at least one task. A team cannot complete and win the game until each team member has done one task.

Before playing the game, ask the group to brainstorm how they can support each other to complete the tasks, particularly if a participant chooses tasks that take them into the stretch zone. What would be helpful/unhelpful?

Make sure this includes something on not pressuring other to do tasks they don't feel comfortable doing. If necessary pause during the activity to prompt participants to support each other, reminding them that the game requires them to work together to negotiate the risky or stretch tasks.

After the activity has finished have a debrief discussion using the following prompts:

- How did people feel during the game?
- Why did you make the decisions that you did (e.g. to choose a comfortable/stretch activity, to do/refuse to do an activity)?
- Why do we take risks? Why do we choose not to take risks?
- Did anyone feel pressured to do a task? What was the pressure?
- How did it feel doing the tasks?
- Did you gain anything from doing the tasks?
- Have your confidence levels changed from the beginning of the exercise?
- What did you learn from taking part in the exercise?

TABLE 2.1 Risk it tasks

Describe yourself in three words	Roll your tongue
Give someone in your team a compliment.	Tell the group three things about yourself – one of them can be a lie.
Describe a time when something happened at school that you thought was unfair.	Say five words in another language.
Close your eyes and write a message to a team mate. They have to be able to understand what you have written to win the coin!	Pat your head and rub your tummy at the same time.
Tell the group about a time when you won something.	Complete the following sentence: If I won the lottery I would…
Tell the group one character trait of yours you think needs improvement.	Tell a joke.
Tell another person in the group one thing that you like about them.	Talk for one minute without stopping.
Choose a team member. Stare into their eyes for one minute without moving, smiling or speaking.	Tell the group one thing you have learnt about yourself through taking part in the programme so far.
Whistle a tune that your team mates have to guess.	Tell the group about a time when you felt really embarrassed.
Pretend you are swimming.	Close your eyes and shake hands with every person in the room (your team mates will need to guide you).
Sing a song of your choice whilst pretending you are in the shower.	Tell the group your favourite part of your body and why.
Tell the group something you don't like about yourself and what you would like to do to change it.	Strike whatever pose the opposite team tells you to do (it has to be a realistic pose that is possible – the educator is the referee!).
Do a stand up comedy routine that lasts one minute.	Do a downward dog (yoga move that involves putting your hands and feet on the floor and pushing your bottom as high into the sky as you can).
Close your eyes and let a team member lead you around.	Dance for one minute to a song selected by the other team (and refereed by the educator).
Walk across the room three times, each time displaying a different emotion. Your team mates have to guess the emotion (and you have to tell the educator which emotion you are acting out to make sure there's no cheating!).	Give a one minute lecture on either: Schools in the UK today; The problems facing young people in the UK today; The current political situation in the UK.

Tasks: remember to allocate whether they are a comfortable/stretch/challenge task based on your knowledge of the young person.

Sex talk

Parts of this activity are based on an activity by Sharon Lamb and her Research Lab at *Umass Boston* as part of the *Sexual Ethics for a Caring Society Curriculum* (SECS-C; see *Useful resources* at the end of the book). Used with permission.

 To explore the language we use to talk about sex in different social situations and reach group consensus about what language is and is not ok in RSE sessions. If you do not have time to complete this activity you may find it useful to pull out the questions at the end of this activity to refer to when discussing with participants whether or not a language or term is ok to use in your working environment. 45 minutes

 Flipchart paper, pens, scissors. 11+

Divide into small groups and give each group three pieces of flipchart paper and pens. Ask each group to brainstorm all the words that they would use to talk about sex when talking to: 1) their friends; 2) their parents/carers; 3) a teacher, nurse or other professional.

Prompt students to think about how they might talk about bodies and body parts, different types of sex, different ways of describing people who have sex or people we are attracted to. Participants should include the words that they actually use or would use in any language. This can include slang/colloquial/made up terms used in families or friendship groups. Ask participants to provide a translation in a different colour for any terms they think you or the rest of the class might be unfamiliar with. This should take about ten minutes.

After groups have finished their initial brainstorms, ask them to cut out each word from the flipchart and think about which of these words they think it is ok to use in their RSE sessions. To do this, ask participants to sort each word into three piles: *Find a replacement: Depends on context: Ok.*

Next ask groups to come together and try and reach a consensus as a whole class and to think of replacement words where needed. Draw three columns on the board/flipchart and write/stick up words once they have been agreed. Where this isn't possible note which terms cause disagreement and the reasons why participants disagree. As a group come to an agreement about whether you will use these contested terms and agree not to use the words that need to be replaced. This should form part of the group working agreement.

The group will need to work out how they are going to come to a consensus in an ethical way. This could be through voting or discussion. As the educator, prompt the group to think about whether they are considering the views of minority groups and listening to the voices of all those in the group. Reflect at the end of the process on the challenges of compromise and consensus building. This could take between 15 and 45 minutes depending on the number of words and nature of the group.

You may find the following discussion questions and points to consider useful to facilitate this activity.

- Is this word gender neutral? Does this matter?
- Does this word objectify or demean anyone?
- Is this word violent or aggressive? Why might this matter?
- What new words and phrases do we need? What might these look/sound like?

Points to consider

- Language is much more than a way of communicating our thoughts and feelings. It helps shape and structure our thoughts, feelings and beliefs.
- Slang can be funny and inventive and can help us to have more relaxed conversations about difficult subjects. It can also reinforce our group identity and separation from other groups. Slang can also be harmful and used (intentionally or not) to objectify, demean or belittle others. Language is never 'just a word' as all language carries meaning, thought, belief or emotion.
- Vague terms are more suggestive which can be more seductive in sexual situations. They can also be misread and lead to a confusion that is awkward or uncomfortable. They can also be unhelpful when we need to get information or advice from an education or health professional.

Pronoun badges

This activity is adapted from the *Sex and History Project* LGBT history resources[5] and shared with permission.

 To explore the use of pronoun badges to find out how pronoun use can help create safer spaces.

 5–10 minutes

 Pronoun badges (can be made or purchased online) or images of pronoun badges such as the one from the People's museum featured on the LGBT+ History month website…

 11+

Show the group a range of pronoun badges (or images of pronoun badges) e.g. she/her, they/them, xe/zem, he/him.

Ask the group:

- What do you think these are?
- Who created them?
- What were they created for?
- Who might wear them?

Explain that these are pronoun badges. Lead a discussion using the following questions:

- What is a pronoun? *Explain to the group that in grammar a pronoun is a word that can be used instead of a noun – like 'it' instead of 'the table' or 'them' instead of 'the flowers'. Some languages, such as English, use gender specific pronouns (he/she, his/hers) and do not always have a gender neutral pronoun available. English has they/them, which can be used for any gender, but is most often used to indicate a plural. This lack of gender neutrality is problematic especially since writers and speakers have traditionally used 'he/his' when referring to a generic individual in the third person. This is known as 'default male'. The dichotomy of 'he and she' in English is also not inclusive of those who identify as trans including transgender, genderqueer and non-binary gender. In the interests of inclusion and equality, attempts have been made to create new gender neutral pronouns.*
- Why might someone wear a pronoun badge? *Explain to the group that pronoun badges are a way of asking for preferred pronouns to be respected, as they clearly identify someone's preferred pronouns so we don't accidentally assume or guess someone's gender based on how*

they look, act or what their name is. Being misgendered can cause upset. Being respectful of people's preferred pronouns is important to ensure people feel accepted and safe. Pronoun badges can also help to open up conversations about gender and raise awareness of gender diversity. Increasingly people are communicating their preferred pronouns in other ways such as including it in their email signature. People could also wear the badge to show that they are inclusive, an ally, that they understand what preferred pronouns are and to try and encourage wider adoption of them.

- How do you think people would respond if you or one of your friends wore one of these badges? *The group may suggest that their peers might think it was strange, they might make fun, they might bully or laugh at you for being different, or they might be intrigued and they might want to have their own badge.*

To extend the activity participants could make and decorate a set of pronoun badges to be used in this or other activities. The badges they make do not necessarily have to reflect their own pronouns to keep this activity safe.

Pass the pronouns

With thanks to Andrew Pembrooke at *Teach SRE* for this idea and all his help with discussions about best practice in pronoun activities.

 A quick fire activity in which participants pass different pronouns around in a circle to practise using different pronouns without being personally asked to share their pronouns with the group.

 5–10 minutes

 Pronouns written on individual cards, if necessary.

 11+

Arrange the group in a circle. The first person turns to the person next to them and they have this exchange. Person 1: I am a he. Person 2: A who? Person 1: A he. Person 2: A he! Person 2 then turns to the third person in the circle and they repeat the exchange. The same exchange is passed around the circle. As it sets off around the circle, Person 1 then starts a similar exchange but in the opposite direction, this time with a different pronoun, she, xe, they, etc. The two different exchanges are now going in different directions and will cross over. A third or fourth exchange can be added to make things even more fun. If necessary you could hand out pronouns for people to use on cards to help with the exchanges.

To close the activity, choose some of the following questions to discuss. See responses to the questions in the 'Pronoun badges' activity on p. 26 for useful discussion points.

- How and why do we currently use pronouns?
- How would it feel to share our own pronouns? Would it make spaces feel safer or less safe?
- Before doing this activity had you thought about what your own or someone else's preferred pronouns might be? Why isn't this something we think about regularly?
- Why is it important to know what someone's preferred pronouns are?
- Do we regularly ask others what their preferred pronouns are? What would it be like if we did?
- Why is it not ok to use 'it' as a pronoun to describe someone else?
- What would happen if we all used the pronoun 'They' to describe each other and ourselves?

The key learning point is that when it comes to pronouns it is ok to ask, it's ok to check and it's not the end of the world if we make mistakes.

Top tips for creating an LGBT+ inclusive space

Research suggests that LGBT+ young people often feel excluded from RSE sessions and from the RSE curriculum. LGBT+ relationships and identities are frequently not discussed or represented, sexual health concerns are not addressed and homophobic, biphobic and transphobic bullying is frequently unchallenged. See Stonewall's *School Reports* for more information about young LGBT+ people's experiences in schools.[6]

Here are some top tips to help educators create an LGBT+ inclusive space when delivering RSE:

- Ensure that you don't make any assumptions about the sexual orientation or gender identity of young people you work with. For example, always use the word 'partner', rather than boyfriend or girlfriend and check what young people's preferred pronouns are. If it doesn't feel appropriate to ask use they/them. Or just use they/them as a default.
- Make sure that the examples that you give are diverse in terms of gender and sexual orientation. For example, don't always use case studies or stories of straight young people.
- A young person may choose to 'come out' (disclose their lesbian, gay, bisexual or transgender identity) to you as a result of your RSE sessions. This is because these activities could signal to them that you are a 'safe' person to talk to. The most important thing to do in this situation is to listen to the young person and show that you accept them for the person they are. Don't brush them off or say they are in a 'phase' or merely 'lacking experience with the opposite sex'. You are not required to pass on information about a young person's sexual orientation or gender identity to anybody else unless you suspect there is an additional safeguarding issue.
- Modern western culture generally sees only two binary genders (male and female). It is frequently assumed that all people are attracted to and have relationships with someone from the binary 'opposite' gender. This is known as heteronormativity and is based on a set of assumptions that we can challenge through RSE. In your practice, talk about people of 'all genders' rather than 'both genders' and challenge heterosexist assumptions. For example, that there are only two genders, that everyone identifies as male or female, that everyone identifies with the gender they were assigned at birth, that being straight/heterosexual is 'normal'.
- In all sessions (not just RSE) do not tolerate homophobic, biphobic or transphobic language such as 'that's so gay'. Young people should be made aware that such language is unacceptable. Likewise, be aware of unintentionally reinforcing a culture of homophobia and gender stereotypes. For example, by telling boys not to 'be such a girl' or telling boys who are play fighting to 'stop cuddling'.
- Language is constantly evolving which means that we won't always get language right – but it is important to try. Today using the term homosexual is offensive to many gay men and lesbian women because 'homosexual' was the medical term to describe being LGB as a medical disorder. Likewise some lesbians don't like to be called gay, but others don't mind. Use the terms lesbian, gay, bisexual and trans and be open to challenge from the young people you work with who may have their own preferred terms.

Is our space safe for LGBT+ young people?

To reflect on how inclusive your school/classroom/youth club is for LGBT+ young people and agree how to make the space more inclusive.

15 minutes

None.

11+

As a group, choose a space that everyone knows (e.g. the classroom/school/youth club). Ask the group to discuss the following questions:

- Is our space LGBT+ friendly?
- How could it be more inclusive?

Brainstorm all the ways that the space is inclusive and all the ways it could be more inclusive. Points to consider include:

- What posters or wall coverings denote this space is safe and LGBT+ friendly?
- What toilets are available – is there a gender neutral toilet?
- What everyday words are said in the space that could be considered sexist, homophobic, biphobic or transphobic (e.g. phrases like 'that's so gay' or terms like 'slag')?
- What assumptions are made in the room that could be considered sexist, homophobic, biphobic or transphobic? How are these expressed?
- What action is taken if someone does express sexist, homophobic, biphobic or transphobic language or assumptions?
- What ground rules should be put in place to make sure a safe space is developed and maintained?

Discuss as a group if and how you want to action any of these suggestions. You may want to create a group action plan or agreement for how to make the space more inclusive or how to makes changes in your school/youth club.

Extension questions

To further this discussion about safe spaces you could unpick how spaces are affected by sex, gender and sexual orientation categories using the following questions:

- What spaces can you think of that are segregated by sex, gender or sexual orientation? (*Answers could include: toilets, changing rooms, hospital wards, night clubs, sports teams, youth clubs.*)
- Why are they segregated? (*Answers could include: to make people feel more comfortable in intimate settings such as toileting or changing; to create safe spaces for boys/men/women/ girls or LGBT+ young people/adults; to protect women from male violence; outdated ideas about keeping men and women separate to preserve modesty; physical differences meaning competitive segregation in sport.*)

- What are some of the problems with these segregations? (*Answers could include: some people don't fit into the categories which means their ability to access the facilities/resources available is compromised; controversy around intersex athletes competing in either male or female categories; segregations can reflect outdated ideas about sexual/gender differences; within the context of wider inequalities women's sports/activities does not have equal status to that of men.*)
- Is providing gender neutral options a good idea? (*Answers could include: important for ensuring inclusivity of people who do not identify with a particular gender or who do not feel comfortable using single sex facilities. However, needs to ensure provision is adequate for all and that the space does not compromise the safety or comfort for any individual, e.g. floor to ceiling enclosed cubicles containing a sink.*)

Section 2: Icebreakers, energisers and warm up activities

Icebreakers are fun, interactive activities that encourage participants to have fun whilst starting to interact with each other and with you. We recommend that you always include at least one icebreaker activity at the start of an RSE lesson as this is an important part of creating a space in which participants feel energised, relaxed and able to participate. These activities can also be used as energisers half way through a session if the energy is dropping.

There are hundreds of ideas for icebreakers available. We have included just three, two of which have a specific RSE focus. For more ideas see the link to free online resource *Low Cost, No Cost Youth Work – 101 Positive Activities for Young People* in *Useful resources* at the end of this book. We have also included three warm up activities. These are gentler and longer activities that you can include at the start of a programme of work. They encourage participants to think about what they do and do not feel safe to share about themselves within the group setting and learning environment you have created. For this reason they may not work well in larger groups, but are fantastic for smaller groups that are going to work together for a period of time.

Would you rather?

 To energise the group and get participants moving around whilst also expressing their personal views and acknowledging the views of others. Being able to do this is important for participation in RSE. 5–15 minutes depending on the number of statements used and amount of discussion

 A list of statements for the educator and space to move around. Rope or tape. 11+ (adapt the statements to suit your group)

Divide the room in half using rope, tape or whatever you have available. Ask the group to stand with one leg either side of the rope. When asked 'would you rather?', participants have to jump to the left or the right as indicated by the educator.

Here are some example questions – have a go at adding your own and make sure you use a combination of silly and more serious examples. You can add some examples that are related to any themes you might be covering later in the session (e.g. social media – never go on snapchat or never watch YouTube):

Would you rather?: Statements for educators

- Be invisible or be able to fly?

- Sit on a beach for a week or go to New York?

- Wear someone else's dirty underwear or use someone else's toothbrush?

- Know *when* you are going to die or *how* you are going to die?

- Never be able to use the internet ever again or never be able to use a car, motorbike, bus or train?

- Always say out loud everything that you are thinking or never be able to speak again?

- Only wash your hair once a year or brush your teeth once a year?

- Fall in love or win the lottery?

- Give up your mobile phone or your best friend for a whole year?

- Snog a complete stranger or lick your friend's face?

- Lie in a bath of spiders or a bath of slugs?

- Have hiccups for the rest of your life or always feel like you are about to sneeze but not be able to?

- Be a multi-millionaire but have no friends and family or be homeless with your friends and family?

Cross the circle

 An icebreaker activity that encourages participants to start sharing their views and experiences with others in a way that feels safe to them. Works best with small to medium sized groups.

 5 minutes

 Set of statements for educator and space to move around.

 11+ (statements will need to be adapted to the age of the group)

Stand in a circle with the participants. Read out a series of statements and ask participants to cross the circle if the statement applies to them. You may want to start with an easy example such as, if you have brown eyes. There are some statements following that can be adapted to suit the group and the theme of the session. Use a combination of fun and more serious statements. Let participants know that they only need to cross the circle if they feel comfortable doing so.

Cross the circle if you...

- Have a brother or sister.
- Laughed out loud this morning.
- Have ever been to Turkey.
- Like the taste of Marmite.
- Have ever had a foot massage.
- Like having your head stroked.
- Have ever loved someone.
- Have ever cried from being so happy.
- Have heard someone making sexist comments.
- Have made a sexist comment yourself.
- Have felt uncomfortable about something you have seen online.
- Have challenged someone online for being out of order to someone else.
- Have ever wished you had someone to talk to about something that is worrying you.
- Have felt unsafe whilst walking around in your local area.
- Have stood up for something you believe in.
- Have argued with someone.
- Have witnessed racism.
- Have said 'yes' to something when you wanted to say 'no'.
- Have lied.

Quick fire debates

 A quick energiser or icebreaker that gets participants talking and interacting with each other. This activity works well at the start of a session, or mid-way through the session to explore key session themes.

 10 minutes

 A list of statements for the educator and space to move around.

 13+ (choose statements that are appropriate to the age of the group and the theme of the session)

This activity involves a series of quick fire debates between two people. After each debate, participants change partners and debate with a new person. This works by everyone standing in two lines (row A and B) facing a partner. The educator reads out a statement which each person must debate with the person opposite them for the allocated amount of time which could last from ten seconds to 45 seconds. When the educator shouts 'stop' everyone in row A moves along one person and row B stands still so that each person has a new partner to debate with. The person at the end of row A needs to run to the end of the line. As the educator you will need to direct this person to the end of the line and make sure participants get moving quickly to keep the energy up.

You can start with ten-second debates on less sensitive issues (cats or dogs, coffee or tea, Snapchat or Instagram) and warm up to longer 45-second debates on some of the key issues you will be exploring in the session. Select five–ten examples from this list that are appropriate to your group and RSE programme or make up your own. There is also a set of statements in Chapter 6 ('Speed debating sex and sexuality', p. 200) that relate to sex, pleasure and consent for use with young people aged 15+.

- I would feel comfortable using the word 'penis' in front of my parents.
- Educating children about relationships is a parent's responsibility, not friend's.
- You need to be in love to really enjoy having sex with someone.
- Boys enjoy sex more than girls.
- Pleasure is the main reason why people have sex.
- If you are in a relationship you need to be having sex for the relationship to work.
- There is always a dominant person in a relationship.
- LGBT people have always existed throughout history, even if the terms 'lesbian', 'gay', 'bisexual' and 'trans' haven't.
- It's easier to be gay today than it was 50 years ago.
- At our school people are very accepting of gender diversity.
- There is no racism at this school/college/town.
- People send nudes because they feel confident about their bodies.
- Watching pornography is a good way to learn about sex.
- Girls should have pubic hair.
- [Our town/city] is a good place to grow up.
- It's easier being a young person today than it was 50 years ago.
- Today men and women are equal.
- Alcohol is a drug and should be made illegal.
- Children and young people who live in the countryside are happier than those who live in cities.
- The police treat all young people equally, it doesn't matter what their race or ethnicity is.
- Social media helps people to make friends and feel connected.
- The legal age of sexual consent should be lowered to 14.
- [Our town/city] has great services to support young people.

After the activity you may want to have a discussion with the group about the key themes that have been debated. You can prompt discussion by asking – which statements did you and your partner agree on? Which caused the most disagreement? Which were the hardest to talk about?

Warm up activities

Feel good Jenga

 A fun activity that encourages participants to think about what they do and do not feel safe sharing about themselves within a group.

 10–15 minutes

 Jenga sets prepared with sentence starters (you will need one set per four–eight participants).

 11+

Before the session get hold of a standard Jenga set (you can buy versions online for about £4) and write a sentence starter on each block (see following list). If you want to do this with a large group (8+) you will need more than one set.

To play the game, set up a tower of Jenga blocks per group of four–eight participants. Each participant then takes it in turn to draw out a block from the tower trying not to knock down the tower in the process. Once a block has been withdrawn the participant should read the sentence starter to themselves and check that they are comfortable sharing something with the group. If yes, the participant should read the sentence out loud and finish it by saying something about themselves. A guiding principle should be 'no self put downs' so the young person should aim to keep their responses positive. The block should then be placed on the top of the tower and it is the next person's turn. If a participant does not want to complete the starter they should place the block in a bag and it is the next person's turn.

The game continues with the tower growing (or blocks being placed into a bag) until the tower is so unstable it collapses.

Example sentence starters:

1. I am awesome because…
2. My favourite thing is…
3. One thing that makes me smile is…
4. My favourite person is…
5. The favourite part of my body is…
6. My hobbies are…
7. Something not many people know about me is…
8. When I was little I wanted to be…
9. My proudest achievement is…
10. When I grow up I want…
11. My best feature is…
12. Something I want to change is…
13. People would say that I am…
14. I would say that I am…
15. The thing I am most proud of is…
16. I like that I can…
17. I wish I could…
18. I want to…
19. If wishes could come true I would wish…
20. I am amazing because…
21. I am brilliant because…
22. I am beautiful because…
23. I am kind because…
24. My party trick is…
25. My earliest memory is…
26. My happiest moment was…
27. My favourite food is…
28. If I was in charge of the world I would…
29. Sometimes I think…
30. I am optimistic about…
31. Something that makes me smile is…
32. Something that makes me laugh is…
33. Something that makes me happy is…
34. The best thing about me is…
35. I feel safe when…

36. My trusted people are…
37. I'm a good friend because…
38. I'm a good human because…
39. Something that sparks joy in me is…
40. I get butterflies when…
41. My best feature is…
42. My last good deed was…
43. I hope…
44. I dream…
45. I want …

46. I can…
47. I will…
48. I am…
49. I love…
50. I love it when…
51. I like it when…
52. I enjoy it when…
53. I feel safe when…
54. I feel loved when…

There is value in revisiting this activity when working with a group over a period of time. In our experience young people value the opportunity to practise being positive about themselves and hearing positive things about each other whilst playing a game. If one member of the group is struggling they will often help each other think of positive statements and become more skilled at this with practice.

What's my label?

This activity works well alongside the 'Identity label tetronimoes' activity on p. 126 in Chapter 4: *Gender and sexual equality*.

 Participants are invited to create identity labels for themselves and look for others with similar labels. This is used to reflect critically on labelling as an experience and social process and to consider how to create spaces in which people feel able to be open up about different aspects of their identity if they choose to. 5–15 minutes

 Sticky labels or post-it notes. 11+

Ask participants to write down their name and three–five of the most important aspects of their identity on individual post-it notes or sticky labels and stick them on their top. They then have 30 seconds to circulate and find a matching partner with a similar characteristic to themselves and introduce themselves, and remove that label. If they can't find a match, they should take a moment to celebrate being unique and then move onto the next label. Repeat this a few times until most labels have been removed.

Once the activity is complete discuss the following questions:

- How was that experience?
- What did it feel like to label yourself?
- Why do we have labels? *(Answers might include: to feel part of a group; to have a shared collective identity; for monitoring and statistics; to be classified and controlled by others for understanding.)*
- Do we need labels? What would it be like if we didn't have any?

- What's the difference between labelling yourself and being labelled by others? *(Answers might include: you have the power if you label yourself; being labelled by others (particularly those in a position of power or authority) may feel disempowering; others may label you incorrectly or in a way that is potentially offensive to you.)* You could revisit the ground rules at this stage around language.
- Why might people feel comfortable sharing some labels and not others? *(Answers might include: some identities may be privileged, others may be taboo; fear of discrimination/ exclusion.)*
- What can we do to make people feel comfortable about sharing their labels? *(Answer might include: using respectful and inclusive language and creating inclusive spaces; challenging inequalities and inequities, put downs and discriminatory/offensive labels; educating others and raising awareness, and how we talk about and with each other.)*

More warm up activity ideas

- **My favourite things:** Ask each participant to bring an object to the session that is their 'favourite thing'. Go around the circle and ask each person to say what their favourite thing is and why it is important to them.
- **Roll the dice:** Stand/sit in a circle. Each person rolls a large dice and the number dictates the number of things they have to say about themselves. After several rolls, the game can be changed so that you have to say things that you have learnt about other people from listening to what they have said.
- **Truth or lies:** Each person has to think of two things about themselves that are true and one lie. They then tell the group and the group has to guess which statement is a lie. If a participant successfully deceives the group they get a prize. Warning – some participants find it takes them a long time to think of what to say so you may need to encourage and prompt them to keep the activity moving!
- **Telling tales:** Stand or sit in a circle and explain that the group is going to tell a story one word at a time. Go around and each participant says one word. You can either ask the group to decide the theme of the story, or you can select a theme that is relevant to the session.

Section 3: Developing a curriculum with young people

RSE should always be based on the needs, interests and concerns of children and young people so that it reflects the realities of their lived experiences of sexualities and relationships. This means that every RSE programme needs to include opportunities for young people to get involved in consultation and co-production of programme design, facilitation and evaluation. This will help you to ensure that the content and style of the programme is appropriate for the young people that you work with and that they feel safe participating in the programme. The following activities are useful for both finding out what is important to young people as well as inspiring them to think critically about their learning needs and to bring about change in their communities. For a range of creative ideas on how to involve young people in evaluating the RSE curriculum, see Chapter 8: *Concluding the learning.*

Note: Although not covered here, remember it is also a good idea to consult and involve parents in developing and reviewing your RSE curriculum.

Stop-start plates

Adapted from *AGENDA: A young people's guide to making positive relationships matter* (see *Useful resources* at the end of this book). Used with permission.

 A creative activity that encourages participants to identify the issues that are important to them and that are impacting on their everyday lives. This can be used as the basis for RSE curriculum design or to take forwards social action projects. It is a simple to use and a powerful method that we refer to throughout the book.   40–60 minutes

 Packs of red and green paper plates (six per participant), marker pens (one per participant), pegs, washing line/string.   11+

Give each participant six paper plates (three red and three green) and one marker pen. Ask them to think of three things in their lives and the world around them that they would like to STOP and three things that they would like to START, e.g. 'STOP calling girls slags', 'STOP ignoring students'/ 'Start respecting girls and women', 'Start listening to what students have to say'. This can work well following a discussion about a particular issue or you can open up the conversation and prompt participants to think about things that are happening in the world that make them angry, frustrated or upset. This could be a tweet, a school rule or comment that offended them or wider global issues.

Use pegs to hang the plates on a washing line that is strung up around the room. Next as a group walk around and view the plates and try to come to a consensus about which of the issues identified on the plates are most important for them to address as part of the RSE curriculum. What do they need to learn more about? Which of the START plates do they most want to put into action? This will be difficult and the group may not agree. Encourage the group to think about not just what is important to them personally but to those in minority groups or to their school/community/ youth club in general. Depending on the amount of time you have for your RSE curriculum, ask the group to agree on five–ten plates or key issues.

If you have time, ask participants to choose one of the START plates and discuss how to put it into action. This can be done in small groups or as a large group.

What jars you?

Adapted from *AGENDA: A young people's guide to making positive relationships matter* (see *Useful resources* at the end of this book). Used with permission. We refer to this simple but powerful method throughout the book.

 A creative activity that encourages participants to think about what is unfair and unequal in society when it comes to relationships, sex, gender and sexuality and what can be done to address this. This can be used to identify key issues and themes to focus on in your RSE curriculum. It is a great way of embedding social change and activism within your curriculum from the start.

 30–40 minutes

 Glass jars, slips of blank paper, coloured marker pens that can write on glass, flipchart and pens.

 11+

If you are working in a large group, divide participants into smaller groups. Give each group slips of paper, a glass jar and a pen. Tell the group that we are going to talk about what 'jars' us when it comes to relationships, sex, gender and sexuality. Show this definition of 'jar' and discuss what it means:

> **Jar** (verb): to jolt, shake, vibrate.
> - send a shock through something (especially the body).
> - strike against something with a vibration or jolt.
> - have a disturbing effect.

Ask each person to work on their own to write down all the things that jar them about how society is unequal or unfair when it comes to relationships, sex, gender and sexuality. Key questions for participants to consider are: What shocks you about relationships, sex, gender and sexuality today? What disturbs you? What disturbs others? What would you like to change about sex and relationships today? Once they have finished they should fold up the bits of paper and put them in their group's glass jar.

When all participants have finished, ask groups to work together to take each comment in turn and discuss what needs to change to turn what is unfair to fair or what is unequal to equal. These can be scribbled down on flipchart paper. Next ask each group to decorate their jar with messages for change, drawing on their brainstormed ideas.

Ask groups to present their jars to each other, explaining the things that jar them and what changes they would like to see. Participants will need to decide as a group whether they want to display their jars anywhere or give them to someone who needs to hear their messages.

Use this activity to identify the issues that are important to the young people that you work with. Use the identified issues and suggested strategies for change as a way of mapping out the themes and projects that you can include within your RSE curriculum.

Key questions for educators to consider when involving young people in RSE curriculum design

These questions are adapted from resources created by the Sex Education Forum[7]:

- Are participants consulted about what is included in RSE and when topics are introduced?
- Are participants asked for their ideas about how RSE is taught (for example, teaching methods and resources)?
- Is the cultural and religious background of participants reflected in the curriculum?
- Are your sessions inclusive in terms of gender, sexual orientation, disability, ethnicity, culture, age, religion or belief or other life-experience particularly HIV status and pregnancy?
- Have the needs of participants with special educational needs been met?

Sort it out

With thanks to Emma Renold for the idea for this activity.

Using images based on the key concepts in the UNESCO (2018) *International Technical Guidance on Sexuality Education* (see *Useful resources* at the end of this book), this open and creative activity allows participants to explore what themes, issues and topics they are interested in covering in RSE. The data and ideas from this activity can be used to inform curriculum planning and/or feedback to senior leaders in your organisation.
 20–30 minutes

One or more copies of the UNESCO (2018) *International Technical Guidance on Sexuality Education* available for free online. Pieces of card, a range of images, pens.
 11+

To prepare for this activity have a look at the UNESCO (2018) *International Technical Guidance on Sexuality Education*. This document draws on international research to create a framework for delivering RSE to children and young people of all ages. It contains eight key concepts to cover in RSE. Each concept is broken down into key topics and each topic into learning objectives for children aged 5–18.

Look at the eight key concepts (Relationships; Values, Rights, Culture and Sexuality; Understanding Gender; Violence and Staying Safe; Skills for Health and Well-being; The Human Body and Development; Sexuality and Sexual Behaviour; Sexual Health). Find or create an image that represents each key concept and use these to make sets of eight cards for participants to use. You can have more than one image for each concept/card. Use the UNESCO topic guide to give you ideas about what each concept covers. Alternatively you can ask participants to find (or create) the images and create the cards themselves as the first step of this activity.

To facilitate the activity divide participants into small groups and give each a set of picture cards. Ask them to sort the cards into groups but don't give them the categories. They have to choose the categories themselves. This will feel strange at first as we are used to being given the categories in card sort exercises but the open ended nature of the activity means that participants can take the discussion in directions that feel relevant and interesting to them. After a few minutes take feedback on each group's categories and the themes that emerged from their discussion. Repeat the exercise two more times with the rule that you are not allowed to re-use any of the categories. Take note of key themes that are emerging from the exercise.

Ask them to imagine that all the cards represent topics that they could learn about in RSE and sort them into an order of the things they would most like to learn about. As they are doing this give each group a blank card and ask them to draw or write on it any other issues or topics they would like to cover in RSE and include this in their card sort. You may find it useful to use the diamond nine technique (see Figure 2.3) to help participants to prioritise the different topics. Ask participants to share the diamonds with others and take photos for your records.

Once the priority topics have been identified and prioritised ask participants to select one topic or issue and write on flipchart paper: 1) what they already think/know/believe about this issue; 2) what questions they have about the issue and what they would like to learn more about; 3) what they would like to change about the way this issue is talked about/managed in their community and beyond. You may want to give them copies of the UNESCO report so that they can see the breakdown of possible topics and learning objectives for each concept for their age groups.

Make sure you are clear and honest with participants about how you will use this data and their ideas to inform your RSE curriculum planning. If there are limits to young people's involvement (e.g. you have to cover certain topics and/or have limited curriculum time, etc.) be honest about this. If you are working within tight constraints you may find it more helpful to focus this activity on one concept that you know you have to cover in the curriculum (e.g. relationships) and create image cards based on the key topics or learning objectives within the concept of relationships. This will allow you to open up the concept in detail and explore participants' needs, interests and concerns.

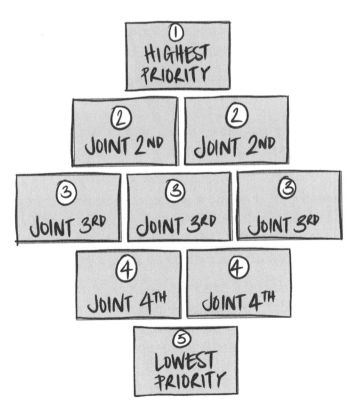

FIGURE 2.3 Diamond 9 technique
Illustration by: Chrissy Baxter

I know but I didn't know

Adapted from *AGENDA: A young people's guide to making positive relationships matter* (see *Useful resources* at the end of this book). Used with permission.

 A creative activity that enables participants to reflect on what they have already learnt in RSE and identify what more they would like know or raise greater awareness of. This can be used to inform the development of an RSE curriculum and to campaign on issues that are important to the group.

 60 minutes

 Paper and pens; phones/tablets/computers to research online and make short films; A3 card and marker pens; a quiet space; post-it notes; pens; large A3+ plain sketchbook; set of resources containing key facts and figures; videocamera/smartphone with recording device.

 11+

Working in small groups give each group some facts and figures about gender, sexuality, relationships and other related issues. Use accessible resources that present information in ways that young people can relate to. Here are some examples:

- NATSAL (The National Survey of Sexual Attitudes and Lifestyles).[8]
- Stonewall's *School Reports*:[9] we have provided the link to the 2017 report in the footnote which was the most recent report at the time of publishing. This survey is completed every 5 years so check that you have the most up to date version.
- Your local area School Health Survey – this will have lots of highly relevant and useful facts about children and young people's health behaviours.
- *Annex 5 SRE and Safeguarding: key facts and figures* in Renold, E and McGeeney, E, (2017) *Informing the Future of the Sex and Relationships Education Curriculum in Wales* (see *Useful resources* at the end of this book).
- Girls Attitudes Survey: Girlguiding.[10]

Working in small groups, ask participants to each identify a fact that they didn't previously know that shocks or surprises them. Ask them to write this on a post-it note starting with the phrase: 'I didn't know…'

Next ask each participant to write down on a different post-it note one thing that they did know already, based on all the things they learn at school. This can be from any subject. This time the sentence should start: 'I know that/I can…'. For example, *I can tell you Pythagoras Theorem, I can recite a soliloquy from Shakespeare's Macbeth, I can score 24 goals in one netball game.*

Go round the class and get everyone to read out their post-it notes, starting with what they did know, followed by what they didn't. For example, *I can tell you pythagoras theorem but I didn't know that almost half of all LGBT+ pupils still face bullying at school for being LGBT+.* Use this to discuss and reflect on what young people do and don't learn in schools. You may find these discussion prompts helpful:

- How many hours per year of RSE do you get at your school? How does this compare to other subjects?
- Should the number of hours be equal to other subjects?

- Who decides what is and is not useful knowledge?
- Should young people be able to decide what they learn?

Ask a group to decide what you want to do with the post-it notes. Here are two ideas:

- Get a large A3 sketch book. On one page write one statement that someone knew and on the opposite page what they didn't know. This creates a powerful visual illustration of young people's learning and the gaps in their knowledge. Participants can use simple sketches or diagrams as well. See page 46 of the *AGENDA* resource for examples of what this can look like.
- Make a flashcard story. A flashcard story is a short film of a person that is usually posted on YouTube where the person silently holds up a series of flashcards each containing a sentence. The words tell the person's story, without them uttering a word. To make your flashcard you will need to write the statements on large pieces of paper or card and film participants holding them up. They can do this covering their faces to remain anonymous if they want to. You can also film people turning the pages of the A3 book. **Note:** make sure you get consent to film from participants who appear in the film and from those whose work and ideas are included in the film.

Decide who needs to see the book, film or other output that the group makes. Young people can use this as a tool to campaign for more, or better, RSE at their school.

Ask it

 To give participants the opportunity to anonymously ask questions and get honest answers. This helps encourage participants to think about what they do and don't know already and helps educators identify what issues and topics participants are curious about.

 20 minutes

 Pens, slips of paper and a box/bag/container.

 11+

Note: This activity can be completed midway through a session or programme to help address the questions that will have arisen for participants so far or near the beginning of the programme to help you ascertain what issues participants are interested in or concerned about. It would be difficult to start a lesson or programme with this activity, however, as participants will need something to get them thinking about the issues first. Try starting with a simple brainstorm or agree/disagree activity before doing this activity.

Give each participant a slip of paper and a pen. Ask each participant to write one question that they have on the piece of paper and put it in the box provided. Explain that you will answer all questions and that all questions are anonymous. You can set the scope for the questions – it could be 'questions about anything we have talked about in the programme so far' or 'any question that you have about sex and relationships' or if you are focusing on a particular topic, be specific about this. If participants are struggling to think of something you may want to list some of the topics that they could ask you about. If participants do not want to participate ask them just to write something on the paper and put it in the box. This helps maintain the anonymity of those who have contributed questions.

Have a look through the questions and answer each one. If you have three questions about the same topic, read all of them. This is important so that participants know that you are addressing all of their questions – even if the question is challenging, silly or impossible to answer! For further advice complete module one of Brook's e-learning programme on Pleasure which has a range of tips and practical advice on how to answer difficult and challenging questions that young people can ask in RSE sessions.[11]

If you don't know how to answer a question, it is ok to say this to the group and to look up the question online in front of the group or to say that you will get back to them in the next session. This helps model to participants that it is ok not to know and where to go for reliable information and advice. Brook's 24/7 tool has answers to lots of frequently asked questions.[12]

Models of sex education

This activity has been adapted from activities in the *Sex and History* resource pack, created by the *University of Exeter*.[13] Used with permission.

 Using an historical object participants reflect on how we learn about sex and relationships from parents and others. This discussion-based activity can be creatively extended to encourage participants to articulate what and how they would like to be educated today. 30 minutes

 Image of the 'embracing couple' object (see Figure 2.4) either on a screen or printed on paper, enough for one copy per pair. Pens and paper. 14+

Note: You can download a free PowerPoint with images and short videos from the *Times Educational Supplement* (TES) website.[14] The resource contains lesson plans using a range of objects so scroll through until you find the embracing couple.

Without explaining what it is show the group the picture of the 'embracing couple' using the slides and/or print-outs of the image. Ask the group to consider the following questions:

- What is this?
- What was it used for?
- When might it have been made?

Give the group a minute to discuss in pairs and then take group feedback about their thoughts. Next reveal the following historical information:

This small ivory model of a couple embracing dates from 19th century, China. Historians don't know exactly who made this and what it was for. Some suggest that in China objects depicting sexual activity might have also been used as something known as a 'trunk-bottom'. Parents would place an object in the bottom of the trunk containing clothes, sheets, and crockery that a daughter would take to her new house when she got married. They are thought to have been a method of sex education.

FIGURE 2.4 Chinese ivory statue of man and woman engaged in sexual foreplay[a]

[a] This image can be downloaded for free from: https://wellcomecollection.org/works/z6p6xwe2

Credit: Wellcome Collection. CC BY

In pairs or as a group discuss the following:

- Why would a parent want to give such an object to a daughter on this occasion? *(Discussion ideas: Parents play a role in preparing their children for sexual relationships. How does this happen today? Is this object meant to be sexually arousing or educational? Or something else? Would a parent today give something like this to their child?)*
- Can you think of words to describe this image of a couple? *(Discussion ideas: Is the depiction intimate? Affectionate? Loving? Equal? Showing mutual pleasure?)*
- Why would parents hide this object at the bottom of the trunk? *(Invite participants to share their ideas. It could be that sex is often seen as a taboo subject that can only be talked about or represented in hidden or secret places. Prompt to think of examples of this today. Alternatively this could be seen as placing the object somewhere safe and a special indicating that sex is something to be treasured.)*
- Do you think they would have given such an object to a son as well? Why or why not? *(Discussion ideas: Do parents today have the same conversations with their daughters as their sons? Are there different expectations of men and women in society? Are girls expected to be more innocent, for example?)*

Working in pairs or small groups task participants with designing a modern day object for parents or teachers to use to help start conversations about relationships and/or sex or to provide young people with information they might need. Ask participants to present their design to the group. Discussion prompts might include: What learning or message would you want your object to convey? What would be the best way to do this? How might new technologies play a part in this?

Notes

1   http://lgbthistory.exeter.ac.uk/
2   www.jkp.com/uk/faith-values-and-sex-relationships-education-2.html
3   www.brook.org.uk
4   www.brook.org.uk
5   http://lgbthistory.exeter.ac.uk/items/show/5
6   www.stonewall.org.uk/school-report-2017
7   www.sexeducationforum.org.uk
8   www.natsal.ac.uk/media/2102/natsal-infographic.pdf
9   www.stonewall.org.uk/school-report-2017
10 www.girlguiding.org.uk/social-action-advocacy-and-campaigns/research/girls-attitudes-survey/
11 http://learn.brook.org.uk/
12 www.brook.org.uk/our-services/ask-brook-a-question-24-7
13 http://sexandhistory.exeter.ac.uk/
14 www.tes.com/teaching-resource/sex-and-history-version-2-sre-pshe-key-stage-4-and-5-11162331

CHAPTER 3

Relationships

Although we are not always aware of it, many of us try to conduct our relationships according to a set of unwritten rules about relationships, sex and gender. These 'rules' shape our expectations about relationships and are themselves shaped by the communities we live in, the media we engage with and the people we have relationships with. The activities in this chapter invite young people to identify and think critically about these 'rules' and explore alternative and perhaps more ethical ways of doing relationships. We draw on the work of researchers Jenny Walsh, Anne Mitchell and Mandy Hudson who have developed an ethical framework for relationships, based on research by Moira Carmody. This framework structures our chapter and underpins our approach to ethical relationships.

In conversations with researchers and educators young people repeatedly say that they don't learn enough about relationships at school and that when they do, there is not enough on positive relationships and relationships skills. The activities in this chapter are designed to address this gap and focus on how to do relationships ethically. Our aim is to give young people the opportunity to practise, explore and reflect on the skills needed to enjoy positive ethical relationships and respond to the many relationship pressures and conflicts that they may experience. Most of the activities can be used to explore any type of human relationship – familial, friendship, romantic and/or sexual and are suitable for young people of all ages.

The structure of this chapter is based on the ethical framework for love, sex and relationships in Walsh, J, Mitchell, A & Hudson, M, (2017) *The Practical Guide to Love, Sex and Relationships* from the Australian Research Centre in Sex, Health and Society, La Trobe University, Melbourne, Australia and based on the original work of Moira Carmody (see *Useful resources* at the end of this book). With thanks to all the researchers involved.

Chapter summary

Section 1: Taking care of me. The activities in this section look at how young people can take care of themselves and their bodies. There are topics on managing risk and personal boundaries and identifying positive and negative qualities within relationships. Activities in this section work well alongside those in Chapter 5: *Bodies* on moving-feeling bodies and those on bodies and pleasure in Chapter 6: *Sex*.

Section 2: Taking care of you. This section includes activities that explore how to manage relationship conflict, tension and competing needs in ethical ways as well as how to express love and care in your relationships with others.

Section 3: Having an equal say. Activities to help young people identify the unwritten rules in relationships and to think critically about power and how to negotiate conflict, pressure and consent in relationships in ethical ways. The activities in this section work well alongside those in Chapter 4: *Gender and sexual equality* on power, privilege and social norms and those in Chapter 6: *Sex* on consent.

Section 4: Learning as we go. Activities that explore ways of learning about our relationships through research, self reflection, discussion and creative projects. Participants are encouraged to observe what they are and are not doing in their relationships and to consider what it means to do relationships ethically.

Points to consider

- Make sure you don't reinforce heteronormative assumptions about relationships and families. Use inclusive language such as 'partner' (rather than boyfriend/girlfriend) and parent or parents (rather than mums and dads) and avoid using phrases such as 'when you get married/when you have a family'.
- Celebrate relationship diversity in your curriculum. Use scenarios and examples of diverse families and relationships that include LGBT+ as well as heterosexual relationships, 'blended' as well as single parent and 'nuclear' families and that involve people from diverse cultural and racial backgrounds. Make sure every young person can see themselves and others reflected in the curriculum. If this feels daunting ask the young people that you work with to help you develop your curriculum and audit your resources.
- Talking about family and intimate relationships can be emotionally charged and challenging at times. Ensure you have created a group agreement that young people are familiar with. Be clear with young people about who is available for them to talk to if they need support and be open and honest about your disclosure policy.
- Try to find a balance opening up spaces to discuss participants' own views and experiences of relationships and making sure you are not inviting them to over share about experiences that may leave them feeling vulnerable or exposed. You can do this by grounding your discussions in relationship scenarios or examples from the media (there are lots of examples in this chapter) and by creating and maintaining a clear group agreement which includes not asking each other personal questions.

- It can be challenging for young people to try and manage their own mental health and wellbeing as well as managing their relationships with friends, families, partners, peers and others. The activities in this chapter aim to support young people to understand the relationship between their own wellbeing, their relationships with others and the places and spaces that they spend time in and to help them develop strategies for taking care of themselves and others.
- Embed work around 'online safety' within your relationships curriculum, rather than as a discrete subject. Talk about ways of keeping safe online in the context of young people's relationships with peers, partners and others. Help young people to develop strategies for keeping safe and enjoying their online relationships that are realistic and that take into account the unequal and gendered power dynamics that shape young people's on- and offline experiences.

Section 1: Taking care of me

Personal universes

 An individual creative activity in which participants map their personal relationships and think about how they feel within different relationship orbits.

 20–30 minutes

 A3 paper and coloured pens.

 11+

Ask participants to draw out their personal universes on sheets of A3 paper. They should be one planet in the solar system and all the other planets orbiting around them are the people important to them in their lives (they can be individuals or groups). The size of the planet and the distance from your planet should denote how important and close they are to you. For example, someone who had a big impact but who is no longer in touch might appear as a large distant planet, whereas an annoying sibling might appear as a close small planet!

Ask participants to think about how they feel in each of their relationships. Is the relationship equal and balanced? Do they feel respected? Think about ways of capturing this in their universes. For example, where there is equality in the relationship this could be depicted as an even round orbit but where sometimes one has more power over the other then an elliptical orbit maybe more suitable. Participants may choose to draw meteorite or asteroid strikes for relationships or relational events that have had a big impact on their lives. Participants can annotate their solar system, planets and orbits to describe how they feel in their different relationships.

Use the following questions for personal reflection or small group discussions. Participants do not have to share their Universes with anyone else unless they want to.

- How do you feel when you are in each of the orbits created by the different relationships in your life?
- Which of your relationships can you choose to be in? Which can't you?
- Why might you choose to spend time in relationships where you feel unsafe or uncomfortable? What pressures do you feel? How much choice do you really have?
- What can you do to take care of yourself within your different relationship orbits?
- What kind of a solar system do you live in? How does the nature of your solar system affect your relationships? (E.g. What kinds of external factors shape what is and is not possible in your relationships?) For example:
  - *The things you do and the physical environment around you*, e.g. having a comfy home or a nice place to spend time makes the relationship more comfortable/enjoyable.
  - *The cultural norms and values at play*, e.g. experiences of discrimination such as racism affect the relationships that we have and how we feel in different spaces.
  - *The laws and policies of the institutions you spend time in*, e.g. schools that keep you safe/unsafe.
- What would need to change in your solar system to help you feel safe and comfortable in all your relationships with others? Which of these changes are possible? Which aren't?

As an alternative to this activity, facilitate the 'Where are my safe spaces?' activity in Chapter 2: *Creating safer spaces* (p. 17) that asks participants to create a map of all the places that they spend time and to think about where they feel safe and comfortable and where they don't. Encourage participants to think about creative ways of showing how they feel in different spaces using colours, symbols or metaphors.

The key learning is that how we feel in different spaces is shaped not just by the physical environment but by the people and relationships that create that space. These relationships shape how much power and control, freedom and choice we have. This is an important starting point for look at self care as it invites young people to think about how they can take care of themselves and others in the context of the social world around them.

Comfort, Stretch and Panic in relationships

 An individual reflective activity that asks participants to consider how they feel in their relationships with others using the Comfort, Stretch and Panic model. This is used to explore how we feel in our relationships with others and to think about ways of supporting those who feel powerless, panicky or out of control within their relationships with others. 15–20 minutes

 Diagram of Comfort, Stretch, Panic model or pens and flipchart to draw one. 11+

Start by completing the 'Comfort, Stretch and Panic' activity in Chapter 2: *Creating safer spaces* (on p. 21). If you have completed this in a previous session or some time ago, refresh participants memories by re-drawing the comfort, stretch, panic diagram and brainstorming how someone might feel in each of these zones (see Figure 3.1).

Ask participants to think of one important relationship in their lives. They do not have to share this information with others. Ask them to consider:

- How do you feel in this relationship? Jot down key words or phrases.
- Which zones does this relationship take you to? Comfort, Stretch and/or Panic?
- Does which zone you are in vary depending on what you are doing? E.g. when watching TV with your partner you might be in your Comfort zone but when arguing you may feel in the Stretch zone.
- How has this changed over time? E.g. when you first met your partner you were always in the Stretch zone but now you are mainly in the Comfort zone.

FIGURE 3.1 Comfort, Stretch, Panic model

Illustration by: Chrissy Baxter

Ask participants to draw the Comfort, Stretch, Panic model. Their task is to map their relationships on to the diagram. They could choose to map multiple relationships on one model (asking themselves the questions above) or to focus on one relationship over time, using arrows to show how the relationship has changed. Models can be annotated with key words, images and phrases to describe how they feel within a relationship. Keep diagrams anonymous so that they can be shared or displayed if needed or desired. The maps can make a powerful display when brought together.

When bringing the models together try and tease out through discussion the idea that in positive relationships we usually switch between Comfort and Stretch zones. The 'Stretch' moments can be important for bringing about changes in our relationships (e.g. plucking up the courage to talk to someone or to address an issue that is worrying you) and providing moments of bonding (e.g. when you tell someone something about yourself, get through a disagreement together). However, feeling regular moments of panic when you are with someone is not ok. This could be because you are someone who finds relationships difficult and communicating with others makes you feel panicky and uncomfortable. Or it could be because you are in a relationship that is abusive or exploitative.

Ask the group to think about how to support someone who feels panicky in their relationships with others (e.g. give them space, go somewhere quiet with them, talk to them about how they feel when they feel less panicky) and someone who has one particular relationship (e.g. a friend, partner or parent) that regularly takes them into the Panic zone (e.g. talk to them about how they feel, challenge the idea that it is 'normal' to feel panicky about your relationship, encourage them to think about who they feel comfortable with and to seek help).

Note: This discussion could lead to the disclosure of exploitative or abusive relationships. This is a safeguarding concern that you should always follow up with the young person after the session has finished – it is never appropriate to do this in the group setting. If this happens, close down the conversation sensitively and move on until you can talk to the young person on their own.

Relationship boundary maps

 This activity explores relationship boundaries by asking participants to create individual visual maps of their relationships. Participants can focus on romantic, family or friendship relationships. 20–30 minutes

 Board/flipchart and pens, pens and A3 paper/blank maps (optional) for each participant. 11+

Introduce the group to the idea of a boundary. To do this draw a shape on the board or flipchart such as a circle or a square. Define the inside as the local school or youth club.

Brainstorm what behaviours are acceptable within the school/club boundaries (e.g. for a school this might be sitting quietly, discussing classroom topics, chatting with friends, using phones at break time) and what behaviours are excluded (e.g. smoking, wearing your own clothes, swearing, etc.) and what is acceptable outside of them. Discuss how these boundaries are established (e.g. school rules) and how they are policed and maintained (e.g. system of punishments and rewards).

Next introduce the idea of a relationship boundary starting with a familiar relationship such as teacher/pupil, youth worker/young person or parent/child. Draw a second shape and write what is acceptable within the relationship boundary and what is unacceptable outside of it. Discuss how these boundaries are established and maintained.

Note: If groups are familiar with the concept of relationship boundaries skip the previous section and start here.

Next ask participants to work individually to think about their own personal boundaries in relationships. They can either choose one type of relationship to focus on – this could be friendships, family relationships or romantic partners – or one relationship in their life. This should be done anonymously and participants do not have to share their work if they don't want to.

Ask participants to create a visual map of their relationship boundaries using the following prompts:

> **Privacy:** Can you look at each other's phones? Diaries? Bedside drawers? Can you be in the same room when one of you is on the loo/in the bath? What about talking about your relationship or your sex life with other people?
>
> **Contact**: How much contact do you want to have throughout the day? How many texts/phone calls is too much? Do you want any physical contact?
>
> **Fidelity:** What does it mean to be unfaithful in this relationship? Can you be friends with others? Can you chat online to others? Can you be in group chats that exclude the other person? Is this an open relationship? Is a drunken kiss a dealbreaker?
>
> **'Banter':** Do you want to have banter in your relationship? At what point for you does gentle teasing become personal attacks? Are there any areas where nobody can comment (e.g. appearance, personality traits)?
>
> **Body and sex:** Is it ok to touch your body? Are there any parts of the body that you do not want to be touched? Do you want to experiment sexually? Any sexual activities you do not want to try? Would you have unprotected sex? Would you have sex with more than one person?
>
> **Boundary crossing:** Do you communicate your boundaries to the other person? Or are they assumed and unspoken? Does the other person have similar or different boundaries? What do you do when they clash? How would you feel if someone crossed one of your boundaries? How would you respond?

Participants will need to think about how to visually represent their relationship boundaries. For example, using shapes, world and country maps depicting islands and borders, or planets in the solar system. Maps can be annotated with boundary statements and boundaries, and the importance or strength of a boundary can be indicated visually, e.g. a high barbed wire wall with security lighting might indicate a boundary that cannot be crossed but a small hedge and flower border might be a boundary that can be crossed with the right person or with some negotiation or it might mean it's not quite such an important boundary.

Participants can share their maps in pairs if they feel comfortable and reflect on what they have learnt from doing this activity. Ask pairs to share any key learning points. Discuss as a group:

- Why is it useful to have boundaries in relationships?
- What can we do if we feel someone is crossing one of our boundaries?
- Who has control over a relationship boundary?
- How can we take care of ourselves in relationships where boundaries are difficult or not as we would wish?

Lean on me

 This activity involves participants doing trust leans in pairs as a way of exploring and reflecting on risk-taking and trust in relationships.

 15–20 minutes

 Room with space for trust exercises, (optional) large paper and pens.

 11+

Ask participants to get into a pair with someone they feel comfortable with. Take it in turns to do a trust lean. This is where partners stand both facing in the same direction (not facing each other). The person at the front needs to lean backwards, keeping their body straight, and the person behind catches them under their arms. The catcher should gently take their partner's weight before pushing them gently back up to standing.

Partners should take it in turns and have a couple of goes each. You may want to ask participants to swap partners. Remember the group ground rules (see Chapter 1, p. 14) and participants' right to pass.

Come back together as a group to share experiences. You can do this verbally using the following questions. Alternatively spread a large sheet of paper on the floor and ask participants to sit around the edge and draw or write their responses.

- How did it feel to do this activity?
- Was it easy or hard for you?
- What were the risks of the activity (think of physical and emotional risks)?
- Why did you do the activity even though there were risks?
- What made it possible for you to trust your partner (or not if that was the case)?

Lead a wider discussion about trust and risk-taking within relationships using the following questions. Emphasise that we all take risks. Having relationships with others involves taking risks as does trying new things on your own and with others. The aim is not to eliminate risk but to take risks safely and to help others to do the same.

- How do you know if you can trust someone?
- Does your past experience of relationships affect how you trust someone?
- If you don't feel you can trust someone what bodily sensations might you be experiencing?
- What does trusting your gut mean?
- If your gut is saying 'don't trust' why do we sometimes override this?

Romance or red flag?

This activity is adapted from an activity called *Healthy and Unhealthy Relationships* from Lesson 3 – *Love* created by Justin Hancock and Alice Hoyle for *DO…RSE for schools* used with permission (see *Useful resources* at the end of this book).

 Using a red, amber and green traffic light system, participants work as a group to discuss the signs and indicators of positive and of abusive relationships.

 30 minutes

 List of situations on card. Individual green, amber and red flags.

 13+

Choose a selection from the following examples and discuss as a whole group whether each example is a relationship green flag (i.e. an indicator of a positive relationship), an amber flag (it depends on the context) or a red flag (a clear sign of an abusive relationship). Remember that many of these can apply to friendships too.

You may want to give each participant three flags (or ask them to make their own) and task them with raising the flag of their choice when you reveal an example. This can help encourage participation in larger groups. Alternatively you can sort the statements on a continuum from positive relationships through to unsupportive and then abusive relationships.

- Saying 'I love you' within first few weeks of a relationship.
- Messaging every night for hours.
- Keeping in contact throughout the day.
- Never stopping talking about a partner.
- Seeing friends less.
- One person pays for everything.
- A big age gap.
- A relationship with no arguments.
- Sending nudes to each other.
- Showing nudes of partner to friends.
- Buying lots of gifts for the other person.
- Making plans for kids, marriage, moving in together.
- Having enjoyable sex.
- Making comments about how you look.
- Always wanting to check in with the other person.
- Being able to be yourself.
- Encouraging you to travel independently and not always rely on your parents.
- Being physically violent.
- Not letting you pay for anything.
- Sharing social media passwords with partner.
- Friends with an ex on Facebook.
- Checking partner's phone without permission.
- Relationship status says single on Facebook (even though they are not!).
- Meeting up in the park every night for a few hours.
- Playing games together on X-box most nights.
- Using messaging to chat about sex and what they want to do with a partner.
- Using text to check where partner is and that they are safe.

For many of the examples, the answer may be amber because whether or not a behaviour is abusive will depend on the context and participants will need more information in order to make their decision. For example, 'seeing friends less' could be part of being in a relationship with someone who you have shared interests with or like spending time with and therefore have less time to see your friends. Or it could be a symptom of an abusive relationship in which one person controls the other and restricts how much time they spend with their friends.

For each amber example, ask participants to imagine scenarios in which the behaviour could be seen as positive and scenarios in which it could be a sign of an abusive relationship. You can do a few examples as a whole group as part of your discussion before breaking into small groups. Ask participants to be imaginative – think of the ages and genders of the couple and the background to their relationship.

For each red flag example, ask the group what they might do in that situation and how they could make the situation more positive:

- How can we support someone in an unsupportive or abusive relationship?
- Where can we find support for people in unsupportive or exploitative relationships? For example, in schools, from the police, family, refuges, counselling services, young people's services (you may be able to signpost to help that can be offered in school or local services).
- What can people do about being in an unsupportive or abusive relationship and what are the risks about trying to change or leave them?
- How can society at large help people to have happier relationships? For example, what do films and TV teach us about love and relationships?

Mind flower

 This activity introduces participants to a model used in Cognitive Behavioural Therapy (CBT) – commonly called the Vicious flower – for exploring the relationship between our thoughts, feelings and actions. Participants work in small groups to consider how our thoughts and feelings about a given situation can affect how we respond in that moment (and vice versa – how our responses can also affect our thoughts and feelings). 40–50 minutes

 Blank flower handout or ask participants to draw the outline of a flower with four petals. 11+

Draw or project a large blank flower and label each petal as: Thoughts, Emotions, Behaviours and Physical feelings (see Figure 3.2). Ask participants to think about a common relationship scenario that young people experience in their everyday lives that is challenging, stressful or difficult. For example, a parent is saying you have to be home at a certain time which is really early and means you either miss out on being with your friends or get home late which causes arguments; your partner is jealous because you are talking to someone online that they don't think you should be talking to; drama is unfolding on a group text because someone said something cruel about one person in the group.

Start by summarising the scenario in the middle of the flower. Next ask participants to brainstorm how they might think and feel in this scenario and what they might do. Try and probe beyond the 'correct' way of responding and think about good and bad thoughts, feelings and actions. Write participants' responses in the relevant petal.

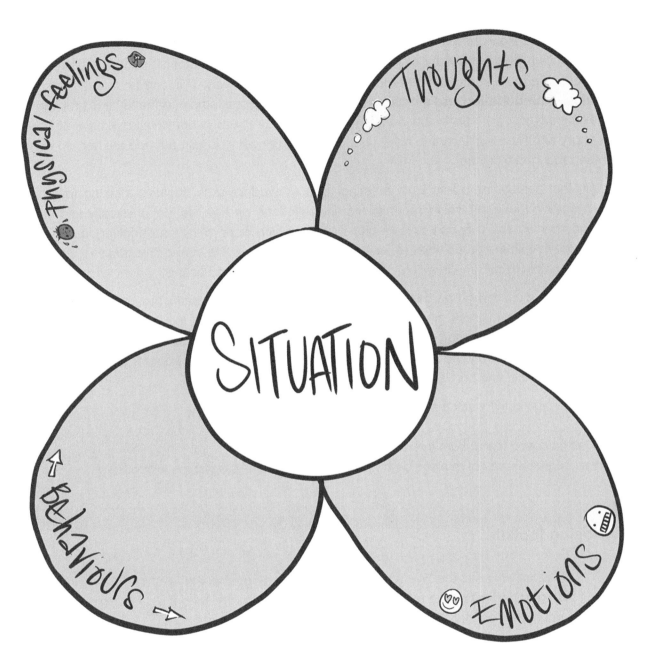

FIGURE 3.2 Mind flower

Illustration by: Chrissy Baxter

Divide participants into small groups and give them a blank copy of the flower (or ask them to draw it). Ask them to repeat the activity for a new scenario. It is helpful to all look at the same scenario.

Once all the groups have filled in their flowers take feedback from each group and explore the similarities and differences in how people could respond to the same scenario. Use the diversity of responses to highlight that it is not the situation itself that makes us feel or act in a certain way (as shown by the diversity of responses across the group). Rather it is our thoughts and assumptions *about* the situation that lead us to feel a certain way. This can be summarised as **situation> interpretation and self talk> emotion-action.** For example: A friend hasn't replied to my text message. This must be because she's annoyed at me and is punishing me. I feel anxious and angry and like I don't want to talk to her anymore. I'm going to text her and tell her I'm done with her and then block her.

Explain that sometimes our internal messaging is skewed towards negative thinking (or automatic negative thoughts) which can then impact negatively on how we feel physically and mentally and how we act. This can cause vicious cycles which work to trap our thinking in negative ways. Explore with the group what we can all do to break this cycle of negative thinking. Suggest pausing to think: What am I thinking? What am I feeling? How am I acting?

Emphasise that changing one petal such as how you act, or the self-talk/thoughts in your head can help shift another petal, such as how you feel. Experiment with this by proposing positive alternative thoughts in relation to your scenario and seeing how this might shift emotions, physical feelings and actions. It can be helpful to do this on the board to show participants the relationships between the petals and between what we think, feel and do.

To reflect on the activity ask the group:

- What have you learnt from this activity?
- How might this way of thinking be helpful for you in your relationships with others?

Wellbeing toolkits

 This activity uses the *Five ways to mental wellbeing* model to support participants to reflect on strategies they currently use and strategies that they could use to support and improve their own wellbeing. 30 minutes (minimum)

 Copies of *Five ways to mental wellbeing* model. Art and craft materials and shoe boxes depending on which toolkit is being made. 11+

Introduce participants to the *Five ways to mental wellbeing* model from the New Economics Foundation. This suggests that there are five actions that are all equally important for improving our wellbeing:

Connect... with the people around you. With family, friends, colleagues and neighbours. At home, at work, or in your local community. Think of these as the cornerstones of your life and invest time in developing them. Building these connections will support and enrich you everyday.

Be Active... Go for a walk or run. Step outside. Cycle. Play a game. Garden. Dance. Exercising makes you feel good. Most importantly, discover a physical activity you enjoy and that suits your level of mobility and fitness.

Take Notice... Be curious. Catch sight of the beautiful. Remark on the unusual. Notice the changing seasons. Savour the moment, whether you are walking to work, eating lunch or talking to friends. Be aware of the world around you and what you are feeling. Reflecting on your experiences will help you appreciate what matters to you.

Keep learning... Try something new. Rediscover an old interest. Sign up for that course. Take on a different responsibility at work. Fix a bike. Learn to play an instrument or how to cook your favourite food. Set a challenge you will enjoy achieving. Learning new things will make you more confident as well as being fun.

Give... Do something nice for a friend, or a stranger. Thank someone. Smile. Volunteer your time. Join a community group. Look out, as well as in. Seeing yourself, and your happiness, linked to the wider community can be incredibly rewarding and creates connections with the people around you.[1]

Ask participants to work on their own to brainstorm strategies that they use to help them look after their own wellbeing and take care of themselves. Write each strategy on a post-it note and see if it is possible to sort their strategies into the five categories. It doesn't matter if some of the strategies don't fit. The aim here is to explore the model and use it to identify which areas you have lots of strategies for and which you don't. For example, some of us are really good at connecting with others and building strong relationships, but not so good at making time to be active or look after our bodies.

Ask the group to consider the answers to the following questions

- What else could I do to look after my wellbeing that I don't currently do?
- What can others do to support me?
- What else do we need to make it possible for us to look after ourselves (e.g. support from parents, safe places, enough money, etc.)?
- If we don't have the things we need to help us, what can we do? (See the extension activity on 'Barriers to self care' on p. 60 to explore this further.)

Encourage participants to jot down any new ideas for how they could support their own wellbeing and any suggestions of organisations and resources that could support them. Encourage participants to focus on areas of their wellbeing that they have less existing strategies for and to ask their peers for suggestions and look online for tips and resources if needed (e.g. local groups they could join or examples of activism that other young people have engaged in).

To pull these ideas together ask participants to create their own wellbeing and self-care toolkit that they can use as and when they need it. This can take any form they wish. For example:

- A small cardboard box of resources that participants can make, find and collect, e.g. a hoody, a book, pajamas, trainers or sports wear, earphones, chocolate, an apple, a pot noodle, bubble bath, song lyrics, letters from close friends, photos, a zine.
- A jar filled with quotes, instructions to self, phone numbers, websites and things to make them laugh. The jar can be decorated with key images and messages.

- A playlist or digital file containing videos, tips, links, images designed to help them relax, reflect, laugh or connect with others.
- A dodecahedron dice (the net for which is widely available online to print onto card). On each of the 12 sides write a strategy for self care that works for you. In times of need roll the dice and do the self-care strategy. (With thanks to 2BU Somerset LGBT+ service for this idea).
- Introduce the HALT (Hungry, Angry, Lonely, Tired) strategy. The idea is that when we notice we aren't feeling good we stop (Halt!) and think: Am I Hungry? Angry? Lonely? Tired? This can help us decide what to do next to look after ourselves as sometimes the solution can be more straightforward than we think (get something to eat, get some sleep, find someone to hang out with). Task participants with creating a card containing information about the strategy that can be kept in a wallet or pocket to remind someone of the strategy when they need it. Or they can explore alternative strategies that they think would be useful to them in taking care of themselves. For example, every day reflecting on and sharing #3goodthings (an exercise in gratitude) or regular mindfulness practice using an app like Headspace.

Extension: Barriers to self care

Make sure that discussions about positive wellbeing and self care do not close down opportunities to talk about the barriers and challenges that young people experience when trying to look after and feel good about themselves. For example, most young people are not economically independent, have limited choice over who they live with and the conditions they live in and may experience multiple forms of discrimination. They will also have lots of relationships with others that they have limited choice over (e.g. parents, teachers, etc.). All of these factors will impact on their wellbeing.

To explore this ask participants to write down (or draw) all the barriers to good self care they experience and wish they could get rid of. Write each one on a piece of paper. Scrunch each piece of paper up and put it inside a jar or a paper box. Decorate the outside of the jar/box with images or words that show what they can do moving forwards to be kind to themselves or to make positive changes in their lives. You can either bring in old jam jars to use or task participants with making simple paper boxes.

Section 2: Taking care of you

Relationships venn diagrams

Adapted from a resource created by Justin Hancock and an activity created by Justin Hancock and Alice Hoyle for *DO…RSE for schools* (see *Useful resources* at the end of this book). Used with permission.

 This is a discussion-based activity that uses visual aids to enable participants to think critically about how to find balance of time, independence, power and control within their relationships with others. The aim is to think about different types of relationships and what makes a relationship positive and enjoyable.

 20–30 minutes

 Paper, pens, flip chart/board, pens.

 11+

Draw six venn diagrams on the board or on flipchart paper. See the examples provided in Figure 3.3. Your drawings don't have to be exact.

Divide the group into pairs or threes and ask them to draw the same six venn diagrams on a large piece of paper. Explain that each diagram is an example of a different type of relationship. Make it clear that we are talking about all kinds of different relationships such as friendships – not just romantic/sexual relationships.

Ask participants to write down words or phrases they would use to describe each relationship that is represented through these diagrams. These could be nouns or adjectives (e.g. friends with benefits, long term relationships, parent/child, groupmates, abusive, positive, close, sexual, romantic).

Ask participants to then share some of their thoughts with the rest of the group. As you go, ask these questions to draw out more comments and views:

- Which of these show positive relationships? What is a 'positive' relationship? (E.g. equal balance of power between all those involved, independence and time to ourselves and time together, care and respect, good communication, etc.)
- Is it important to have parts of a circle that don't overlap? Why? (e.g. so we still have a relationship with ourselves/time on our own)
- What might be left of the circles if (when) the relationships end? What might that mean for us? (e.g. in some of these examples we might have very little of our own interests/friends at the end of the relationship)
- Which relationships look like they might be exploitative or abusive? What makes a relationship abusive? (e.g. unequal power balance, no independence or freedom, lack of care and respect)
- How do we know if our own relationships are balanced and equal? (e.g. checking in with yourself – do I have enough time/independence/freedom/choices? Check in with friends, discuss with partner)

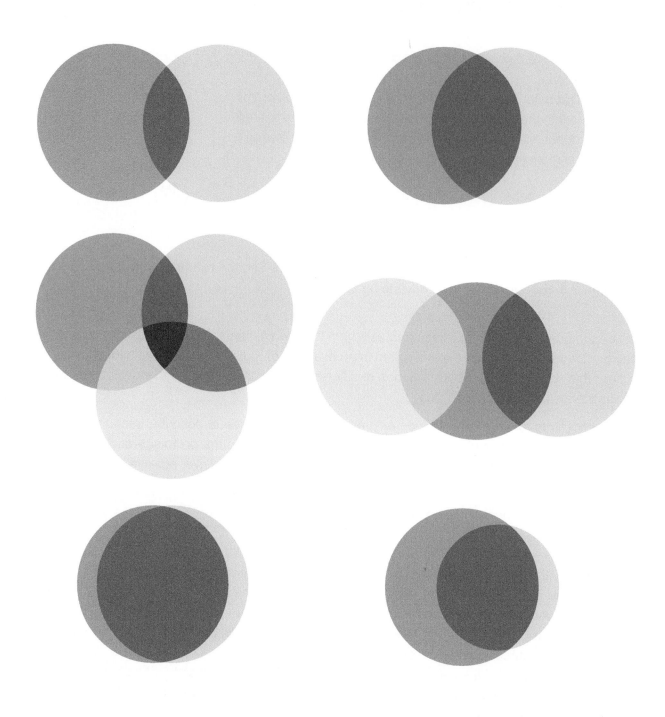

FIGURE 3.3 Relationships venn diagrams

Digital dilemmas

 This activity uses scenarios to provoke discussion about consent, trust and safety when using technology within relationships. It encourages participants to think about the role of friends and peers, as well as those in relationships, in facilitating ethical relationships and decision making.

 30 minutes

 Scenarios printed out.

 14+

Divide into small groups and give each a case study to read and discuss. Go around and prompt discussion about what each person in the case study should do to ensure that they are using technology ethically. Encourage discussion of the role of peers and bystanders – not just the couple – in creating positive, consensual relationships. To prompt participants you can use the ethical framework developed by Walsh, et al. (2017 – see *Useful resources* at the end of this book) that structures this chapter: taking care of me, taking care of you, having an equal say, learning as we go.

Feedback to the wider group and lead a plenary discussion using the following questions as a guide:

- How can we use technology ethically within our relationships – without harm to ourselves or to others? What kind of ground rules/code of conduct might be useful?
- How can friends and peers support couples to enjoy positive relationships?
- What can we all do to create positive relationship cultures online and offline?

Digital Dilemmas: Scenarios for participants

Ali and Becky

Ali and Becky met through a friend and started going out straight away. They have both been in relationships before, but this is Becky's first relationship with a woman. After a few weeks Ali changes her relationship status and starts putting photos on Instagram of romantic walks and time spent together, with descriptions like 'date night with my girl' and hashtags like #girlfriend, #love and #mygirl. She doesn't tag Becky because Becky told her not to. Becky doesn't ever post anything about Ali. This makes Ali feel like Becky doesn't care about her or is embarrassed about their relationship. Becky doesn't want her family to know she's seeing Ali as she can't face all the questions that will follow. She wants to be with Ali but just wants to keep it between them.

What should Ali and Becky do?

Matt and Laurie

Matt and his girlfriend Laurie met at school in year 7. They knew each other a bit and then became friends in year 10 when they had science together. Later in the year they started going out and went 'Facebook Official' after about three weeks. They often have matching profile pictures although they don't use Facebook much to chat.

Both Laurie and Matt have photos of themselves on Facebook with other people – in some of them it looks like Matt is flirting with other girls. Laurie doesn't like it and wants Matt to delete those photos and block some of the girls in the photos from his profile. Matt doesn't care that Laurie has photos of her with other boys on Facebook but he doesn't like it when she snapchats with other boys in their year. He wonders what she is sending. It is starting to cause arguments.

What should Laurie and Matt do?

Latoya, Max and Lara

It's Friday night and Latoya is very drunk at a house party. She is snogging Max and they end up sneaking upstairs to have sex. Unknown to Latoya, her friend Lara secretly films Latoya and Max having sex and then puts the film on a group chat.

What should Latoya, Max, Lara and the members of the group chat do?

Luca and Jasmine

Luca and Jasmine have been together for three months. At first Jasmine wasn't sure how much Luca liked her as he was always chatting to other girls. Now he has changed and is always telling her how much he loves her and how he wants to be with her forever – as long as he can trust her. She's shared her passwords with him and stopped using snapchat when he asked. Now she only uses it to message him and to send him photos and videos when he asks for them. Jasmine is happy but her best friend Tash is worried. She knows that Luca shows everyone nudes of Jasmine and still chats to other girls online. Recently Luca filmed them having sex and everyone is saying that he is showing it around, although Tash hasn't seen it.

What should Luca, Tash and Jasmine do?

Jono and Zee

Jono is 15 and has been playing PS4 for years. He has met lots of friends online over the years. They chat during games and sometimes in between but have never met up. Recently Jono has met a guy who he really likes called Zee. They chat on snapchat and Facebook too. It's started getting really flirty and they have been sending lots of topless photos to each other. Zee suggests that they meet up and Jono agrees. When Jono tells his friend Kyle about his plans to meet up with Zee, Kyle says he is mad – he has no idea who this guy really is and he might be some kind of weirdo. Jono disagrees. He has been chatting to Zee for months and has told him things he has never told Kyle. Besides, it's hard to meet other gay guys his age where he lives and this could be his only chance to have a real relationship.

What should Jono, Zee and Kyle do?

Ask a rellie

 A 'homework' activity that tasks participants with having conversations with family and friends about positive relationships and what makes a relationship work. An alternative research task is provided for young people who are unable to do this.

 This is a 'homework' activity that needs a minimum of 20 minutes discussion time in the session. Can be extended to a longer activity of up to an hour.

 Online access may be required.

 11+

Task participants with identifying someone in their life who they think is in a positive long term relationship with a partner or a friend. Participants should contact that person and ask to 'interview' them by email, phone or face to face and ask them what they think has made their relationship work well over time. Participants may need to be prepared to discover that what they thought was a happy relationship is actually more complicated!

Possible questions to ask include:

- What do you think has made your relationship work over the years?
- How do you give care and respect for the other person? How do they do this for you?
- Is this an equal relationship? In what ways is it equal/unequal?
- What do you do if/when you want different things? How do you manage this?
- What have you learnt about your relationship over the years?

Participants will need to get the consent of the person they are interviewing to record or take notes on their answers and to share them anonymously with the rest of the group. This can be done through changing the person's name and the way you describe your relationship (e.g. say it's a friend's aunt, rather than your aunt, etc.).

In the session ask participants to collate their responses and discuss as a group. See if there are any common factors that the group can identify in the responses. You may want to create a display that showcases quotes and/or key factors from participants' research.

Ask participants to reflect on what they have learnt from the activity, in particular about how people can manage competing interests and needs and how people can give care and respect.

If participants are not able to find someone to interview they can look at the findings from the *Enduring Love* study[2] as an alternative. The findings from this study, which involved over 5,000 adults in the UK, have been summarised in a free e-learning module for the *Brook Learn* platform[3] called *Relationships and Enduring Love*. Participants will need to sign up for free to access the course. Although it is aimed at professionals working with young people the material is suitable and accessible for young people. Task participants with looking at module 2: *The secrets to a lasting relationship* and ask them to share key findings; anything that surprised them; any thoughts on whether the findings would have been any different if the research had been conducted with young people.

100 ways to show I love you

 A fun and creative activity that explores ways of showing love and care within a relationship.

 20 minutes

 Pen and paper, other creative and craft materials and online access as required.

 11+

The task is to brainstorm 100 ways of showing someone that you love them. For example, giving someone a hug, making someone a cup of tea, asking someone how their day has been, etc. This can be a family relationship, friendship or sexual relationship. Participants can do this individually or in small or large groups. Responses can be displayed however the group choose. Ideas include a series of tweets with an agreed hashtag, written on origami birds, a paper chain across the room, heart shaped post-it notes or biscuits, a PowerPoint or poster.

For ideas and inspiration participants can look at the findings from *Enduring Love*, a study of adults in the UK and what makes their relationships work (see 'Ask a rellie' activity on p. 66). Go to the *Brook Learn Relationships and Enduring Love* online learning programme modules 2 and 3 to see examples of things that people do together that they enjoy and that make them feel valued and appreciated. Examples include: laughing together, talking and listening, being made a cup of tea and your partner doing the household chores.

Love is...?

 A creative activity that explores ideas about love and romance using the Love is... cartoons created by Kim Casali in the late 1960s.

 10–20 minutes

 Cartoons to show to participants digitally. Post-it notes and pens. Arts materials.

 11+

Kim Casali was a New Zealand cartoonist who created the cartoon feature *Love is...* in the late 1960s. These single frame cartoons consist of the words 'Love is...' and then an image representing different ideas about love and romance. Google 'Kim Casali' and have a look at the hundreds of examples from the last five decades available online.

To facilitate the activity show participants a range of the cartoons. Ask participants to call out key words that they think of when they see the cartoons. Brainstorm these to build a picture of what love is (according to these cartoons). Once you have finished, discuss with the participants what the cartoons *don't* show us about relationships. Ideas include: all the cartoons show a boy and girl so we don't necessarily see LGBT+ relationships represented; most of the cartoons don't show the tensions and challenges involved in loving someone; the cartoons focus on adult relationships.

Next ask participants to create their own cartoon that captures their own ideas about what love is. This can be done as a quick fire activity using anonymous post-it notes containing words and/ or images. (The cartoons apparently began as notes that Kim Casali left around the house for her husband.)

Look at the post-it notes as a whole group and consider:

- You may find participants' responses vary between idealistic and cynical responses. It is worth discussing with the group the difference between idealistic and realistic relationship expectations. Where do we get our ideas from about what a relationship *should* be like? How do we learn how to resolve tensions and difficulties in relationships in ways that are respectful? How do we maintain an equal balance in a relationship?
- Some of the ideas captured in the cartoons from the 1970s and 1980s seem outdated and/or sexist (e.g. love is babysitting so she can go to her part-time job; love is buying her an Easter bonnet) but others seem timeless (e.g. still hearing fireworks go off when you kiss/wishing she was there to enjoy the view with you). Explore this with participants through comparing some of the examples found online with those created by participants. Be sure to check the date of any found online as there are lots of contemporary examples too. You can also turn this into a quiz by reading out an example and getting participants to guess the decade.

As a group, decide if and how you want to curate your cartoon ideas. For example, by selecting key examples to develop into larger cartoons/images to display in your place of work, by taking photos of the quick ideas sketched out on post-it notes and sharing these online using an agreed hashtag. This can be extended to a longer creative project where everyone spends time creating their own A5/A4 image to create a 'Love is…' gallery.

A complement of compliments

This activity provides the opportunity to practise giving and receiving compliments – something that many of us often find difficult to give.

15 minutes

Room with space for participants to move around.

11+

Ask participants to stand in two rows or two circles with each person facing a partner. Each person needs to give their partner a compliment and receive one in return. Once this has been done, row A moves along one person so that everyone has a go at complimenting each other. Keep going until the exercise starts to feel repetitive (this can happen in larger groups). If this feels too difficult / daunting for participants you can use the compliment cards from the activity 'The gift of a compliment' in Chapter 8: *Concluding the learning* (p. 319).

To lead a discussion and extend the activity use one or more of the following questions:

- How did it feel to take part in this activity? (e.g. *awkward, nice, positive, hard, etc.*)
- How does it feel to be *required* to compliment someone? (e.g. *Makes the compliment feel less valid because you know someone was forced to give it to you; feels coercive having to compliment someone you don't know very well or don't like; encourages you to think about others in the group and be kind and positive.*)
- What kinds of things did people say to accept or acknowledge a compliment? (*Thank you, nothing, disagreed, agreed.*)
- Why can it be difficult to accept compliments? (*We are not used to doing it; feels arrogant to accept them; we don't often say kind and positive things to each other. Note if there are any gender differences here.*)

- Did anyone receive any compliments about their looks? How did this feel? (*Answers may include awkward or flattered and some people may feel objectified and that all that matters about them is their appearance. If this is the case explore some non-appearance related compliments that participants can use in the future – this is something we may need to practise as we can often focus on how people look – especially when it comes to girls and women. See the examples in 'The gift of a compliment' activity on p. 319 of this book for suggestions.*)
- What's the difference between a compliment and a sexist comment? (*see following activity, 'Is it a compliment?'*)

Is it a compliment?

 An interactive activity that explores the concepts of sexism and objectification using the flow diagram created by Kate Meaner, shared here with permission. Works as a standalone activity or as an extension to the previous activity: 'A complement of compliments'. 40 minutes

 Post-it notes and pens. 11+

Ask the group to brainstorm a list of compliments they have heard in their everyday lives on individual post-it notes. They may want to use the ones observed in the 'Complement of compliments' activity just given, but do this anonymously and be careful not to attribute these compliments to any one person.

Ask the group:

- What are some of the ways that compliments can make us feel uncomfortable? (*e.g. complements that focus on appearance or are sexist/objectifying; those from someone you don't trust/feel comfortable with; those that are actually put downs; those that are designed to manipulate you – e.g. being nice to you to get you to do something.*)
- What's the difference between a compliment and a sexist comment? (*Compliments show appreciation/gratitude to a person, sexist comments seek to objectify someone/put them down/show power over them.*)
- What makes a compliment sexist? (*e.g. a compliment that objectifies someone.*)
- What does it mean 'to objectify' someone? (*e.g. to treat a person like a tool, toy or object of desire rather than a person, as if they had no feelings, opinions or rights of their own.*)

Ask the group to use Kate Meaner's flow diagram: 'Is it a compliment or is it *a bit sexist*' (see Figure 3.4) to sort the post-it notes into categories. The categories are up to the group but there are usually three categories: compliments; sexist comments; hmmm/possibly sexist comments.

You will find that some comments are well intended but end up being sexist. Thinking about the concept of objectification (the degrading practice of treating people like things instead of human beings) is a good way of checking whether or not a comment could be sexist and offensive. The key learning here is that sexism is not always intentional, but that doesn't make it ok.

You may find that some participants become angry or defensive about the idea that compliments can also be sexist and may accuse you and others of being ridiculous or 'too politically correct'. It is important to challenge this and to question why there is often so much rage about 'political correctness gone mad' in the media and in everyday conversations, and such an absence of rage about the sexist and racist words that are used every day and don't get challenged. When people are accused of being 'too PC' they are usually trying to be inclusive, caring and considerate.

Finally discuss with participants: *How can we respond when someone gives a compliment that we think is sexist or manipulative? Either to us or others around us?* Explore safe strategies and responses, including how we can intervene safely as peers and bystanders when we hear comments that are sexist or manipulative. If participants do not feel that it is safe/realistic to stand up for themselves or for others focus on what we can all do in our everyday lives to create cultures and communities that are inclusive, equal and safe. See Section 1 of Chapter 4: *Gender and sexual equality* for ideas for social activism.

Is it a compliment or is it *a bit sexist?*

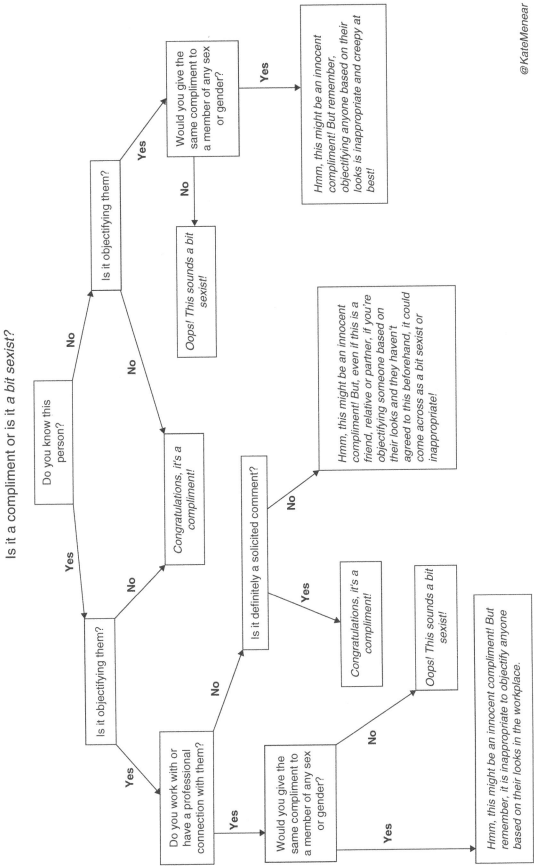

FIGURE 3.4 Is it a compliment or is it a bit sexist?

Section 3: Having an equal say

Unwritten gender rules

This activity is adapted from the Unwritten Rules activity in the *Expect Respect Education Toolkit* from Women's Aid (the toolkit is quality assured by the PSHE Association and includes primary and secondary lessons – see *Useful resources* at the end of this book).

 This is a discussion-based activity that invites participants to identify the unwritten rules relating to gender norms and consider how these impact on our relationships with others. 20–30 minutes

 Large roll of paper and marker pens. Other creative materials as required (see later). 11+

Explain that in society we have laws which dictate how people should behave but we also have a set of 'unwritten rules'. Use the following questions to prompt discussion about what we mean by an 'unwritten rule':

- Can anybody think of any other unwritten rules? (e.g. *speaking with your mouth full; if you bump into somebody, say sorry; if somebody gives you something, say thank you; wait your turn in the queue*)
- Who makes these unwritten rules?
- How are they enforced?
- How are those who break these rules punished?

Next roll out a long roll of paper across the floor and give each participant a pen. Ask the group: can anybody think of a rule that is different for men and women or boys and girls? Ask them to write their rule on the roll of paper.

As a group move around and take a look at the rules and discuss:

- How might these rules make some people feel or behave?
- Do we have choices about whether we follow the rules?
- What happens if we don't follow the rules?
- How do these rules affect our relationships with others?

In your discussion explore how gender rules (e.g. about men being 'macho' and women 'gentle') create a power imbalance within relationships that makes it difficult for both partners to have an equal say. For example, some men believe they should be the dominant partner and some women feel that they are expected to put up with bad behaviour because they care about their partner or think they might be able to change them.

To conclude the activity, ask participants to rewrite one of the rules discussed to make it more ethical, equal or fair. For example,

- 'Men should never walk away from a fight' could be replaced with: 'Nobody needs to fight to prove themselves whatever their gender'.

- 'Men should open doors for women' could be replaced with 'Acts of kindness don't need to be gendered'.
- 'Girls who have a lot of sex are sluts' could be replaced with. 'It's ok to have and enjoy sex whatever your gender. What matters is that the sex is consensual and mutually enjoyable for all involved'.

This activity can be followed by 'Rewriting relationship rules'.

Rewriting relationship rules

 Participants work in small groups to identify the 'unwritten rules' about different types of relationships. They are invited to think critically about these rules and create their own more equal and fair alternative. This activity can work well alongside the previous activity, or as a standalone activity.

 20–30 minutes

 Post-it notes and pens, rulers and marker pens.

 11+

Following on from the 'Unwritten gender rules' activity on p. 72 (if not done explain concept of unwritten rules) ask participants to work in small groups to brainstorm all the unwritten rules they can think of for relationships. This could be for romantic relationships, family relationships, casual sexual relationships, relationships with ex-partners, etc.

Ask for feedback from each group and discuss the following:

- What are some of the unwritten rules in relationships?
- If they are 'unwritten', who writes them?
- What happens if you don't follow the rules? Are the consequences different for people of different genders?
- Are the rules fair?
- Do the rules help people to enjoy their relationships and treat each other with respect?
- What might an alternative set of rules look like that would be more fair, kind and respectful?
- What would relationships be like if we didn't have any rules?

Give each participant a ruler (or a printed paper ruler if you don't have real ones available). Ask participants to rewrite an unwritten rule that they feel needs to change on the ruler.

Come together as a group and share the rules participants want to change. Next destroy the rule(r)s by snapping or tearing the rule(r)s in half. Use your torn and shattered rulers to make something – a sculpture, display, object or item of clothing. For example, you could stick the broken rulers together to create a tree or set of branches. Put your tree in a pot and create leaves from paper, then write new ethical principles or messages for change and hang these on the tree branches. Think about where to display your sculpture to best communicate your message with others. See 'Reassembling the rules' in Chapter 4: *Gender and sexual equality* and *AGENDA: A young people's guide to making positive relationships matter* (see *Useful resources* at the end of this book) for more ideas.

(Re)imagining power

 This activity uses scenarios and discussion to explore the key concept of power. It is based on a theory developed by VeneKlasen, L, & Miller, V (eds) (2006) *A New Weave of Power, People and Politics*. Practical Action Publishing, who articulated four different types of power. This activity introduces participants to this typology to help them understand power as a force for individual and collective change and not just as a negative force that people are unable to fight against.

 35–45 minutes

 Scenario from the 'Digital dilemmas' activity (see p. 63).

 13+

Explain to the group that this activity explores the concept of power. Ask the group what they think 'power' means and to give some examples of power being used. Collate examples.

Read out one of the examples from the 'Digital dilemmas' activity (see p. 63) and discuss the following in small groups:

- Who has power in this scenario?
- What kind of power do they have?
- What are some of the positive ways in which the people in this scenario might use their power? What are some of the negative ways?

Take feedback from groups. Explain that we often think of power as a negative force of something that one person has over another. Another way of thinking about power is as a force that can be used positively or negatively, collectively or individually. Introduce participants to the following four types of power.

Power over: This is the most common understanding of power, as someone having power over another and using it to control or dominate. This tends to be quite a negative understanding of power and is associated with coercion, force, corruption and abuse. Examples may include an abusive relationship or a government having power over its citizens and controlling resources and access to land.

Power to: This refers to each person's unique ability to shape their own lives, to decide what they want to do and to go ahead and do it. There will be many everyday examples of people doing this in your community. Where there is mutual support between individuals, *power to* opens up possibilities for collective action or *power with.*

Power with: This is a collective sense of power and is based on the idea that through collaboration and collective support, we are more powerful as a group than as a series of individuals. Examples could include unions, self help groups or groups of community activists.

Power within: This is the power to imagine, hope and dream, to feel like you can do something and bring about change. This is similar to self confidence and is linked with a sense of awareness and self-worth.

Refer back to the opening scenario.

- Which of these types of power can we see operating in this scenario?
- What are some of the ways in which people within the scenario (including those indirectly referred to such as parents, friends, social media platforms, etc.) could mobilise power to, power with and power within in positive ways?

To conclude ask participants to privately reflect on some of the ways that the different sorts of power explored play out in their lives in positive and negative ways. This can be followed by imagining some positive ways in which they would like power to play out in their lives in the future. If participants feel comfortable these future imaginings could be shared and displayed on a power wall in your place of work.

To explore these concepts further make sure you do the following two activities from Chapter 4: *Gender and sexual equality.* The activity 'Power and privilege' asks participants to explore how certain individual identities are privileged above others, and the '(Re)imagining power in action' activity asks participants to apply these four concepts to everyday situations and imagine opportunities for social activism.

Relationships represented

 Participants research the portrayal of relationships in a television programme, box set, novel or play and think critically about how diversity, difference and power are represented. Participants then create their own scene to explore ways of representing more ethical and positive relationships through tv drama or literature. One hour (minimum)

 Access to television and a range of channels or box sets. 11+

Divide participants into small groups and ask each group to research the portrayal of relationships within a particular drama, reality tv programme or box set of their choice. They can focus on partner relationships, family relationships or friendships. You can also use a novel or play for this task to weave the activity into a literature curriculum.

Participants need to examine the different types of relationships depicted and to consider the answers to the following questions:

- **What kinds of relationships are shown?**
- **What kinds of diversity and difference are visible? Which aren't?** (*Answers might include: relationships are often heterosexual, some are monogamous, many aren't, actors are often (although not always!) white, able bodied, slim and conventionally attractive. Although we do now see LGBT+ relationships and relationships between disabled people on television this is often in specific programmes focussed on these groups. This reinforces the idea that certain people and relationships are 'normal' and others are on the margins.*)
- **What does the representation of relationships teach us about the unwritten rules of relationships?** (*Answers might include: that relationships should be monogamous but this is an impossible ideal, that relationships should be fun; relationships should be heterosexual; sex is important in partner relationships, etc.*)

- **What specific examples of positive/toxic relationships behaviours can you see?** (*Answers might include: self care and caring for others; listening and assertive behaviours; lots of 'drama' (e.g. arguments, shouting, jealousy, etc.); portrayals of toxic masculinity/narrow gender roles and expectations for women – to explore further see 'The Bechdel test' activity on p. 103 in Chapter 4.*)
- **How does power play out in the relationships you can observe? Can you see examples of power over, power to, power with and power within being used in positive and negative ways?** (see '(Re)imagining power' activity on p. 142.)

To explore these questions further task participants with creating a new episode or scene for their television drama, play or novel that does one or more of the following:

- Makes invisible forms of diversity and difference visible.
- Constructs a set of relationship rules that are realistic and/or ethical.
- Shows examples of how power (over, with and within) can be used in positive ways to bring about positive personal or social change.

Ask participants to present or perform their scenes to each other and consider as a group: Can relationships in the media/literature be both ethical and entertaining? Can they be realistic and entertaining? Does realism make relationship portrayals boring? Do we need hyper-romance and portrayals of violence and toxic relationships to pull in an audience?

Pets and consent

This activity was inspired by an activity called 'Caring' (a lesson for Key Stage 1, p. 88) within Martinez, A, Cooper, V and Lees, J, (2012) *Laying the Foundations: A Practical Guide to Sex and Relationships Education in Primary Schools.* (Second edition.) Sex Education Forum/NCB and Jessica Kingsley Publishers. Used with permission.

 This is a quick and fun way of opening up gentle conversations about consent and safe touch. Participants are asked to think about how they know when and how to pet animals and use these reflections to think critically about human consent. This activity can work particularly well with special educational needs (SEND) participants. 10–15 minutes + longer creative extension

 Pet visit if appropriate, pictures of a range of pets. 11+

Either bring in a real pet or use pictures of a range of pets to start a discussion about consent using the following questions:

- How do you know if your pet wants petting?
- What noises do they make when they want petting? What is their body language like?
- How do you know HOW to pet them?
- What signals do they give to stop or change how you are petting them?

To round off the discussion ask the group: What can we learn from petting animals about negotiating safe touch and consent with humans?

As a creative extension to this activity ask participants to imagine they are writing an instruction manual for looking after humans, which has to include details of when and how to 'pet' them. This can be a written document or a short video meme or documentary. Participants could use the widely watched *Tea and consent* video[4] as a starting point for inspiration. This video, although popular, is somewhat problematic as it explains consent as a passive activity (being given or receiving tea) rather than an active process of continuous negotiation. This is something that participants can try and address and overcome in their own instruction videos. For a lengthier critique on the *Tea and consent* video see blogpost by BISHtraining entitled: 'Have you seen the tea and consent video?'[5]

The phone game

 A role play activity in which participants practice identifying when consent has, or has not, been negotiated. 10–15 minutes

 Room with space to move around. Mobile phones or equivalent. Printed instructions for volunteers. 11+

You will need ten volunteers for this role play activity: five to play person A and five to play person B. Each A–B pair will play out a short scenario. In each scenario person A is trying to get person B's phone.

Give each person a different instruction (see list on p. 78) and do not let them see each other's instructions. Give person B a phone at the start of each scenario. Ask each pair to role play their scenario, whilst the rest of the group watches.

After each role play discuss:

- Did person A have person B's consent to take the phone? (Answers: No for scenarios 1, 2, 3 and 4. Yes for 5. See following key points.)
- Who has power in this scenario? (Both A and B have power except for in scenario 3 where B is asleep and is powerless. In 1, 2, 4 and 5, Person B has power because they have the phone, which A wants. But in 1, 2, 3 and 4 person A uses/abuses their power to threaten and steal from person B. In 5, power feels equal and negotiated.)

Key points to emphasise in your discussion include:

- Getting consent and getting the phone are not the same thing. You can get one, without getting the other.
- If someone is asleep, scared or pressured they cannot consent.
- Consent is not just a case of giving a yes or no. It should include a negotiation around boundaries of what is okay and not okay and can be revisited at any time.
- You always have the right to say no to anything you don't want to do. Just because you have the right, this doesn't mean it is easy to do. See the following activities to practise saying no.

To conclude you may want to watch the Campus Clarity YouTube video *2 minutes will change how you think about consent*[6] which plays out the scenarios participants have roleplayed.

Role play statements for volunteers (one per person)

Scenario 1:

> *Person A1:* Your task is to do what you can to get persons B's phone. Even if the person says no, just take the phone anyway.

> *Person B1:* Someone wants to take your phone but you do not want to give it to them. Do not give the phone away. If asked, just say no.

-- ✂

Scenario 2:

> *Person A2:* Your task is to do what you can to get persons B's phone. If the person doesn't give you the phone, threaten them.

> *Person B2:* Someone wants to take your phone but you do not want to give it to them. Do not give the phone away unless you are threatened. If someone threatens you – give them the phone.

-- ✂

Scenario 3:

> *Person A3:* Your task is to do what you can to get persons B's phone. If the person is asleep just take the phone.

> *Person B3:* Someone wants to take your phone; you are asleep and don't know anything about it. Stay asleep throughout the interaction.

-- ✂

Scenario 4:

> *Person A4:* Your task is to do what you can to get persons B's phone. If the person won't give you the phone, keep pressuring and persuading them until they do.

> *Person B4:* Someone wants to take your phone but you do not want to give it to them. Don't give the phone away unless someone keeps pressuring you. If you feel pressured give the phone away.

-- ✂

Scenario 5:

> *Person A5:* Ask to borrow the phone and negotiate what you can and can't use it for. You would like to play games and listen to music.

> *Person B5:* Someone wants to take your phone. You don't mind giving away the phone but you want to make sure that no-one reads your texts or emails. You don't mind someone playing your games but you don't want them to beat your high score. You are happy for someone to listen to music on your phone. If you are able to negotiate this with person A, give them the phone.

Pressure cooker

This lesson was adapted from the Jo Adams 'Pressure Cooker' activity from the *RU Ready* program (unpublished training manual) and is used with permission.

 This activity explores two scenarios in which young people are being pressured into something they don't want to do. It uses drama techniques to help participants analyse the thoughts and feelings that can emerge during peer pressure and create solutions to help them. The scenarios can be altered to explore a range of situations in which young people may feel pressured or coerced.

 20–30 minutes

 Scenarios displayed on flipchart or board. Space to move about.

 13+

Display the following scenario:

> Ana is 13. She met her boyfriend, who is 15, online and has been going out with him for three weeks. He has been asking her for naked photos. She doesn't want to send any but is worried that she'll loose him if she keeps saying no. Ana asks her school friend Jasmine for advice. Jasmine has sent nudes before and doesn't understand why Ana thinks it's such a big deal.

Divide into three groups and allocate each group a persona: 1) Ana, 2) the boyfriend, 3) Jasmine. Ask each group to have a one-minute brainstorm of all the things that their character might be thinking and feeling.

Ask participants to stay in role as those in groups 2 and 3 create a 'pressure cooker alley' for those playing Ana to walk through. To do this, participants in groups 2 (boyfriend) and 3 (Jasmine) stand in two lines facing the person opposite them with a gap between them of no more than a metre.

Participants playing Ana should slowly walk through the 'alley' one at a time. As they do so the rest of the group say ('in character') what they are thinking and feeling. This creates a pressure cooker effect for 'Ana' as she is bombarded with the needs, thoughts and wishes of others.

Break up the alley and come into a circle and ask the participants playing Ana 'How was that for you? What thoughts and feelings do you have when experiencing that kind of pressure?'

Listen to Ana's thoughts and feelings and allow participants the opportunity to raise any questions or concerns they may have about the scenario. (You may get questions about the law – it is illegal for young people under 18 to send sexually explicit images.)

Split back into three groups. Ask all participants in groups 2 and 3 to imagine that they are Ana's on- or offline friends. Ask them to think of just one thing that they'd like to say to Ana to relieve the pressure she's feeling. Ask each 'Ana' to walk slowly down the line again as each person offers solidarity and support.

Display the next scenario:

> Dev is 15. All his friends have nudes on their phones that they say are from girls they've met online. Dev doesn't. His friends call him 'gay' and go on about how he'll never get any girls. Dev wants to get hold of some photos to get his friends off his back.

Run the pressure cooker alley experience again as outlined for Ana. This time divide into two groups; a small group of participants to play Dev and the rest to play Dev's friends. Each group brainstorms thoughts and feelings, followed by a pressure cooker alley walk, a circle reflection and a supportive alleywalk.

At the end of the exercise put Ana and Dev's scenarios up side by side and ask the group 'Does anything strike you about this?' Participants will realise (if they have not already) that Ana and Dev may well be a couple who are considering sharing images they don't really want to in order to meet a completely different set of needs.

To conclude, task participants with imagining scenarios in which it would be possible for Ana and Dev to feel able to make relationship choices free from pressure and coercion. This can be done through discussion or as a written task. Participants will need to consider not just what Ana, Dev and their friends can do differently but what else might need to change within the wider culture.

Saying no

 This is a role play activity in which participants practice saying no in situations that they find challenging. This activity is best followed by the 'Saying no assertively' activity that follows, which gives participants the opportunity to explore what assertive behaviour looks like and to practise saying no in an assertive way. 20 minutes

 Slips of paper and pen for each participant, box or bag to hold slips of paper, flipchart paper and pens, post-it notes. 11+

Ask participants to choose a partner that they feel comfortable working with. Each person should think of something that they find hard to say no to and write this down on a slip of paper.

Partners should exchange slips of paper and take it in turns to practise saying no. To do this, person A should repeatedly ask person B to do the thing that they find it difficult to say no to. Person A should be as persuasive as possible and imaginative about different scenarios in which the request might be put to person B. Person B has to try and keep saying no.

As the educator, observe participants' behaviours closely as this will come in handy if you are doing the extension activity.

After five minutes stop the activity and ask participants to step out of role. This can be done by saying their real name and something true but mundane about themselves (what they had for breakfast, what form they are in, etc.). This activity can be quite intense and emotional if participants really get into it. Taking a moment to step out of role helps maintain a safe working space.

Swap over so that person B is asking person A to do the thing that they find it difficult to say no to. After five minutes stop and ask participants to step out of role.

Come together as a group and debrief the activity:

- How did it feel to take part in this activity?
- What did you learn?
- How easy was it to say no?
- What strategies did you use? Which strategies did you observe your partner using?

- As a group is there any gender difference in how easy or difficult you found it to say no? (Analysis of people's conversations in research suggests that women find it harder to say the word 'no' in everyday conversations compared to men.[7] Discuss with the group why this might be, e.g. women feel more pressured to be 'nice' and accommodating to others, women have less experience of being given power, etc.)

Saying no assertively

 This activity extends the previous role play exercise by encouraging participants to think about the difference between passive, aggressive and assertive behaviours and to practise saying no assertively.

 20 minutes (minimum)

 Flipchart paper and pens.

 11+

As a group create a list of all the strategies for saying no that participants used during the role plays – whether they were effective or not. Encourage participants to think about their tone of voice, facial expressions and body language as well as what they did or did not say. Share any observations you have from watching the role plays.

Next introduce participants to the concepts of passive, aggressive and assertive behaviour if you have not covered this in the curriculum already. This works best as a brainstorm of aggressive, passive and assertive behaviours, starting with aggressive, which is the easiest to describe.

Go back to your list of refusal strategies and ask participants to identify whether the strategies are passive, aggressive or assertive. Where possible, ask participants to reenact some of the strategies so that the group can all observe what passive, aggressive and assertive behaviours look like.

If they have not been discussed already introduce the following assertive behaviours to the group:

Stance: Stand firmly on both legs (standing makes breathing easier), arms loosely by your side, shoulders dropped, head up. If seated uncross legs.

Eye Contact: Get eye contact with the person you are about to speak to.

Other Body Language: Minimise gestures, no pointing or arm waving. Face the other person with your body.

Breathing: Relax your breathing by slowing down, letting your belly drop and take a deep breath before speaking, breathe deeply.

Voice: Slow your speech down, keep your voice even toned and at a level volume (under stress we speak faster and louder than normal).

Repeat the role play activity to give participants the opportunity to try out some of these strategies. This time person A should be persuasive but should also respect person B when they say no. This can be a powerful experience for participants to communicate clearly and assertively what they want and to have this heard and respected.

If you have time you may want to try doing this with one pair acting at a time with the rest of the group observing. Observers can shout 'Freeze!' at any time and give directions to the actors. The aim should be to guide the actors to use the assertive behaviours listed previously. Remember your group ground rules and participants' right to pass.

Rewriting the script

With thanks to Andy McGeeney for his input on assertive behaviour techniques.

 This activity introduces participants to assertive behaviour techniques and provides the opportunity to practise using them through role play.

 40 minutes+

 Assertiveness techniques handout.

 11+

Give each participant a handout on assertiveness techniques (see p. 84 in this activity). Give participants the opportunity to read through each technique and express any initial reactions (including feeling that some of these are unrealistic!).

Working in small groups, ask participants to create a short script of a conflict scenario. This can be based on a scenario in a novel, reality tv programme or drama to create a script of the conflict scenario. Alternatively if there are particular conflict scenarios that you would like to explore with the participants you are working with (e.g. jealousy within romantic relationships or 'drama' within friendship groups), ask each group to create a script of how they think this type of conflict often unfolds.

If participants are struggling to think of conflict scenarios give them one of the scenarios on the following page to get them started.

If you have time, ask each group to act out their conflict script (these can be very short – only one minute long – conflict can unfold very quickly!).

Next ask groups to rewrite their script using the assertiveness techniques provided in this activity. They should select the techniques that feel most appropriate and plausible in the given scenario.

Ask participants to act out their new scenarios to the rest of the group. The audience should identify where assertiveness techniques have been used and provide feedback on body language and tone of voice.

Rewriting the script: Conflict scenarios

--✂

- Your brother/sister has borrowed your new trainers without asking. You bought them especially for a PE competition at school and when you look in your wardrobe they are not there. You get them back later, covered in mud. What do you do?

--✂

- Somebody tells you that they have seen your partner flirting with somebody else at the youth club. What do you do?

--✂

- You are out with your sister who is disabled and is in a wheelchair. A group comes up to you both and starts telling her she is hot and pushing her round by her chair. What do you do?

--✂

- You want to go to a party that finishes at midnight. Your friends have got permission to stay but your parents/carers say you have to be in by 10 o'clock at the latest. What do you say to them?

--✂

- You have asked people to use a new name and pronouns for you but a few people in your life keep using your old name and pronouns. You don't mind if people accidentally forget but you feel this is deliberate. What do you do?

Assertiveness techniques:

Broken Record: Using a calm, even toned voice state your request. If you do not get the positive response you desire, repeat the statement again. It is important in your repetition not to sound like a robot. Even if you change the words slightly each time, continue to be brief. For example, if you are taking a pair of shoes back to a shop to get a refund, keep calmly stating that you would like a refund, e.g. 'I understand you have a policy but I would like an exchange for a new pair or a refund.'

Mirror Technique: It is useful to reflect back the other person's thoughts and feelings without agreeing with them so that the other person knows they have been heard.

Stay on Topic: Stay focussed on your request and do not get sidelined into other issues. For example, you may ask a person not to smoke outside your front door and they bring up the fact that they don't like your loud music. Stay on topic by saying something like, I am willing to talk about my music playing later and right now I want you to stop smoking outside my door please.

Fogging: The fogging technique is a bit like judo; you absorb what another person is saying rather than get into conflict by pushing back. Agree with the aspects of what the other person says that are true, or could be true, without necessarily apologising or taking responsibility for the other person's feelings. For example, when someone is angry with you for being late you can say: 'I am late. I did intend to be here much earlier. I can see you are annoyed with me being late.' Here you are empathising with the other person's thoughts and feelings without agreeing you are the cause of them.

Negative Enquiry: Negative comments and criticism can be hurtful even though it is only another person's opinion. This can often lead to escalating conflict and close down assertive communication. To key is to focus on the facts and ignore the emotion of the critic.

Person A: You take rubbish photos. I don't know why you bother!
Person B: Well who are you to talk?! I think my pictures are great, so there.
Or assertively:
Person B: What is it you don't like about my pictures? How do you think I could improve?

Using *Negative Enquiry* defuses the emotion and flushes out any genuine criticism which you might be able to learn from as opposed to put downs which are emotional and unhelpful.

Using 'I' Statements: A person who behaves assertively takes responsibility for their feelings and avoids making judgements or attributing blame to others. For example, saying things like: 'you make me feel angry' or 'you are ignoring me' are not helpful to good communication. No-one can make us feel anything, however nasty they are. These statements can be translated into assertive 'I' statements in which the speaker owns the responsibility for the feeling such as, 'I feel angry when you say that' and 'I feel I am being ignored by you'. These subtle differences are really important.

Section 4: Learning as we go

Relationship duplo bridges

With thanks to Sexual Health Youth Worker, Glen Wiseman, for helping develop the original idea for this activity, and to Year 4 primary school pupils for helping test and refine the idea.

 Using duplo or Jenga, this activity invites participants to consider what makes a strong and robust relationship and what causes relationships to weaken or collapse. The activity encourages play and experimentation which is great fun for children, young people (and adults!) of all ages. It can be used to explore friendships, romantic or family relationships.

 20–30 minutes + extension activity of 15+ minutes

 Flipchart and pens, at least three–six duplo blocks per participant or Jenga set for alternative. One dry wipe marker per participant. Wet wipes. Duplo figures (optional).

 11+

Give each participant three–six duplo blocks and a dry wipe pen. Ask participants to write one quality of a strong relationship on each building block, choosing the qualities that are most important to them. Depending on the duplo pieces you have available, you could also allow the group to denote the importance of each quality by the size of the chosen block. Biggest blocks being most important, smaller blocks being less important.

Set up two tables about 10cm apart. Ask participants to use their duplo pieces to build relationship bridge(s) across the tables. For younger participants you may want to use duplo characters and set this up so that the characters have to build a relationship bridge so that they can meet in the middle.

Once the bridge is successfully built ask participants to brainstorm the following question: What factors destabilise relationships? E.g. What can cause arguments or friction?

Each time a new factor is mentioned try and see if it is possible to take away the relevant block from the bridge (e.g. if jealousy is mentioned then the trust block might be removed, or telling lies might mean the honesty block is removed). This won't be an exact science but the group will enjoy working out which block could have been destabilised by the factor. The value is in the discussion and not the perfect answer.

Some brick removals will leave the bridge intact but less stable and others will cause the bridge to instantly collapse. Introduce the idea of rupture/repair in relationships. All relationships will go through moments of 'rupture' where there is conflict in the relationship. This can happen very quickly for just a few moments (quick moments of irritation, disagreement, anger, etc.) or they can last for days, weeks, months or years. The key is recognising these moments when they are happening (or after they happened) and focusing on what can be repaired and rebuilt to move forwards. This may mean ending the relationship or rebuilding it in a way that makes it stronger. This sounds simple but it can be difficult to know when to rebuild and when a relationship is beyond repair. Focussing on what's important to you in a relationship, understanding what's important to your friend and drawing on support from those around you can help you to learn and reflect.

As a group discuss what qualities strengthen and build relationships and what qualities can cause them to weaken or rupture. Task participants with rebuilding the bridge and thinking about what qualities they want to include/exclude to repair and rebuild the relationship bridge and make it robust.

At the end of the activity use wet wipes to wipe the writing off from the blocks before the next session.

Jenga alternative: You can also try this activity using a giant garden set of Jenga blocks and chalk. Build the Jenga tower with qualities of relationships written on each layer, then look at how the relationships can be destabilised by taking a relevant block away from the Jenga tower. The game ends when the tower topples. As described for the duplo exercise, use participants' ideas about what qualities strengthen a relationship and which weaken it and consider rebuilding the tower with this in mind. Consider what qualities to include/exclude to make the relationship tower robust. This time you can experiment with introducing a new rule in which the tower creator identifies five blocks that cannot be removed by their opponent. These should be the qualities that they think will help keep their relationship strong and robust but also those that are strategically placed to prevent the tower from falling!

Extension: Make your own relationship bridge, tower or structure

Task participants with creating their own relationship or friendship bridge or tower or other structure using duplo or other building blocks. Participants can work individually or in pairs or small groups. Their structure should be given a name and a short description of why it is built that way. Each block should be labelled with the qualities that they want in a relationship and built in a way that reflects how they want their relationships to grow and develop. Showcase the creations to the rest of the group and take photos to share online.

Relationship values auction

With thanks to the education teams in Brook Wirral and Liverpool for this idea.

 This is a fun, competitive activity that encourages participants to think about the qualities they value in a partner and what they want from a relationship.

 25 minutes

 Printed 'auction card' worksheets – one per small group, pens.

 13+

Ask participants to get into small groups of approximately two–five people. Give each group an auction sheet containing a list of relationship qualities (see p. 88).

Ask participants to read through the list of relationship qualities and add four extra qualities that are important to them in the blank boxes provided. They will need to discuss and agree these as a group. You can ask each group to share their additional qualities with the larger group and note down any common/shared themes.

Inform participants that each group has £10,000 to spend on an ideal partner. To get their ideal partner they need to participate in a values auction against other groups. Explain that the starting bid must be £100 and any increases need to be by at least £50. Give groups time to think about which qualities they really want to bid for and which they are less interested in. They should write the maximum bid for each of the qualities they are interested in on the worksheet and cross out any qualities they are not interested in bidding for.

Pick one of the qualities and start the bidding process until the quality has been won by one group. Ask the winning group to circle the quality and the remaining groups to cross it off their list. Keep a note of how much money each group has spent on the board and get participants to do the maths for you!

Repeat this process until all the qualities have been bought or until each group has no money left. Once this has happened ask each group in turn to present their values.

Lead a discussion using the following questions and prompts:

- Are there any qualities you wish you had won? (Why?)
- What do you think of the set of qualities that you have?
- What would you change about this person?
- Would this person also make an ideal friend? Are there any differences in what we want from a partner and a friend?
- What can you do if your partner doesn't have all the qualities you want? Or you don't have all the qualities that they would like?
- Imagine you are aged 50 – Do you think you would bid for the same qualities? What might change over time?
- Would men and women bid for the same qualities? What about people who don't identify as male or female? (Note: this often evokes stereotypical responses about what men and women want. Allow space for participants to voice these but then challenge them.)

Auction card worksheet

Buys me things Max Bid:	**Caring** Max Bid:	**Dresses nice** Max Bid:	**Takes me to nice places** Max Bid:
Good looking Max Bid:	**Funny** Max Bid:	**Honest** Max Bid:	**Has a lovely family** Max Bid:
Has money Max Bid:	**Someone I can trust** Max Bid:	**Talks to me** Max Bid:	**A good listener** Max Bid:
Kind to me Max Bid:	**Independent** Max Bid:	**Gets on well with my friends** Max Bid:	**Interested in politics** Max Bid:
Looks after me Max Bid:	**Gives me compliments** Max Bid:	**Sees me as an equal** Max Bid:	**Intelligent** Max Bid:
Ambitious Max Bid:	**Respects my boundaries** Max Bid:	**Does not play games** Max Bid:	**Shares their feelings** Max Bid:
Gives good hugs Max Bid:	**Turns me on** Max Bid:	**Sexy** Max Bid:	**Would make a good parent** Max Bid:
Takes charge Max Bid:	**Tidy** Max Bid:	**Good cook** Max Bid:	**Keeps my secrets** Max Bid:
Makes me feel safe Max Bid:	**Makes me feel excited** Max Bid:	**Has good hygiene** Max Bid:	**Shaven** Max Bid:

Positive relationship webs

Adapted from *AGENDA: A young people's guide to making positive relationships matter* (p. 49) (see *Useful resources* at the end of this book) and BISH UK Relationships Graph. Used with permission.

 An individual activity to help think about which positive relationship qualities are important to us and to evaluate them within our relationships with others.

 20–30 minutes. Can be extended to longer creative project.

 Blank copies of the relationship graph, optional copies of the BISH relationship graph[8], pens. Optional – arts, crafts and sculpture making materials.

 11+

List all the different positive relationships that you enjoy as a group. Think about relationships with partners, friends, family, pets, special places, objects (e.g. mobile phones).

Next brainstorm what it is about these relationships that participants enjoy. Think about the qualities that they value such as honesty, trust, fun times together, communication, support.

Give each participant a relationship graph (see Figure 3.5). Each person should label the 12 points on the graph with the 12 different relationship qualities – selecting the 12 that are most important to them. For work with older groups (age 14+) on sexual/partner relationships you can print off BISH's relationship graph which already has 12 relationship qualities in place.

Next ask participants to choose their favourite relationship (e.g. dog, gran, partner, best mate) and use their graph to map this relationship. To do this give the relationship a score out of 10 for each of the 12 qualities and place a dot in the appropriate place on each line of the graph. Once they have finished join the dots to make a relationship web. This helps us to see the good bits in a relationship and the bits we need to work on.

The activity can be repeated for different relationships, using a different coloured pen each time. This helps to highlight the strengths and weaknesses of different relationships in one person's life.

Extension: Building webs

To extend this activity, task participants with creating a sculpture or object based on their relationship web. Participants can cut out their web and use the shape as a stencil to create the shape out of waste card, material, old CDs, wood or whatever materials you have available. Participants can decorate their objects with words, images or messages about relationships, reflecting what they have learned about relationships or about themselves. Decide if and where to display these objects and what message you want to give as a group about human relationships. For more sculpture ideas and images see *AGENDA: A young people's guide to making positive relationships matter*, p. 39.

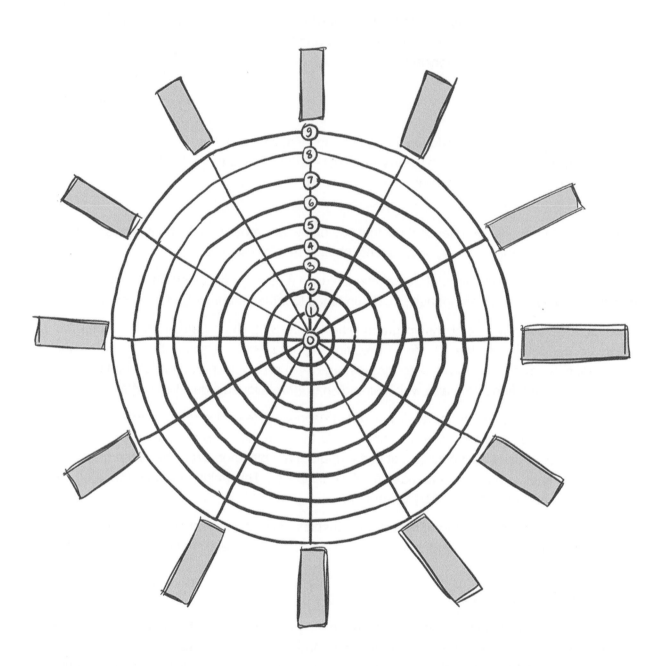

FIGURE 3.5 Relationships graph

Illustration by: Chrissy Baxter, adapted from BISH How is my Relationship? www.bishuk.com/relationships/how-is-my-relationship/

Digital romance

Research on young people's use of technology suggests that technology is widely used by young people in their romantic relationships, but has not replaced face to face contact. This activity uses findings from a 2017 study to encourage critical reflection about the benefits and risks of using tech within romantic relationships.

 50 minutes

Four copies of McGeeney, E, & Hanson, E, (2017) *Digital Romance: A Research Project Exploring Young People's Use of Technology in Their Romantic Relationships and Love Lives.* London: National Crime Agency and Brook. Available for free online.

 13+

Divide into four groups and assign each group one of the following relationship practices:

- Flirting and getting together,
- Sending nude or sexual images,
- Communicating in relationships,
- Breaking up and surviving post breakup.

Ask each group to create a two–three-minute drama that presents a snapshot of how young people today flirt, communicate, break up, send nudes, etc. Encourage participants to present an everyday or 'normal' scenario rather than an extreme scenario and perform it to each other.

Next introduce *Digital Romance* as a study of the role of technology in young people's romantic relationships conducted in 2017. The study involved over 2,000 young people across the UK and set out to explore in detail how young people aged 11–25 use technology to start, maintain and end relationships. Give each group a copy of the report and invite them to go through the report and spend at least ten minutes reading the sections of the report that are relevant to their topic. The task is to present another performance to the rest of the group that highlights:

- Key findings, quotes and facts.
- Things that surprised you
- Positives and negatives of using online technologies for flirting/nude sharing/communicating/ breaking up.
- Any relevant thoughts or observations from your own lives and communities that you want to share (remember the ground rules here – see Chapter 1).
- Suggested ways that we can help each other to enjoy having relationships online and offline.

The aim of this activity is to encourage reflection on the role of technology in young people's love lives – not to suggest that using technology is risky, wrong or inferior to face to face relationship contact. Highlight the benefits as well as the risks and encourage groups to think about ways in which they can work together to create positive and supportive online/offline communities. After each group has presented discuss:

- What are the similarities and differences between our own observations of our peers and those captured in the research?
- How realistic are our own observations of ourselves and our peers? Why do we tend to think that we are worse than we really are?

- What can we learn about ourselves from engaging with the research and reflecting on our own peer groups and communities?

Extension: Acting out digital romance

To engage with the research more deeply use the activity 'Acting out' on p. 115 of Chapter 4: *Gender and sexual equality*. This is a creative activity in which participants read through the research report to pull out powerful quotes that can be used to rewrite scripts, music or short stories. As well as short quotes, the *Digital Romance* report contains four case studies or 'stories' that could be dramatised or developed through creative work.

You can also follow this activity with 'Communicating online and offline' to help participants to reflect on how they communicate within their relationships.

Communicating online and offline

 This is a self reflection task in which participants reflect on how and why they communicate using different on- and offline modes of communication.

 20–30 minutes

 One worksheet and pen per participant.

 11+

Give each participant a copy of the worksheet on p. 93 and ask them to find a space on their own where they can work unobserved and uninterrupted. Emphasise that this is a personal activity and that participants do not have to hand in the worksheets or share them with anyone.

Think of an important relationship in your life. It may be a positive or negative relationship, a friend or partner. Then ask participants to fill in the worksheet answering the following questions:

1. In this relationship have you used any of these ways of communicating when doing the listed activities?
2. Circle where you have had positive experiences using a particular communication mode (e.g. using private messaging to sort out an argument).
3. Draw a jagged circle where you have had a difficult or negative experience using a particular communication mode.
4. In a different colour pen go through the worksheet again and tick how you *would like* to communicate within this relationship.

Ask participants to talk in pairs about how they felt during one positive and one negative experience and discuss whether or not the communication mode made things better or worse in these situations.

Come together as a whole group and ask participants to share an example of how they would like to communicate. Use this to explore the strengths of each form of communication, weighed against its limitations and risks.

The key learning here is *not* that online or offline communication is better but rather that each mode of communication has limitations, risks and benefits depending on the context in which they are used. This means that we have to make wise choices about how we communicate with others, which is tricky when communication often happens very fast. Taking time to reflect on how we communicate in our relationships can help.

Communicating online and offline: Self reflection worksheet

	Private message (e.g. text/ email/ messenger)	Public post on social media	Voice note	Video call	Audio call	Face to face	Never/ N/A
Talked about something that is worrying you							
Talked about what you want from the relationship							
Talked about hopes and dreams for the future							
Said that you care about or love the other person							
Laughed until your stomach hurt							
Argued							
Sorted out an argument							
Talked about sex							
Got naked							
Had a sexual experience							
Felt turned on							

Extension: STOP/START communication

To extend this activity task participants with writing a set of statements about how they want to communicate and be communicated with by others. It may help to focus on communication within a particular community or location (e.g. communication with teachers/parents/friends, communication on Instagram, in the youth club, school corridors, etc.). You can use the 'Stop-start plates' activity to help you do this (see Chapter 2, p. 38). Think about how to display and circulate these positive messages online and/or offline. Ideas include printing or painting statements on cups used in your youth club, or on T-shirts that can be worn, photographed and shared online, or on large posters or banners displayed around school.

Ethical relationships

 A concluding activity that invites participants to explore what ethical relationships look like in practice. To do this, participants use the ethical framework developed by researchers Jenny Walsh, Anne Mitchell and Mandy Hudson based on work by Moira Carmody that structures this chapter and apply it to real life scenarios. 60 minutes (can be extended to longer project)

 Copy of ethical framework and linked questions for educator to share with the group, set of scenarios, pens and paper for participants. 11+

This activity works after activities such as 'Unwritten gender rules' (p. 72), 'Rewriting relationship rules' (p. 73) or 'Relationships represented' (p. 75) that ask participants to identify the unwritten relationship rules in the media and/or their communities. Start this activity by recapping on the learning from these activities and sharing some examples of relationship rules that are unhelpful, unjust and unequal.

Introduce participants to the following ethical framework that was developed by researchers in Australia[9] as an alternative approach to doing relationships:

Taking care of me: This means asking, 'Is this what I really want to do?' Am I safe emotionally and physically? Is the other person treating me with respect and concern?

Taking care of you: How does what I want affect the other person? How do I know? I've got to check.

Having an equal say: Do we have equal power, or is one person getting their way most of the time?

Learning as we go: Few of us are born knowing how to 'do' relationships. We can learn, and learn from our mistakes. What would have made the situation better? What am I doing, what am I not doing? What can I learn from this?

Ask participants to share ideas about what each of these principles might mean and discuss how these principles differ from common relationship rules that participants encounter in their everyday lives.

To have a go at using the framework give participants a set of scenarios to work with. You can use the scenarios from the 'Digital dilemmas' activity, or from a television programme discussed in 'Relationships represented', an example from 'Problem pages' on p. 327 in Chapter 8: *Concluding the learning*, or an example from participants' own lives.

Working in small groups or pairs ask participants to apply the ethical principles to their scenario, using the following questions as a guide:

Taking care of me: What reflective questions can the characters ask themselves to increase awareness of their feelings and thoughts (instead of just going along with someone else's desires or with gender norms and unwritten relationship rules)?

Taking care of you: What questions can the characters ask of each other to check what they are thinking and feeling and to see how their own needs and desires are affecting the other person?

Having an equal say: How might conversations between the characters play out in which they try to resolve their dilemma? Why might it be hard to have this conversation? What are some of the possible barriers? (e.g. relationship rules and gendered expectations about how we should behave, not having the language for talking about emotions/sex.)

Learning as we go: What can the characters do after their conversation to help them reflect on what has happened and learn about themselves and their relationship? Imagine what might they say to these questions:

- What happened?
- What were you thinking and feeling?
- What was good and bad about the experience?
- How can you make sense of what happened?
- What were the alternative conclusions?
- What would you do if it happened again?

To pull the learning together ask participants to write a script, story, journalistic report or Twitter exchange that documents the previous process of doing ethical relationships and brings it to life. Use this to show how ethical relationships can be done in practice, as well as the challenges and potential awkwardness of working in this way. It is important when doing this work to emphasise that doing relationships ethically isn't easy and can often feel strange, stilted or awkward since we are used to following a different set of rules. Although our relationship rules may be flawed, they can feel comfortable so being asked to leave them behind can feel uncomfortable or exposing.

Ask participants to share their ethical scenarios with each other. As a group reflect on the activity using the following questions:

- What have we learnt from doing this activity?
- How might it feel to put these principles into practice in our own lives and relationships? What barriers might we come across?
- What small steps can we take to practise doing relationships ethically? Who can support us?
- Would we change any of these principles? Or add any extras?

Extension: Can you make ethical relationships go viral?

To extend the activity task participants with identifying key messages or learning from the activity (or from your wider curriculum) about ethical relationships that they would like to make go viral. Brainstorm ways of making these messages go viral and decide together which ideas to put into practice. Ideas could include crafting the ethical framework ditty (Taking care of...) onto fabric and using it to 'yarnbomb' your local area. For other ideas on spreading a message look at the 'Craftivism' activity on p. 116 of Chapter 4: *Gender and sexual equality*. Take photos and share them online using an agreed hashtag.

Notes

1   New Economics Foundation (2008) Five ways to wellbeing https://neweconomics.org/uploads/files/8984c5089d5c2285ee_t4m6bhqq5.pdf
2   www.open.ac.uk/researchprojects/enduringlove/
3   https://learn.brook.org.uk/
4   www.youtube.com/watch?v=pZwvrxVavnQ
5   https://bishtraining.com/Have+you+seen+that+tea+and+consent+video
6   www.youtube.com/watch?v=laMtr-rUEmY
7   Kitzinger, C & Frith, H, (1999) 'Just say no? The use of conversation analysis in developing a feminist perspective on sexual refusal', Discourse & Society, 10(3), pp. 293–316. doi: 10.1177/0957926599010003002.
8   www.bishuk.com/relationships/how-is-my-relationship/
9   From Walsh et al. (2017) *The Practical Guide to Love, Sex and Relationships*. Used with permission. See *Useful resources* at the end of this book.

CHAPTER 4

Gender and sexual equality

International research states that the most effective RSE programmes are those that adopt a rights- and gender-based approach. This means creating opportunities with your RSE programme for young people to explore the impact of gender norms on themselves, others and society and to think critically about the role that gender norms play in discrimination, conflict and oppression. The activities in this chapter will help you do this, but there are others woven throughout the book. This reflects the fact that gender underpins all the work that we do in RSE. In Chapter 7: *Sexual health*, for example, we have an activity to help you explore with young people how gender norms and identities can impact on contraception choices and decision making (p. 293). In Chapter 6: *Sex*, we have an activity that explores the gendered myths and assumptions about masturbation and pleasure (p. 233) and in Chapter 5: *Bodies*, we have an activity on 'Gendered bodies' (p. 193) that explores how gender norms and stereotypes affect how we move, act, perform and feel in our bodies.

Exploring gender and sexual norms and inequalities is an area of RSE that can provoke lively and passionate debate, but also tensions and disagreement. This makes it an exciting but challenging area of learning. The activities in this chapter are designed to help you engage young people in safe, creative and inclusive conversations about gender and sexuality. Not all of the activities will be safe for you to facilitate, however, it depends on the group you are working with, the context that you work in and your own confidence, skills and experience. We've provided points to consider at the start of the chapter and throughout to help you to make decisions about which activities to use and develop in your place of work. Since gender underpins all the work that we do in RSE you may find that you need to keep coming back to these activities and weaving them into your education programmes and conversations with young people.

Chapter summary

Section 1: Heteronorms. Activities to identify gender and sexual norms and engage in social activism to challenge or change unequal and/or oppressive norms. Includes activities that cross over with media studies, careers guidance, creative writing, history, geography, drama, music, film and art.

Section 2: Key terms and definitions. Four activities that help clarify key terms and definitions in relation to gender, sex and sexual orientation.

Section 3: Diversity, power and privilege. Activities that explore key concepts such as power, privilege and heteronormativity and those that recognise and celebrate gender and sexual diversity and difference.

Points to consider

- Modern western culture generally sees only two binary genders (male and female). It is frequently assumed that all people are attracted to and have relationships with someone from the binary 'opposite' gender. This is known as heteronormativity and is based on a set of assumptions that we can challenge through RSE. The activities in this chapter help to expose heterosexual privilege and normativity and explore how this can be challenged.

- When doing this it is important not to position participants who challenge gender and sexual norms as 'good' (progressive) and those who invest or hold onto gender sexuality norms as 'bad' (regressive). This creates an unhelpful dichotomy. Rather it is your role to create safe spaces for participants to explore and reflect on their own values and the gender and sexual norms that they encounter in their lives and communities, to enable participants to explore what gender and sexual equality might look like and to think about what they would like to change in their own communities.

- In this chapter (and in the book more generally) we focus on gender and sexuality as key forms of difference, power and privilege. It is important that we don't see these in isolation and work within our communities and schools to think about how gender and sexuality intersect with other forms of difference such as race, faith, disability, citizenship.

- This chapter covers challenging topics such as inequality, privilege and power. It asks young people to think critically about the norms and inequalities in their everyday lives. This can provoke angry, defensive and uncomfortable emotions. Ensure that you always create and maintain a safe enough space to do this work. See Chapter 2: *Creating safer spaces* for activities to help you do this and for tips on how to maintain an inclusive space.

- Remember that in any group you are likely to be working with young people who are LGBT+ who may or may not be public about their gender or sexual identity. Never assume someone's gender or sexuality and never require them to 'come out' in a session.

- The language that we have for talking about gender and sexuality is always changing and is contested. Always check that participants understand the terminology used within a group (including terms like 'gender') and be open about the fact that there are multiple definitions and ideas for many of the terms that we use. This means that we have to be reflective, critical and open-minded about the language that we use. There are two activities in this chapter to help clarify key terms.

- There are regular news stories, films, dramas and adverts that provoke public debate about gender. Draw on these in your RSE programmes, using the key concepts in this chapter to encourage critical thinking and social action.

Section 1: Heteronorms

The focus in this section is to encourage young people to voice their own experiences of gender and sexuality, including experiences of harassment, inequality and discrimination. You may also hear positive stories of acceptance and celebration. The activities invite young people to reflect on their experiences and think critically about ideas about what is 'normal'. Many of these activities also encourage young people to take action to change the rules and norms that are oppressive and discriminatory.

Gender boxes

With thanks to *Good Lad Initiative* and David Bartlett (Good Lad Consultant) for the inspiration for this exercise.

 This activity explores participants' own experiences of gender, using the simple idea of the gender box to explore complex processes of socialisation.   30 minutes

 Pen and paper. Access to internet, display screen and sound.   14+

This activity works particularly well with single gender groups as a way of unpacking masculinity and femininity in a safe space (although can also be done with mixed gender groups).

Note: Remember that to create and maintain a safe space (whatever group you are working with) it is important to establish a working agreement and facilitate relevant activities from Chapter 2: *Creating Safer Spaces* to help develop group relationships and ways of working before doing this activity, or others in this chapter that explore gender norms and stereotypes.

Introduce your group to the idea of the 'gender box'. This is the idea of a box that contains all the things that society says you have to do to be a 'real man/real woman'.

In small groups ask participants to draw and write the contents of either a 'man box' or a 'woman box'. This may be a set of rules that men/women have to follow in order to be 'real men/women' such as a series of statements that start with 'It's ok to…/it's not ok to…'. Alternatively, it might be stories that men/women are told to warn against certain behaviours or encourage others.

Ask each group to feedback and present the contents of their gender box. Use the following questions to facilitate a discussion:

- What do you like and enjoy about your gender box and its rules?
- What don't you like?
- How do these rules impact on how men see girls and women and behave towards them/how women see boys and young men and behave towards them?
- What would life be like for you if you didn't have to adhere to this gender box?
- Which of these things would you like to take out of the gender box?
- What would you like to put in there instead?
- What would it be like if we didn't have any 'gender boxes' at all?

Explain that what you are discussing is a process called socialisation in which women/men are socialised to act and behave in certain ways. Whilst there are many ways of being a woman/man that are enjoyable, rewarding and fun, much of the restrictive content of the gender box is toxic and directly linked to wider harms. For example, we can link high suicide rates among men to man box rules such as 'Don't cry/man up/don't talk about emotions/don't ask for help'. Ask the group to think about what these harms may be, if you have not discussed this already. In your discussion be sure to explore what people enjoy about their gender boxes as well as the potential harms of gender norms.

To explore further you can show the group The TED Talk: *Tony porter, A call to men.* (2010, 11 minutes)[1] to aid your discussion. Consider whether the 'man box' that Tony describes based on his experiences as a Black man growing up in Harlem, New York, match the experiences of your participants and unpick his comments about how 'man box' rules are directly linked to the objectification and violence towards women.

Ensure that you conclude by considering the possible contents of more fair and equal gender boxes and the possibility of having no gender boxes at all. The aim of this activity is to create a space to explore more fluid and holistic ideas about masculinity/femininity – not to learn the 'right way' to behave as a man or woman! To do this we need to first identify and critique gender stereotypes and then start to imagine alternative ways of 'doing' gender.

Extension: Act like a man or Be ladylike

An alternative to this activity would be to write the phrases *Act like a man* and *Be ladylike* on two pieces of flipchart and ask participants to write down at least one word they associate with each phrase. This activity is based on an activity included in *Sexuality Education Matters* (2013), created by Debbie Ollis and used with permission. (See *Useful resources* at the end of this book.)

- What kinds of situations might we feel pressured to 'act like a man' or 'be ladylike'?
- What do these terms tell us about what is expected of men and women?
- How might these expectations lead to negative outcomes?
- Are there situations when these expectations could lead to positive outcomes?
- Are there any expectations you would like to see changed?
- Are there any expectations you would like to remain?
- On this basis, would you want to be male or female?
- Can you see any problems with the categories?
- How do individuals, groups and communities resist or challenge the representations?

Gender documentary

Working in small groups, participants create a short documentary about gender norms and present it to the rest of the class. The task encourages participants to conduct independent research in small groups and take time to observe gender norms and differences in everyday life. Where it is not possible to film, participants can find alternative ways of presenting their findings.

Minimum of two one-hour sessions. One to research and create the documentary and one to present and discuss the films. Can be extended to a much longer project.

Cameras and editing software.

11+

The task is for participants to research gender norms and create a short film documentary to share their findings. This can be a 'rough and ready' film created using camera phones and edited using freely available software or a more polished piece if you have access to the skills and resources required. Groups will need to carefully consider issues of consent when filming (see below).

Working in small groups, participants can choose to focus on a particular ethnic group, profession or life stage (e.g. parenting, toddlers, teenagers) or to look at gender norms across the life course and population. Participants will need to draw on their own experiences, talk to family and friends and conduct internet-based research to find out more about gender norms and how gender influences what people do.

Here are some points for groups to consider:

- Dress and presentation,
- Play and leisure,
- Behaviour in the home environment,
- Behaviour in the work or school environment.

Where possible, ask participants to create a documentary style film (e.g. 'The secret life of...' series or a wildlife documentary) that focuses on close observation of the subject. The aim is to document and report what you see and to consider what this behaviour might mean.

Participants will need to carefully negotiate consent to film. Where consent to film is not possible, participants can still conduct research. It may be that participants will only be able to film each other and draw on their own experiences, or they may need to stage common scenarios they have witnessed or experienced and film these. If filming isn't possible, participants can conduct their research and present their reports 'live' to the rest of the group.

Once all participants have presented their work, lead a discussion using the following questions:

- What are the key gender differences that we can observe from these documentaries?
- In your role of documentary maker what did you observe about gender that you don't normally see?
- Were there gender differences that you are aware of but couldn't capture in your documentary?
- How do the gender differences we have observed affect people's expectations and everyday lives?
- Documentary makers don't intervene in the lives of the people or animals they observe. How did it feel to watch without intervening? If you could have intervened, what would you like to have done or said?

In your discussion emphasise that we don't always notice gender differences and gender norms, often because they are so normalised and ubiquitous. This activity helps to make gender differences strange and to observe how they impact on people's everyday lives and contribute towards creating and sustaining gender inequality and inequity.

To conclude the project, consider if and where the films can be shown. If you have consent, can the films, or extracts from the films, be shared online? Or can you host an event to raise awareness of issues highlighted in the films?

Gender audit

 In small groups participants are tasked with doing a gender audit of their school or college to identify where gender equalities and equities are supported and celebrated and where they are not. This activity can be used as an alternative to the previous 'Gender documentary' activity on p. 100.   30 minutes

 Access to school curriculum and policies, large sheets of paper, pens and other craft materials.   11+

Ask participants to work in small groups to create a gender audit of their school or college (or adapt for workplace). Things to consider could include:

- Uniform policy.
- Gender of staff in senior management.
- Gender of staff in each department.
- Toilets – are toilets safe for people of all genders?
- Sexual bullying/aggression.
- Curriculum resources, e.g. case studies and examples used in lessons.
- Seating plans.
- Sports options.

Ask participants to display the findings of their audit visually, uses colours, diagrams, arrows, maps and other materials. For example, create a large map of the school that highlights areas in which girls and women, boys and genderqueer/non-binary students feel safe/not safe. Annotate with words and images to show how safety is supported/undermined by policies and environmental issues.

Share audit displays and work out as a group if there is anything that participants want to change at their school or college.

An alternative version of this activity would be to use the *Gender Watch Bingo* tool found within *Primary AGENDA: Supporting Children in making positive relationships matter* (see *Useful resources* at the end of this book). This is a creative and participatory audit tool that you can download and print to help participants identify how their school is doing when it comes to gender equality.

Pink or blue?

 A creative activity that uses poetry and spoken word to explore gender stereotypes and our personal responses to them. Participants can work on their own or in small groups.   60+ minutes

 Pink or Blue by Holly McNish (available on YouTube), online access and screen to watch YouTube video.[2]   14+

Note: The poem contains some language and images that may be considered suggestive or explicit (depending on your point of view!). Watch it first before showing it to your group to check that it is suitable to be played in your place of work.

Explain to participants that you are going to listen to a poem on gender stereotypes and have a go at writing your own. Before listening to the poem, ask participants to make a brainstorm of all the gender stereotypes that they can think of. Give them two or three minutes to complete this task.

Next ask them to silently read their own list and to jot down any key words or phrases that come into their heads as they read through the list. Ask participants: How do you feel when you reflect on the gender stereotypes that you observe or experience in your everyday life – both online or offline?

Watch *Pink or Blue* by performance poet Holly McNish (available on YouTube – three minutes long) and ask participants to consider the following questions. Play the poem for a second time as they complete their answers.

- List some of the gender stereotypes that Holly McNish identifies in this poem.
- List the key words, phrases or images that stand out for you in this poem.
- Write down three words to explain what you think and/or feel when you watch this poem.

Individually or in small groups ask participants to write their own poem about gender stereotypes, using the words and phrases from their initial brainstorm and their responses to Holly McNish's poem.

Prompt participants to consider how gender stereotypes are often linked to sexuality stereotypes, e.g. that a boy who likes daisy chains is 'gay', that a man who wears makeup is 'gay'. These stereotypes assume that a man or boy who expresses their gender in a typically feminine way is assumed to be 'gay'. In reality someone's gender expression cannot tell us anything about who they are romantically or sexually attracted to. (See 'The Genderbread person' activity on p. 118 to explore this further.)

Participants can choose how to display or perform their poems and whether or not they want to include visual images and music/sound as well as text and/or spoken word. Ideas include a display of poems and images in the school/youth club; a spoken word event; a set of audio visual pieces displayed in a public space.

The Bechdel test

With thanks to Jo Taylor, Associate Assistant Head, Head of Department Health (PSHE), Philosophy, Beliefs and Ethics (PBE) and Psychology, Chestnut Grove School for the idea for this activity.

 This activity explores the representation of women in films using the simple concept of the *Bechdel test*. This asks whether a work features at least two women who talk to each other about something other than a man. We also include the requirement that the two women must be named.

 20 minutes. Can be extended to longer activity/ project if required.

 Flipchart/board and pens.

 11+

Ask the group what their favourite films are. Responses can be written on a post-it note and shared with the rest of the group or called out as part of a whole group brainstorm.

Introduce the concept of the *Bechdel test*. The *Bechdel test* asks whether a film or work of fiction:

1) Features at least two women,
2) These two women talk to each other about something other than a man,
3) The two women are named.

Ask each participant to apply the concept of the Bechdel test to their favourite film. The activity could be extended by applying the test more widely to a particular genre of films as part of individual/small group research projects.

Create a large pass/fail table on the board and ask participants to write their films in the pass or fail column and go through all three steps of the test.

To close the activity, discuss the following questions:

1. Can you think of any other films that do pass the Bechdel test?
2. Why do so many films fail the Bechdel test? Why do so many stories feature men or women talking about men?
3. Why does it matter?
4. How are other kinds of diversity represented/not represented/mis-represented in films?
5. What needs to happen to increase diversity in films? (Discussion prompts include: who has power and influence in the film industry; who is paid the most money for appearing in films; the impact of sexism and sexual harassment within the film industry.)

Task participants with rewriting the script or plot-line of films they love but that don't pass the test. Or write a new film outline altogether. This can be an individual or small group task.

StereoTOYpes

Adapted from ideas included in *AGENDA: A young people's guide to making positive relationships matter* (see *Useful resources* at the end of this book). Used with permission.

 A range of fun, lively activities that look at gender stereotypes in children's toys and toy advertising. These activities would also work in media studies or careers sessions.

 From 5 minutes to extended research projects

 Depending on which of the following activities you select, you may need Tablets or computers with online access, coloured pens, paper and other arts materials, large set of Lego for participants to use, online gaming console.

 11+

Choose one of more of the following activities and use the discussion questions to engage participants in critical discussion about gender norms and stereotypes in children's toys and toy advertising. All of these activities work as individual, pair or small group tasks.

Gender Remixer.[3] Use the simple drag and drop function on this website to mix up the images and audio from children's toy adverts. Participants can overlay images from 'boys' toys' adverts with audio from 'girls' toys' adverts to see what effect this creates. This remixing makes the seemingly 'normal' or 'natural' gender of toys and toy advertising seem strange and invites critical thinking about why any one gender is assigned to particular toys and activities.

Unisex Toys. Ask participants to design a unisex toy, complete with packaging and associated marketing campaign. Ask them to reflect on the process, the challenges they faced and what they think about how toys and play are gendered in our society.

Lego Then, Now and the Future. Compare and contrast the 1981 Lego advert 'what it is its beautiful' with the current Lego advertising (examples available on Gender Remixer website). Look at debates online about Lego and gender stereotypes to help with this. Next give participants Lego to use to make a machine or create a scenario that combats corporate or commercial sexism. Participants should name their machine or scene. Finished products can be photographed and shared online or as part of a display in your place of work. See *AGENDA: A young people's guide to making positive relationships matter*, pp. 57–58 for further details of how to create a 'commercial sexism crushing machine'!

Gender Avatar. Task participants with playing online games using avatars of different genders. Observe and record how people respond to them, depending on their gender. In response, create an Avatar that can smash online sexism. See *AGENDA: A young people's guide to making positive relationships matter*, p. 43 for further details.

Discussion questions:

- What techniques are used to market toys to different genders (e.g. imagery, language)?
- What messages does toy marketing give to children about what it means to be a girl/boy?
- Why do you think there are so few gender neutral toys?
- What would it be like if toys were marketed to all children regardless of gender?
- What skills get developed with stereotypical 'boys' toys' vs. 'girls' toys'?
- Did the kind of toys you played with as a child influence your current skills and interests?
- What is the impact of toy stereotyping on children as they grow into adulthood?

Career choice?

 A couple of quick suggestions for quick, fun activities that open up conversations about gender and career 'choices'. Choose one of these activities to facilitate with your group and use the following discussion questions to explore the impact that gender stereotypes and assumptions can have on children and young people's education and career 'choices'. These activities can be included in career guidance sessions, as well as in RSE. 5–10 minutes

 Pen, paper, riddle and/or list of professions for educator, copies of Chambers, N, Kashefpakdel, Dr Elnaz T, Rehill, J & Percy, C, (2018) *Drawing the Future*. Education and Employers. 11+

Idea one
Tell the group the following riddle:

A father and son get in a car crash and are rushed to the hospital. The father dies. The boy is taken to the operating room and the surgeon says, 'I can't operate on this boy, because he's my son.'

How is this possible?

Answer: The surgeon is the boy's mother. If the group haven't heard this riddle before they will often think that the scenario is impossible because they will assume that the surgeon is a man and therefore has to be the boy's father. Occasionally participants might assume two gay dads before they assume a female surgeon. Use the discussion questions on p. 107 to explore further.

Idea two

Ask participants to write numbers 1–25 on a piece of paper. As the educator, read out the following list of professions. For each one ask participants to close their eyes and imagine what gender the person is when they hear the profession. This should be the first image they see in their mind's eye on hearing the profession. They should not overthink it – just what they initially see. They should not discuss it at this stage but should write down M (male) or F (female) or Q (where someone has imagined more than one gender simultaneously or someone whose gender cannot be read in the mind's eye or someone who is non-binary or genderqueer) against the number corresponding to that profession. Read the list quite quickly as follows:

1. nurse
2. engineer
3. business manager
4. cleaner
5. model
6. footballer
7. hairdresser
8. dancer
9. firefighter
10. secretary
11. lawyer
12. care assistant
13. singer
14. computer programmer
15. builder
16. florist
17. nursery teacher
18. scientist
19. teacher
20. dress maker
21. surgeon
22. driver
23. farmer
24. chef
25. electrician

As a whole group discuss what gender was assigned to each profession. Use the following discussion questions to explore further.

Discussion questions:

- Do we make gendered assumptions about different jobs and careers? Where do these ideas come from?
- How do these gendered assumptions affect young people's career and education choices?
- If our career decisions are shaped by gender norms and expectations to what extent do we have a 'choice' about what jobs we do?
- What can we do to challenge these stereotypes about gender, jobs and career choices?

To support your discussion or as further reading for the group look at Chambers et al. (2018) *Drawing the Future*. This report is based on findings from a global survey of 20,000 primary school children that asked the children to draw a picture of the job they want to do when they grow up. The survey found that gender stereotyping about jobs is set from a young age and that family, tv, radio and film have the biggest influence on children's choices. Toy choices are also found to influence careers. You and your participants may want to extend this activity by conducting your own research on younger children in your school or youth club to find out more about gendered expectations in your community.

Nail bar

This activity is based on an activity developed by Nelta M. Edwards and published as Edwards, Nelta M, (2010) 'Using nail polish to teach about gender and homophobia'. *Teaching Sociology*, 38(4), pp. 362–372.

 Through experimenting with painting each other's nails and wearing nail varnish, participants explore and reflect on how people express their gender and how gender expression is judged and policed by others.

 30–40 minutes over two sessions a week apart

 Wide range of nail varnish colours. Nail varnish remover and cotton wool, masks if ventilation is an issue.

 13+

Note: This activity invites participants to experiment with their gender expression and reflect on how others in their community react to this. It was developed for use in a university setting and has been adapted for use with younger participants in community settings. In some settings and with some groups, however, this would not be a safe activity to do. Use your judgement and discuss with your group if and why this would be a safe/unsafe activity to explore. Also see note on opting out on p. 108.

Ask participants to find a partner and to paint each other's nails. Participants can choose any colour, except for clear. Task participants with volunteering to wear the nail varnish for one week. Give participants a set of questions (following) to consider over the course of the week and to make a note of any thoughts that they have. The following week ask participants to discuss the following in their pairs:

- What colour did you choose? Why?
- How did it feel to have your nails painted? What made it comfortable? What made it awkward?
- What did you think when you first finished painting and looked at your hands?

- How did you feel about yourself when you looked at your nails?
- Did you change your behaviour in any way when you had painted nails (e.g. showing them off, hiding them, making jokes about them)?
- How did people react to your painted nails?
- What did you think about their reaction?
- How long did you wear the nail polish? If you removed it rather soon, what influenced your decision to do so?
- Did your gender and the gender of the person painting your nails affect this activity?
- What assumptions do we sometimes jump to about nail varnish use? How does this vary by gender? (e.g. vain, stylish, pretty, slutty for girls, belonging to a particular subculture for all genders, for boys being gay as nail varnish is considered feminine.)

Create opportunities for participants to feedback on how it felt to participate in the activity in small groups.

Ask groups to feedback if they feel comfortable. As a whole group discuss why painting nails is a gendered activity and use this to lead into a discussion of the social construction of gender roles. Discussion points might include:

- Nail varnish is often considered to be 'feminine' but there is nothing inherently gendered about nail varnish – this is something we have ascribed to it culturally.
- Different colours have gendered connotations. These are culturally and historically specific (e.g. in the west pink used to be considered a boy's colour).
- When someone is considered to be gender non-conforming it is often assumed that they are also not heterosexual (e.g. effeminate men are 'gay'). In reality someone's gender expression cannot tell us anything about who they are romantically or sexually attracted to. This confusion often happens because heteronormativity is based on very narrow and limited gender stereotypes that don't give much wriggle room for creative and diverse self expression.
- Consider what it would be like if we didn't have rigid gender rules about colours, dress and fashion. What would this be like?

A note on opting out: Participants do not have to take part in this activity if they feel uncomfortable. Try asking participants what it is about the activity that makes them uncomfortable. Try and establish if there is any version of the activity they might find acceptable – e.g. painting their own nail(s) just for the session duration. Remember to draw these participants into the discussion at the end of the activity so that they can contribute.

Rights over time (and around the world)

 Participants research women's and/or LGBT+ rights over time in small groups and use their findings to create a visual timeline that can be hung in your place of work. This sparks conversations about gender, sexuality and social change. This is a cross-curricular activity that links with the history and/or geography curriculum. One hour

 Website access. Colouring pens, string, coloured A6 pieces of paper or card. Paper clips. 11+

Divide participants into small groups. Explain the task which is to research the history of women's rights and/or LGBT+ rights. For each key date participants should write details of the historical moment onto a piece of A6 card and attach it with a paper clip to a string that is hung across the room. Areas to cover include:

- Women's rights (e.g. reproductive rights, violence against women, political representation, employment and equal pay, property rights, marriage/divorce law, access to education). Useful resources include The Fawcett Society's report: *Equality – it's about time: Timeline of women's rights 1866–2016*).[4]
- Lesbian, gay, bisexual and trans rights (e.g. age of sexual consent, criminalisation/decriminalisation of sex between two men, marriage rights, parenting rights). There are a number of LGBT+ history timelines available online. See, for example, Stonewall's *Key Dates For Lesbian, Gay, Bi and Trans Equality*[5].

You can choose to work together to create one timeline with each group researching a specific set of rights (e.g. trans healthcare rights; women's property rights) or rights in a particular country or region. Or you can create multiple timelines crossing the room with each group/timeline having a different focus.

As a final plenary and/or as participants are working use the following questions to spark discussions about gender, sexuality and social change:

- What has changed over time? What has stayed the same? How has this varied across different communities and countries?
- In your opinion have the changes largely been positive or negative?
- What changes would you like to see in the future?
- Do you feel optimistic about the future in terms of women's and LGBT+ rights? What hopes and fears do you have?

Extension: A bill of rights

As an extension activity ask participants to create a Bill of Sexual Rights/Bill of Gender rights that outlines their hopes and vision for the future. Participants can choose whether to have a global, regional or national focus.

To extend the activity (or as an alternative), task participants with mapping the same set of rights around the world. Try using the *Sexual Rights Database*[6] or other information provided by organisations such as Amnesty International, The World Bank and UN data on Education, Gender and Social Development. Give each group a blank world map and task them with using coloured pens and post-it notes to map rights across a selection of different countries. For example, they could colour code their findings with green (equal rights achieved), yellow (some examples of equal rights, more work needed) and red (examples of rights being denied). Each group should present their findings to each other and talk about what they learnt and what surprised them. Participants can opt to create one large map to be displayed that includes participants' collective findings on rights for women and LGBT+ people around the world.

Reassembling the rules

Based on an activity that was developed by Professor Emma Renold and a group of young women at a school in Wales. It is included in *AGENDA: A young people's guide to making positive relationships matter* (see *Useful resources* at the end of this book). Used with permission.

 This activity asks participants to think about the unwritten rules in society that they think are unequal, unjust or unfair and invites them to engage in creative forms of gender activism. One hour

 Rulers (preferably those with holes in the top), permanent marker pens, digital camera. 11+

Pick a rule. In groups discuss what rules you want to change to make the world a more gender equal and gender fair place to live. Rules can be laws, policies, social norms and stereotypes – anything that you want to change about the way things are that reinforce or create inequality.

Graffiti. The ruler with one or more messages for change.

Ruler relfies. Ask all participants to stand in a long line. Each participant should hold two rulers up to their face and have their photo taken. If you use the rulers to block out eyes and other parts of the face an element of anonymity is provided.

Rattle those rules. Ask each participant to choose an object in the room such as a chair, table or radiator and rattle their ruler against it to make as much noise as possible. Record the sound.

Tweet. Use the images and audio you have created to make a short video to share online with other schools. Create your own hashtags.

Create. Ask participants to think about what else they can do with their rulers. For example, make a ruler skirt and wear it at public events, string up the rulers somewhere they will be seen.

An alternative idea is to print out paper rulers and put them on every seat in your youth club or assembly hall. Invite everyone to write on the back of the ruler what rules they want to change. Collect them back up and deliver them to whoever holds power within your organisation.

Is this sexual harassment?

 An interactive continuum activity that asks participants to consider whether different behaviours can be categorised as sexual harassment or not. The activity explores how sexual harassment can become normalised creating hostile and unsafe environments.

 25 minutes

 List of statements for educator, projection of statements on to a board or lists of statements for participants. Three large pieces of card or paper containing the words: Always, Sometimes, Never.

 14+

Set up a continuum along a wall using large cards containing the words *Always*, *Sometimes* and *Never.* Make sure there is space between each card for participants to move around.

Explain to participants that this is an activity about sexual harassment. You are going to read out a series of statements describing different behaviours. Participants need to decide whether they think the behaviour is 'sometimes' sexual harassment, is 'always' sexual harassment or 'never' sexual harassment. After you have read out each statement ask a number of participants to explain why they have chosen to stand where they are. Encourage participants to debate with each other and move along the continuum if they change their mind. Make sure you unpick why a behaviour might 'sometimes' be harassment and 'sometimes' not.

Note: It is highly likely that you will have participants in your group who have experienced sexual harassment as a victim and/or aggressor. We would recommend only facilitating this activity with groups that you have already worked with to establish working relationships and create a safe working environment (particularly as this is a whole group activity). Before facilitating this activity create or remind participants of the group working agreement and the importance of a safe space using some of the activities in Chapter 2 of this book.

Is this sexual harassment?: Statements for educators (please choose a selection of these)

- Commenting on someone's body shape or size.

- Commenting on someone's dress sense or personal appearance.

- Making jokes about sex.

- Making jokes about rape.

- Sharing a short film of two people from the year above having sex.

- Discussing someone else's sex life.

- Calling someone a slapper/slag/whore.

- Saying 'that's gay!'

- Looking at topless photos of women in the newspaper.

- Staring at someone's body for a long time.

- Pulling up a girl's skirt or pinging her bra strap.

- Asking someone what their genitals are like.

- Writing graffiti about someone's sex life in the toilets.

- Upskirting (taking a photo up someone's skirt).

- Repeating rumours or gossip about someone's sex life or sexual identity.

- Touching someone's body.

- Posting images of someone's naked body on a social network site.

- Making graphic remarks about sex (e.g. she would look good naked on my bed) within earshot of others.

- Wolf-whistling and cat-calling.

Participants will have different opinions about what does and does not count as sexual harassment. Challenge participants to think about whether each of the behaviours is *ethical* using the following questions:

- Why might someone do this? What might be their intention?
- Has consent been given in this scenario? Is consent needed? [Answer = yes!]
- How might someone feel if this behaviour was happening around them?
- How might someone feel if this behaviour was directed towards them?
- Does it make a difference what the genders of the people involved are?*

*Sexual violence and sexual harassment can occur between two children of any age and gender but all the evidence available suggests that girls experience much higher levels of unwanted sexual touch, pressure to share nudes, unwanted sexual messages and sexual assault. For a summary of the evidence see The Department for Education's 2018 Report: *Sexual Violence and Sexual Harassment Between Children in Schools and Colleges: Advice for Governing Bodies, Proprietors, Headteachers, Principals, Senior Leadership Teams and Designated Safeguarding Leads.*[7]

At the end of the activity share the following definition of sexual harassment and explain key terms.

Sexual harassment is unwanted behaviour of a sexual nature (e.g. something sexual, or related to your gender), which does any of the following:

- violates your dignity (e.g. makes you feel disrespected) OR
- makes you feel intimidated, degraded or humiliated OR
- creates a hostile or offensive environment.

Distribute a printed list of the statements or project them on to a wall. Ask the group to read the list and think about which ones 1) violate someone's dignity and 2) create a hostile environment. Take feedback from participants. Emphasise that any of the behaviours listed *could* be considered as sexual harassment. You may find it useful to introduce the concept of rape culture by showing an example of the rape culture pyramid (available online).[8] This theory suggests that behaviours such as some of those listed earlier on p. 112 help to normalise sexual and gender violence and create a hostile, unsafe environment.

To explore these statements using an ethical framework see the 'Ethical decision making' activity in Chapter 6: *Sex* on p. 256.

Stamping out sexual harassment

All of the following methods are adapted from ideas from *AGENDA: A young people's guide to making positive relationships matter* (see *Useful resources* at the end of this book). Used here with permission.

 The following activities give ideas about how you can open up conversations with the young people that you work with about sexual harassment and gender inequalities and support them to engage in social activism around the issues that are important to them.

 Minimum one hour

 Various – see the following text.

 13+

Choose one of the following methods to start conversations about sexual harassment. Choose the method most suited to the needs of your group. Given the high rates of reported sexual harassment among young people, especially young women, it is very likely that some of the young people you are working with will have experienced sexual harassment themselves, even if they may not call it as such. Remember the ground rules and every participant's right to pass. Make sure you create space to support participants outside of the session if necessary or signpost them to someone who can.

Stamp it out. Get a large roll of paper and roll it out on the floor. Give each participant a pen and ask them write down any words, thoughts or statements that they can think of about sexual harassment. This can be facts, figures, stories, feelings, questions. As prompts you can cut out key figures and statements about sexual harassment taken from the Department for Education's 2018 Report: *Sexual Violence and Sexual Harassment Between Children in Schools and Colleges: Advice for Governing Bodies, Proprietors, Headteachers, Principals, Senior Leadership Teams and Designated Safeguarding Leads.*[9] Alternatively you can use this activity to start conversations about tackling homophobia, biphobia and transphobia. Use Stonewall's annual *School Report*[10] for details of research on this issue for young people in schools and adapt the following techniques. When everyone is finished invite participants to read the roll and decide which of the statements, words or stories they want to stamp out. Invite participants to stamp on these with their shoes. You can also use an old shoe to make paint footprints to block out words, phrases, rules or policies that the group feel strongly about.

What jars you? Give each participant a glass jar, pens and slips of paper or post-it notes. Ask them to write down all the things that 'jar' them about sexual harassment. Collect in the jars and invite participants to share their experiences in pairs or small groups if this feels safe. After a discussion, participants can decorate the outside of the jars with positive messages for change.

Stop-start. Give each participant one red and one green paper plate and pens. Ask them to write one thing that they would like to start and one thing that they would like to stop when it comes to sexual harassment. String up the plates and negotiate with participants whether there is anywhere that they can be hung for others to see. You can also take photos of some of the plates (with consent) and share online.

Create a mood board. Write the topic of gender at the top of a large piece of paper. Working individually or in small groups ask participants to use magazines or newspapers or images found online and cut and paste them on to their 'board'. Encourage participants to pick out words and quotes that express their feelings about the topic.

Feeling it. If strong feelings emerge in your discussion encourage participants to write down key words or phrases that capture how they feel – or alternatively you can do this for them as the discussion emerges. Ask participants to then scrunch or rip up the paper to create a big pile of feelings. Rather than throwing these feelings away get creative with them. One idea is to use the feelings to create a heart and decorate it with messages for the outside world. These could be examples of feelings that the group wants others to hear or messages about what they experiencing or what they want to change.

Based on the key issue that emerges within your group, think about ways of raising awareness about the issues that are affecting participants. For example, create a pop-up shop in your school or youth club. Design and print T-shirts. Attach a clothes tag to each item that tells of participants' experiences of harassment. On the T-shirts print messages for positive social change.

Alternatively look at the street art created by Tatyana Fazlalizadeh as part of the 'Stop Telling Women to Smile' project, which contains statements such as 'My worth extends far beyond my body', 'My outfit is not an invitation and I am not here for you'. Task participants with creating their own street art in your youth club or school.

Acting out

 A creative activity that uses quotes from research with young people as the basis for creative writing, song writing and/ or performance. This gives participants the opportunity to become familiar with research on children and young people's lives and to discuss issues such as consent and inequality without having to talk about their own experiences. 30 minutes (minimum). Can be extended to a longer project.

 Printed copies of research reports that can be downloaded for free. Scissors or highlighters, pens and paper. Performance space and musical equipment may also be required. 11+

Choose a research project on children, young people and gender that has been published in an accessible format. We have given some examples in the following list but we know that new research comes out all the time so there may be new examples by the time you read this.

- Stonewall's *School Report* – published every year.[11]
- *'Sex without consent, I suppose that is rape" How young people understand consent to sex.* By the Children's Commission.[12]
- *BOYS AND GIRLS SPEAK OUT: A Qualitative Study of Children's Gender and Sexual Cultures (age 10–12)* by Emma Renold.[13]
- McGeeney, E, & Hanson, E, (2017) *Digital Romance: A Research Project Exploring Young People's Use of Technology in Their Romantic Relationships and Love Lives.* London: National Crime Agency and Brook. Available for free online.

Go through the research and pull out the quotes from young people. You can either do this your-self in preparation or, if possible, ask participants to go through and cut these out themselves. Use these as the basis for writing a short story, play, poem or song. There are some examples that follow. Some participants may find the content of the research projects challenging and triggering. Remember a participant's right to pass and opt out of participating in an activity and ensure you are able to signpost participants to a safe place and person to talk to if needed.

- Read out a series of quotes one after the other. Ask participants to listen silently with their eyes closed. When they open their eyes ask them to write non-stop for two minutes as if they are one of the people in the research. Working in pairs or small groups think of a story line that could link together the monologues. Write a script, adding in movement, gesture and tone. Work with the drama department or local performance groups to develop the script and put on a live performance in your community.
- Give participants a list of quotes and ask them to select the two that they feel are the most powerful. Share these in small groups and use them as the basis for creating a song that only initially uses quotes from the research. After ten minutes ask participants to write another verse that includes their reactions to the quotes they have read. Work with the music depart-ment or musicians in your team to develop and record your song. Perform it live or record and share it online. Look at the Wellcome Collection's *Sounds of Sexology*[14] initiative for examples of songs written and performed by young people that are inspired by research.

Craftivism

 Craftivism is where craft is used as a tool for social action with the aim of bringing about long term social change. This is a creative activity in which participants engage in craftivism with a view to bringing about change in their local school, youth club or community. Minimum one hour

 Art and craft materials, stones, etc. 11+

Engage participants in a craftivist project that tackles an area of sex, gender or sexual inequality that you are addressing through the curriculum. You can use one of the following ideas or invent your own! Encourage participants to consider how and where they might want to use and dis-play their projects. Who needs to hear their voices and engage with their messages for change? Participants can work individually, in pairs or small groups.

Equality rocks. Decorate pebbles with acrylic paints and LGBT+ inclusive or feminist messages. Hide them about towns. Locally there are often [town name] rocks movements where images of found rocks are shared on Facebook and then rehidden in a new location. See if your rocks get shared and how far they travel.

Tiny placards. Make tiny placards out of matchsticks and small squares of card with small polit-ical statements. Laminate the cards and then plant the placards in plant pots out and about. Think about where to place your placards in order to raise awareness of the change needed.

Genderbread humans. Buy or bake a batch gingerbread people. Use a wide range of icing sugar colours and decorations to create a Genderbread person displaying its gender or sexual identity in its own unique way. This can also be done with cardboard body shapes or people paper chains. Where will you display, hand out or sell your Genderbread people?

Equality rainbow paper chains. Make paper chains in rainbow colours and on each chain have people write a statement or a pledge about equality. Display these equality chains in a prominent location where you can target those groups or individuals who need to see your message.

Badge making. Borrow or buy a badge maker and make a series of badges with feminist and/or LGBT+ equality slogans.

Claymation/Lego stop–start animation. Create a short animation using Lego or modelling clay to make a statement about equality. What will you do with your creations? Where will they be curated and displayed to maximise the impact?

Leaf it out. Cut out large coloured leaves. Write an experience on one side and a message for change on the other. Hang leaves on a tree in your community or place of work.

All I want for Christmas is Equality. Politicise your Christmas tree by decorating baubles with equality slogans and making clay or cardboard figures that celebrate and/or symbolise equality.

I'm Sew CROSSstitch. Make a cross stitch with a political statement or image to frame and display. Consider where you would like to curate and display your creation in order to bring about the change required.

Equality Star Awards (with thanks to Louise Pope and the E-Team at Chew Valley School for the original idea). Design and create an award for a person, institution, place or space. Decide on the criteria for awarding the award and award it! Perhaps plan and create an awards ceremony to go with it.

Music to change the world. Rewrite the lyrics to a song you love (but whose lyrics you hate!) or write lyrics for a new song that celebrates equality or social change. Pin up your lyrics or record your song, play it live or post it online.

Section 2: Key terms and definitions

The words that we use for talking about sex and gender are constantly changing. Here are two activities that capture some of the key terms and definitions used at the time of writing, followed by two activities that invite participants to respond to key terms creatively. These activities help clarify the distinction between sex and gender and between gender and sexual orientation and help to develop a more nuanced understanding of what gender is in all its complexity.

The Genderbread Person

This activity uses the image of the Genderbread person produced by The Proud Trust and is used with permission. It is based on an original concept by itspronouncedmetrosexual.com.

 In this activity participants explore the difference between sex, gender identity, gender expression and sexual orientation. This helps develop a vocabulary for talking about different aspects of our own identities and examine some of the assumptions that we make about others.

 30 minutes

 Printed colour copies of the Genderbread person, pre-prepared images of famous people, with name and job title (see p. 119), copy of definitions (for educator).

 11+

Note: There are a range of different models of the Genderbread person and gender unicorn that you can find online. Each model uses slightly different scales and categories. For example, some have separate scales for romantic and sexual attraction. We like this one but there is value in exploring some of the differences between the models with young people and asking them to create their own.

Start by explaining that this is an activity about gender. Gender is something we all know something about and all have some experience of. It is also something that is more complicated than it may seem at first glance.

Show the group an image of the Genderbread person. Use the following definitions to talk through with the group what each of the headings mean.

Gender identity: How you think about yourself and define your gender, based on the options that you think you have available to you. Some people do not feel as though they have a gender identity.

Gender expression: This is how you present your gender. For example, how you act, dress and relate to others and how these expressions are interpreted by others, based on gender norms and expectations in society. Gender expressions are usually described as masculine and/or feminine.

Sex (also referred to as *sex assigned at birth* and *biological sex*): This the sex category that you are given at birth or in utero. It is usually based on observation of your genitals.

THE GENDERBREAD PERSON

Original concept by
itspronouncedmetrosexual.com

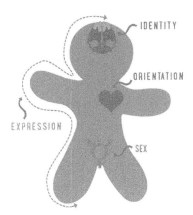

GENDER IDENTITY

WOMAN   NON-BINARY   MAN

Your gender identity is how you think about yourself, the gender that you identify
with and/or feel that you are. Some people feel as though they do not have a gender
at all, and may refer to themselves as agender or non-gendered.

GENDER EXPRESSION

FEMININE   ANDROGYNOUS   MASCULINE

This is how you display your gender and is demonstrated through the ways that you act, dress,
behave and interact in the world, in relation to the gender expectations of your society.

BIOLOGICAL SEX

FEMALE   INTERSEX   MALE

This is usually determined at birth, based on observation of your genitals. However, your chromosomes,
hormones, genes and internal sex organs also contribute to the make-up of your biological sex.

SEXUAL ORIENTATION

ATTRACTED   BI/PANSEXUAL   ATTRACTED
TO WOMEN   TO MEN

The types of people (often based on gender) that you find yourself attracted to, can help you
determine your sexual orientation. Attraction can be emotional, sexual, physical and/or spiritual.
Some people experience little or no sexual attraction, and may refer to themselves as asexual.

FIGURE 4.1 The Genderbread Person

Give participants the opportunity to reflect on the model and share their opinions in pairs or small groups. You may want to prompt by asking if they have seen it before, if they are familiar with the terms used and whether they find it helpful to see identity as sitting along a continuum rather than as a series of boxes that they need to tick.

Next, still working in small groups distribute images of famous people and ask participants to consider: Where do you think these famous people would plot themselves on each of the gender scales?

You will need to select a diverse group of famous people that your group will be familiar with. This changes over time and depends on the communities in which you work. Some examples we might use at the time of writing include: Kirsten Stewart, Tom Daley, Rain Dove, Caitlyn Jenner, Caster Semenya, Nicola Adams, Harnaam Kaur, Joe Sugg, Zoe 'Zoella' Sugg, Laverne Cox, David Bowie, Cara Delevingne, Ellen Degeneres, Barack Obama. It is a good idea to show participants an image of each person with their name and job title and to be open to suggestions from the group.

Once groups have finished plotting each person, come back together as a whole group and share the examples. Prompt discussion and challenge assumptions using the following questions:

- Why have you plotted people where you have? How do you know where to plot someone? (*Answers may include: because they are 'out', because this is what the media or public assume/say they are, because this is how we read them visually or how we interpret their actions.*)
- What assumptions have we made when doing this activity? (*Answers may include: that you can tell someone's sex, gender or sexual orientation just by looking at them or by what other people say about them – prompt participants to reflect on specific examples of assumptions made.*)
- What are some of the assumptions that we make in real life? (*Answers may include: a woman with short hair is a lesbian, a man wearing makeup is gay, etc.*)
- What are some of the problems with making these assumptions? (*Answers may include: they may reflect our own prejudice, they may be inaccurate, they may be offensive or harmful to others, they may affect how we respond to people and the opportunities we do/don't give them.*)
- Why might some people feel like they have to hide aspects of their identity? (*Answers may include: to stay safe due to sexism, homophobia, biphobia, transphobia, because one aspect of their identity may feel incompatible with another – e.g. being gay may be incompatible with a religious, cultural or ethnic identity.*)
- Does it matter where somebody sits on the gender scales? (*Answer: no*)
- Ultimately who decides where someone sits on the gender scales? (*Answer: The person themselves is the only person who can make this decision. This leads us to question of why we make these assumptions in the first place and whether it is ok to apply identities to someone without asking.*)

Sex, gender and sexual orientation venn diagram

This activity is developed from a workshop plan created by Brighton and Hove's *Standards and Achievement Team* and *Allsorts Youth Project*. Shared with permission.

 An interactive activity that enables participants to discuss and clarify key terms relating to sex, gender and sexual orientation. This helps to create shared understandings about terminology within groups and increases participants' confidence in talking about gender and sexuality. This activity takes a while to set up but it's worth it!

 20–30 minutes

 Three large plastic hula hoops of equal sizes or A3 paper and flipchart pens; set of three large labels stating *Sex, Gender, Sexual orientation*; set of small labels containing words from the list on p. 123; dictionaries including an LGBTQ+ dictionary or glossary, e.g. The Proud Trust or Stonewall (see *Useful resources* at the end of this book).

 11+

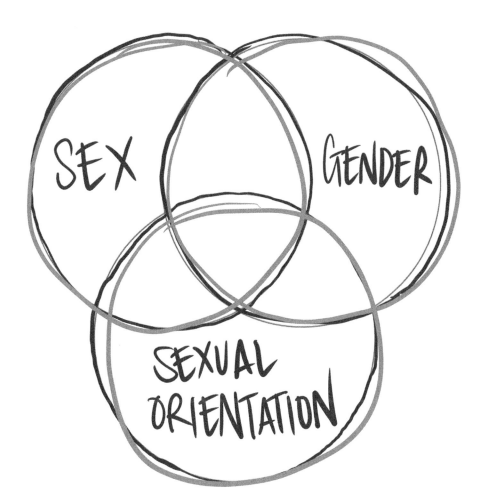

FIGURE 4.2 Sex, Gender and Sexual Orientation venn diagram
Illustration by: Chrissy Baxter

To set up the activity place three hoops to form a venn diagram or draw a three-circle venn diagram on A3 paper. Label each of the three circles as *Sex*, *Gender*, *Sexual orientation* using the large label cards or by writing on your diagram. As you place the labels on the diagram ask participants to say what they think each word means. Use the online glossaries from Stonewall and The Proud Trust to explain these terms – it is helpful to use more than one definition to show that these terms are contested and not everyone agrees on what words we should use or what they precisely mean.

To facilitate the activity divide into small groups and give each group a few small cards, each containing a word from the following list. You do not have to use all of the terms on the list just the ones you feel best to use with your group. Give participants a few minutes to discuss where each word might go. Use the Stonewall and The Proud Trust online glossaries to support understanding of terms.

Ask one person from each group to place their words on the diagram and explain why they chose that position. Use the questions on p. 123 to encourage discussion between participants. We have given some guidance as to where you may want to place some terms but be clear with the group that answers may not always be clear cut as many of these terms are contested and can be placed in more than one hoop.

Words that could be placed in 'Sex' (but may be placed elsewhere on the venn):

- **Chromosomes**. Most bodies have a pair of XY chromosomes or a pair of XX chromosomes. This is one of the ways in which humans are classified as female (XX) or male (XY)
- **Vagina/vulva/penis.** Humans are often classified as male or female and this is generally assigned at birth based on genital observations. Could also go in gender as for some people their gender is strongly associated with their genitalia. However, people could also object to the idea that someone's sex or gender can be defined by their genitals so you could put these outside of the venn.
- **Hormones.** Sex is often classified based on whether the main sex hormones produced by the body are oestrogen and progesterone (female), or the androgen – testosterone (male). This could also go in 'Gender' as some people take hormones to help align their physical body with their gender identity.

Sex, gender and sexual orientation venn diagram: Key terms

Male	Cisgender	Facial hair
Female	Cross-dresser	Breasts
Man (boy)	Drag Queen	Womb
Woman (girl)	Drag King	Queer
Masculine	Asexual	Tomboy
Feminine	Lesbian	Effeminate
Intersex	Bisexual	Camp
Trans	Gay	Butch
Transsexual	Heterosexual	Skinhead
Transgender	Pansexual	High heels
Genderqueer or Gender Fluid	Penis	Short hair
Hormones	Vagina	Baggy T-shirt
Chromosomes	Vulva	

Words that could be placed in 'Sexual orientation' (but may be placed elsewhere on the venn):

- **Lesbian.** Refers to a woman who feels emotional, romantic and/or sexual attraction towards women.
- **Bisexual.** Refers to someone who feels emotional, romantic and/or sexual attraction towards males or females.
- **Gay.** Refers to someone who feels emotional, romantic and/or sexual attraction towards someone of the same gender as them, e.g. a man who is attracted to men or a woman who is attracted to women. 'Gay' is an identity and not all people who have sex with someone of the same gender as them would identify as gay.
- **Heterosexual.** Refers to a person who feels emotional, romantic and/or sexual attraction towards people of a different gender to themselves. Usually only refers to men attracted to women and women attracted to men.
- **Queer.** Sometimes used as an umbrella term for LGBT+ people or to refer to any sexual or gender minority. However, some people who identify as 'queer' would not identify as Lesbian, Gay, Bisexual or Trans. Queer can also refer, like pansexual, to people who are attracted to people of any gender as well as to someone who doesn't see themselves as fitting into cultural norms around gender and sexuality. Could also be placed in 'Gender'.
- **Pansexual.** Refers to a person whose emotional, romantic and/or sexual attraction towards others is not limited or defined by sex, gender or gender identity. Could also be placed in 'Gender'.
- **Asexual.** Someone who does not experience sexual desire or sexual feelings.

Words that could be placed in 'Gender' (but may be placed elsewhere on the venn):

- **Masculine.** Having qualities or appearance traditionally associated with men. People of all genders can choose to present themselves or can be read by others as 'masculine'. This could also be placed in 'Sexual orientation' as women who present as masculine are sometimes read as gay or lesbian. These assumptions and stereotypes are often unhelpful and based on prejudice and/or misunderstandings about gender and sexuality.
- **Feminine.** Having qualities or appearance traditionally associated with women.
- **Trans.** An umbrella term to describe people whose gender is not the same as, or does not sit comfortably with, the sex they were assigned at birth.
- **Transsexual.** Medical term to refer to someone who transitioned to live in the 'opposite' sex to the one assigned at birth. This term is old fashioned and less commonly used today but some trans people do identify as transsexual.
- **Transgender.** Someone who is transitioning or has transitioned to live in a different gender to their sex assigned at birth.

- **Genderqueer/Gender fluid.** A person or approach that sees gender as fluid, rather than fixed and binary. This means that someone may move between one or more genders over a lifetime or day to day.
- **Cisgender.** People whose gender identity matches the sex that they were assigned at birth. For example, a female who identifies as a woman, or a male who identifies as a man. It is often used to describe people who are not trans. It can be a controversial term, because it implies a binary between trans and cisgender (rather than suggesting that gender is fluid). It also doesn't acknowledge that many people who are not trans will have strong feelings about, and questions towards, the gender roles and stereotypes assigned to them based on their sex.
- **Cross-dresser.** Someone who dresses in clothing more commonly associated with someone of a different gender from the sex they were assigned at birth. Participants may place this in 'Sexual orientation' as cross-dressing is often associated with gay culture and gay people. Challenge the idea that you can tell who someone is sexually or romantically attracted to based on what they wear.
- **Tomboy.** Term used to describe a girl who behaves or presents 'like a boy'. Again, unhelpful assumptions can be made about the sexual orientation of girls who present in a masculine way.
- **Effeminate.** A term used to describe a man who is feminine in actions or appearance.
- **Butch.** A woman who exhibits 'masculine' qualities. This is often associated with lesbian women but women who are butch are not necessarily lesbian and vice versa.
- **Camp.** A male who exhibits 'feminine' qualities. This is often associated with gay men, but men who are camp are not necessarily gay and vice versa.

Once you have placed all the terms in the diagram, use the following questions to reflect on the activity:

- What was difficult/easy about this activity?
- What did you learn from this activity?
- Is it useful to have different categories and labels for talking about sex, gender and sexual orientation?
- What would it be like if we didn't have these categories and labels?

The key learning from this activity should be that sex, gender and sexual orientation are all distinct but overlapping and interlinked categories. Sometimes these categories are useful and important categories for making sense of ourselves and the world (e.g. for making sense of why some people earn more than others or why some experience more violence than others) but other times they are not (e.g. they lead to stereotypes, assumptions, etc.). *Sex, Gender* and *Sexual orientation* are legal as well as social and cultural categories that vary across cultures and over time. They overlap with other social and legal categories such as race, class and dis/ability.

QUILTBAGS!

A creative activity in which participants create a patchwork quilt bag to represent some of the key gender and sexuality identity labels.

One hour

Range of fabrics, needles, embroidery and cotton threads.

11+

QUILTBAGS is an acronym which stands for Queer, Undecided, Intersex, Lesbian, Trans, Bisexual, Asexual, Gay, Straight. Introduce the group to this acronym and recap or discuss what each of these terms means.

Task the group with making patchwork 'quiltbags'. At least nine of the squares should be used to represent the nine identities (QUILTBAGS). For example, by sewing a large letter, image, symbol or creative text onto the square. Sew all the squares together to make a patchwork storage bag. As you are creating your bags discuss some of the key messages covered in this chapter and think about how to weave them into your creations. For example, that gender and sexual identities are varied and diverse, that mixed together they make up what it means to be human, that identities change over time and vary across and within different communities.

Identity label Tetrominoes

This activity is based on the idea of a creative display of Freedominos/Polyominos used by *Freedom Youth* a project within *Off The Record* Bristol at the 2018 Critically Queer Conference.[15] Shared with permission.

A creative and interactive activity that explores how we label ourselves and others. This activity complements the 'What's my label?' activity on p. 36 of Chapter 2: *Creating safer spaces*.

20–30 minutes

A wide range of 'Tetromino' pieces (a shape consisting of four squares) cut out in different colours and shapes, e.g. S-shape, Z-shape, T-shape, L-shape, Line-shape, Mirrored L-shape and a Square-shape.

11+

This activity asks participants to think about the ways in which they are labelled by others and label themselves and invites them to share some of these labels and their feelings about them in the group. It was originally developed as an activity for adult participants, facilitated by LGBT+ young people. It could be used as a training activity for staff in your workplace or as an education activity with young people. If using with young people or adults ensure that you have worked with the group to establish a safe working environment and have conducted some of the activities in Chapter 2 of this book to build working relationships within the group. Explain that this is an activity about how we label ourselves and others.

Ask the group to brainstorm the identity labels they would use to describe themselves, writing each label on a post-it note. Labels can be related to sex, gender, ethnicity, skin colour, religion, age, sexual orientation, interests, music, fashion, etc. For example, girl, working class, student,

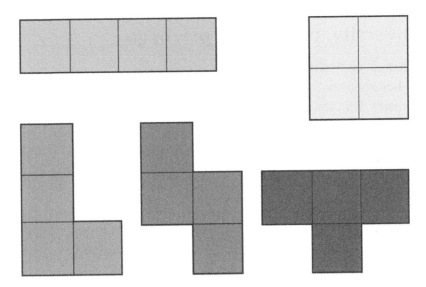

FIGURE 4.3 Tetromino shapes

pianist, goth, Indian. Participants can write as many as they wish and do not need to share their responses with others if they don't want to.

Lay out a range of 'Tetromino' pieces and ask each participant to choose one of the shapes. Their task is to choose four identity labels that they would be comfortable sharing with the group and write these on each of the four squares – one label per square. On the back of the card they can write some thoughts about what the labels means to them, its value, power and significance. This can be done anonymously.

Using sellotape ask participants to stick their label shapes to themselves. Ask participants to walk around and read each other's labels, asking questions and discussing the labels amongst themselves. After a few minutes, ask participants to pause and use the following questions to prompt group discussion:

- How do you feel wearing this set of labels?
- Is there anywhere you would feel uncomfortable wearing this label?
- Without wearing written labels, how else do we signify our identities to others?
- Are there aspects of our identity that we would like to hide? How does it feel to do this?
- What would your Tetromino look like if it only contained labels given to you by others?
- What are some of the ways that we get labelled by others?
- How does it feel to have an identity given to you by others?
- Are we free to choose our own labels?
- Why do we use labels?
- Do labels given to us by others stick?
- How can we push back against labels we don't want or don't like?
- Is it ok not to have a label?

To finish, ask the group to use the Tetronimo pieces to build a whole shape with no gaps between the shapes. The work then becomes a collage, depicting the group's identities and labels.

Section 3: Diversity, power and privilege

The activities in this section explore key concepts such as privilege, power, equity and inequality. There is a focus on heteronormativity as a key form of privilege and on the homophobia and sexism experienced as a result. The aim is to make these complex concepts relevant to young people's lives. We recommend running these activities alongside those from the first section that inspire young people to engage in social activism to bring about positive change in their communities.

Power and privilege

This activity is based on an original activity from the *Them and Us* teaching pack produced by *Metro Youth and Little Fish Theatre Company* (2011). Used with permission.

 An interactive activity that explores key concepts of power and privilege. 15–20 minutes

 Identities printed onto individual cards. 13+

You will need a large empty room or to be outside for this activity as it requires a lot of space. Line up the group at one end of the space you are using so that they are facing you.

Give each person in the group one of the following roles printed onto card (or written on a post-it note). You can edit the list to make up a range of ages, ethnicities, genders, abilities to cover the number of identities needed for your group. Ask participants to keep their roles to themselves and try to avoid giving a role to a person it might apply to.

Note: This activity asks participants to think about power and privilege in relation to age, race, gender, sexuality and ability. When deciding if and how to do this activity think about the group that you are working with and make sure that it won't place a burden on one or more of the individuals in the group because they are the only 'minority' participants. Before facilitating this activity make sure you remind participants of the group working agreement and remember participants' right to pass and opt out of any activity.

Power and Privilege: Identity labels

Adult White heterosexual man.	Trans man, White, mid-30s, heterosexual.
Adult White heterosexual woman, mother of two children.	Trans woman, mixed-race, mid-20s, bisexual.
Woman in her 70s, Asian, heterosexual.	Black gay man, 20s.
Man in his 70s, White, heterosexual.	Black (or other ethnic minority), lesbian woman.
White teenage girl, bisexual.	Bisexual man, aged 20, White.
Black teenage girl, heterosexual	Bisexual woman, aged 20, Black.
Asian teenage boy, heterosexual.	Pregnant woman, White, lesbian.
Girl (under 11), White.	Disabled man, White, heterosexual.
Boy (under 11), mixed ethnicity.	Disabled woman, White, heterosexual.
Black (or other ethnic minority), teenager.	Man who has sex with other men in secret, publicly identifies as heterosexual, White, mid-40s.
LGBT+ teenager.	Non-binary teenager, mixed ethnicity, bisexual.

Once each participant has been assigned an identity, read out the following list of activities and ask participants to take a step forward if they think they can do the activity as their assigned identity. Where a participant's answer is 'no', 'sometimes' or 'depends on the situation' they should stay where they are. Use the following notes to encourage discussion.

Activity	Notes
Feel safe kissing your lover in public	Discuss views with participants whether they think LGBT+ people could kiss safely in public in their communities. Does this depend on their ethnicity? For bisexuals does it depend on whether they are kissing someone with the same or a different gender?
Feel safe holding hands with your lover in public	See above.
Expect your family to accept your girlfriend or partner.	Answer will depend on your family's views.
Marry your partner in the UK	Gay marriage is now legal in the UK. Not all religious authorities recognise gay marriage.
Marry your partner abroad	Many countries do not permit gay marriage and in some countries gay sex is illegal and punishable by death. See the International lesbian, gay, bisexual, trans and intersex association's annual *State-Sponsored Homophobia report*.[16]
Feel safe to walk the streets after dark	Discuss with students whether your race, age, ability, gender (or assumed gender) or appearance might affect this answer.
Give blood	Men who have had sex with men in the last three months are not permitted to give blood in the UK. Under 17s or over 66-year-olds cannot donate blood.
Adopt a child	Lesbian and gay couples have been able to do this since 2002 in the UK. You need to be over 18.
Expect to receive helpful sex education at school	Answer may depend on the attitude of the school and staff. Research suggests that many LGBT+ young people feel excluded by their school RSE programmes and that disabled people's and women's experiences of pleasure are often left out of sex education.
Have access to affordable social meeting places	Discuss what meeting places are available in your community. Think about age, gender, race, sexuality and disability and possibilities for young parents.
Have sex legally at 16	The legal age of consent was changed to 16 for gay men in 2003 – previously gay men had to be 18. For heterosexual people the legal age of consent is also 16.

Activity	Notes
Expect to be fairly treated by the police and get justice for crime committed against them	The police and criminal justice system have been accused of being institutionally racist with Black young people being eight times more likely to be stopped and searched than White people and nine times more likely to end up in prison (Lammy Review, 2017).[17] Violence against women and girls makes up 1/5th of all convictions (huge increase on previous years) BUT only one in four domestic violence incidents are prosecuted and less than 6% of reported rapes end up in a conviction for the perpetrator (CPS VAWG Report, 2017).[18] 'One in five LGBT people have experienced a hate crime or incident because of their sexual orientation and/or gender identity in the last 12 months. Two in five trans people have experienced a hate crime or incident because of their gender identity in the last 12 months. Four in five anti-LGBT hate crimes and incidents go unreported, with younger LGBT people particularly reluctant to go to the police' (Stonewall *School Report*, 2017).[19]
Join the army	Gay men and lesbians can serve in armed forces and all armed forces are now Stonewall diversity champions. This means that they are officially committed to equality for people who identify as LGBT+.
Have your relationship supported by your religion	The answer will depend on the religious community you are part of and the kind of relationship you are in – discuss with participants.
Expect promotion at work	Answers will depend on the type of work and how equalities are championed and respected in a workplace. One in nine pregnant women experienced discrimination or were made redundant or dismissed from their job due to pregnancy.[20] LGBT+ – A quarter (26%) of lesbian, gay and bi workers are not at all open to colleagues about their sexual orientation.
Be represented positively in the media	Ask participants for their views. LGBT+ characters are more commonly represented in the media now, compared to two decades ago. A range of ethnic backgrounds, abilities, faiths are also shown in the media but there is still a bias towards White heterosexual people being shown. There are concerns about the objectification of women in the media and half of all films fail the Bechdel test (see p. 103).
Be represented positively on children's television	There is often an absence of LGBT+ identities portrayed in children's television.
Expect positive role models at school	Discuss reasons why there may be no LGBT+/female/Black and Minority Ethnic (BME)/disabled role models at schools.

Activity	Notes
Go on holiday to anywhere in the world you want to	While it is not illegal to be gay anywhere in the world there are a high number of countries in the world which ban gay sex including popular holiday destinations such as Malaysia, Maldives, Jamaica, Kenya, Seychelles, Dubai. Therefore, LGB people may be at risk of imprisonment, torture and even a death sentence in certain countries.
Feel able to be yourself while at school	Discuss participants' perceptions of equalities in their schools.
Expect to have a toilet that meets your needs	Disabled toilets are available in most schools, shopping centres, cinemas, but provision can be patchy in smaller buildings. Gender neutral toilet provision is variable.
Be able to vote	In the UK you can't vote if you are under 16 (Scotland) or under 18 (rest of the UK). Women have only had the right to vote for 100 years. Severe mental or physical impairments do not affect your right to vote.

Once you have read out the list, and the initial line of participants is now spread out across the space, check in which identities were able to take the most steps forward (White adult male usually). Use this to lead a discussion about power and privilege and the effect of gender, race, age and sexual orientation on people's experiences of school and community life. Use the following discussion questions and explain the concept of intersectionality to guide your discussion.

Intersectionality: the way in which different types of discrimination (=unfair treatment because of a person's sex, race, etc.) are linked to and affect each other.

Discussion questions:

- Thinking about the categories of age, gender, sexual orientation and race is there one factor that is more influential than others in this activity? Or is it the combination, or intersection, of factors that makes a difference?
- Are there any other categories not explored in this list that also confer privilege (e.g. height, body size, wealth, popularity, attractiveness, education level, job, who their network of friends and family are)?
- How does this activity compare to the way that discrimination works at your school/community?
- How easy is it for someone to see privilege in their own community? Why might those in privileged positions be less likely to see their privilege compared to those in less privileged positions?
- What do we need to do to challenge discrimination within our community?
- No space is ever entirely equal, including ours. What can we do so that everyone in the group feels safe and able to participate in the work we do together?

In your discussion explore the idea that some people have more power because they have more access to resources (money, education, etc.) and others because they live in a society that privileges their identity over others. Highlight that those who are members of privileged groups tend not to see their privilege because it just seems normal or natural. However, people in less privileged groups can often see the inequality or unfairness because they are faced with what they can't access and what doesn't work for them (e.g. disabled and trans people experiencing issues accessing appropriate toilets or changing facilities, Black children not seeing themselves reflected in cartoons, children's books or school curricula). The activity '(Re)imagining power' on p. 74 in Chapter 3: *Relationships* may serve as a useful follow on to this activity.

Riddle's scale of attitudes

This activity is based on an activity included in *Sexuality Education Matters* (2013), created by Debbie Ollis, Lyn Harrison and Claire Maharaj and used with permission. (See *Useful resources* at the end of this book.)

 This activity explores homophobia using an attitudes scale that ranges from repulsion through to celebration. This enables participants to unpick the difference between tolerating and accepting the LGBT+ community compared to admiring and celebrating it. What is challenging about this activity is that acceptance and tolerance are viewed as negative attitudes. For many participants this may be the first time they have considered that to tolerate someone from the LGBT+ community can be homophobic.

 20–25 minutes

 A set of scale of attitudes cards. You can create these by adapting the text below for your group and sticking it to the back of a large piece of card. On the front of the card write the name of the attitude in large writing. A4-size card is recommended.

 16+

This activity is based on a continuum of homophobic attitudes that was developed by Dorothy Riddle, a psychologist from the US.[21] She identified four homophobic attitudes and four more positive attitudes that she argued needed to replace the homophobic ones. These are detailed in the box that follows.

Riddles scale of attitudes

Repulsion: Here homosexuality is understood as a 'crime against nature'. People who identify as homosexual are seen as sick, crazy, immoral, sinful, wicked, etc. Therefore any measure which is designed to change them and make them more 'normal' - such as prison or hospitals - is justified.

Pity: People who adopt this attitude prefer heterosexuality and think that gay people should be supported to 'become straight' if possible and pitied for being 'born that way'.

Tolerance: Homosexuality is understood as a phase of adolescent development that most people 'grow out of'. Gay people are treated like children - behaviours are tolerated as they are seen as vulnerable and in need of extra protection and support. Gay people should not hold positions of authority because they are still immature and haven't 'grown up' yet.

Acceptance: This attitude implies that there is something to accept. It is characterised by such statements as 'what you do behind closed doors is fine, just don't flaunt it', which ignores the social and legal realities of being gay and experiencing homophobia. It also puts the person giving acceptance in a position of power to be the one to 'accept' or reject others. It ignores the pain and stress of having to hide, manage or conceal an aspect of your life and identity. This is where many of us find ourselves, even though we might like to think we are not homophobic.

Support: This position involves supporting gay people and working to safeguard their rights. People who have this attitude may still feel uncomfortable with homosexuality themselves, but they are aware that homophobia is unfair and unjust.

Admiration: This attitude acknowledges that being gay in our society takes strength. These people are able to look at their own attitudes and challenge their own homophobia.

Appreciation: These people value living in a diverse society and see gay people as an important part of that diversity. These people are able to challenge homophobic attitudes in others.

Celebration: These people celebrate gay people as an indispensable part of society. They are able to be advocates for gay people.

Ask participants to get into pairs and stand opposite each other about two metres apart. Inform them that the aim of this exercise is to examine issues related to homophobia. Place the scale of attitudes cards on the floor in the middle of the room (with the attitudes side up). A good way to do this is to read the scale out as you place it on the floor. Suggest to the large group that understanding attitudes works best if they are 'broken down'.

Inform the line on the right that for the purpose of this activity they are to imagine they are gay. Inform the line on the left that for the purpose of this activity they are to imagine they are straight. Ask participants to visualise the last/current school they are at.

Ask them to physically move and place themselves on the attitude that reflects how their school would position their sexuality. Briefly look at where the sexualities are positioned. Swap the line so that the gay people become straight and the straight people become gay. Observe any differences.

Note: If it feels difficult to do this activity about the current school you work at you can make the activity retrospective by saying 'when you were in years 7–9', etc.

Now ask the entire group to move to the attitude that reflects that of their last school to their sexuality if they were gay. In other words, the entire group is positioning their last school in relation to being gay. Ask for a volunteer who feels like sharing with the group why they have placed themselves in that spot.

Next turn each of the cards over and describe the meaning of each attitude. Discuss which attitudes are positive sexnd which are negative and why. As each attitude is described, ask the participants to give an example of how that particular attitude may be displayed in a school setting.

Finally, in small groups, get participants' teachers to discuss, develop and record strategies to support positive attitudes and combat negative attitudes to homophobia. This will work best if each group has one positive and one negative attitude to consider. Groups then report back. The large group can then brainstorm strategies for developing positive attitudes in a school context.

Same/different visualisation

This activity is adapted from an original visualisation provided by Dr Linda Kirkham. Shared with permission.

 This is a visualisation activity in which participants are asked to imagine they have a 'mainstream' or 'othered' identity and consider how they feel in each of these scenarios. 10–15 minutes

 Copy of visualisation for educator. 11+

The purpose of this exercise is to experience a sense of how it feels to have a mainstream identity, and non-mainstream identity in the world. We have focused on non/mainstream gender and sexual identities, however these can be substituted for whatever facets of identity are being studied, e.g. ability, ethnicity, religion, immigration status, etc.

This activity is powerful because it allows the participants to be themselves, and experience safety as themselves, which for non-mainstream people can be very powerful. Participants are also invited to imagine what it feels like to be non-mainstream, which can be a powerful experience for those whose privileged identities protect them from experiencing discrimination and/ or social isolation. In the discussion no-one has to say who they are, so everyone can discuss responses.

Explain to the group that you are going to guide them through a visualisation and ask them to follow the instructions that they hear. Encourage everyone taking part to get into a comfortable position and listen:

Same/Different visualisation (for educators)

Imagine you are you; with the gender and sexual identity that represents the you who you feel you are. This information is not for sharing. Close your eyes and feel a sense of yourself and your identity. Imagine that who you are is mainstream for the rest of the world; if you are looking for a partner, want to talk about your identity for any reason, it is safe to do so. If you apply for a job or to rent a flat you can be who you are without fearing discrimination. Life isn't perfect however your identity is absolutely ok for you, and for the wider world. Stay with the feeling of belonging and safety. What is this like?

Pause for a moment then tell the group:

We are going to repeat the visualisation, with some changes. You are still you, with the gender and sexuality that feels right for you. However, most of the rest of the world is different from you, and who you are is not mainstream. Finding a partner or talking about your identity is only safe in certain limited contexts. You have to pretend to be like the others, and not be true to who you are in order to be safe. If you apply for a job or to rent a flat you have to be careful to pass as mainstream in order to avoid discrimination. How does it feel to be you in this world? What is it like?

Pause for a moment and then say: 'When you are ready, bring yourself back to the room and ground yourself. Open your eyes and take a deep breath.'

Ask participants the following questions. Depending on your group ask participants to discuss in pairs, small groups or as a whole group if this feels safe.

- How did it feel to be part of the mainstream?
- How did it feel to be different?
- What parts in the visualisation were unexpected or really made you think?
- What are some of the ways that heterosexual privilege* plays out in our school/culture/community?
- What are some of the ways that we can challenge heterosexual privilege in our school/community?

* See definition of heteronormativity in 'Points to consider' on p. 138. This refers to a cultural logic in which heterosexuality is seen as the norm and that all other sexual identities are therefore stigmatised or unacknowledged. Heterosexual privilege gives advantages and rewards to heterosexual people usually without question or challenge. These same benefits are not granted to LGBT+ people.

Beyond the binary

 This is a research and present activity that tasks participants with researching non-binary gender identities and histories. This activity would work well in a cross-curricular programme intersecting with geography, history and science. 30 minutes + (can be an extended research project)

 Internet access, pens and paper, A3 paper, coloured pens. 12+

Here is a list of terms used to describe people who are gender non-binary/gender variant (e.g. those who cannot easily be categorised as male/female). Some are inherited genetic conditions, some of historical terms no longer in use and others are culturally specific terms used in particular communities. Working individually or in small groups ask participants to research one of these terms and present their findings to the rest of the group. You can do this as a quick two–three-minute presentation task or as an extended research project. Encourage groups to ask each other questions and compare and contrast terms and ideas. Be mindful that there may be participants in your group who will have lived experience of non-binary gender identity and possibly some of the syndromes included in this list. Remember to always work with participants to create a safe space before facilitating this and other activities and remind participants of the working agreement and right to pass.

- Two Spirit (term used in North American Indigenous cultures to describe gender variant/non-binary people).
- Khatoeys (a Thai term used to refer to people of a third gender and/or to transwomen).
- Māhū (means 'in the middle' and is used to refer to people of a third gender in Hawaiian and Tahitian cultures).
- Hijras (a term given to eunuchs, intersex people and transgender people in the Indian subcontinent).
- Sworn virgins/burrnesha (women who live as men in patriarchal northern Albanian society, in exchange for a vow of chastity).
- Bacha Posh (means 'dressed like a boy' in Dari (Persian) and refers to a cultural practice in which some families in parts of Afghanistan and Pakistan will pick a daughter to live and behave as a boy).
- Fa'afafine (a recognised 'third' gender in traditional Samoan society, fa'afafine are assigned male at birth, and explicitly embody both masculine and feminine gender traits).
- Guevedoces (officially called 5-alpha reductase deficiency, this is a rare genetic condition associated with a small community of people in the Dominican Republic who were assigned as female at birth but later developed a penis and testes at the onset of puberty).
- Inverts (a historical term used in the late 19th and early 20th century to refer to gay people who were believed to have an inborn reversal of gender traits).
- Turner's Syndrome (condition in which a female (generally XX chromosomes) is partly or completely missing an X chromosome).
- Klinefelter's Syndrome (people born with XXY chromosomes, usually classified at birth as male).
- Androgen Insensitivity Syndrome (a rare condition affecting people born genetically male (with XY chromosomes) but who are resistant to androgens, affecting the development of their genitalia).

What's behind the door?

 A creative activity that explores the concept of being in and out of the 'closet'. This is a private, reflective task in which participants explore which parts of themselves and their identities they choose to keep hidden and/or share with others.

 20–30 minutes

 Arts and craft materials.

 11+

Introduce participants to the concept of a 'closet'. 'Coming out of the closet' refers to coming out as gay in a predominantly heterosexual and heteronormative culture (see definition of heteronormativity on p. 138). Being 'in the closet' refers to the choice to conceal your sexual identity from the outside world. People also use the term 'coming out' to refer to telling people that your gender identity is not the same as your birth sex.

In small groups, ask participants to discuss the following:

- How might it feel to be in the closet?
- Why might someone choose to stay in the closet?

- What kinds of relationships, identities and/or experiences do people in our community have to keep hidden from others?
- What would need to change in our community so that everyone felt able to live 'out of the closet'?

Take feedback from groups. Next ask participants to respond to this discussion through engaging in a creative exercise in which they think about what aspects of their own lives and identities they want to keep in and out of 'the closet'. To do this, give each participant two pieces of card. On the first piece of card ask participants to use magazines, pens and other creative materials to create an image or representation of who they are and how they feel inside themselves. They may want to represent their 'true self' or the person that they would really like to show to the world (but maybe don't always feel able to).

Take the second piece of card and cut out a door that can be opened or closed. This piece of card should be lain over the first piece of card and attached at both sides. Points to consider include:

- What gets hidden behind the door and what can be seen when you open the door.
- How many doors. They can have more than one door if they want to and can choose the size, shape and position of the door to reflect what they want to be seen by the outside world.
- Who you would let open the door (e.g. friends vs. acquaintance, online vs. offline friends, family, teachers and others) and how wide they could open it. They may also want to think about whether there is anyone who they would invite in to see everything that is hidden behind the wall.

Participants do not have to share their cards with others but you may want to discuss as a group how it can feel to keep a part of yourself private from people you care about and how it can feel to reveal things about yourself. Discussion points may include: feeling vulnerable/exposed, feelings of trust/intimacy, feeling trapped/isolated, feeling guilty/ashamed. Remember participants' right to opt out and not contribute to the discussion here – this is part of the key learning from this task – that we all have aspects of our lives and selves that we choose not to share with others. This is an important part of maintaining our privacy and keeping ourselves safe as we meet new people and build relationships both online and offline. Revealing parts of ourselves and sharing things about our lives with people we trust is one way of building intimacy in our relationships and can feel really positive. We can also feel exposed and vulnerable when someone we thought we trusted exposes our secrets. Some people and groups also experience violence, discrimination, exclusion and hate for revealing things about ourselves. You may want to explore with the group how best to support someone who wants to 'come out' about an aspect of their identity to ensure that this is a positive and affirmative experience.

Who are we? Spoken word poetry

In this activity the group creates a spoken word poem together exploring themes of identity, belong, visibility and invisibility. This works well as a way of extending and consolidating learning about gender and sexual identity and opening up the conversation to include other aspects of identity that are important to the participants in your group.

    One hour

    Pen and paper

    11+

Explain the task to the group which is to create spoken word poetry initially in groups and later by ourselves.

Introduce the group to the themes which can be: Who are we…; Where are we from…; This is us. Choose a theme to focus on. Ask each person to write one line, or a collection of words about this theme. Encourage the group to think about different aspects of identity that you have covered in your group discussions such as race, culture, faith, sex, gender, sexuality, age, dis/ability, mental and physical health. You may also want to explore themes of visibility and invisibility if you and your participants feel this is a safe space to do so.

Ask participants to work in small groups. In each group participants should take it in turns to read out their line. One group member can act as a scribe and write down the lines, using them as the basis of writing a poem. It may be helpful to give participants a poem template to use, or they may prefer to free write. Encourage participants to play around with the words until they have created a poem that they are all happy with. Next encourage groups to practise performing the poem. How best does it work? With one person performing? With each person performing a line each? With the whole group speaking together?

If groups feel comfortable, ask them to each perform their poem. To extend the activity you can ask participants to write their own poems on one of the themes. These can be finished at home and shared at a subsequent session or displayed anonymously if participants prefer. Alternatively the poems created by each group can be used to create one meta-poem.

Extension: Who am I? – Creative response

As an extension or alternative task, participants can do an individual creative response to the question: Who am I? Using modelling clay, art materials, photography, collaging or any other medium they wish to use to answer the question. Finish with an exhibition of all their work. This can serve as a celebratory close activity at the end of a group working together.

Equity vs. equality

 An interactive activity that uses craft, play and images to explore the difference between equity and equality. One hour

 Range of wooden spoons of different lengths/heights, wool, pens and paper. A cardboard box/box file, a box of toy wooden blocks or duplo. Series of equity vs. equality images (found online – see p. 142). 11+

Divide the class into small groups and give each group a wooden spoon to make into a character. It is important that the spoons are different lengths/heights or the activity won't work. Participants can create an identity and persona for their 'spoon' by adding a face, hair (wool), hats (paper) and clothes (fabrics). Explain that this is a competition and you will award a prize to the best designed character.

At the front of the room you will need to set up a 'wall'. You can create this using a cardboard box or box file and placing it on a table. Decorate your box with brick effect wrapping paper or your own brick design. Each of the wooden character spoons will need to stand behind the wall at the same time. This means that for larger groups you will need to have two boxes next to each other so that your 'wall' is at least 60cm long.

When participants have finished creating their wooden spoon characters, ask one person from each group to bring their spoon characters to the front and stand them behind the wall. Ask the rest of the group to sit in front of the box, like an audience watching a puppet show. As the educator and judge of the spoon making competition, sit with the audience.

The rule is that each spoon must be touching the table. You will find that due to the different lengths of the spoons, some will be able to be seen by the audience over the top of the box and some won't.

State that you are now going to judge the characters, but don't reference the fact that you can't see some of the spoons because they are behind the wall. Choose a winner and award a prize to that group.

You will find that participants will be puzzled or annoyed by this part of the activity and inform you that the competition is pointless or unfair as some of the spoons can't be seen over the wall. Initially play devil's advocate by saying that it's not your fault that some spoons are smaller than others and can't be seen, these are the rules of the game and this is just how it is. Listen to participants' protests and note that yes, the competition was unfair and unjust.

Next ask the group what you could do to make the show fairer and to give each group's spoon an equal chance at participating and winning. The one thing you cannot do at this stage is remove the wall or change its height. Get out your box of duplo/wooden toy blocks and give each group one block for this spoon to stand on. Explain that you are treating everyone equally by giving each team/spoon the same boost.

Again the group will protest that this is unfair as some of the spoons will still not be seen completely over the wall. Reflect that the addition of the block has not evened out the inequality, although it has enabled some additional spoons to be seen. Ask the group for a solution that would even out the inequality. The obvious solution will be to give some groups more duplo/wooden blocks than others. Do this and allow each group to create a structure for their spoon that enables them to be seen over the wall.

Judge the activity again and award the winning group a prize.

To reflect on this activity, show the group the 'Injustice, Equality, Equity and Liberation' image (Figure 4.4). The first image shows three children of different heights standing behind a fence. All of the children are too small to see over the fence and see what's beyond it. The ground is uneven so some of the children are further away from the top of the fence than others. In the second image the children are all standing on the same sized block. This has helped two of the children see over the fence, but not the third.

Explain that in this picture there is an equal distribution of resources (everyone has the same sized block) but that does not mean that the situation is fair or that the outcome is equal. In the third image the children are all standing on different sized objects and can all see over the fence.

In this picture there is an unequal distribution of resources (some of the people have managed to get more help/blocks than others) but the outcome is fair. Everyone can see over the fence. In the fourth image the children have brought down the fence and are liberated from the barriers that stop them from accessing opportunities.

FIGURE 4.4 Injustice, Equality, Equity, Liberation

Illustration by: Chrissy Baxter

Ask the group to reflect on the metaphors within this activity.

- What kinds of real situations are represented by this image and in the spoon activity? What are some of the things in life that not all people have an equal chance at? (e.g. educational achievement, good health, financial security)
- Why doesn't giving everyone an equal amount of help lead to a fair society? (e.g. with reference to educational achievement – if everyone is given the exact same education they won't all do well because some people need more support than others for a range of reasons including class, income and racial inequality and disability/health needs)
- What does the wall/fence represent? What are some of the barriers that people face? (e.g. racism, sexism etc./negative assumptions and stereotypes; lack of money/access to resources such as technology, libraries, good quality healthcare)
- What do the blocks represent? What are some of the ways in which we can ensure that all people have an equal chance? (e.g. giving extra help in education to some children, extra health resources for some groups, positive discrimination in employment, wealth redistribution through tax and benefits)

Finally, explore with participants what is wrong with the image as a way of explaining equality and equity. This is a question that some participants may find tricky! Explain that the image suggests that the 'problem' is the person/spoon for not being tall enough. This suggests that the problem is inherent to the people themselves, which could be seen as victim blaming. Someone growing up in poverty may be less likely to do well in education, but this is not because they are inherently less clever or capable but because of the environment around them.

To explore this further and rethink some of the key concepts you have been discussing ask participants to create new images or models using the wall, blocks and spoons. Use the following resources to inspire you:

- The *injustice, equality and equity* image in the *AGENDA* resource. Images created by Adam Croaton and Emma Renold.[22]
- 'Why we need to step into #the4thbox' created by *The Centre for Story Based Strategy*.[23] Contains an accessible critique of the 'equity vs. equality' image and an example of a 'liberation' image and other free downloadable tools.

(Re)imagining power in action

 A small group activity in which participants reflect on how power can limit and enable positive social change and activist projects. This activity follows on well from the '(Re) imagining power' activity on p. 74.

 30–40 minutes

 Scenarios (see later).

 14+

Start by doing the activity '(Re)imagining power' in Chapter 3: *Relationships*, p. 74, which introduces participants to four different types of power: power over, power to, power with and power within. Follow this with the following activity which helps participants to use these concepts to think about social activism projects within their communities.

Divide participants into small groups and give each group one of the following scenarios or ask them to come up with their own.

Ask participants the following questions:

- Who has power in this scenario? How is this power being used?
- What are some of the ways in which power is being used in negative ways?
- What are some of the ways in which power is being used in positive ways?
- Imagine you are in this situation. What are you thinking? What are you feeling?
- What are some of the ways that you can mobilise your power to bring about positive change?
- What barriers might you face? How might these be tackled? (Think about power to, power with and power within.)

Share general responses as a group. Collect together all the strategies that participants suggest using to harness power with and within and making a positive change. Finally, consider:

- What are the risks of harnessing our 'power within' to bring about change in our schools/ families/communities?
- How can we look after ourselves and others when working to bring about positive change?

These scenarios may trigger participants to discuss similar issues that are currently happening in their schools or communities. Use some of the ideas in this chapter and in *AGENDA: A young people's guide to making positive relationships matter* (see *Useful resources* at the end of this book) to inspire and support young people to engage in activism and bring about positive change in their communities.

(Re)imagining power in action scenarios

--✂

You and some friends have been talking about the sexual harassment girls experience at your school every day. When you try and stand up to the boys who do this they get abusive. You decide to start a feminist society to try and do something about this.

--✂

A young person in your school has recently come out as trans and is unsure which toilet they should be using. The school has said it isn't possible to create a gender neutral toilet because the building is so old and there have always been boys and girls toilets and changing rooms. You decide to start a campaign for gender neutral toilet and changing room options.

--✂

You are fed up of people not using the correct pronouns towards you at your youth club. Even when you correct them they keep calling you the wrong pronoun. You make a new pronoun badge which you decide to wear to your local youth group.

--✂

You a hear a story about someone in your community who has been unable to get an abortion when they requested one from their GP. You decide to write a letter about abortion rights to your local newspaper. The letter is published.

--✂

You start an online petition to allow an LGBT+ lunch time club to start at your school after the school said you couldn't have one. It goes viral.

--✂

You start an anonymous activist blog documenting the incidents of hate speech such as racism, disablism, homophobia, biphobia, transphobia you hear in your local community. For everything negative you hear and record you write suggested possible responses for tackling that episode of hate including suggestions for bystanders to intervene. For every post you encourage members of your local community to do a counterbalancing gesture of justice, kindness and respect.

The gender and power plot

A creative activity in which participants write a plot synopsis for a new novel that reimagines gender and power relations. Inspired by feminist sci fi novels such as *The Handmaid's Tale* and *The Left Hand of Darkness* this activity encourages participants to imagine worlds in which the usual gender rules no longer apply.

One hour. Could be extended into a longer creative writing project.

Paper and pens. Copies of the following may be helpful but are not essential: Ursula Le Guin, *The Left Hand of Darkness* (1969); Margaret Atwood, *The Handmaid's Tale* (1985) (or episodes of the box set series); Naomi Alderman, *The Power* (2016).

14+

Working individually or in groups, the task is to write a plot for a new novel that disrupts or challenges how we think about gender/sex and power. Ideas include:

A. Reimagine gender and power relations on a new planet. For inspiration participants may want to read or look up the plot synopsis of Ursula Le Guin's *The Left Hand of Darkness*.
B. Reimagine a dramatic shift in politics and governance gender and power. For inspiration participants may want to read or look up the plot synopsis of Margaret Atwood's *The Handmaid's Tale*. The novel has also been recently dramatised as a critically acclaimed television series.
C. Imagine a change in the human body that would cause a dramatic shift in gender and power relations. For inspiration participants may want to read or look up the plot synopsis of Naomi Alderman's *The Power*.

Encourage participants to focus on mapping out the society and cultures that their novel will depict. Points to consider include:

- *Relationships and families:* How do people group together? What are their relationships? What are customs and traditions relating to growing up and forming partnerships? Are there families? What do families look like? How do people negotiate sex? Is there rape and sexual violence?
- *Society and governance:* Who has power to make decisions in society? Who makes laws (if there are any)? Who decides whether to go to war? Who controls the economy?
- *Religion:* Are there any religions? Can people choose what religion they want to worship? How powerful are religious institutions? What do they tell us about gender?
- *Work and leisure:* Do people work? Can everyone work? What kinds of leisure activities are enjoyed?
- *Fashion and clothing:* What do people wear? What is considered cool/fashionable/ attractive? Is clothing gendered?
- *Health and body:* What do bodies look like? What body parts are desirable? What health issues are there? Are they different for different types of bodies?
- *Education:* Who gets to learn? What do they learn? Who decides what knowledge is valuable and what isn't?
- *Media and advertising:* Who is represented in media? Who is missing? What products are available? Is censorship in the media?

Notes

1   www.ted.com/talks/tony_porter_a_call_to_men?language=en
2   www.youtube.com/watch?v=NybJ-xHUpdc&vl=en
3   www.genderremixer.com/html5/#
4   www.fawcettsociety.org.uk/equality-its-about-time-timeline-of-womens-rights-1866–2016
5   https://www.stonewall.org.uk/about-us/key-dates-lesbian-gay-bi-and-trans-equality
6   http://sexualrightsdatabase.org/map
7   www.gov.uk/government/publications/sexual-violence-and-sexual-harassment-between-children-in-schools-and-colleges
8   www.11thprincipleconsent.org/consent-propaganda/rape-culture-pyramid/
9   www.gov.uk/government/publications/sexual-violence-and-sexual-harassment-between-children-in-schools-and-colleges
10   www.stonewall.org.uk/school-report-2017
11   www.stonewall.org.uk/school-report-2017
12   www.childrenscommissioner.gov.uk/wp-content/uploads/2014/02/Sex_without_consent_I_suppose_that_is_rape.pdf
13   https://childhub.org/en/system/tdf/library/attachments/1705_boys-and-girls-report_wdf100416_original.pdf?file=1&type=node&id=6238
14   http://prev.wellcomecollection.org/whats/sounds-sexology
15   https://criticallyqueer.wordpress.com/
16   https://ilga.org/state-sponsored-homophobia-report
17   https://assets.publishing.service.gov.uk/government/uploads/system/uploads/attachment_data/file/643001/lammy-review-final-report.pdf
18   www.cps.gov.uk/sites/default/files/documents/publications/cps-vawg-report-2018.pdf
19   www.stonewall.org.uk/school-report-2017
20   www.equalityhumanrights.com/en/managing-pregnancy-and-maternity-workplace/pregnancy-and-maternity-discrimination-research-findings
21   Riddle, D, *The Riddle scale. Alone no more: Developing a school support system for gay, lesbian and bisexual youth*. State Department: St Paul, Minnesota
22   http://agendaonline.co.uk/what-if-this-is-me/
23   www.storybasedstrategy.org/the4thbox

CHAPTER 5
Bodies

This chapter will give you the ideas that you need to facilitate sessions about the human body. This is an area which can often get missed out of RSE programmes. Too often we teach young people about contraception first before stopping to explore how their bodies work. Or we focus on the function of the reproductive organs without ever talking about how the body feels and changes during arousal. Sometimes we talk about body image, but not always in a way that connects low confidence and self-esteem with the wider gender inequalities and social pressures that shape how we feel about our bodies and ourselves.

This chapter aims to address these gaps by providing activities that support young people to understand how their bodies work and change, what they can do, how they feel and how all of this is shaped by social norms and other influences around us. We also look at how to identify feelings, personal preferences and body boundaries, how to communicate about consent and how to relax our bodies and take care of our ourselves and those around us. Our aim is to think critically about the body whilst also celebrating what the body can do. Our approach is to have fun, get messy, get moving, whilst also learning the vital knowledge that young people need in order to talk about, understand and enjoy their bodies.

Chapter summary

Section 1: Our bodies, ourselves. This section explores the social norms and politics that shape how we feel about our bodies and ourselves and how we can take care of ourselves and each other within this context. This section includes activities on body image, self care and relaxation, consent and body boundaries.

Section 2: Sexual bodies. Activities for developing a vocabulary for talking about the sexual body and thinking critically about the myths, norms and assumptions that shape how we talk and think about our bodies. Includes activities on the vulva, penis, clitoris and hymen/vaginal corona. This section also includes activities to help develop an understanding of the whole body as a potential site of pleasure and sensuality. Includes activities on pleasure, consent, safe touch and the senses.

Section 3: Reproductive bodies. Fun and creative ideas for learning about reproduction, puberty, periods and period stigma, body fluids, menstrual, hygiene and other 'beauty' products.

Section 4: Moving-feeling bodies. A series of activities to help young people notice and share their emotions with others and connect their emotions with wider politics and social issues. Many young people find it hard to name and express the feelings that surface as they have to manage gendered social pressure to look or act in a certain way. These activities use craft, dance and movement to support them to try and explore this.

Points to consider

- Too often RSE programmes focus on the reproductive function of the body, which leads to a heteronormative view of sex and a focus on the genitals. You can avoid this by making sure that you start with an activity that looks at the whole body (such as 'Pleasurable bodies' on p. 156) before moving on to look at the genitals, fertility and reproduction (if these are areas you want to cover). Also make sure you include activities on the social, emotional and sensual aspects of the body. There are lots of examples in this chapter to help you do this.
- If you have not already looked at the difference between gender identity, gender expression, biological sex and sexual orientation with young people, we suggest you cover this first using activities from Chapter 4: *Gender and sexual equality.* This will help develop an inclusive vocabulary for talking about sex, gender and the body.
- It is important not to make assumptions about what body parts someone has based on their appearance or gender identity. For example, not everyone who identifies as a 'woman' will have a vulva and not everyone who identifies as a 'man' will have a penis. To be inclusive of trans and non-binary gender people try to just name the body part rather than make assumptions about the person's gender identity. For example, you can just say 'penis' and 'vulva', rather than 'male penis', 'his penis' or 'women's vulvas'.
- Being inclusive doesn't mean that you can't talk about the different physical and biological processes and attributes that societies assign as male, female and intersex. This is important for understanding human anatomy and reproduction and for thinking about how different sexed bodies are subject to violence and oppression in unequal and inequitable ways. Female Genital Mutilation is one example of this (see pp. 168–70). When doing this be clear that you are talking about biological attributes to which societies assign a 'sex' and not making assumptions about the gender identities of those bodies.
- We have found that this can be challenging to do, particularly since at the time of writing (2018–19) the language for talking about sex, gender and bodies is changing rapidly and is contested, with different communities using different language and terms. Our aim is to write and educate in ways that are inclusive and equitable of all young people and that challenge the inequalities that young people face. We hope that after publication of this book the language for talking about this key area of RSE evolves to offer young people and educators more options for talking about the gendered, sexed and sexual body. If you feel unsure about this area of work seek advice from organisations that offer specialist support around gender and sexuality (e.g. The Proud Trust) or around particular issues such as FGM (e.g. Forward).

- Learning about the genitals, what they can look like and how they work is one important element of RSE and we include a number of activities to help you do this. Think carefully about how you choose to display images of genitals in your classroom or work space as some young people may find it challenging to see images of genitals suddenly projected on a large screen. For some young people this may be culturally taboo and quite shocking – for others it will be uneventful! If you are unsure choose an activity where young people draw their own images and do their own research (e.g. 'My genitals: getting to know you' on p. 159) and reflect on how this works with your group.

Section 1: Our bodies, ourselves

Bodies in the media

This activity is adapted from the *Consent Teaching Pack* written by Justin Hancock. Available online at www.bishtraining.com for purchase. Shared with permission.

 A group work activity that explores how bodies are represented in the media. Through discussion participants are invited to think critically about the impact that media representation can have on how we feel about our own bodies.

 20 minutes

 A1 paper, pens.

 14+

In small groups ask participants to draw or write on a large sheet of paper what kinds of bodies they might expect to see in the following places. This can be done through drawing, describing, brainstorming keywords, or printing, cutting and pasting images from websites, magazines and social media.

- A Hollywood sex scene.
- A how to have sex manual.
- A mainstream porn clip.
- 'Position of the month' sex advice.
- A sex scene in a TV programme.
- A fitness magazine.
- A clothing catalogue.
- A woman's magazine aimed at over 40s.
- A 'lads mag'.

Ask groups to present their findings to the whole group and describe the bodies they discussed. Prompt participants to think about age, ability, race, sexuality, gender, etc. and reflect on the relationship between the characters in the drawings (e.g. mixed age groups, mix of races, etc.).

Lead a discussion with the whole group, using these questions as a guide:

- Who do we expect to see in each of the situations? (*answers might reflect the fact media can often reflect thin, muscled, White, heterosexual, able bodies*)
- Who do we not see? (*e.g. we don't often see disabled bodies, Black and ethnic minority bodies, fat, curvy, skinny bodies, scared bodies, gay relationships, trans bodies, etc.*)
- What message does that send out to the kinds of people not seen? (*e.g. that only able bodied, White, straight people are allowed to have their bodies celebrated and have sex*)
- How does this make us feel? (*e.g. self conscious, angry, excluded, awkward, not good enough, wanting to make changes to bodies to get the perfect ideal*)
- What kind of sex is depicted? What message does this send to the kinds of people featured in the drawings? (*e.g. sex is only about penis in vagina, men are supposed to want it, it is not necessarily pleasurable for women, you have to have sex in relationships, etc.*)

To extend the activity explore what needs to change to improve the representation of diversity in the media. Give each participant one red and one green paper plate. Ask them to write one thing they want to STOP on the red plate and one thing they want to START on the green plate. Work out where to hang or display your plates for maximum impact. They can be pegged on a line or photographed and shared on social media. See Chapter 1: *Creating safer spaces* for further details of this activity (see p. 38) which is taken from *AGENDA: A young people's guide to making positive relationships matter* (see *Useful resources* at the end of this book).

Body image

Adapted from N. Hutchinson and C. Calland (2011) *Body Image in the Primary School*. Routledge. A great practical resource to teach body confidence and emotional resilience for 6–13-year-olds. Shared with permission.

 A discussion-based activity that introduces participants to the concept of body image and has a surprise reveal! 20 minutes

 Two envelopes with a picture of the same person in it – one named A and one named B. Each envelope also contains a copy of the instructions and some questions. 11+

Write the word 'body image' on the board and ask participants to consider in pairs what it might mean.

Explain that body image is what we believe and feel about how we look. It is not *how* we look but what we believe and feel about our appearance that creates our body image.

Split the group in half. Where possible ask the two groups to work in separate spaces where they can't see and hear each other working. Give one group the envelope with Person A in it. Tell the group that this person has a very good body image and ask them to consider what might have helped this person feel positive about how they look. The envelope also contains some questions to help with the answer.

Show the other group Person B and tell them that Person B has a very bad body image and ask them to consider why this person might feel so bad about their looks.

Ensure that neither group sees the picture the other group is working with at this stage.

Collect in the pictures from both groups. Take feedback from each group about what has created good body image in group A and what has created bad body image in group B.

Reveal the pictures of Person A and Person B, which are actually the same person. Explore the idea that it doesn't matter what you actually look like, but how you feel about yourself and how you are treated by others.

Introduce the idea that we are not all treated equally. Some types of bodies are discriminated against far more than others. Prompt the group to consider differences in how bodies are treated across gender, race, size, age and disability.

Body image scenarios

Person A

This person has a very good body image. Consider what might have helped this person feel positive about how they look. You could consider the following questions to help you:

- What messages might they have heard in their life?
- What experiences might they have had?
- What messages do they tell themselves?
- How might their idea about their looks affect other things that they think about themselves?

Person B

Person B has a very bad body image. Consider why this person might feel so bad about their looks. You could consider the following questions to help you:

- What messages might they have heard in their life?
- What experiences might they have had?
- What messages do they tell themselves?
- How might their idea about their looks affect other things that they think about themselves?

Finally ask the group to imagine they know a Person B (taking care not to mention names of anyone known to the group) and discuss in pairs what they could do to help Person B feel good about themselves and their body. Share the ideas as a group. You can also explore ways of addressing the unequal treatment and representation of different bodies. One way of doing this is to use the 'Stop-start plates' activity described Chapter 2 (see p. 38).

Body traffic lights

 A group activity in which participants identify the unwritten rules about body boundaries in their school, group or youth club. 20 minutes

 Large roll of paper, or sheets of paper taped together; red, green and amber stickers. 11+

Task participants with creating two large body outlines on a sheet or roll of paper. The best way to do this is for some of the group to draw around one of the participants, negotiating body boundaries as they do this! Label one body as the front of a body, one as the back.

Participants' task is to place red, green and amber stickers on the body as follows.

- Green = at our school/youth club it is ok to touch someone here without asking.
- Amber = at our school/youth club it is ok to touch someone here if you ask and gain consent.
- Red = at our school/youth club it is never ok to touch someone here.

To do this, participants will need to discuss and agree with each other what they think the unwritten rules are at their school, group or youth club.

Once they have finished consider the following questions:

- Is it ever ok to touch someone without asking? Does it depend on who is doing the touching?
- If these are the unwritten rules, what is the reality? Do people respect these body boundaries? Would you move any of the stickers to reflect the reality of your own and others' experiences?
- How should we respond when someone touches a red area? How often does this happen in our school/local area? What parts of the body/types of bodies are targeted? What impact does this have*?
- What are some of the ways that we can communicate with others about our own *and* their body boundaries? (Remember it's all of our responsibility to seek consent – not just to give it when it's requested.)

*It may be useful to get hold of the data from your local area school survey or national surveys which collect data on sexual harassment in schools. For example, in the Girls Attitudes Survey conducted in 2017 by *Girl Guiding*, 19% of girls aged 13–21 reported unwanted touching at school in the past year, 39% of girls aged 11–21 reported having their bra strap pulled by boys in school and 27% reported having their skirts pulled up by boys in school (Girlguiding, 2017).[1] This data can be useful for highlighting that respect for body boundaries is gendered, with girls and women experiencing more sexual harassment and violence.

My body boundaries: too close for comfort.

This activity has been developed and adapted from the *PSHE Association Guidance on Teaching of Consent* published in 2015, co-authored by Alice Hoyle, Nick Boddington, Jenny Barksfield, Joe Hayman and Sarah Lyles. Shared with permission.

 An interactive activity in which participants use their bodies to think about body boundaries and practise communicating about consent. 10–15 minutes

 None. 13+

Line the group up in two lines facing each other about three metres apart and identify them as row A and row B. Ask row A to slowly take small steps forward, asking their partner each time 'can I take another step?'. The facing person in row B should say 'stop' once they feel uncomfortable with the proximity of the person opposite them. Person A must stop when requested and remain in that position.

Continue until everyone on the opposite line has said 'stop'. It is likely that participants will have asked each other to stop at different points. Keep the participants in their lines for a discussion of the following questions:

- Who has responsibility for making things stop? (*The person seeking consent (Person A) is responsible for ensuring that they have Person B's consent. This is an ethical issue but is also reflected in law.*)
- Why do you think people in row B said stop at different distances (*Answers might include: people have different body boundaries/levels of comfort with personal space; depends on the relationship between Person A and Person B; depends on how clear the communication was between Person A and Person B*).
- For row Bs: How did it feel to say 'stop'? How easy or difficult was it? How did it feel to have that listened to and respected?
- For row Bs: How would it have felt if the person opposite you had kept taking a step forward even when you asked them to stop?
- For row As: How did it feel to hear stop? How did it feel seeing that other people were able to go further/less far than you?

To extend the activity go down each line quickly and ask participants to show how someone might have communicated non-verbally (with body language/facial expressions) that they wanted the other person to stop walking towards them. You can repeat the activity using non-verbal signals and reflect on which row As and row Bs found easier and more comfortable – verbal or non-verbal.

Emphasise that consent is not just about saying yes or no and that it is always the responsibility of the seeker of consent to be sure of whether consent is being freely given or not given. This shouldn't be considered as a one-off since people can change their minds or consent to one activity but not another. This makes continued checking each step of the way very important.

Body scan

With thanks to Georgie Bassford from *Bright Blue Yoga* for sharing this self compassion body scan for us to use.

 Developed by a yoga teacher, this activity provides the opportunity for participants to pay attention to their bodies and their breathing. Through this activity young people can learn techniques that can be repeated in their everyday lives to help with relaxation, bodily awareness and self care.

 20 minutes

 Copy of the script for educator.

 11+

If possible, ask a local yoga teacher to come in and facilitate a session with your group as a way of teaching participants techniques for relaxation and bodily awareness. Where this is not possible guide participants through this simple body scan.

Ask participants to sit or lie down somewhere comfortable. Read out the following script slowly, making sure you take your time.

Once the body scan has finished ask participants to sit in a circle and reflect on the activity:

- How do you feel after taking part in that activity?
- What did you enjoy?
- Was there any part of your body you paid attention to in particular whilst doing this? Did any part of your body feel particularly stiff, sore or relaxed?
- When doing the activity how did you feel about your body in that moment compared to how you feel about your body in other situations and environments?
- What might be the benefits to doing this activity every day/regularly?

Where possible see if participants are interested in trying to do this activity regularly to see if it affects how they feel about their bodies. Where there is interest ask participants to agree how often they will try the activity and for how long and whether this will be individually or as a group. Agree to discuss again as a group after the agreed time period to see if participants have observed any differences in how relaxed they feel/any changes in bodily tension, etc.

Body scan: script for educators

Ensure your body is comfortable and that you are able to breathe comfortably with no restrictions.

Close your eyes. During this activity there is no need to move your body unless you become uncomfortable. Ideally try to remain still.

Start by taking your attention to your whole body. Your body is now resting. Say to yourself: 'There's nothing for me to do, I can be still and rest'. Take a few slow, deep breaths through the nose.

Draw your awareness to your feet – toes, heels, the whole foot, left and right side. Really focus on the sensations and feeling in your feet, totally aware of any sensations as they arise inside the feet or on the surface of the feet. Notice any tenderness, pain, discomfort, warmth – any sensation at all. Try to stay present and rather than think, just notice and be aware. You have nothing else to do and nowhere else to be. Continue to breathe and send your breath into your feet – imagine your breath flowing through your body and into your feet.

Next draw your awareness to your legs. Notice any sensations as they arise in the backs of your legs or your knees, thighs. Breathe in and imagine your breath travelling through your body to your legs.

Now focus on your back. Can you feel any tightness, pain or discomfort in your back? Notice and be aware of this. Send your breath down and through your back.

Next focus on your belly and your chest. Feel your body fill with air as you breathe in and empty of air as you breathe out. Feel your chest and belly rise as you breathe in and fall as you breathe out, rise as you breathe in and fall as you breathe out.

Continue with arms, hands, neck, head.

Now notice the gentle movement of the whole body as you breathe. Notice how soft your body can be and how quiet and still the mind can be underneath the turmoil of thoughts and when the body is still.

Now drop your awareness into the space behind your chest. Imagine there is a ball of light where your heart is, with each breath the light gets brighter and spreads through your whole body – down your arms, back and legs, down to your toes, fingers, ears and right up through your scalp.

Stay with this for a few breaths, as long as you like, filling your whole body with light and calm. You are at one with your body, you are at peace with your body.

When you are ready, drop your awareness down to the belly and take a few breaths noticing the rise and fall of the belly and chest as you breathe. Become aware of where you are, visualise yourself in the room and deepen your breath until you feel ready to stretch a little and start to move your body. Open your eyes.

Section 2: Sexual bodies

Pleasurable bodies

 A simple activity that enables participants to start thinking about the whole body as a potential site of pleasure. The activity helps to provoke discussions about consent and communication, bodily anatomy and good touch.

 20 minutes

 Large sheets or rolls of paper and different coloured pens.

 13+

In small groups ask participants to draw the outline of a body. It works best to draw round one person in the group and create a lifesize body.

Ask participants to start at the top of the paper and work their way down to the toes thinking about *where* on the body it feels good to be touched and *how* it feels to be touched in that way. For example, some people enjoy having their head stroked and this can feel relaxing. Participants should write or draw the type of touch and feeling on their body map. Emphasise that the activity is about what can feel good for people in general and not about participants' personal preferences.

Next ask participants to think about what it feels good to *do* with their bodies. Again, annotate or draw to show the movement/action and to describe what the good feeling is.

You will find that some participants mention the genitals and sexual activity whereas others don't. A strength of this activity is that it allows participants to set their own pace and agenda and for you to find out what is important to them.

Ask participants to feedback some examples and lead a discussion that covers the following key points:

- Where does it feel good to be touched on the body? Do we all enjoy the same sensations? (*Everyone has different preferences when it comes to touch and pleasure – some people love having their feet massaged and find this relaxing, others find it tickly, others hate it and some might find it arousing.*)
- Which parts of the body do *not* feel good when they are moved, used or touched? (*The whole body is a potential site of pleasure – it can feel good to be touched by others and by ourselves and it can feel good to move and use our bodies in different ways. Equally any part of the body can feel uncomfortable or painful – particularly if you are using muscles you don't normally use, moving in an unsafe way or being touched with force, violence or without consent.*)
- How do we know which parts of our body we enjoy moving, using and being touched? (*We have to experiment in ways that feel safe and comfortable. For example, trying yoga and stretching different parts of our body, trying out different types of dance, sports and exercises; touching our own bodies and seeing how it feels, having massages from friends, family or partners.*)
- We all like being touched in different places and in different ways – how do you know what kind of touch someone else likes? (*You need to ask them and talk about their preferences, be careful not to make assumptions, always ask before you touch someone, ask for feedback after you have given someone a massage.*)
- If someone in the street came up to you and started giving you a head massage how might you feel? Would it be different if it was a parent, friend or partner? (*Touch can feel good/bad depending on the context; factors such as privacy, intimacy and consent shape how enjoyable touch can feel.*)

Emphasise that pleasure is a whole body experience that can involve all our senses whether we are experiencing pleasure through exercise, food, intimacy, playing music or having sex. Understanding what feels good in your own body can help you to maximise the enjoyable experiences you have and communicate to others what you do and do not enjoy.

To extend the activity deliver the 'Meet and greet' activity in Chapter 6: *Sex* (see p. 250) which enables participants to practise communicating about their preferences for good and safe touch and opens up conversations about consent.

Playdoh pleasure anatomies

 A creative activity using playdoh that challenges the preconception that sexual pleasure and enjoyment has to involve the genitals and increases awareness that sexual pleasure is a whole body experience. 10–15 minutes

 Playdoh. 14+

Ask participants to use playdoh to sculpt a body part that is involved in sexual pleasure. Don't suggest anything in particular. Once everyone has finished ask each participant to show what they've made and explain why they chose that particular body part. If skin, brain, eyes, nose, mouth, waist, tummy, toes, feet, fingers, ears, neck, nipples, vulva, penis or anus, etc. aren't made, ask the group why they think this might be. Here are some more discussion questions to help you explore the models:

- Why do you think there is such a focus on the genitals when it comes to thinking about sex, pleasure and desire? (*Answers could include: understandings of sex are often based around reproduction which leads to a focus on the penis and the vagina; there is a high concentration of nerve endings in the penis and the vagina which can make it enjoyable to have sex using these body parts.*)
- Often when we do this activity lots of people create a penis, why do you think this might be? Why is it strange to identify the penis as the *most* important part of the body when it comes to pleasure? (*Answers may include: it's strange to prioritise the penis when lots of people have sex without a penis! Even for people who do have a penis, they may not use it when having sex – e.g. oral sex on a vulva. There are many more nerve endings on a clitoris compared to a penis so why is this not what we first think of? Culturally the penis/phallus is given greater significance than other parts of the sexual body – think of examples from pornography and school graffiti!; male pleasure is prioritised in mainstream understandings of sex and strongly associated with the penis and there is more stigma and shame associated with female sexuality and pleasure and with associated body parts such as the vulva.*)
- Do you think young people in other countries would have created similar body parts as you have? (*Answers could include: perceptions of which body parts are 'sexy' vary across cultures, as well as between individuals.*)

Emphasise that sexual pleasure is a holistic, whole body experience as opposed to the understanding of sex that many of us have which is based around reproduction. This leads to a heteronormative understanding of sex as always involving penetrative sex between a man with a penis and a woman with a vulva.

What's in a name?

 A variation on a much loved RSE activity that explores the language that we use to talk about our sexual organs. It is a great starter activity to do with a new group as it lets out lots of the giggles associated with using 'rude' words, whilst also developing important conversations about sexual language, misogyny and taboos. 10–15 minutes

 Flipchart paper, pens. 13+

Divide the group into four groups and assign each group a part of the sexual anatomy: penis, vulva, bottom and breasts. You may need to explain what the vulva is as most young people are more familiar with the term vagina. Clarify the difference between the vulva and the vagina. If you are not confident explaining (or drawing) the difference, Planned parenthood have a one-minute animation on YouTube to help you do this: *Episode 1: Get to Know Your Vulva & Vagina Anatomy Planned Parenthood Video.*[2]

Ask each group to write down as many words as they can think of for this part of the body, writing one word per post-it note. Let participants know that rude or slang words *are* permitted.

Once the brainstorm is complete ask each group to divide their set of words as follows:

1. Words that could be offensive.
2. Words that are mainly used by and with children.
3. Words that someone would use with a sexual partner.
4. Words that you might expect a doctor or nurse to use.

Look at the sets of words as a whole group. Participants may want to add new words and adjust the groupings.

Lead a discussion using the following questions:

*   Are there more words for the penis compared to the vulva or vice versa? Why might this be? (*We often have more words for the penis and are more used to seeing images of penises on graffiti; in many cultures there is more shame and stigma associated with female sexuality and sexual bodies.*)
*   Which are the most offensive words when used as insults? What does that say about how we view male and female sexuality in society? (*Some of the most offensive words – e.g. cunt – are associated with female sexuality and the shame, stigma and violence directed towards women and their bodies.*)
*   What words are young boys given to name their genitals? (*e.g. willy, penis*) What about young girls? (*e.g. twinkle, flower, front bottom, minnie, vagina, vulva*) Why is there no consistent name for the vulva, as there is for the penis? (*more shame and stigma associated with female sexuality and girls and women's bodies; less confidence talking about the vulva*)
*   What word can adults use to talk about their own or a partner's vulva or penis that is strong, sexy and powerful?

To conclude, agree as a group what words you will use for the remainder of the RSE session/programme. It is important that everyone in the group, including the educator, feels comfortable with the words chosen.

Extension: Body sign language

To enrich your discussion research the British Sign Language (BSL) signs for key anatomical words. For example, the BSL sign for vulva is a diamond shape made by bringing the thumbs and forefingers together on both hands to create a beautifully visual sign that reflects the shape of the vulva. However, some people in the deaf community might find this sign offensive in some contexts as it can also signal 'cunt'. Whether this word is anatomical or offensive can be conveyed with the use of fingerspelling and facial expressions as well as micro expressions of the hands and arms, for example conveying the sign aggressively or gently. Use this to revisit the discussion questions on p. 158 and explore possibilities and challenges of communicating about the sexual body given the stigma, shame and violence that is so closely linked with the sexual body, in particular the bodies of women, trans and non-binary people.

My genitals: getting to know you

 An interactive, team work activity in which participants learn more about the genitals and how they change during arousal. Knowledge is tested through creating quizzes and testing opposing teams. The aim is to equip young people to better understand their own bodies, and those of current or future partners. 35 minutes

 Paper and pens, laptops or tablets to give groups online access to resources; a prize for the winning team. 13+

Ask participants to draw an image of a vulva and a penis and label as many parts of their drawings as possible. Ask participants to share their images and note what participants do and do not know about the genitals.

Divide the group in half and allocate one group the penis and the other the vulva (do NOT do this according to a participant's gender!). Ask each group to research their organ using the following suggested resources. Their task is to use the information to create a quiz for the other group.

- The *Brook Learn Anatomy of Pleasure* module, which is free to use, and forms part of the e-learning course of Pleasure.[3] There are two slides on the vulva and two slides on the penis. Groups should not cheat and look at the other group's slides until given permission to do so!
- The *Pussypedia*[4] and the *Dicktionary*[5] created by the RFSU, which are free downloadable resources (may not be suitable for low literacy and younger age groups).
- Betty Dodson's vulva illustrations and internal clitoris short film, which can be accessed for free online.[6]
- Brook; the Royal College of Obstetricians & Gynaecologists (RCOG); and the British Society for Paediatric & Adolescent Gynaecology (BritSPAG) leaflet *So what is a vulva anyway*.

Once this has been completed, each group gets two minutes to read up on the other group's body part using the two slides from the *Brook Learn* module. Each group then delivers their quiz – the winning team is the team that answers the most questions correctly. As the educator you may also want to ask your own questions to both teams!

To conclude, return to the original drawings that each participant created and reflect on what they have learnt, what has surprised them and what they found useful. If you have time (or if needed for assessment purposes) you may want to ask participants to create new drawings to demonstrate what they have learnt, including what happens to the genitals during arousal.

Genital gallery

This activity is developed from an activity from The Proud Trust published in *Sexuality aGender v2: An Inclusive Sexual Health Toolkit* (see *Useful resources* at the end of this book). Shared with permission.

 This activity provides the opportunity to explore the variation that exists in people's genitals and talk about how social norms shape ideas of what is normal, sexy and/or attractive.   10 minutes

 Copies of The Proud Trust's *Genital Gallery*[7]; Jamie McCartney's *Spice of Life* and *Great wall of Vagina* images[8]; RFSU *Pussypedia*[9] and *Dicktionary*[10] resources; 'So what is a vulva anyway' leaflet by Brook, the RCOG; and BritSPAG 'Doodle your Down there' by Colette Joan Nolan – a colouring book of self portraits of people's genitals.   13+

Look at some images of genitals with your group. We recommend the *Genital Gallery* created by The Proud Trust. Alternatively, you can use the work of artist Jamie McCartney, who has created plaster casts of people's vulvas, penises and breasts to celebrate how diverse our anatomy is and to challenge notions of shame and stigma about what is normal. (**Note:** If using McCartney's work remember to point out that the images of the plaster casts feature no pubic hair because of the obvious issues of casting hair! Many of the models will have removed their hair just for the casting.) Other resources are also listed at the start of this activity.

Make sure you include bodies with a range of shapes, sizes, skin tones, abilities, disabilities, scars, stretch marks or other distinguishing marks.

Note: The activity works best if you print and laminate your set of images onto A3 to pass around the group. This allows participants to look at the images in more detail and gives participants more choice over which images they want to look at and which they don't. See the final point to consider at the start of this chapter for more advice on using images of genitals in sessions. Remember that participants always have the right to pass and the choice to not participate in activities that make them feel uncomfortable.

Give participants time to look at the images and ask questions if needed. If you have not already covered bodily anatomy with your group you may need to spend some time identifying and naming different parts of the vulva and penis.

Working in groups, ask participants to select the images of genitals that they:

- are likely to see in textbooks.
- are likely to see in pornography.
- are likely to see in a doctor's surgery.

This can be done as a card sort if you have printed and laminated the images, or by pointing to the images.

Ask groups to feedback and discuss as a group:

- What surprises you about the images you have seen?
- Do every person's genitals look the same?
- Which genitals from the gallery might we not see in textbooks, pornography or a doctor's surgery? Why might this be?
- Which of the images reflects what you understand to be 'normal' or 'ideal'?
- Where do our ideas about what's normal or ideal come from?
- How do ideas about what's 'normal' make us feel about our own bodies?
- Does being 'normal' help us to feel happier? Would you rather be happy or 'normal'?

In your discussion emphasise the diversity of vulvas and penises and that no two vulvas or penises look the same. This means that there is no such thing as a 'normal' body. As with all parts of the body there are powerful social norms that shape what we think is 'normal', 'sexy' or 'beautiful'. These norms can be powerful and shape how we feel about ourselves and respond to others. Celebrating body diversity and recognising the power and pleasure of what our bodies can do (as well as what they look like!) can help push back against some of the pressures to look 'normal' that we all experience in different ways.

You can follow this activity with 'Design your own' to creatively explore the diversity of people's genitals and beauty ideals.

Design your own

This activity is created by The Proud Trust and published in *Sexuality aGender v2: An Inclusive Sexual Health Toolkit* (see *Useful resources* at the end of this book). Used with permission.

 Works well as an extension to 'The genital gallery'. This activity allows participants to creatively explore the diversity and variation in genitalia and ideals of attractiveness. 30 minutes+

 Coloured pens, pencils, craft materials, fabrics, playdoh, etc. 13+

Task participants to design a set of genitals, with or without accessories. Give participants access to different coloured pens and pencils and other arts and crafts materials such as glitter, tissue paper and fabrics. They can also work in 3D using playdoh or modelling clay if they choose (see https://squishsquashsquelch.com/2018/10/28/playing-around/ for a blogpost link explaining how to do this). Encourage participants to take their time. If you have purchased the *Sexuality and aGender Toolkit* you can use their illustrations of tattoos, moustaches, bow ties, piercings, a monocle, comb, padlock and glasses. If not, you may want to provide a range of similar images to encourage young people to think creatively, beyond the norms that they may be more accustomed to seeing.

Ask participants to place the images/models on a table or a wall grouping the penis and the vulva images together so that you have created a genital gallery. Draw attention to how much variation there is in the genital gallery that has been created and discuss with the group how well the gallery reflects the variation that exists in human genitals.

Phallic objects

This activity is adapted from a lesson on Roman phallic objects in the *Sex and History Starter Resource*. The resource is free to download[11] and is shared and adapted with permission.

 Using images of historical objects this activity invites participants to compare historical and modern day norms about sexuality and the human body.

 30 minutes

 Images of the phallic amulet and the phallic street sign (optional) available on a slide or on colour print outs.

 13+

Without explaining what it is show participants the image of the phallic amulet using a slide or coloured print out of the image. Ask the group:

- What is this?
- What was it used for?
- When might it have been made?
- Who would have one and why?

Give the group a minute to discuss in pairs and then take group feedback about their thoughts.

Reveal the following information:

> This is a small, ivory model of an erect penis, or 'phallus'. It was made around the 1st century AD in Roman Italy. It has a hole at one end so that it could be threaded onto a necklace. In Roman times the image of the erect penis or 'phallus' was thought to bring good luck. This type of necklace was worn by soldiers as they moved around the Roman Empire, meaning we find lots in Britain. They were also given to young boys by their parents to keep them safe.

Ask the group:

- What do you think about young children wearing something like this? What would happen if a child today wore a phallic amulet?
- Would you wear an amulet like this? Or other jewellery relating to the genitals such as vulva rings or earrings? Would it depend where you were?

You may also want to show the group images of the phallic street sign and explain that it was made in the 1st century AD, and found in the ancient Roman city of Pompeii, Italy. It was probably mounted on the outside wall of a house, shop or bar to protect the occupants from harm. This was a common site in Rome at the time.

Use the following questions to guide a discussion about the different meanings and values given to body parts throughout history and across different cultures:

- Imagine you have gone back in time to Roman times. How do you think you would react seeing phallic objects like the amulet and the street sign? (*e.g. embarrassed, shocked, amused, happy, maybe you would get used to it*)
- Where do we see images of the phallus today? (*e.g. graffiti, pornography, sex education textbook, sculptures and other art*) How would you describe these images? (*e.g. funny, offensive, beautiful, arousing*)

- In modern times showing an erect penis could be classified as pornography. What do you think about this? (*Discussion ideas: the difference between art, erotica and pornography; the difficulty of finding out what different genitalia look like because we can only see images of erect penises in pornography; different views on censorship and whether it is necessary or not*)

- What can we learn from these objects and our reflections on modern day society about the meaning and value of the phallus? (*e.g. meanings change over time and between cultures, the phallus/penis itself doesn't have meaning – it's what we attach to it, the fact that meanings have changed over time suggests that they will change in the future*)

Storm in a D-cup

 An agree/disagree activity that uses a bra to explore knowledge, attitudes and values relating to breasts.

 10–20 minutes

 Large white plain cup bra (such bras can be purchased relatively cheaply online or in the sales). We advise educators not to use one of their own if they wear them! Printed out and cut up agree disagree statements, safety pins, colored permanent markers.

 11+

Hang the bra horizontally so the cups are pointing downwards with the clasps connected. Label one cup 'Agree' and the other cup 'Disagree' so that each cup will serve as a collection cup for the relevant statement. If a bra is not available or this does not feel appropriate to do with your group you can do this activity as a standard agree/disagree continuum instead. However, it would be worth discussing with your group (or reflecting for yourself) as to why doing an activity using a bra is a problem. Is the bra seen as a sexual object for example? Would it be the same if the activity involved using pants?

Have the following statements in bold printed onto individual pieces of paper and ask participants whether they want to place the statement in the Agree or Disagree cup. Use the discussion comments to help you facilitate the discussion. Where there is dissensus in the group both sides of the argument should air their views and if agreement can't be reached then the statement can be pinned to the back support section of the bra. Take photos of where the statements end up on the bra for your records.

Storm in a D cup statements

Breastfeeding in public should be more common.

Wearing a bra that fits and is comfortable is more important than wearing a bra that is 'sexy'.

The purpose of a bra is to hide the breasts from show.

Having moobs or 'manboobs' can be really upsetting.

It's fine for men to show their nipples in public, but not women.

The main function of breasts is for visual arousal and sexual pleasure.

Teenagers don't need to worry about breast self examination.

The main function of breasts is for feeding a baby.

The most visually attractive breasts are ones that are large, rounded and pert with nipples that are not too small or large.

#Freethenipple campaigners are attention seekers.

Discussion points

Breastfeeding in public should be more common. (Discussion points include: the UK has one of lowest breastfeeding rates in the world; there is social stigma related to breastfeeding in public; if you don't see others doing it you are less likely to feel comfortable doing it yourself; some people don't want to breastfeed their babies and shouldn't be pressured to if they don't want to.)

The purpose of a bra is to hide the breasts from show. (Discussion points include: the range and types of bras – sports, minimiser, padded, push up, etc. which have a range of different purposes, e.g. support, discretion, to look/feel sexy, to hide nipples, to conform to ideals about attractive breasts, etc.)

It's fine for men to show their nipples in public, but not women. (Discussion points include: in the UK men who are topless in the summer are able to go to lots of different places without judgement unlike women who would usually be restricted to certain beaches and private spaces (e.g. at home); whether it is acceptable to show your breasts in public varies across cultures – e.g. in some indigenous cultures it is common for breasts to be bare.)

Teenagers don't need to worry about breast self examination. (Discussion points include: breast cancer is most common in women over the ages of 50 and that it is common for breasts to feel lumpy especially near the armpit or around menstruation. It is important to be aware of how your breasts feel at different times of the month and while most changes in teenage years would be nothing to worry about it is always a good idea to see your doctor if you are worried.)

The most visually attractive breasts are ones that are large, rounded and pert with nipples that are not too small or large. (Discussion points include: what attractiveness means and how it varies between people; what surgically enhanced breasts look like vs. natural breasts; where these ideas have come from and whether these attitudes are different for people of different genders.)

Wearing a bra that fits and is comfortable is more important than wearing a bra that is 'sexy'. (Discussion points include: the importance of correctly fitted bras and that many women wear incorrect sizes for their bodies; discussion of 'sexy' vs. 'comfort' and whether the two are mutually exclusive; reported recent increases in the sales of non-underwired bras that are meant to be designed for comfort rather than creating pert breasts.)

Having moobs or 'manboobs' can be really upsetting. (Discussion points include: the condition gynecomastia (an enlargement or swelling of breast tissue in people with biologically male bodies) is common and temporary in puberty; gynecomastia can also be a consequence of being overweight or cannabis/steroid misuse. People of all genders can experience pressure to conform to beauty ideals although some would argue that women experience more pressure than men to conform to beauty ideals.)

The main function of breasts is for visual arousal and sexual pleasure. (Discussion points include: that breasts can be sexually pleasurable for both the owner of the breasts and their partner; whether it is ethically ok to get pleasure from looking at someone's breasts without their knowledge/ consent; what visual arousal means relating to breasts; what other functions of breasts exist.)

The main function of breasts is for feeding a baby. (Discussion could include: what other functions of breasts exist; the pleasure of breasts for the owner and others; the importance of breastfeeding and how this has decreased at a time when we have also seen high levels of sexualisation of breasts.)

#Freethenipple campaigners are attention seekers. (Discussion could include: what #freethenipple campaign is (a global movement for equality that has involved in some cases getting breasts out in public); the power of social movements; what someone's motives might be for taking part in such activism; what attention seeking is; what rights we have as individuals to conceal or display our bodies.)

To finish, ask participants to choose an aspect of the session they have been most interested in and use colored permanent markers to decorate the bra with slogans and statements about what they have learned and what they think and feel about breasts. The bra can then be displayed and used as a tool to facilitate further discussions and raise awareness of some of the issues explored in this activity.

Busting myths about the hymen and introducing the vaginal corona

  An interactive activity in which participants identify myths about the hymen and virginity loss and research accurate information to bust these myths.   30 minutes

  Images of the vaginal corona; copies of or access to *My Corona: The Hymen & the Myths That Surround It* by Anna Knöfel Magnusson/RSFU, which is a short article on the teen sex education site Scarleteen[12] and/or Vaginal corona: myths surrounding virginity – your questions answered by the RFSU, which is a free downloadable booklet.[13]   13+

Show participants images of the vaginal corona. You can access these online via the RFSU resource or by photocopying the images included in Figure 5.1. Used with permission.

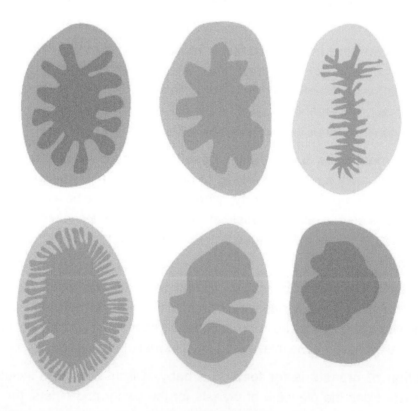

FIGURE 5.1 Examples of how vaginal corona might appear (formerly known as hymen)
Credit: © RFSU

Ask participants:

- What do you think these are images of? (Vaginal corona)
- Has anyone has heard of the vaginal corona before? (Most will not)
- What part of the body might this be? (Tip: vaginal = vagina and corona = latin for crown)
- Has anyone heard of the hymen? (Many will have heard of this. Explain that the vaginal corona and the hymen are the same thing.)

Divide your white board in half or stick up two sheets of flipchart. On one half/piece of paper write 'hymen' in the middle of the board and ask the group to brainstorm everything they know about the hymen. Write down all young people's words and comments even if they are untrue and/or offensive. Write a question mark after each statement to indicate that it may, or may not, be true. One the other half of the board write 'vaginal corona' in the middle and leave the rest blank.

Divide participants into small groups and ask them to research the vaginal corona/hymen to find out which of the words and statements on the board/flipchart are true and which are myths. We recommend the following resources:

- *My Corona: The Hymen & the Myths That Surround It* by Anna Knöfel Magnusson/RSFU. This is a short article on the teen sex education site Scarleteen
- *Vaginal corona: myths surrounding virginity* – your questions answered by the RFSU.

As participants discover new information they should walk up to the board and underline the word or statement to indicate whether it is myth or fact. Agree one colour for myth and one for fact. If it is a myth, participants should write the corresponding fact on the blank half of the board. Other interesting statements and facts can also be added to create a new, accurate word cloud.

When all words and statements on the original brainstorm have been addressed, close the activity and discuss the two spider diagrams you have created using the following questions:

- What were our initial ideas about the hymen and about virginity loss?
- What did you learn that surprised you?
- Why do you think there are so many myths about the hymen and about virginity loss?
- Are myths about virginity and virginity loss different for young men and young women?
- What do some of the myths about the hymen tell us about popular views about gender and sexuality?
- How can we challenge these views?

The key myth that you need to dispel is that the hymen is a membrane that covers the vagina like the skin of a drum that is broken during penetrative sex, causing bleeding and pain. As the images of the vaginal corona show, the cells of the 'hymen' take many different forms but never completely cover the inside of the vagina. Some people with vaginas bleed the first time they have sex but some don't so bleeding cannot be taken as evidence of first sex or 'virginity loss'. First sex can be uncomfortable for some people but it shouldn't hurt – it is not normal or expected for sex to be painful. If sex hurts this may be because you are not aroused or relaxed so it is a good idea to stop and try a different sexual activity or try again another time.

Many of the myths about the hymen tell us more about cultural attitudes to female sexuality then they do about human anatomy. The hymen is associated with ideas about purity, chastity and the need to control female sexuality and women's bodies. Renaming the hymen the vaginal corona is an attempt to leave these myths behind and find new ways of talking about bodies and sexuality that are more empowering, inclusive and equitable.

This activity would be good to do alongside the 'First sex and virginity cards' activity in Chapter 6: *Sex* on p. 221.

Cliteracy

 A creative activity in which participants write articles, stories, poems and songs about the clitoris with the aim of raising awareness about the anatomy and potential of this often forgotten part of the sexual body. 40–50 minutes

 3D Printed Clitoris models (open source files for printing your own models if you have access to a 3D printer[14]) or pre-printed models (purchasable online). Diagrams of the clitoris (available online). Access to the internet. 13+

Note: Although this activity is best suited for 13+, knowledge that the clitoris is a part of the body and information about FGM should be covered earlier than this in primary school when girls are most at risk of FGM.

Pass round a model of the clitoris and ask participants what they think it is and what part of the body it represents.

Explain that it is a model of the clitoris which is a part of the vulva. It looks unfamiliar because, until recently, the clitoris was rarely talked about or represented in education materials. When included in textbooks it often lacked detail or was inaccurately drawn or described. Ask the group why they think it took so long for the clitoral anatomy to be more widely known and discussed.

Tell the group that we can only see a tiny part of the clitoris (the glans) from the outside of the body. It is on average 10cm long but it is like an iceberg where the majority of it is located underneath the skin. To help participants visualise this, push your thumb between your second and third finger and stick out your four fingers pointing down. Here the tip of your thumb is the clitoral glans and the webbing between your fingers can demonstrate the clitoral hood with the inner and outer labia represented by your fingers. This is the only part that is visible in people who have a clitoris. If someone has experienced Female Genital Mutilation (FGM – see p. pp. 168–70) then this may not be visible. The rest of the clitoris is not visible. In total the clitoris contains around 8,000 nerve endings which are why it is such a sensitive and potentially pleasurable area of the body (the head of the penis contains 4,000 by comparison).

Ask participants if they know what the function of the clitoris is and explain that it is the only organ in the body that has the sole purpose of pleasure.

Provide a 'Cliteracy' Task for participants such as writing articles, stories, poems or songs that raise wider awareness of the full anatomy and potential of the clitoris such as:

- Rewrite the research article: O'Connell, Helen E, Kalavampara, V, Sanjeevan, & Hutson, John M, (2005) 'Anatomy of the clitoris.' The Journal of Urology 174(4), pp. 1189–1195, for a teenage audience.[15]
- Write a song called an *Ode to the Clitoris* using the example from Refinery29.[16]
- Adapt Laurie Mintz's Psychology Today article 'A Linguistic Sexual Revolution: Naming the Clitoris'[17] into a series of campaign messages.
- Write an imaginative short story about the discovery of the clitoris written from the perspective of a nerve cell or a scientist.

Depending on the group you may wish to share RFSU 'A Guide to Clitoral Sex'[18] to finish the session. This would be more suitable for older groups with good literacy.

Female Genital Mutilation (FGM)

Female Genital Mutilation (FGM) is the term used to describe all procedures that involve partial or total removal of the female external genitalia for non-medical reasons (see World Health Organization for full definition[20]). There are four main types of FGM:

Type 1 (clitoridectomy) involves removing part or all of the clitoris.
Type 2 (excision) involves removing part or all of the clitoris and the inner labia (lips that surround the vagina), with or without removal of the labia majora (larger outer lips).
Type 3 (infibulation) involves the narrowing of the vaginal opening by creating a seal, formed by cutting and repositioning the labia.
Type 4 involves other harmful procedures to the female genitals, including pricking, piercing, cutting, scraping or burning the area.

FGM is usually carried out on young girls between infancy and the age of 15, usually before puberty starts. FGM is illegal in the UK and can be very painful, leading to possible long term problems with sex, childbirth and mental health.

FGM is sometimes called Female Genital Cutting (FGC), Female Circumcision (FC) or excision. Many communities affected by FGM also use local names to refer to the practice, including 'Tahor' or 'Sunna' (both Arabic terms).

For more information about FGM see the information pages created by the NHS, the World Health Organization or FORWARD (Foundation for Women's Health Research and Development) which is the leading African women-led organisation working on FGM, child marriage and other forms of violence against women and girls in the UK and Africa.

Note: Elsewhere in this chapter we have argued that it is important not to talk about body parts in gendered ways (e.g. let's talk about 'vaginas' not 'female vaginas'). We have chosen to use the term FGM as this is the term that is widely used by activists within communities affected by FGM. The term also highlights the fact that this is a form of gender-based violence experienced by girls and women.

Extension: Campaigning against Female Genital Mutilation

To extend the activity and provoke further discussion show participants the 'My Clitoris'[19] song and video made by young people at *Integrate UK* to raise awareness that FGM is not acceptable and to push back against the control of women's bodies and female sexuality.

Task participants with creating their own campaign to end FGM.

Section 3: Reproductive bodies

Modelling the reproductive body

 This activity uses objects, models and other visual prompts to facilitate learning about the reproductive organs.

 20–30 minutes

 3D scientific models or diagrams of uterus, fallopian tubes, the vulva, the clitoris, the penis, the testicles. You can also get 3D printed versions. If possible, include model testicles and breasts with lumps in, knitted or crocheted models of sexual organs. Playdoh.

 11+

You can purchase Pelvis models[21] or look at purchasing the Body Sense Wendy Model[22]: this model reproductive tract is an excellent resource for showing how the internal anatomy of the uterus, fallopian tubes and ovaries connect to the external genitalia (vulva). Originally developed for learners with additional needs, it has also proved very successful in mainstream sessions to discuss pleasure, pubic hair, anatomy. It can also be used to partially demonstrate how to use a tampon, menstrual cup, dental dam, femidom, diaphragm, contraceptive ring.

Pass round models or show diagrams of the uterus, fallopian tubes, ovaries and vulva. (Also referred to as the female reproductive or sexual organs. See 'Points to consider' on p. 197 for further discussion on using inclusive language to talk about parts of the body.)

Ask participants to identify the different parts of the body and their function. See Table 5.1 and Figures 5.4–5.8 for details.

To support participants to visualise and remember the positioning of the womb, cervix and ovaries clench your fist and stick your thumb and little finger out to the side. Here your arm is the vagina, the wrist is the cervix, your closed fist is the womb and thumb and little finger the fallopian tubes. The fallopian tubes and vaginal canal are way out of scale but the fist part is broadly the same size as

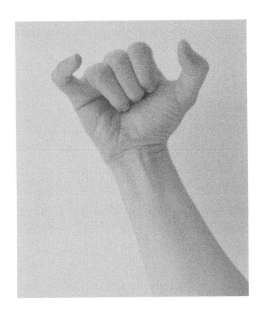

FIGURE 5.2 Using the hand to model the front view of the uterus
Credit: © Bertil Mulvad

FIGURE 5.3 Using the hand to model a side view of the uterus
Credit: © Bertil Mulvad

the uterus and the bend in the wrist shows how the uterus bends forward (and in some people can bend the other way, which is called a retroverted uterus). (See Figures 5.2 and 5.3.)

Follow this by passing round an object or diagram of the vulva and ask participants to identify the different parts of the anatomy and their function:

- Clarify which parts of the vulva have a function for reproduction and which have other functions (e.g. pleasure, to urinate).
- Also clarify the difference between a vagina and a vulva as this is often not widely understood (see the 'What's in a name?' activity on p. 158 for details of a short animation to help you do this).
- You can also model a vulva out of playdoh. This can also be used to explain the four types of FGM (see box on p. 169).

In your discussion mention the following hygiene pointers:

- Vaginas are self cleaning and the vulva just needs washing with water not soap to prevent infections or irritations.
- If you have a vagina, get familiar with your usual monthly variations in vaginal discharge. If you notice any unusual changes in the appearance or smell or any itching or pain go to a doctor or sexual health clinic.
- If you have a vagina it is a good idea to go for a wee after having sex. This can help prevent urine infections.

When talking about the clitoris you can help participants visualise the organ by making the hand shape described in the 'Cliteracy' activity on p. 168. You can also pass round 3D models and diagrams of the clitoris and talk through the different parts of the organ and their sole function which is pleasure!

Next pass round an object or show a diagram of the penis and the testicles (also referred to as the male reproductive or sexual organs or genitalia). (See 'Points to consider' on p. 197 for further discussion on the use of inclusive language when talking about parts of the body.)

Ask participants to identify the different parts of the organs and talk about their function. See Table 5.1 and Figures 5.4–5.8.

- It is useful to use a condom demonstrator or other model of the penis to show young people what the average size of an erect adult penis looks like.
- Where possible show images of penises with and without a foreskin and talk about circumcision.
- Explain what the frenulum is and show where this is on the penis (you can place an elastic band around the condom demonstrator to help visualise this, to help explain that if the frenulum (also known as the 'banjo string') is too tight it stops the foreskin from being able to move up and down causing discomfort during masturbation or sex. If this happens, go to the doctor. There is a simple operation that can loosen the frenulum and make sex more comfortable.

In your discussion mention the following hygiene and health pointers:

- If you have a foreskin it should be gently rolled back and cleaned underneath with water every day to help prevent any buildup of skin cells, etc. that can smell unpleasant and lead to infection.
- Ensure the foreskin is pulled back when putting on a condom.
- If you notice any changes to what is usual for your testicles, including any lumps, you should go to the doctors to get this checked out.
- If you have any pain or unusual discharge from the penis, go to the doctor.

Table 5.1 contains basic information about the reproductive and sex organs. For more detailed information we recommend you visit Brook, BISH or Scarleteen for excellent diagrams, short films and explanations. See *Useful resources* at the end of this book for details.

TABLE 5.1 Information for educators about the reproductive and sex organs

Organ	*Function*
ovary	Where eggs are stored and released once a month. There are two ovaries, which are connected to the womb by the fallopian tubes. Usually only one egg is released each month.
fallopian tube	These are the tubes that connect the ovaries and the womb. The egg travels down the fallopian tube. Fertilisation can only take place here.
womb (uterus)	A muscular organ located in the abdomen. It has a lining that is shed once a month – this is called a period. If a fertilised egg implants in the lining this is where a foetus can grow.
cervix	The neck of the womb that connects the womb and the vagina.
vagina	When people talk about the 'vagina' they are normally talking about the vulva. The vulva includes the vagina and the labia, clitoris, etc. (see Figure 5.4). The vagina is the muscular tube that connects the uterus and cervix to the outside of the body, allowing for menstruation, intercourse and childbirth. This is not where you urinate (wee) from.
vulva	This is the external genital organ (the part of the body you can see). We often refer to this as the vagina, but it is actually called the vulva. As part of your vulva you have two sets of labia – the outer labia and the inner labia – a clitoris, vagina and urethra.
outer labia	The external lips of the vulva. These are covered in pubic hair (from puberty onwards), and can be very fleshy.
inner labia	The inner labia are inside your outer labia, and don't have any pubic hair on them.
clitoris	Below the mons pubis, at the top of the labia is the clitoris. It looks like a small pea-sized bump with a hood covering it. It is the only part of human body where the sole function is pleasure. Contains 8,000 nerve endings and fills with blood and becomes erect when aroused.

TABLE 5.1 (Cont.)

Organ	Function
urethra	The tube where urine is passed from your bladder to outside of the body. In penises the urethra can also carry semen from the testicles. If you have a vulva you can find your urethra above the vagina and below the clitoris.
mons pubis	This is the soft area below your belly button where pubic hair grows from puberty onwards.
anus	The anus leads to the sphincter (bum-hole), which is the tight circle of muscle that contracts and loosens to allow the passage of faeces (poo) out of the body. The rectum is that part of the digestive tract that leads to the anus. For many people the anus and surrounding area are very sensitive and are sexually arousing.
penis	Part of the external genital organs (the bits you can see) that has two main functions: urination (carrying urine or wee out of the body) and ejaculation (delivering semen from the testicles). It is mainly made up of the shaft and the glans.
testicles	This is where sperm is produced and stored. Testicles hang behind the penis in a pouch of skin called the scrotum. Sperm is carried from the testicles via the prostate gland. Here prostate fluid is added to the sperm for nourishment, making semen. The semen travels out of the body through the urethra.
scrotum	The pouch of skin that holds the testicles.
shaft	The main part of the penis from the base to the head (glans). Between the shaft and the head is the corona, which is a sort of ridge that separates the two.
foreskin	The foreskin is the fold of skin that covers the head of the penis (glans).
glans	This is the head of the penis and is usually covered by the foreskin. It can be very sensitive.
vas deferens/ sperm duct	This is the tube in which semen travels from the testicles to the urethra.
prostate	The prostate is a walnut-sized gland located between the bladder and the penis. The prostate secretes fluid that nourishes and protects sperm.

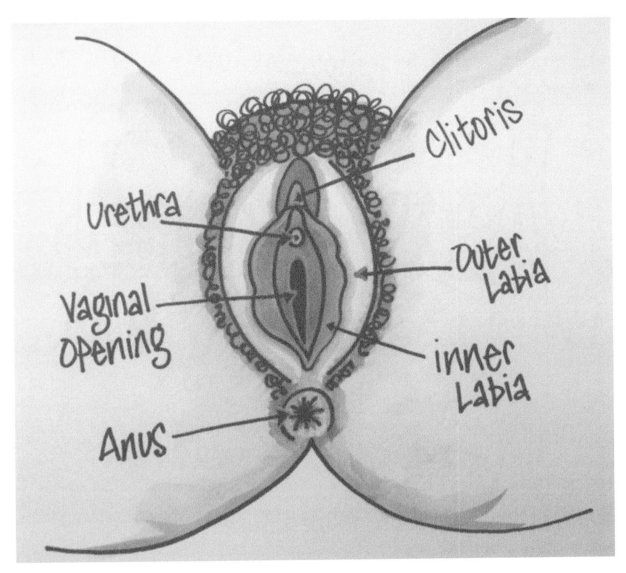

FIGURE 5.4 The vulva

Illustration by: Chrissy Baxter

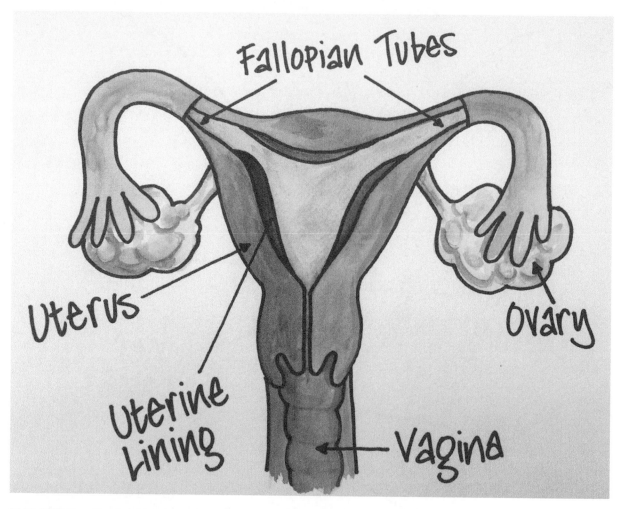

FIGURE 5.5 Internal view of the uterus, fallopian tubes, ovaries and vagina

Illustration by: Chrissy Baxter

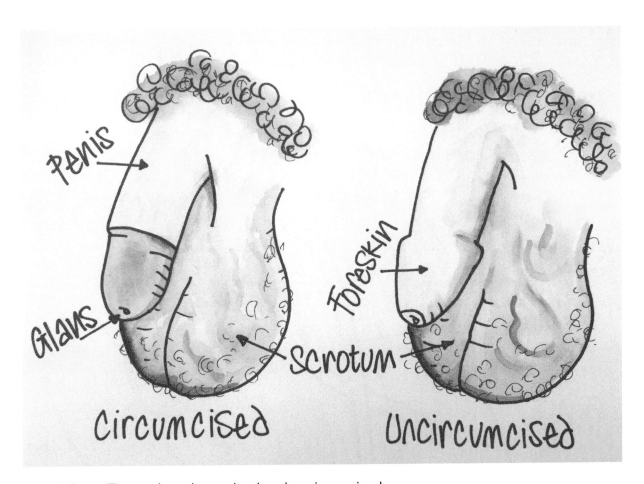

FIGURE 5.6 The penis – circumcised and uncircumcised

Illustration by: Chrissy Baxter

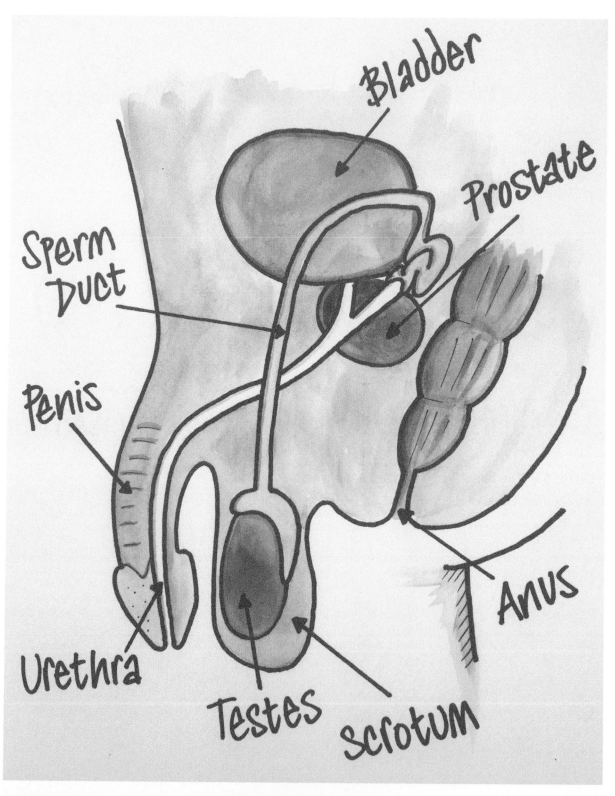

FIGURE 5.7 Internal view of the penis and testicles

Illustration by: Chrissy Baxter

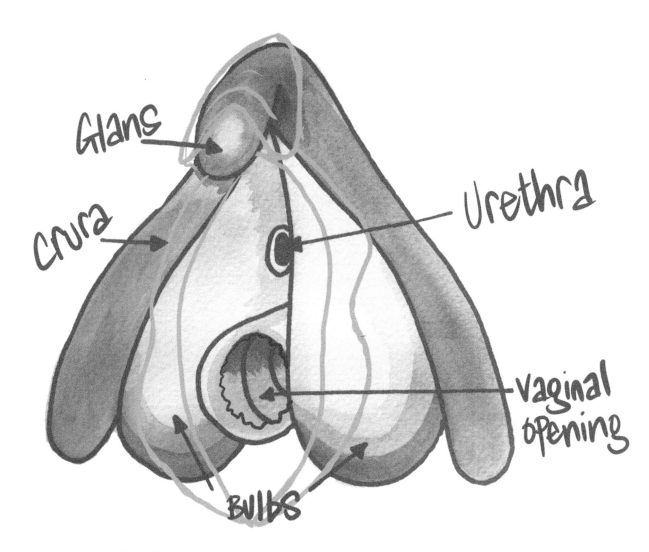

FIGURE 5.8 The clitoris
Illustration by: Chrissy Baxter

To consolidate the learning from this activity, task participants with designing their own model or diagram of one or more of the reproductive organs. The following materials may be useful:

- Playdoh – A guide to making the genitals from playdoh can be found at https://squishsquashsquelch.com/2018/10/28/playing-around/
- Modelling materials, e.g. lots of pink tissue paper, string (pubic hair), buttons (e.g. clitoris), table tennis balls (testicles), toilet rolls (penis external or vagina internal), tennis ball (bladder or womb), anything else suitable such as glue, scissors, sticky tape, colouring pens, pipe cleaners, etc.
- Food, e.g. slices of apples, tangerines, spaghetti, bananas, carrots, plums, pears, raisins, etc.

Ask participants to present their model to the group and discuss how this part of the body works. Ensure that they identify why this organ is important for reproduction and whether it is also important for sex and/or pleasure.

Puberty party!

 A fun, interactive way of finding out what participants already know about puberty, identifying gaps in knowledge and setting puberty in a celebratory context. 45 minutes

 Party materials, pens, paper. 11+

Ask participants to plan a puberty party to celebrate an individual becoming fertile through the process of puberty. This might mean someone has started their periods, changing body shape, is growing new body hair or started producing semen and having wet dreams. Or it could be a celebration of any other signifier they choose. For example, they could think about the following:

- What reasons would someone throw a puberty party? How is/was 'coming of age' celebrated historically and geographically?
- What games, activities and rituals would you include at the puberty party? What party games will help you to educate friends about puberty and the changes in our bodies including being mindful of personal and body boundaries?
- What key messages would you want party-goers to take away from the party and the experience?
- What products and other items might you put in their party bags to celebrate and support puberty?
- How would you decorate the party venue to celebrate growing up?
- Would you have a cake? What key icon relating to puberty would it look like?
- What food and drink would you have? What foods are most nourishing for growing bodies? E.g. mood boosting foods, or hormone balancing foods.
- What would you write in a card to the person whose party it is? Think of messages of support, information, celebration and/or encouragement? (e.g. accepting that puberty affects our moods and being kind to ourselves and each other when feeling the effects of hormones; being willing to talk about and share experiences if needed)

Task participants with designing a puberty piñata *or* an alternative game of their choice. Ask them to consider what their puberty piñata would look like (e.g. the shape of body, organ or symbol) and what they would put inside. If you have time, make the piñata, which can be stuffed or decorated with statements and affirmations to celebrate and support the process of puberty. If not ask participants to draw a design and write the statements and affirmations they would include.

Other game ideas include puberty pass-the-parcel in which party-goers pass around a wrapped gift (ask participants to consider what the gift would be) and each time the parcel is passed to a person they must state a change of puberty such as growing pubic hair around the genitals, increase in spots, mood changes due to hormone production. Each change has to be followed by a tip to others on how to manage this change so that growing up and becoming fertile can be enjoyed. Ask participants to identify a list of changes and tips (and play the game if you have time!).

The Womb room

 A fun and creative activity in which participants create an art gallery of images of menstruation and reproduction to visualise and explore how the womb changes during the monthly cycle, reproduction and pregnancy.

 30 minutes+

 A2 or A3 uterus outlines (printed on thicker paper or backed onto card for display in a gallery), paints, pens, glitter, red and pink tissue paper, white and grey tissue paper, modelling clay.

 11+

Ask participants to imagine that you are commissioning a body of work called the *Womb room* which requires a visual representation of a series of uteruses in different stages of the menstrual cycle, conception and pregnancy.

Divide participants into small groups and assign each group a stage or series of stages of the menstrual cycle, conception or pregnancy, as described on the following pages. Alternatively participants can work individually and bring their works together to create a collective gallery.

The task is to create a visual display of what is happening within the uterus at the given stage using the range of modelling and arts-based materials available. If access to the art materials and scale of this project is a problem then a quicker alternative is to give participants blank uterus diagrams that have to be coloured and labelled to create a storyboard for display.

Some groups or individuals could also be asked to represent contraception or assisted conception (IUI or IVF) in their *Womb room* displays, showing how the method works to prevent or assist conception and pregnancy. For example, when representing contraception, e.g. the combined oral contraceptive pill (usually just called 'the pill'), it contains artificial versions of the hormones oestrogen and progesterone, which are produced naturally in the ovaries. The contraceptive pill prevents the ovaries from releasing an egg each month (ovulation). It also thickens the mucus in the neck of the womb, so it is harder for sperm to penetrate the womb and reach an egg. It also thins the lining of the womb, so there is less chance of a fertilised egg implanting into the womb and being able to grow. With the assisted conception the displays could seek to explain the artificial hormonal stimulation of the ovaries to release more than one egg, the fertlistation of the sperm and egg outside of the body before transferring the embryo directly into the uterus (IVF) or the insertion of semen directly into the uterus (IUI).

Display the groups' gallery creations together to create a *Womb room* and ask each group or individual to share their learning.

Here is a list of stages of menstruation, conception and pregnancy which can be allocated to groups or individuals. You may want to start by showing participants a short film about the menstrual cycle such as the NHS *Menstrual cycle: animation*[23] or show some of the images from the *My beautiful cervix* project[24] to give some context and generate ideas.

The menstrual cycle

- The menstrual cycle starts on the first day of the menstrual period (day one) and ends the day before the next period begins. The length of the menstrual cycle is often approximately 28 days, however it can vary between cycles and between individuals and can last anywhere from 21 to 35 days and still be within average range. There are a range of apps that can be used to track the menstrual cycle.
- Each month the womb lining thickens between approximately day 6–14 ready for a fertilised egg to implant. Cervical mucus (which can be seen as discharge) thins and becomes more slippery to support sperm to reach the egg.
- During ovulation an egg is released from the ovary; this happens once per cycle on approximately day 14, but this varies per person, and over the course of the menovulatory lifetime.
- The egg is released into a fallopian tube. If the egg is not fertilised by sperm then approximately 14 days after ovulation the thickened womb lining leaves the body through the vagina. This is known as menstruation, or a period (short for menstrual period), which lasts around four–seven days (usually the same length of cycle and period for each person, though this can vary between people and change throughout one's life).

Stages of conception

- Conception stage 1: If two people have penis-in-vagina sex without a condom or diaphragm to act as a barrier, semen containing sperm is released at the top of the vagina and can enter the cervix. The sperm cells will swim through the cervix and womb and into the fallopian tubes. Sperm can also be placed in the vagina, uterus or fallopian tube to aid conception without having penis-in-vagina sex.
- Conception stage 2: If there is an egg in the fallopian tube the sperm and egg will join together. This is called fertilisation and the fertilised egg and sperm are known as a zygote. It won't happen if one person is taking hormonal contraception such as the pill, implant or injection as this can prevent an egg from being released from the ovary and/or make the cervix inhospitable to sperm. With some IUDs fertilisation can still take place but the presence of the IUD means that implantation cannot take place.
- Conception stage 3: As the fertilised egg is moved down the tube the cells start to divide and multiply so the ball of cells (known as a blastocyst) starts to grow.
- Conception stage 4: The ball of cells is fixed to the lining of the uterus. This is called implantation. Pregnancy has occurred. However, one in four pregnancies will end in miscarriage and possibly more, as in many cases miscarriage occurs before the pregnancy is discovered.

Stages of pregnancy

- Pregnancy stage 1: The first trimester: weeks 1–12 of pregnancy – the implanted ball of cells (known as an embryo) continue to grow and divide. Between six and seven weeks the heart starts to beat. By week 12 the embryo is fully formed with bones, muscles and all the organs of the body and it is about the size of a lime. It is now known as a foetus. The pregnant person may feel morning sickness and more tired.
- Pregnancy stage 2: The second trimester: weeks 13–28 of pregnancy – the foetus continues to grow and develop. A pregnancy bump becomes more prominent and movements can be felt. The ligaments around the uterus will soften to allow for changes in weight and size, and to prepare for a vaginal birth.
- Pregnancy stage 3: The third trimester: weeks 29–40 of pregnancy – the foetus grows to the size it will be at birth. Bump increases in size and movements felt much more regularly. The foetus will usually move to position head down ready to be born in final weeks of pregnancy. In the person's breasts milk ducts will begin to be able to produce milk ready for breastfeeding.

Dicktionary

A research, create and present activity to address common areas of sexual health that affect people with penises that are not always covered in sufficient detail for young people.

One hour (minimum)

Pens, paper, computer access.

11+

Explain to the group that the following areas of sexual health are not always fully understood by, or explained to, young people. They are all issues that affect people with penises:

1. Normal variations in penis and testicle shape, size and appearance.
2. Prostate location, purpose and importance.
3. Erections (timing, appearance, size, duration).
4. Ejaculation (when desired and premature).
5. Masturbation and pleasure.
6. Foreskins – keeping them clean and healthy and facts about circumcision (surgical removal of the foreskin).
7. Fertility factors affecting sperm count, sperm health and motility.
8. Common infections and cancers affecting the penis, testicles and prostate and how they are diagnosed and treated.
9. Body image and confidence relating to anatomy and sexual performance.
10. Seeking help and advice when needed about sexual health.

Divide the group into ten smaller groups or pairs and task each with coming up with individual education campaigns on each of the topic areas listed previously. Each group should think about the following:

- What's the issue?
- What are some of the common myths on this issue?
- What information is needed to counter these myths?

Groups may find the *Brook, BISH UK* and *Scarleteen* websites (links in *Useful resources* on at the end of this book) useful to help with this task.

Encourage participants to be creative with their response. They could do advertising campaigns (videos, leaflets, posters) or create teaching tools with associated guides on 'how to use' (e.g. a range of penis and testicle models made out of clay, or knitted – if knitted you could include a small bead in the testicle to encourage checking for lumps). Testicle checking models can also be purchased. Each group needs to present their education campaign topic area to the whole group while the rest of the group assesses the quality of their work. Use the 'Research, present and assess' activity in Chapter 8: *Concluding the learning*, on p. 328, for how to do this. You may choose to do an exhibition of both Dicktionary and the *Womb room* (p. 181) as a celebration of some of the learning from these activities.

Body fluids

Using 'homemade' samples of bodily fluids this interactive activity helps participants to understand what different bodily fluids look like, what is normal and healthy and when to seek help. This is rarely covered in RSE leading to a lack of knowledge, in particular about how vaginal fluid and discharge changes throughout the menstrual cycle.

20–30 minutes

Pre-prepared petri dishes with a range of fluid types as outlined in the following. Tape up petri dishes so participants can't smell or touch them. Fluid labels or cards. Underwear and menstrual pads (optional).

11+

Preparation

Using the ingredients listed in Table 5.2, create a range of bodily fluids. Put one–two teaspoons of each fluid in a sealed petri dish and add 'smell' labels as instructed. Number each petri dish clearly. This can be time consuming and is a great activity to ask peer educators/young volunteers to help you prepare as it can be good, messy, educational fun!

Facilitation

Place the petri dishes on a table and ask participants to gather round. Encourage participants to look at each dish in turn and describe what it is they can see. Give participants a set of labels or cards, each containing a name of a bodily fluid. Their task is to match each dish to a bodily fluid.

Reveal the correct answers and discuss why and when each bodily fluid may be visible and what this can tell us about our bodies, using the information in Table 5.2.

Emphasise to participants that if a fluid is not smelly or causing irritation it's likely that it's entirely normal. As you go through each fluid you may want to demonstrate how it appears in the gusset of underwear or on a disposable menstrual pad. Make sure you remind participants that pads don't need to be worn all the time as most fluids (except menstrual blood) will be absorbed by underwear.

Some young people may find this demonstration disgusting but there is also high potential for them being privately reassured that their leaky bodies are normal.

TABLE 5.2 Information for educators on bodily fluids and the ingredients required for the activity

Fluid	Ingredients	Information
Cervical mucus	Egg white for fertile stretchy cervical mucus produced around ovulation (5–10ml).	Produced around ovulation. Normally stretchy and stringy and looks like egg white.
Normal vaginal fluid	Small amount of watered down milk for entirely normal milky discharge pre or post ovulation.	Produced throughout the month as a way of the vagina self cleaning. Can be milky thin liquid. The vagina is naturally acidic which helps good bacteria to thrive and keeps harmful bacteria in check.
Vaginal lubricant	Watered down water-based lube for clear discharge produced by vagina on arousal.	Produced on arousal. Clear slippery fluid.
Pre-cum	Watered down water-based lube for clear discharge produced by penis on arousal.	Clear liquid produced by the tip of the penis when aroused.
Semen	Translucent whitish hair conditioner for sperm (3–5ml).	Produced by the testicles and exits the tip of the penis; contains sperm. Semen is naturally alkaline.
Period/ menstruation	Watered down red food colouring, seedless strawberry jam (clots), a bit of soy sauce (brownish colour at different stages). The average is approximately two–six tablespoons of blood and tissue, and the colour and consistency can vary throughout a period. You could provide these on different petri dishes to show beginning, middle and end of a period.	Produced during menstruation.
Yeast infection (Thrush)	Watered down cottage cheese to indicate possible yeast infection (Thrush) labelled with 'can smell yeasty'.	Infection of the vaginal canal. Caused by yeast organism Candida albicans can cause a thick cream coloured itchy discharge.
Trichomonas vaginalis	Small amount of green washing up liquid in water to create foamy pale greenish tinged discharge (trichomonas vaginalis infection) labelled with 'can smell very unpleasant'.	Infection of the vaginal canal. Caused by parasite Trichomonas vaginalis. Can cause a pale greenish tinged frothy foul smelling discharge.
Bacterial vaginosis	Excess of small amount of thin flour and water paste, perhaps with small amount of black pepper to give a greyish tinges for possible bacterial vaginosis infection. Labelled with 'can smell unpleasant (fishy)'.	Infection of the vaginal canal. Caused by overgrowth of bacteria often when the acidic pH balance has been upset, can cause a grey fishy smelling discharge.

The menstrual product experiment

With thanks to Chella Quint at #periodpositive for her help with the development of this activity.

A practical activity that uses object-based learning methods to introduce or re-familiarise participants with a range of menstrual products. This activity can be used to provoke discussion about the lack of awareness about reusable menstrual products and the shame and stigma around periods in the UK and worldwide.

 25 minutes

Applicator and non-applicator tampons with different levels of absorbency, disposable and reusable menstrual pads, different brands of menstrual cups and pairs of menstrual pants/period underwear. Containers of red liquid (water + food dye/grape juice/blackcurrant squash, etc., as long as it is the same liquid for every group), measuring spoons or 10ml syringes, jugs.

 11+

Divide participants into small groups and give each group one of each type of product. Encourage participants to take the products out of their packaging, touch and feel them and ask for a description of how each product works. If you do not have enough menstrual cups or menstrual pants to have one per group (they are expensive) then pass round the products that you do have available for each group to look at in turn. Alternatively, you can write to reusable menstrual product companies and request a sample. They will often send example cups/pants which cannot be used and are for display purposes only.

Ask each group to test how much liquid each product can absorb or hold, starting with 5ml or one teaspoon and working their way upward. Groups should write down their results to the nearest millimetre or teaspoon in a comparison chart. It is useful if groups have more than one tampon or pad to experiment with, preferably of different sizes, materials (such as plastic, organic cotton, gel core, fleece, PUL) and brands. You may want to ask groups to predict how much liquid each product can hold before they conduct their experiment.

Ask groups to wash the menstrual cups, cloth pads and pants and hang them on a rack or radiator at the end of the experiment to make it clear that these are reusable products that can be cleaned, unlike the tampon and the disposable pad.

Ask groups to answer the following questions, based on their own research and further research online. Participants will need to complete the necessary calculations presenting a good opportunity to test their mathematical skills!

- Which product held the most liquid? What was it made of?
- How much does each product cost to buy in the UK?
- What is the cost of using each product over a five-year period in the UK? (Estimate the cost based on someone having a 28-day cycle and a period that lasts five days.)
- Which products are reusable and which are disposable? What are the advantages and disadvantages of both options? A combination?

Ask participants to feedback their findings and discuss the following:

- Given that menstrual cups hold the most liquid and are among the cheapest products available, why do you think they not more widely used? (*Answers can include: reusable products are less profitable and are therefore less aggressively marketed; there is discomfort/shame around menstrual blood or putting something in your vagina that means people prefer disposable products; not enough awareness of the environmental benefits of reusable products)*

- How can we increase awareness and availability of reusable products in the UK and globally?

For a lively extension to this activity and a fun mnemonic for the different types of products, try doing the menstrual product mambo, designed by Chella Quint at #periodpositive.[25] A dance card that teaches the steps can be or printed or displayed.[26]

Menstruation education top tips

- Teaching about menstruation should not be a one-off event at the end of primary school. Make sure you include activities about attitudes to menstruation (including taboo, stigma and consequences like fear of discussing medical issues and period poverty), the biology of menstruation, media literacy around corporate messages about menstruation and how to choose and use different menstrual products, throughout your RSE curriculum with young people of all ages.
- It's not just girls who need menstruation education. Make sure you are inclusive of boys and non-binary young people and teach young people together about the physical, social and personal aspects of menstruation.
- Always talk about 'menstrual products' and not 'sanitary products'. Menstruation is not unsanitary. Try to use the words 'menstruation' and 'menstrual' rather than euphemisms.
- Work with participants and consider signing up to the #periodpositive charter to examine the policies and facilities at your school/youth club/community centre to assess the extent to which they support/hinder period stigma. For example, are visits to the toilet allowed at all times? Do toilets have hot water, soap, private cubicles? Are emergency menstrual products of different types freely available? How is this information shared? Do pupils know whom they can ask if they have questions about menstruation?

For more information, tips and activity ideas follow @chellaquint on Twitter and go to #periodpositive.[27]

STAINS™: leak chic

These activity ideas were originally developed by Chella Quint of #periodpositive who coined the phrase and developed the idea of period positivity. Shared with permission.

 A series of creative activities that aim to empower young people to challenge menstrual stigma, improve their media literacy and promote period positivity. Creating space to discuss the fear and taboos around period leaks is an important part of good quality menstruation education. 45 minutes to an hour

 Images of adverts and period leaks, STAINS™ templates and art materials. 12+

Vintage and modern day menstrual product advertising

Show participants images of vintage and modern day menstrual product adverts, followed by a series of images of menstrual blood in the media.

Vintage images which can be found by entering these search phrases in the Duke University Ad Access Archive (https://repository.duke.edu/dc/adaccess):

1. Modess: 'Women! End Accident-Panic!'
2. Modess: 'Wrapped, it looks like a box of note paper...or bath salts...or candy...or facial tissues.'
3. Kotex: 'A Great Hygienic Handicap that Your Daughter will be Spared'

Examples of modern menstrual product adverts include:

1. Tampax: '100% leak free periods are possible'.
2. Tampax: 'Made to go unnoticed' or Always Infinity: 'Magician'.
3. Kotex: 'For the ultimate care down there'.

First show the vintage ads. Ask participants to look at them in pairs or small groups, discuss what techniques the companies use to sell their product, and have them write down or circle language and images the adverts use to make consumers worry about period stains and blood leaks.

Do the same for the modern adverts. Ask the group to draw comparisons between vintage advert 1 and modern advert 1, vintage and modern advert 2 and vintage and modern advert 3, respectively.

Ask the group the following investigative questions:

- Have the techniques changed?
- Are the messages the same?
- Why do you think product advertising hasn't evolved over time?
- What impact could this have on attitudes towards menstruation today?

Beauty in blood

Explore how else the media has represented menstruation using the following images.

Suggested images or articles:

- Photo of marathon runner Kiran Ghandi who ran the London marathon without using a menstrual product in 2015. Photos available online via various UK news platforms.
- Photo or video of Fu Yuanhui who explained her poor performance in an Olympics swimming event was down to her period.
- Rupi Kaur's photo story of her menstrual cycle[28] and an article about one photo being banned by Instagram.
- Abstract images from Jen Lewis's work *Beauty in Blood*.[29]

Ask participants to write down the first three words that come into their heads when they see each image.

Ask participants to share some of their words if they feel comfortable and use these, and the following questions, to discuss the possible shame and stigma around menstrual blood and fear of period leaks. Then lead a discussion using the following questions:

- Where else do we see blood in the media? Does this have the same association?
- Most menstrual product adverts use blue liquid instead of blood – why do you think this is? Why do you think activists want this to change?
- Many people consider Jen Lewis's images beautiful. Does knowing that they are images of menstrual blood change how you feel about the images?
- Would you display her art if you ran a gallery?
- Do you think Instagram should have deleted Rupi Kaur's image?

STAINS ™

Task participants with creating a new advertising campaign that turns the period stain into a fashion item. To do this visit www.stainstm.com (or print materials in advance), look at the fashion emblem and read out the 'sales pitch' for STAINS™ – a spoof fashion line that uses a trademarked image of a menstrual leak to help young people 'debunk, demystify and disempower leakage fear by turning the stain into an object of desire'. If you have internet access or can download the video to watch offline, share the STAINS™ at BLOOD video for a performance of the sales pitch.[30]

Trace the STAINS™ pattern and follow the brand identity guidelines to make a print or live action advert for STAINS™ including #periodpositive slogans that reverse and reclaim the advertising message about leaking. Groups should then present or perform their adverts for each other.

You could also show how some companies are capitalising on the #periodpositive movement to sell products by making their advertising campaigns seem like activism:

- Bodyform: Periods are normal, showing them should be too.
- Libresse: Viva la Vulva – using humour.

Ask the group to think about why it might it be seen as problematic for brands to capitalise on the #periodpositive movement in this way.

Finally, let participants know that in several studies[31], young people have reported period leaks as their biggest fear around menstruation. Discuss how this activity could help other young people. Also discuss with the group whether their feelings about period leaks have changed, and whether they will look at menstrual product adverts differently from now on. As a whole group, come up with three recommendations for companies to improve advertising messages in the future. Share the adverts and recommendations online with permission using the hashtags #stainstm and #periodpositive.

Essential products?

 This activity uses object-based learning to enable participants to think critically about products that are marketed as necessary or essential for our bodies.

 20–30 minutes

 A range of products from the following: disposable menstrual pads (scented and unscented), tampons, menstrual cups and reusable pads, deodorants, antiperspirants, body sprays, intimate wipes (for vulvas or anuses) or intimate washes, soaps, razors, whitening cream, fake tan, makeup products, hair dye, comb, toothbrush, hair straighteners, protein shakes, Pilates balls, false eyelashes, eyebrow brush and pencil set, plasters.

 11+

Note: You can use advertising materials instead of the products themselves.

In small or large groups set out a range of products and give participants time to look at them and consider:

- What is this used for?
- Who might use it?
- Who is this product advertised to?
- What do you think and feel about this product?

Ask the group to sort the products three times as follows:

1. Products we need to take care of ourselves and our bodies (and those that we don't).
2. Products we choose to use to feel good about ourselves and our bodies (and those that we don't).
3. Products that we feel we need to fit in and avoid judgement (and those that we don't).

After each product sort, pause and ask:

- Which products have you placed in each pile? How and why did you decide to organise the products in this way?
- Which groups in society are these products aimed at? Why might this be?
- What do each of these products tell us about how we should look and feel about our bodies?
- Does our own age, ethnic background and gender identity shape how we feel about these products and how valuable/important we think they are?

Finally ask participants to agree which of these products are *necessary* and which are *optional.* It is important that the grounds for decision making are made explicit. It is likely that participants will have different views on what products are essential for them. Steer the conversation away from stigmatising individual beauty/consumer choices to explore the ways in which beauty norms are constructed and circulated by companies and media outlets with a vested interest in the sales of these products.

To finish ask participants to discuss the following statement: 'In a society that profits from your self doubt, liking yourself is a rebellious act' (Caroline Caldwell Twitter: @DIRT_WORSHIP).

Section 4: Moving-feeling bodies

Moving with our feelings

Based on an activity created through the EveryBody Matters project by dance teacher and choreographer Jên Angharad; visual artist and film-maker Heloise Godfrey-Talbot; sound artist Rowan Talbot and Professor at Cardiff University Emma Renold. Used with permission.

 Many young people find it hard to name and express the feelings they experience as they have to manage gendered social pressures to look or act in a certain way. This activity invites participants to practise and experience using their bodies to express different emotions and to notice how emotions feel in the body.

 15–20 minutes

 None.

 11+

Ask participants to move around the room (you will need lots of space). Call out instructions to participants such as walk, bend, stretch. After each instruction pause and ask participants to call out one word to describe how the movement feels in their body.

Next ask participants to move around the room with different feelings such as joy, sadness and anger. You can start naming the emotions and then ask participants to join in. After all emotions have been explored pause to reflect how different feelings travel through the body, into our arms, faces and backs. Consider:

- What do we notice about the way that we move and feel when we are expressing different emotions?
- Has anyone noticed any of these sensations in their bodies in their day to day lives?

Body language game

This activity is also taken from the EveryBody Matters project (see 'Moving with our feelings activity on p. 192).

 This activity uses movement to encourage participants to read each other's bodies and emotions and respond with their own.

 5–10 minutes

 None.

 11+

Ask participants to stand in a circle. In silence one person strikes a pose in the middle of the circle. This can be a pose that reflects how they are feeling that day, or how they are feeling about a particular issue or event that has happened. Another person has to join them and without speaking has to respond to their stance with their own pose. For example, if the first person looked angry, the second may respond with more anger, or they may hide or be running away. Alternatively if the first person looks distressed, the second may respond by offering care and support, or by turning away if they find it too difficult. The key is for participants to read and interpret each other's body language and think about how to use their bodies to express different emotions.

Depending on the scenario you can ask more people to step in. If the activity is working well you can ask participants to start moving and responding to each other's movements. This becomes a form of dance that is also a conversation between different bodies.

If participants are struggling at the beginning prompt by giving them suggestions for feelings to express with their bodies and work with the group to unpick and interpret what a body might be saying and discuss ways of responding to this. Avoid doing this if you can as the activity works best in silence but participants may need a bit of help to get going.

Gendered bodies

 Using movement participants explore how bodies can be used to express gender roles and stereotypes. Participants are invited to notice how this feels and looks in others and to experiment with using and stretching their bodies in less restrictive and explicitly gendered ways.

 10–15 minutes

 None.

 11+

Ask participants to move around the room. They have to freeze when you call out a gendered role: perfect man, perfect woman. After each freeze, ask half the group to unfreeze and walk around to observe the stances adopted by others, then swap over so that everybody gets a chance to see each other's poses. Participants may want to call out their own gendered roles for the group to embody.

Next ask the group to move around the room and then act out your instruction: 'run like a boy' and then 'run like a girl'. Again allow the group to observe each other moving in role.

Ask the group to move around the room a final time and call out non-gendered roles for the group to embody and observe: 'perfect person', 'leader', 'carer', 'lover'. Follow this with a series of movements – 'giant leap', 'high jump', 'huge hug', 'reaching up', 'standing still', 'free wheeling', 'big stretch'.

Discuss as a group:

- What did we notice about the way our bodies responded and embodied the gendered roles?
- What did we observe in each other's bodies?
- What did we notice about how our bodies felt when we weren't instructed to express a gender? What did we observe in others?
- What did we learn about what our bodies can do?

Guess what I'm feeling

This activity is also taken from the *EveryBody Matters* project (see 'Moving with our feelings activity on p. 192).

 Working in pairs, participants practice using their bodies to express their own feelings and to model the feelings of their partner. Participants are able to see their own feelings reflected back at them in their partner's pose. The activity helps participants to notice what they and others are feeling and consider how they express their own emotions and read the emotions and bodies of others.

 15–20 minutes

 None.

 11+

Ask participants to work in pairs. One person has to express a feeling without using any words and their partner has to guess what the feeling is. Encourage participants to express how they are feeling right now, or in relation to an issue you have been discussing. Partners should swap roles before coming back as a whole group and sharing examples that were easy/difficult to decipher. Ask participants: What was this exercise like? Was it difficult? Did you guess right?

Flip the activity round so that one partner (Partner A) has to tell the other partner (Partner B) how they are feeling (e.g. I am feeling unsure or awkward). Partner B then shows Partner A what that feeling might look like through a movement or a pose, and then asks: 'Is this how you're feeling?' Partner A then directs Partner B to alter their movement to show more accurately how they are feeling. They then swap, so each gets a turn to 'feel how I feel'.

Reflect on the series of activities with the group:

- Have you ever had to work out how someone is feeling just by looking at them?
- Is it easier to work out how someone is feeling by looking at them (no words) or by texting them (words but no visual cues)?
- What makes it harder or easier to guess the feelings?
- Do you want others to know how you are feeling?

Wiring our bodies

This activity is also taken from the *EveryBody Matters* project (see 'Moving with our feelings activity on p. 192).

 Participants are invited to craft a wire body using pipe cleaners and other materials to express their own emotions and to interpret and explore the emotions of others. 30 minutes

 Different coloured pipe cleaners, a box (i.e. shoe box). Other materials such as buttons, pieces of cloth, paper and pens are optional. 11+

Give participants different coloured wire pipe cleaners and ask them to create a pipe cleaner body that expresses how they are feeling on that day. You can adapt this to focus on how the group is feeling in response to events in the world or at your place of work. You can use additional craft materials if available.

Ask participants to each carefully place their wire body in a box.

Pass the box round and ask each participant to select a wire body. Working in small groups or one large group, ask participants to try out the pose and imagine the emotion that their wire body is expressing. As a group explore ways of capturing the poses to create a visual display that can be shared with others, alongside the wire dolls as a record of the group's emotional responses to a given event, or issue being discussed. For example, participants can draw round each other's poses on large sheets of paper and paint or colour these or they can take anonymous silhouette photos. Think about how and where to share these images online or display them in your place of work.

As they are doing this activity participants will need to be careful with the pipe cleaner bodies as they are fragile and break easily. Taking care of this fragile body form and the emotion it conveys is part of the activity and can be used to spark conversations about how we take care of ourselves, our bodies and of others.

Notes

1 Girlguiding (2017) Girls Attitude survey www.girlguiding.org.uk/globalassets/docs-and-resources/research-and-campaigns/girls-attitudes-survey-2017.pdf

2 www.youtube.com/watch?v=SiOE7DsCJIM

3 www.brook.org.uk/our-work/pleasure

4 www.rfsu.se/globalassets/pdf/pussypedia.pdf

5 www.rfsu.se/globalassets/pdf/dicktionary.pdf

6 www.scarleteen.com/resource/advice/betty_dodsons_vulva_illustrations and www.youtube.com/watch?v=YhoSUoZ_uJ0&t=1s

7 Available to purchase as part of their *Sexuality and aGender Toolkit*, version two. Available at: www.theproudtrust.org/shop/general-shop/educational-resources-secondary/sexuality-agender-v2/

8 https://jamiemccartney.com/genital-art/

9 www.rfsu.se/globalassets/pdf/pussypedia.pdf

10 www.rfsu.se/globalassets/pdf/dicktionary.pdf

11 www.tes.com/teaching-resource/sex-and-history-version-2-sre-pshe-key-stage-4-and-5-11162331

12 www.scarleteen.com/article/bodies/my_corona_the_anatomy_formerly_known_as_the_hymen_the_myths_that_surround_it

13 www.rfsu.se/globalassets/pdf/vaginal-corona-english.pdf

14 www.thingiverse.com/thing:1876288; www.ufunk.net/en/tech/imprimer-un-clitoris-en-3d/; and http://amystenzel.wixsite.com/vulvacademy/printable-3d-files

15 www.jurology.com/article/S0022-5347(01)68572-0/abstract

16 www.youtube.com/watch?v=k3E2pBC1R2A

17 www.psychologytoday.com/gb/blog/stress-and-sex/201506/linguistic-sexual-revolution-naming-the-clitoris

18 www.rfsu.se/globalassets/pdf/a-clitoral-guide.pdf

19 https://vimeo.com/195012798

20 www.who.int/news-room/fact-sheets/detail/female-genital-mutilation

21 www.3bscientific.co.uk/genital-and-pelvis-models,pg_31.html

22 www.bodysense.org.uk/wendygenitalia.shtml

23 www.nhs.uk/video/Pages/Menstrualcycleanimation.aspx

24 https://beautifulcervix.com/

25 www.periodpositive.com/

26 https://periodpositive.files.wordpress.com/2016/02/menstrual-product-mambo1.jpg?w=1680

27 www.periodpositive.com/

28 https://rupikaur.com/period/

29 www.beautyinblood.com/

30 www.youtube.com/watch?v=mtVkBWWqbxk

31 Quint, Chella, (2019) 'From embodied shame to reclaiming the stain: reflections on a career in menstrual activism' The Sociological Review, 67(4), pp. 927–942. https://journals.sagepub.com/doi/10.1177/0038026119854275

CHAPTER 6
Sex

Introduction

Historically sex education has focussed on the negative aspects of sex such as unwanted pregnancy, sexually transmitted infections and sexual violence. These are important concerns to cover in RSE, but the negative focus means that educators often neglect important issues such as intimacy, sensuality, pleasure and consent and the potential positive impact that safe, enjoyable sexual experiences can have on our relationships and wellbeing.

Similarly consent education is often delivered to young people using a legal framework that focuses on how consent and rape are defined and understood in UK law. Whilst it is important that young people understand the law and their legal rights and responsibilities within this framework, such an approach can be limited in helping young people to navigate complex real life situations and make informed ethical decisions about sex. This chapter aims to redress the balance and provide the lesson ideas needed to educate young people on these important topics and provide honest, realistic and balanced education.

Chapter summary

Section 1: Sex and sexuality - starting the conversation. Activities to open up conversations about sexual behaviours, attitudes and values. These activities also help to clarify key meanings and definitions and expand understandings of what 'counts' as sex and sexuality.

Section 2: Sexual norms and expectations. Activities to help identify and explore sexual norms and expectations, whilst also problematising the process of labeling types of sex and relationships as 'normal' or 'not normal'. There are activities here on first sex, pornography, sex and social change.

Section 3: Masturbation. Safe and interactive ways of exploring this important topic that remains taboo in many communities and often gets left out of RSE programmes.

Section 4: Pleasure and sensuality. A set of creative and interactive activities on pleasure, sensuality, safe touch and establishing your boundaries. Don't miss out this often ignored but much requested area of learning!

Section 5: Sexual ethics and consent. Some of the best activities we know of for exploring the vital topic of sexual consent, sexual communication and ethical decision making.

Points to consider

- There are many different ways that one or more people can have sex. Naming and talking about these different sexual practices can help give young people a language for talking about what they do and do not enjoy or want to explore. These discussions also help break down the myth that the only sex that counts as real sex is penis-in-vagina sex, when in fact there are many ways that people can come together to enjoy intimacy, touch and pleasure.

- Supporting young people to understand how their body works and what feels good physically, mentally and emotionally can help them to negotiate safe and enjoyable sexual experiences. This is a vital part of ensuring that young people can recognise and draw their own boundaries.

- When talking about different sexual practices keep it factual. It's not your job to give sex tips about how to have good sex or discuss your own sexual preferences but it is your job to give accurate information about sex and to be open and honest about what you do and don't know. It is also useful to explain slang terms for different sexual practices such as 'giving head', 'going down'. Even if you think everyone knows what they mean, there will likely be someone who isn't sure or who is grateful for having you clarify things. If you don't know what a word that a young person uses means, just ask.

- In the UK the legal age of sexual consent is 16 for all young people. Children under the age of 13 are not deemed to have capacity to consent under any circumstances. Young people aged 13–15 can be viewed as competent to consent in circumstances where they are close in age and there are no obvious power imbalances.

- The average age that people in the UK first have intercourse is 16. Between a quarter and a third of young people have sex under 16, but the majority do not. You will find that most young people think the opposite and believe that the majority of young people are having sex under 16. This is a useful myth to bust and it's worth exploring why young people are so convinced that all their peers are having sex.

- Unequal gender norms can make it more difficult for young people to negotiate sex, consent and pleasure. There is often an expectation that young men always want and enjoy sex (with women) and that girls aren't as interested in sex and hold the responsibility for saying no (to men). Good RSE needs to unpick and challenge these norms and offer more equitable and diverse accounts of sex and pleasure.

- The topic of consent is often approached as a simplistic matter of yes or no, sex or rape, often using legal frameworks to shape how we teach about this difficult topic. However, this rarely matches young people's sex and relationship experiences. Love, desire, trust, loyalty, social norms and expectations all influence how we 'do' consent. When we teach about consent only using legal frameworks we can end up reinforcing a black and white model by suggesting that there is a clear distinction between consensual sex and rape. Research suggests that sometimes this can inadvertently prevent young people from recognising lower levels of sexual violence and coercion. The activities in this chapter offer an alternative approach to consent education that takes account of the 'grey areas' of consent.

Section 1: Sex and sexuality - starting the conversation

Sexuality collage

 This is an interactive activity in which participants sort and respond to a range of objects and images working individually or in small groups. This activity consists of two tasks that can be facilitated together or as standalone tasks. Both work well as an introduction to the concept of sexuality as they allow participants to set the tone and pace of the conversation and explore aspects of sexuality that they are interested in.  15 minutes per task

 Large roll of paper, pens. Copy of the WHO definition of sexuality. Range of objects and images relating to sexuality (see examples in the following). 11+

To set up the activity, place a large sheet of paper on the floor and write 'Sexuality' in the middle in large letters. Below this paste or write the following definition of sexuality from the World Health Organization:

Sexuality is a central aspect of being human throughout life and encompasses sex, gender identities and roles, sexual orientation, eroticism, pleasure, intimacy and reproduction. Sexuality is experienced and expressed in thoughts, fantasies, desires, beliefs, attitudes, values, behaviours, practices, roles and relationships. While sexuality can include all of these dimensions, not all of them are always experienced or expressed. Sexuality is influenced by the interaction of biological, psychological, social, economic, political, cultural, legal, historical, religious and spiritual factors.

(World Health Organization 2006)[1]

Place a pile of objects/images relating to sexuality next to the paper. Choose a range of objects or images that relate to the different aspects of sexuality captured in the WHO definition. For example:

- **Social, political and legal:** Law books; a prison door; rainbow flag; passport or identity card; HIV red ribbon; wedding veil; choora (wedding bangles); religious texts or quotations.
- **Sensuality and pleasure:** Massage oil; candle; chocolate; CD; dancing figures; trainers; yoga mat; sunshine; lubricant; massage tool (e.g. head massager/wooden massager); a mobile phone; a computer screen; infographics from NATSAL-3 (available online – cut up and isolate key charts[2]).
- **Emotions:** Range of emojis or faces expressing different emotions – joy, sadness, guilt, anger, longing.
- **Sexual health:** Reproductive organs model; contraception (condom, coil, pill packet, etc.); baby/doll.
- **Gender norms:** Pink and blue baby clothing; images from advertising aimed at men/women.
- **Sexual behaviour:** Infographics from NATSAL-3 (available online – cut up and isolate key charts).

If you are not able to source any of these items, or similar objects, you can access a set of images and case studies to use instead at www.agendaonline.co.uk

To facilitate the activity start by introducing the topic of sexuality and reading the definition. Ask participants to highlight or underline any key words and explain any unknown terms.

Task one: Ask participants to work in small groups. Each group should take a selection of the objects. Their task is to group the objects into three or more categories. Do not give them the category headings. They will need to decide this for themselves. This may feel strange at first as participants are used to being given the categories but you will find that it quickly generates open discussion about a wide range of issues and allows participants to set the pace and tone of the discussion. Participants may want to refer to the title and definition in the centre of the paper but they do not need to. After five minutes ask groups to share their categories with the whole group. Repeat the exercise two more times with the rule that they are not allowed to use any of the categories already used.

Task two: Ask participants to sit around the edge of the paper and work individually. They should browse the selection of objects and images and choose one that they think says something important about sexuality. Their task is to place the object on the paper and write around it how it relates to sexuality and why this is important. If possible, stick the object to the collage. If it cannot be glued ask participants to draw or represent the object in some way.

Once everyone has finished, give participants time to walk around and read each other's examples.

Finally, look at the pile of left over objects and images:

- Are there any that the group find challenging or do not think are related to sexuality?
- Are there any objects or images missing that need to be included in the collage?
- How does the collage challenge understandings about sexuality and what it means?
- Who needs to see this collage and where should it be displayed (if at all)?

What is 'sex'?

 A quick brainstorm that can be used to break down myths and assumptions about 'real' and 'gay' sex. 15 minutes

 Flipchart paper and pens. 14+

Working in small or large groups ask participants to brainstorm all the different ways that people can have sex. Remind the groups that knowing about sex and different sexual practices does not mean anything about the person who said it!

You may need to encourage participants to think broadly about all the different ways people have intimate and/or erotic experiences on their own and with others including kissing, hugging, different kinds of touch, mutual masturbation, sex using sex toys, etc. Prompt with questions such as: What about sex for older people? Young people? Sex for people with physical disabilities? Sex with someone of the same/different gender? Sex on your own?

The list may end up including some of the more extreme sexual practices that young people may have heard about. If the conversation is getting derailed into listing these, we suggest bringing it back to the kinds of sex it is common for many people to experience (avoid using loaded terms like 'normal').

Remind participants that this is not the creation of a 'to do' list, and try to avoid the passing of value judgements on the different kinds of sex. Instead remind participants that the key here is any sex act is entered into consensually and enthusiastically by all parties.

There are two key learning points from this brainstorm.

1. **To challenge the assumption that when someone refers to 'having sex' they mean penis-in-vagina sex.**
   Explore this common assumption using the following questions:

   ● Which of these sexual activities count as 'having sex'? (circle responses)
   ● Why do we categorise some sexual activities as 'real' sex and not others? Why does it matter? What assumptions lie behind these categories?

   Key assumptions include: that sex always takes place between a person with a penis and a person with a vagina; sex is always potentially reproductive; the most pleasurable way of having sex is penis-in-vagina sex (even though we know that for many women in particular this is not the case).

   Note: You can also explore which activities count as 'virginity loss' as a way of exploring virginity myths.

2. **To clarify that there is no such thing as 'gay sex' (despite many people's fascination with this question!)**
   A common question that comes up in RSE sessions is – what is gay sex? Or, how do two women/two men have sex? Use the following questions to explore this and make the point that this isn't a helpful way of looking at things:

   ● Which types of sex can ONLY be enjoyed by straight people? (circle responses)
   ● Which types of sex can ONLY be enjoyed by gay people? (circle in different colour)

   You will find that almost all of the sexual activities could be done by any couple or individual regardless of their sexual orientation or identity. There are some sexual activities that may require particular anatomy, e.g. penis-in-vagina sex, although if this is reframed as 'penetrative sex' then anyone can engage in this activity if they have a sex toy or a penis. Further, we need to be careful about making assumptions about someone's anatomy since a 'straight' couple could refer to a relationship between a cis woman and a trans man – neither of whom may have a penis.

   The key learning here is that it doesn't make sense to talk about 'gay sex' or 'straight sex' as there are many different ways that two bodies can come together to have sex. It may involve mutual masturbation, oral sex, penetrative sex (vaginal or anal), using sex toys and having orgasms together. These activities can be enjoyed (or not) by people of any sex, gender or sexuality.

Speed debating sex and sexuality

 A quick, fun starter activity to open up conversations about sex and sexuality. 10 minutes

 List of statements. 15+

Ask participants to get into two lines, each facing a partner. Identify the lines as row A and row B. Explain that you will read out a statement for participants to debate with the person opposite them for 45 seconds only. After 45 seconds you will shout 'stop' and all those in row A will move down one person and start the next debate with a new person.

Keep the activity moving quickly and intervene if a pair seems to be struggling to engage in debate. Use a selection of the following statements, pulling out those that best relate to themes that you want to cover in your session.

Statements:

- Good sex is when you are in love with the person you are having sex with.
- Everyone is bisexual really, it's just that some people don't admit it.
- Sex is like football – the more you practice, the better you get.
- To be happy in life, you need to be having good sex.
- Everyone should be able to get free contraception – whatever their age.
- Ultimately, the point of having sex is to have babies.
- Only gay people have anal sex.
- The age of sexual consent in the UK should be higher than 16.
- The point of sex is to have fun and enjoy yourself.
- Everyone has a right to sexual pleasure – regardless of their age, gender or sexuality.
- Women who have sex with women have the best sex.
- Sex education should start in primary schools.
- Men should show an interest in contraception but ultimately it is women's responsibility.
- Pornography is a useful way of learning about sex.
- Only single people masturbate.
- Masturbation is good for your wellbeing.

After using five–ten statements (depending on the group energy and participation levels) draw the group together and use the following questions to guide a discussion. Be sure to pick up on and challenge any stereotypes or myths that emerge from the discussion (e.g. that only single people masturbate, that lesbians have the best sex or that only gay men have anal sex).

- Which statements did you and your partner instantly agree on?
- Which statements did you really disagree on?
- Which statements did you find difficult to discuss?
- Was there anything you wanted to find out more about?

Sexual stats quiz

 Create your own quiz using research data on sexual attitudes and behaviours. Use this to inform participants, bust some myths and start conversations. 20–30 minutes

 Paper, pens, a prize for the winning team. 13+

Create your own quiz from research into sexual behaviours using data from the available data sets such as The *National Survey of Sexual Attitudes and Lifestyles* (NATSAL). This is a large British representative survey of sexual attitudes and behaviours. It is conducted every ten years so allows us to see how attitudes and behaviours have changed over time. The last survey was NATSAL-3 and this time the team produced handy infographics that summarise some of the key findings. They are free to download and are a great resource for RSE.[3] There may be other data sets released over time that give you more up to date data.

If you have time, divide participants into small groups or teams and task each one with using the NATSAL data to create their own quiz to challenge other teams or to use as part of a peer education programme. Alternatively we have provided some example starter questions taken from NATSAL-3 which you can use to facilitate a quick quiz to your group. If you have time it is a good idea to create a PowerPoint with the questions and answers included so that you can share some of the infographics and details from the research. Follow the quiz with a discussion using the following questions:

- Were you surprised by any of the questions and answers?
- How do you think these answers will change over the next 10, 20 and 30 years?

Example quiz questions

1. On average how many times per month do you think people in Britain have sex?
   Answer: Three
2. Over the past two decades has there been an increase or decrease in how often people say they have sex? (Bonus points for average 20 years ago and average 10 years ago!)
   Answer: Decrease. 20 years ago the average was five times every four weeks, ten years ago it was four times every four weeks (once a week) and now the average is three.
3. On average, how many opposite sex partners have a) women and b) men aged 16–44 had in their lifetime?
   Answer: a) 8 b) 12 (rounded up to the nearest whole number)
4. What percentage of a) women and b) men had ever had a same sex experience with genital contact?
   Answer: (a) 8% (b) 5%. This has increased over the past 30 years for men and women.
5. What percentage of 16–24-year-olds said they had anal sex in the last year?
   Answer: 18% (19% of men and 17% of women). This proportion was higher for 16–24-year-olds than for any other age group.
6. What percentage of the British population has had heterosexual sex under 16?
   Answer: Nearly a third (30.9%) of men and a quarter (29.2%) of women aged 16–24 reported heterosexual intercourse before age 16. Bear in mind that in NATSAL, 'intercourse' is defined as vaginal, anal or oral sex.
7. True or false? More people today think that it is ok to have extra marital relationships than they did in the past.
   Answer: False. Today 69.8% of women and 62.5% of men think that non-exclusivity in marriage is 'always wrong', compared to 53.2% and 44.7% 30 years ago.

Types of sex – know, think, feel

 An interactive activity that helps you to gather information about what participants know, think and feel about different sexual practices. This can be used to challenge myths and misinformation about sex and discuss social taboos or particular sexual practices. It can also help you to work with participants to shape your RSE programme. It is a good idea to first facilitate the 'What is 'sex'?' activity on p. 199.   30–40 minutes

 Flipchart paper and pens. A5 pieces of paper for handouts (see the following) – five per participant.   13+

Preparation: Update your own knowledge about different sexual practices. Brook, BISH and Scarleteen websites all have good information on the different types of sex (see *Useful resources* at the end of this book). NATSAL-3 infographics provide accessible research evidence on different sexual behaviours. It is always ok to refer to these sources whilst facilitating a session.

To set up the activity place five boxes in different areas of the room. Label each with a different type of sex: Anal sex, Oral sex, Penis-in-vagina sex, Solo sex (masturbation), Mutual masturbation.

Hand out five pieces of A5 paper to each participant. Ask them to fold each piece of paper in half to create two columns and to label each column as 'KNOW' (facts I know about this type of sex) and 'THINK/FEEL' (what I think and feel about this type of sex). To save time you can create handouts with pre-labelled columns.

To facilitate the activity ask participants to move silently around the five boxes. They should individually complete an answer sheet for each type of sex noting down what they know about this type of sex (facts, figures, etc.) and what they think and feel about it. Once this has been completed the educator will open the boxes and read out the responses.

Remind the group that the answers are anonymous.

The educator should open the first box and start by reading out what participants KNOW about that type of sex. Make sure you correct any myths or misunderstandings and challenge any prejudice. If you are unsure of anything write a question on the board for you or the class to research and come back to later. If possible, research the answer together using a good online resource such as brook. org.uk, bishuk.com or scarleteen.com. This helps you to model to the group that it is ok not to know everything about sex and how to find out information from reliable sources.

Next explore what participants think and feel about that type of sex. Read out the thoughts and feelings without judgement, acknowledging discomfort, awkwardness and prejudice and using the following discussion questions to explore this further.

As you move through the different boxes you will be able to compare levels of knowledge and thoughts and feelings about different sexual practices.

- Which of the sexual practices do we know more about as a group? Why might this be?
- What are some of the differences in what we think and feel about different sexual practices?
- What shapes our thoughts and feelings about sex and different sexual practices? Where do we get our ideas about what is good, bad, normal, disgusting, etc.?
- Would our responses have been different if we had written them publicly on flipchart paper rather than privately and anonymously?
- Why is penis-in-vagina sex often considered to be 'good' and 'normal' whereas other types of sex are considered shameful, disgusting or taboo?
- As a group what do we need to learn more about in RSE?

Section 2: Sexual norms and expectations

What's my normal?

This activity is created by The Proud Trust and published in *Sexuality aGender v2: An Inclusive Sexual Health Toolkit* (see *Useful resources* at the end of this book). Used with permission.

An individual activity in which participants identify activities that are 'normal' for them. These are shared in small groups to stimulate discussion about what we mean by the term 'normal' and how it can be used in problematic and judgemental ways.
 20 minutes

A4 paper and pens or star worksheets, questions for educator.
 11+

Ask each participant to draw a five-point star on an A4 sheet of paper (or to save time hand out worksheets with a star printed on and the title: 'What's my normal?'). Explain the task which is for participants to write on each point of the star an activity or thing that they do that is normal for them. For example, doing a hobby or exercise a few times a week; eating a particular snack food combination; praying before eating dinner; having to watch TV to fall asleep.

In pairs or small groups ask participants to share some of the things they have written on their star and then feedback as a whole group. Facilitate a whole group discussion using the following questions:

* Is everybody's normal the same?
* If not how do we decide who is more 'normal'?
* Do we judge people in this way?
* How would it make a person feel if something they enjoyed doing was described as 'not normal' by others?
* Can we really say anything is 'normal or not normal'?
* Are there more positive words that could be used instead of 'normal' or 'not normal' when considering our own and other people's likes, thoughts and behaviours? Suggestions could include 'common' and 'uncommon' and 'usual' and 'unusual'.

For older age groups, follow this with the 'Is it safe? Is it normal?' activity that follows.

Is it safe? Is it normal?

This activity is created by The Proud Trust and published in *Sexuality aGender v2: An Inclusive Sexual Health Toolkit* (see *Useful resources* at the end of this book). Used with permission.

A discussion-based activity that explores what is 'normal' and what is 'safe' when considering a range of activities relating to sex. We recommend that you first facilitate the previous activity, 'What's my normal?', to help problematise the process of labeling activities as 'normal/not normal'.
 35 minutes

Scenario cards, safe/normal quadrant sheets or one large quadrant (can be created using four large cards containing the words 'normal', 'safe', 'not normal' and 'harmful' and two pieces of rope).
 14+

Divide participants into pairs or small groups and hand each a copy of the safe/normal quadrant sheet. Alternatively you can draw a big quadrant in the centre of the room and run this as a whole group activity. Explain to the group that the words 'normal' and 'not normal' have been used in this exercise (despite the reservations raised through the prior activity) as they are words that a lot of people use and are familiar with.

Pass round a box or bag containing different scenarios, each printed on a piece of paper or card. Allow participants to randomly select and read out to their group or pair the scenario to be discussed. After each has been read ask participants to plot where they think the scenario sits on the safe/normal quadrant, i.e. is it:

- Normal and safe; or
- Safe but not normal; or
- Normal yet harmful; or
- Not normal and harmful?

Allow time for discussion before feeding back as a whole group. Use the supplementary questions in Table 6.1 to help you facilitate discussion of the scenarios. Pick and choose the most useful questions for your group, depending on the nature and direction of the discussion. Remember that there is not necessarily a right or wrong answer. Your role is to help participants explore why they think an activity or situation is 'normal', 'not normal', 'harmful' or 'safe'.

To conclude, ask participants to reflect on the activity using the following questions:

- What did you learn from doing this activity?
- What did you enjoy about this activity?

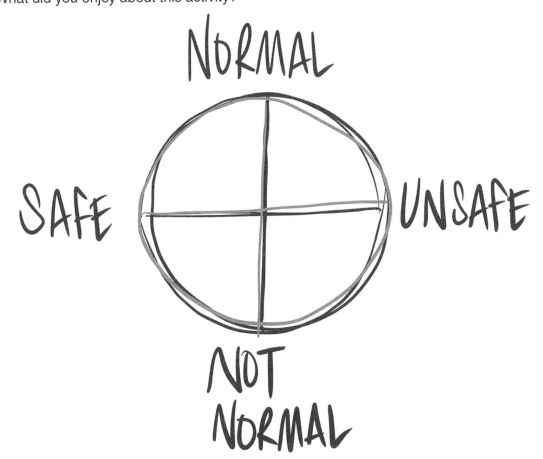

TABLE 6.1 Is it safe? Is it normal? Scenarios and supplementary questions for educators

Scenarios (to be printed on card and given to participants)	Supplementary questions for educators only
Making a list with your partner of the things that you like to do sexually.	• Would this be useful? Why? • How easy is it to communicate verbally about sex and what you like or dislike? • How might you go about making such a list?
Having sex if you don't feel like it, your partner asks you to.	• How would you signal to someone that you don't want to have sex with them? • How might you feel to hear or know that your partner does not want to have sex with you? • How would your body respond in this situation where you don't really want to have sex? • If someone agrees to have sex with you just so that you stop asking is this consensual sex? (Answer = no!)
Having no desire to have sex.	• Is this usual? (note that you don't have to desire sex all the time) • What term do people use to describe this feeling? (some people might describe themselves as not being in the mood whereas other people may be asexual) • Would you feel able to talk to a partner about this feeling?
Watching pornography.	• Why do people watch pornography? • Does porn reflect real life sexual activity or relationships? • What stereotypes might be created or reinforced in pornography? • Is pornography a good place to learn about sex? • Is anybody involved in porn exploited? In what way?
Having a sexual relationship with somebody five years older than you.	• Does it matter how old the younger/older partner is? • Why might someone want a partner that is significantly older or younger than them? • Are there any moral or legal aspects that need to be considered? For more information on legal issues go to: www.bishuk.com/sex/sex-and-the-law/
Not using protection when having sex, such as a latex glove, a condom, or the pill.	• What does using 'protection' mean and why do people use it? • How many methods of protection can you name? • Should you always use protection during sexual activities? • How easy is it to talk to a partner about using protection?

Scenarios (to be printed on card and given to participants)	Supplementary questions for educators only
Receiving a gift from somebody in exchange for sex.	• Are gifts in a relationship a positive thing? Always? • Is there an expectation of sex when a gift of money is accepted? • What about if someone pays for you during a date?
Having a sexual dream about: - someone who is a different gender to you. - someone who is the same gender as you - a mythical creature - someone who is not your partner.	• What does it mean if you have this type of dream? • How reflective are dreams of our actual thoughts and desires? • What might you do if this was a reoccurring dream?
Having sex if someone involved is on their period.	• What is a period? Who has them? How often? (Remember that anyone with a uterus can have a period which includes trans men, non-binary people and cis women.) • Whose decision is it whether to have sex when someone is having a period? • If you do have sex during a period what might you need to consider?
Feeling pain whilst having sex.	• Why might sex be painful? • What should you do if sex is painful? • Do you think some people might want to experience pain during sex? • Is there anything wrong with enjoying experiencing pain? • What if you like pain from 'rough' sex but your partner prefers to be more gentle?
Having an orgasm or reaching your climax within a few minutes.	• Is this usual? (The average time it takes a man to orgasm from penetrative sex is on average three–five minutes. People can also orgasm quickly from other types of sex, including masturbation. Some people don't orgasm from some types of sex and some take much longer.) • Is this a problem? • Can sex still continue if this has happened? • Is the only reason to have sex to have an orgasm?

Scenarios (to be printed on card and given to participants)	Supplementary questions for educators only
Feeling like you need to be under the influence of drugs or alcohol to have sex.	• Why might someone feel as though they need drugs or alcohol to have sex? • How might alcohol or drugs impact on your ability to make decisions and communicate with others?
Sending a photo of your genitals to somebody.	• Why might someone like to send a photo of their genitals to someone? • Are there any risks to doing this? • What moral and legal aspects need to be considered? For more info on the legal aspects go to: www.nspcc.org.uk/preventing-abuse/keeping-children-safe/sexting
Having anal sex.	• Who can have anal sex? (Anyone can have anal sex, it doesn't matter what their sexual identity is. Anal sex is penetration of the anus with a penis, finger or sex toy so can be enjoyed by people of all genders and sexual identities.) • Is this activity pleasurable? • What might you need to consider if having or thinking about having anal sex? • Does anal sex hurt? (Unlike the penis and the vagina the anus doesn't naturally produce any lubrication so it is important to use artificial lube. If you are relaxed and turned on anal sex can be a pleasurable option for people of all genders and sexual orientations.)
Having more than one partner at a time.	• What's this type of relationship called? (Polyamorous) • Who might have this type of relationship? • Can this type of relationship be fair for everyone involved?
Kissing your partner in public.	• Can all people do this? • Are there any risks involved for people doing this?

Is it safe? Is it normal?: Worksheet for participants.

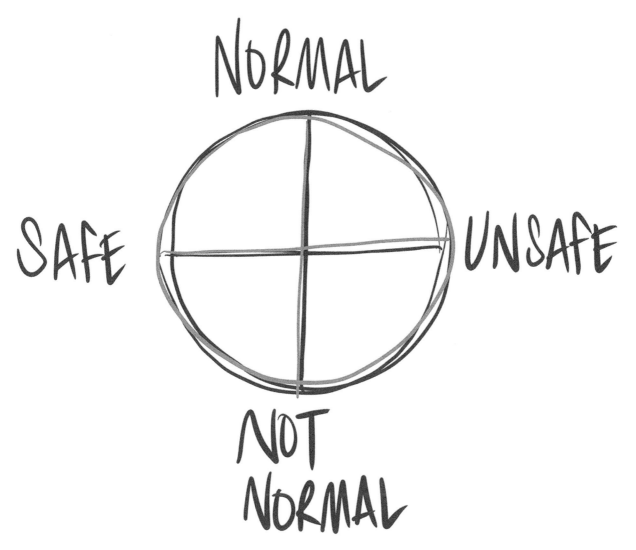

FIGURE 6.1 Safe/normal quadrant

Illustration by: Chrissy Baxter

'Normal' sex: unpacking our stereotypes

Based on an activity developed by Sharon Lamb and her research lab as part of the *Sexual Ethics for a Caring Society Curriculum* (SECS-C; see *Useful resources* at the end of this book). Used with permission.

 An individual activity that seeks to unpick gendered assumptions and stereotypes around sex. This can be used to think critically about what shapes our ideas about what is and is not normal and to problematise the idea of 'normal sex'. 20–30 minutes

 One Normal sex? worksheet per participant. 13+

Give each participant the following Normal Sex? worksheet and ask participants to complete it.

Once participants have completed their worksheet ask them to share and discuss their pie charts in pairs or small groups. Next try putting all of the pie charts together on one table and see what they look like all together or make one big pie chart at the front of the room on a board.

Consider:

- What are some of the similarities and differences?
- What can we learn about youth culture and young people's norms and expectations?
- Which sources are the most accurate? Which the least?

Finally as a group discuss the following questions. You may want to ask participants to write down their thoughts on their worksheets.

- Why do you think everyone is concerned about what is 'normal sex'?
- Why so much focus on 'normal sex' instead of what is 'good sex'?
- Is 'normal sex' also 'good sex'? Think of both meanings of the word good? (Pleasurable, and ethically good.)

Normal sex? A worksheet

Task one: Fill in the following worksheet with what you think is 'normal':

- How much a teen boy should think about sex.

- How much a teen girl should think about sex.

- Who has the most and least sex? (Does it differ by gender? By race? By age? By sexual orientation?)

- How often a person should masturbate. (Does it differ by gender? By race? By age? By sexual orientation?)

- What does 'good' sex looks like. Jot down all your images and thoughts.

- What does healthy experimentation look like. Jot down images and thoughts.

- When should someone lose their virginity? Do you have ideas about what's 'normal'?

- What to look for to know if someone is experiencing pleasure. Where do you get ideas about pleasure from?

- Who has the most pleasure in sex and why?

- Where do you think your ideas of sexual normality came from? Your parents? Your teachers/ relationship and sex education educators? The media? Your friends? Your siblings? Books?

- Draw a pie chart to show what influences your thinking about how much each person or source has influenced you.

Good sex, bad sex, depends

Based on an activity created by Malin Strenstrom and adapted for the *Good Sex Project*. A digital version of this activity can be viewed on the *Brook Learn* platform, Pleasure course, module 4.[4]

 A discussion-based activity that aims to create a safe space for critical discussion about sexual values and norms in relation to good sex and bad sex.

 45 minutes

 Four sets of three A4 cards with 'Good sex', 'Bad sex' and 'Depends on'. One set of prompt cards. These can be downloaded and printed from *Brook Learn* (see above and link in footnote).

 15+

Divide participants into four small groups. Give each group a set of three A4 cards/paper with 'Good sex', 'Bad sex' and 'Depends on' written on them. Ask each group to lay out the cards on the table or floor as a continuum. Also give each group one pack of small prompt cards (see the following) and ask them to place each card on the continuum depending on whether they think it is good sex, bad sex or depends. The group will need to try and come to a compromise/consensus through discussing their opinions with each other.

Before the activity starts remind the group of the ground rules and draw participants' attention to the fact that the aim of the activity is *not* to share personal experiences or to ask other people to share theirs. Instead the idea is to talk about what we think and believe and listen to the views of others. Encourage participants to listen without judgement and empathise with the views and experiences of others.

As an educator you may need to think about how you are going to respond to negative feelings that some participants may have ('that's wrong', 'that's dirty', 'that's disgusting', etc.). Try to keep a balance between letting participants express their thoughts and feelings and encouraging participants to be non-judgemental and to accept that we are all different in our preferences.

Prompt cards (These can be downloaded and printed from the *Brook Learn* platform)

KNOWLEDGE	TIMES AND PLACES
Knows where the sexual health service is	Sex in a nightclub
Knows the signs and symptoms of sexually transmitted infections (STIs)	Sex in a car
	Sex in the bedroom
Knows how pregnancy happens	Sex in pornography
Knows about own and partner's body parts	First time sex
Knows about HIV	Make up sex
Knows about types of contraception	Sex in a school toilet
Knows how to request and give consent	Sex in a park
Knows laws related to sexual violence	Sex on holiday
Knows about different sexual positions	Sex when drunk
Knows what turns them on and off	
TYPES OF SEX	**FEELINGS**
Anal sex	Affection
Vaginal sex	Guilt
Underage sex	Pleasure
Oral sex	Embarrassment
Group sex	Feeling pressured
Masturbation	Fear
Using sex toys	Feeling safe
BDSM sex (Bondage & Discipline Sadomasochism)	Physical pain or discomfort
	Love
Sex in a relationship	Regret
Casual sex ('one-night-stand')	Shame

When each group has finished go round and discuss each of the continuums. Discuss each of the continuums as a whole group using the following prompts. Remember – try not to give your own opinion about what is 'good' or 'bad' sex. Instead encourage participants to listen to and challenge each other.

- How did you decide where to put each card?
- Which of the cards did you disagree on as a group/find hard to place?
- Why did you put these cards in 'Depends'? What kinds of things does this depend on?
- If everyone involved is giving consent, and enjoying themselves, does it matter what type of sex they are having?
- Why are some types of sex by society seen as 'good' and others as 'bad'?
- Why might it be easier to have a good time in some locations compared to others?
- Is it ever ok to feel pain or discomfort during sex?
- Is there a difference between feeling fear and feeling nervous when it comes to sex?

It can be a good idea to leave Feelings until last. Here you can emphasise that love and affection are often important parts of good sex, but not always. For others good sex is quick, rough and anonymous. You can also explore the fact that some people enjoy feeling pain during sex, which is often referred to as kink or BDSM. As with all sexual practices what matters is that sex is consensual and that partners are able to listen and respect each other's wishes and desires.

Finally you may want to explore the fact that many people do feel embarrassed before, during or after sex. These feelings can be difficult and can get in the way of you having sex but don't mean that you can't enjoy an experience. Fear, however, definitely belongs in bad sex. It's common to feel nervous when having sex and trying something new but this is not the same as feeling fearful because you don't have choice and control over what happens to you and your body.

For other key learning points sign up to the *Brook Learn* platform and look at module three of the Pleasure course where you will find a digital version of this activity that can be used by young people and/or practitioners.[5]

The charmed circle

 This activity uses anthropologist Gayle Rubin's 1984 concept of the charmed circle to think critically about sexual values and social change. 30 minutes

 Paper or electronic image of Gayle Rubin's 1984 'charmed circle' which is available online or found within Rubin, G, (2012) 'Thinking sex: notes for a radical theory of politics of sexuality', in *Deviations*, pp. 137–181. Duke University Press. Copyright, 2012, Gayle Rubin. Paper and pens. 14+

Show participants an image of the charmed circle. Explain that this model was created by anthropologist and activist Gayle Rubin in the 1980s to show the ways in which different sexual behaviours are given value in society. In the inner 'charmed' circle Rubin put all the sexual behaviours and acts that society deems to be 'good' and 'natural'. In the outer circle she put all the sexual behaviours that are deemed 'bad' or 'unnatural'. This is not a model of Rubin's view about sexuality but her view of the hierarchical system of sexual values in 1980s western culture. Rubin was critical of this hierarchy and argued for greater acceptance and celebration of sexual diversity and variation.

The charmed circle:
Good, Normal, Natural, Blessed Sexuality

Heterosexual
Married
Monogamous
Procreative
Non-commerical
In pairs
In a relationship
Same generation
In private
No pomography
Bodies only
Vanilla

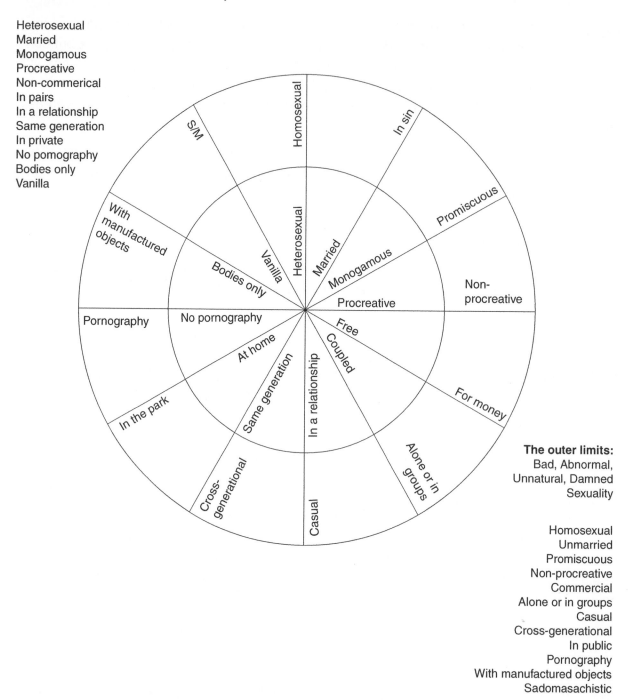

The outer limits:
Bad, Abnormal,
Unnatural, Damned
Sexuality

Homosexual
Unmarried
Promiscuous
Non-procreative
Commercial
Alone or in groups
Casual
Cross-generational
In public
Pornography
With manufactured objects
Sadomasachistic

FIGURE 6.2 The charmed circle

Credit: The charmed circle by Gayle Rubin (from Rubin, G, (2012) 'Thinking sex: notes for a radical theory of politics of sexuality', in *Deviations*, pp. 137–181. Duke University Press. Copyright, 2012, Gayle Rubin. All rights reserved. Republished by permission of the copyright holder and the publisher Duke University Press. www.dukeupress.edu

Divide participants into small groups and task each group with creating a new version of the 'charmed circle' that reflects social norms and sexual values in modern day western culture. Here are some questions to help:

- Are there any behaviours that are in the outer circle in the 1980s that you think are no longer taboo and should be placed in the inner circle today?
- Are there any new behaviours that you would add to the inner or outer circle based on what you think is viewed as 'normal' or acceptable today?
- How can you use your diagram to show what has changed in the past three decades and what has stayed the same?

Ask participants to share and discuss their models. As a group consider what changes participants would like to see over the next 40 years:

- What changes would you like to see to these models over the next 40 years?
- In an ideal world would there be a line between acceptable and unacceptable sexual behaviours? Why would this be necessary? (*e.g. to protect vulnerable people such as children; to prevent a public health crisis; for moral reasons*)
- What other ways can we think about sexuality that are not hierarchical and that celebrate sexual diversity and variation?

The chastity belt and the sexual double standard

This activity has been adapted from the *Sex and History Project* at the *University of Exeter*. We recommend that you download the free *Sex and History* resource from tes.com so that you can use the images, PowerPoint and videos that are designed to accompany this activity.[6]

 The activity uses a historical image of a chastity belt to open up conversations about gender, sexuality, power and control. By asking participants to guess what the unnamed object is they become intrigued and engaged in the discussion as it unfolds. This is a novel and engaging approach to an enduring and ever relevant social issue. 45 minutes

 Digital or paper image of the chastity belt, arts materials such as cardboard, paper, tape, plastic, etc. 14+

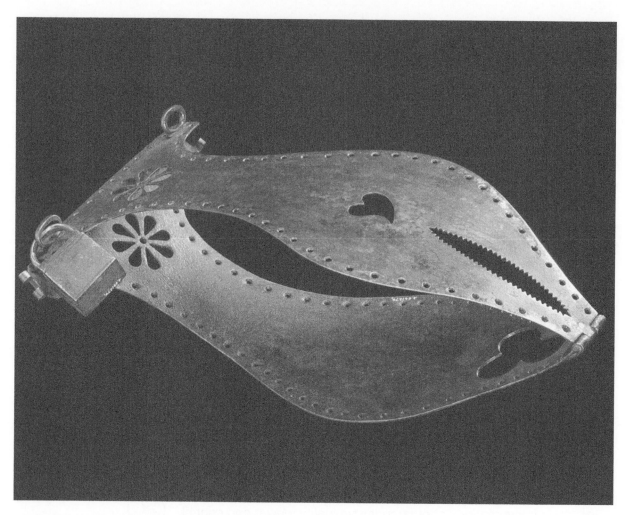

FIGURE 6.3 Iron chastity belt, Europe–1600
Credit: Science Museum, London. CC BY

Show participants an image of the object, without saying anything about it. Ask participants to work in pairs or small groups and discuss the following questions. You may want to give participants a copy of the image and ask them to annotate it with their thoughts.

- What is this?
- What was it used for?
- When might it have been made?
- How would it work?
- Who would wear it and why?

Next ask participants to feedback their thoughts and ideas to the group and then reveal the following historical information:

- This is a chastity belt. It is a metal gusset made of two panels hinged together, designed to be fitted to a waist strap to prevent sexual access to the genitals.
- The two openings allow the woman wearing it to urinate and defecate.
- It has been dated to the 15th or 16th centuries.
- Today we associate chastity belts with Medieval knights and the quest to ensure that their wives remained faithful while they were away at the crusades.

Use this information about the chastity belt to lead a discussion with the group about what it may have been like for women to wear a chastity belt. Where possible, ask each group to make a chastity belt using whatever arts materials you have available (cardboard, tape, paper, plastic). Ask participants to model wearing the belts and to think about how they might walk, sit, dance, etc. if it were made of metal. Discuss:

- Do you think people ever really wore this object?
- Would a woman be happy to wear this? If so, why?
- Why might someone want to control sexual access to a woman?
- Who would have held the key to the chastity belt? What difference does it make?
- Why does society place value on fidelity and virginity? Are these values different for men and women?

Following your discussion, inform the group that the chastity belt is almost certainly a fake that was never actually worn. Use this to have a final discussion about what sorts of 'myths' about sex, sexuality and gender still exist today. Other key questions to explore include:

- Why might someone craft a chastity belt, like this one, which could never actually be worn?
- Does the idea of the chastity belt seem very alien today? Or are there modern day parallels we can think of? (e.g. ways that female sexuality is controlled and/or the sexual double standard is maintained)
- How 'fake' are our images about sex/femininity today? What ideas or myths about sex and femininity do they give us?

Planet Porn

This activity is adapted from *Planet Porn* created by Justin Hancock and shared with permission. A comprehensive version of this activity that contains cards, images and complete instructions can be purchased from BISH Training.[7]

 Participants create a game called *Planet Porn* in which players have to distinguish between sexual and gender norms in pornography and real life sexual relationships. Alternatively you can purchase a pre-prepared version of the game from bishtraining.com and play with your participants.   One hour

 Blank cards for writing statements and discussion points on, Optional – reference copy of *Planet Porn* game.   14+

Explain to the group that they are going to be creating an educational game called *Planet Porn* which will be played by young people aged 14+. The game is a simple card sort in which players sort cards into two piles – Planet Porn and Planet Earth. Each card contains a statement about sex and players have to decide whether this statement describes Planet Earth or Planet Porn. The aim of the game is for young people to think critically about the difference between sex in pornography and sex in real life.

For this task participants need to create the cards for the game. Each card should contain a statement that describes Planet Porn or Planet Earth. For example:

- Where sex is very loud.
- Where people usually have pubic hair.
- Where sex ends when the man ejaculates.
- Where women always orgasm from penetrative sex.

Participants should also include discussion points and/or facts and further information on the back of the card. They can also type them up, add graphics, print and laminate them.

Participants can work together as one group, or do an initial brainstorm in pairs and then share ideas and decide which statements to include/exclude from the game. Encourage participants to create examples that are varied and reflect a variety of knowledge and assumptions about porn. Take time to challenge myths and stereotypes relating to what participants write on the cards.

Also encourage participants to use a wide range of critical sources to develop their statements. Emphasise that the statements that they write will not be judged as a reflection of their personal knowledge and experience of sex or porn. Here are some suggested resources for participants to use:

- *Porn Sex vs Real Sex: The Differences Explained With Food*. Created by *KB Creative Lab*. Available on YouTube.
- *Porn Vs. Reality*. Created by *The Mix*. Available on YouTube.
- Series of articles by *BISH on Porn* such as *An Educational Guide to Porn; What Women Look Like In Porn; What Men Look Like In Porn*. Available from bishuk.com/porn/.
- *Making Sense of Sexual Media* by Scarleteen. Available from scarleteen.com.

Once games have been developed, ask participants to play the game with each other to check that the statements and discussion points work. Encourage discussion throughout the activity and remind participants that the focus of the activity should not be on getting the right answer but on engaging in critical discussion. Alternatively play the game using the pre-prepared BISH Training version. Participants may enjoy seeing how their statements compare to those in the pre-prepared version.

If you have an established peer education programme at your place of work ask participants to try facilitating this activity with younger age groups (14+).

First sex and virginity cards

 A card sort exercise that generates open discussion in small groups about first sex and virginity loss. This is a good introductory activity that creates a safe space for participants to explore issues and questions that are important to them. 20 minutes

 Sets of cards containing images relating to first sex and virginity (see the following pages). One set per group of four–six participants. 14+

Divide participants into small groups. Give each group a set of cards and ask them to sort them into groups. They get to choose the categories and the number of groups. Initially, participants may find this challenging as they are more used to being given categories. Give them time and you will find that this exercise generates discussion about the issues in a way that lets participants set the tone and pace.

After five minutes, ask groups to feedback about the categories that they have chosen. Next ask them to repeat the exercise, creating new sets of categories. They are not allowed to use any of the categories already used.

Feedback and repeat for a third time. Finally ask participants to turn the cards over and read the quotes and stories on the back. Explain that these are quotes from research with young people in the UK. Having read the quotes and stories ask participants to sort the cards one final time.

Note: The first four quotes are taken from the verbatim theatre production SPILL which was written and performed by Propolis theatre and based on peer research with young people. The remaining quotes are from McGeeney, E (2013) What is good sex?: Young people, sexual pleasure and sexual health services. Unpublished doctoral thesis.[8]

First sex and virginity cards

Print each quote on a piece of A4 paper or card. On the back of the paper/card print the suggested image. All images can be found online. Laminate your cards if possible so that they can be reused.

This activity would work well alongside the 'Busting myths about the hymen and introducing the vaginal corona' activity in Chapter 5: *Bodies*, on p. 166.

PURITY RING OR CHASTITY BELT:

'Virginity means something really sacred and something really important and something you need to kinda hold on to as long as possible and share with someone special you know.'

A DRAWING OR SKETCH OF A PHALLUS:

'I think virginity's like a state of mind, more than anything else. Because, it can't really be defined by, having done or not done any physical acts really. If you define virginity by, you haven't had a penis inside your vagina, then what if you don't want a penis inside your vagina and you wanna sleep with women, then, that doesn't make sense.'

ALTON TOWERS:

'It's the first time you have sex! It's not special! It's special in the sense that like the first time you go to Alton towers is special. But, it doesn't mean anything.'

NOTCHES ON A BED POST:

'I don't believe in it [virginity] – it's stupid! It's a stupid made up idea! I think it's a way to kind've quantify female sexuality and kind've you know – it's held in a regard that it shouldn't be.'

AN XXX RATED STAMP ON AN IMAGE:

When it was happening, I was worried, because I didn't know where to put it, what to do and how to move…Like I didn't know what to do. I felt uncomfortable, man. Proper bad. Like I felt like I was all getting itchy and like I was thinking, oh, what do I do? How do I do this and that? And obviously I thought back to watching that bluey and just like doing….It half worked out in the end.

A CONDOM:

When I was younger, the first time I had sex, the condom ripped and I thought it was nothing. I thought that was what happened at the end. I thought, oh, that's supposed to happen. Like obviously I told my mum, told my dad, like what happened. Like I run in. I was like, 'Dad! I'm a man! I'm a man today!' He's like, what you done? I told him what I done. He went, 'You stupid idiot.' And then he just told me. He said, was everything alright? What happened and that? I asked him that question, like you see the thing…it's supposed to rip? He's like, no. You're screwed. But then obviously like I covered myself up and I said I didn't like ejaculate or anything like that and I said I didn't, I didn't, it was just quick. Do you see what I mean? Like, just to try it. I promise you, dad, and all that. Worst promise I ever made.

A CLOCK:

It sort of confused me cos where she knew what to do I was only a beginner, but she was the same age as me. So, I got it a bit confused cos I thought that if someone the same age as me, how would they know how to do it? So I thought, well if she knows how to do it then I'll let her take over. So I let her take over and then she stopped and then it finished. Afterwards, in a way I felt good but I felt like, now I felt like she rushed into things. Like cos we could still be together now and I could have never met any other girl, I could have just stuck with one girl and just, I could have recently just, just had, like just lost my virginity but she decided that she wanted to do it, like go for it quick.

A HAND:

We were sitting down and under the table I could feel him touching my leg and you know and when he was doing it I was very excitable. He, I think we started kissing, I can't remember that well, but I remember him he gave me head and I came and he came. We both did it to each other and yes that was that. I remember feeling like I should be feeling that this is wrong but it didn't, it was fine and it was good and it was more pleasure than, because I had kissed girls and I have had sex with a girl as well and it was just better it was just so much more natural, it just felt so much more natural and right.

A RED ROSE:

I thought it was going to be like one of those like, you know movie, cliche movie moments where there's like screaming but it was more like, you know, I felt like…blah! It was like – an activity. Not like passion. It was just like doing something. It was really disappointing, now I mean, just thinking about it, it wasn't what it was cracked up to be. Also looking back at it now, like my first time, who I lost it to, it was like, was that worth it? Afterwards, I felt like – so, ok – this is going to sound stupid. I felt like grown up. Like now I can join the club. So yeah I think I did it for all the wrong reasons. I am a terrible human being (laughs) I guess everyone has different reasons, like some people are like I'm going to do this for pleasure even if I'm a virgin, if that's why you wanna do it then I think that's the right reason.

The sexual fairytale

 A creative writing exercise that explores participants' sexual expectations and ideals. Through discussion, groups are able to unpick the differences between fantasy and reality when it comes to sex and explore the benefits and limitations of each having our own idea of what the sexual fairytale looks like. 20–30 minutes

 A4 sexual fairytale sheets, pens, highlighter pens. 15+

Divide participants into groups of two–four participants and give each group a sexual fairytale sheet (see p. 225). Ask each group to create a fairytale story about a couple having sex for the first time together (they may or may not have had sexual partners before). They should consider what the characters are wearing, where they are and how the sex proceeds. They may also want to consider what positions the characters adopt and if, how and when they orgasm. The content of the story and points considered will depend on participants' level of knowledge, interest and experience.

Pin all the sheets to a display board and ask the whole group to compare and contrast the narratives. To do this give each group highlighter pens and ask them to underline common themes in the narratives and to circle moments or themes that they feel are unique. Use the following discussion questions to explore the narratives further:

- What are the common themes in these narratives?
- Where do we get our ideas from about what a fairytale sexual experience should be like? (*Answers may include: conversations with siblings, parents, other family, friends and peers; pornography; films and TV; books.*)
- How are ideas about equality, safety, pleasure and consent represented in our narratives?
- What kinds of people and experiences are missing from our narratives?
- How do these narratives compare to real life sexual experiences?
- How do we know what real life experiences are like? How reliable are our resources/ sources?
- Why might it be useful to have an idea about what an ideal or good sexual experience might be like? (*Answers may include: helps to make sure that we don't normalise or put up with bad sex; helps us to know what to ask for and expect from a relationship, e.g. equality, safety, trust and consent.*)
- How might our ideals and fairytales be a problem for us? (*Answers may include: could lead to unrealistic expectations; could lead to people feeling pressured to have great sex/be sexually empowered when they don't feel this way; doesn't allow for average, mundane sexual experiences which are ok.*)

To explore further you may want to share with participants the 'red rose' quote (on p. 223) from a young person, where he explains his disappointment at his first sexual experience not being like a 'movie cliche'. If participants are interested in finding out more about 'real life' experiences of first sex you may want to watch some of the short films from the *Good Sex Project* created by Brook and the University of Sussex in which actors voice young people's experiences. These are available from brook.org.uk or goodsexproject.wordpress.com.

The Sexual Fairytale

Once upon a time...

...and they all lived happily ever after?

Screwball

 This activity uses a short video clip to stimulate for discussion in pairs about first sex.

 20–30 minutes

 Access to TrueTube or vimeo to see the BAFTA award winning *Screwball* short film.

 14+

Watch the *TrueTube Screwball comedy* which is a 12-minute video that features two young people, Ryan and Natalie, negotiating a sexual experience for the first time.

Divide the group into pairs and allocate each one of the pair one of the following roles (the genders of participants do not need to match that of the characters):

- Ryan
- Natalie

Ask each group to think about how each character might be thinking and feeling before, during and after the encounter. Share these as a whole group and explore whether the group felt there are any gender differences in how each character might have responded. Also consider if/how the scenario might have played out differently were it to feature an LGBT+ couple. To finish ask each individual to note down one take home message they felt the video clip was trying to portray.

Section 3: Masturbation

Masturbation can be defined as touching, rubbing or stroking your own sexual organs for pleasure. You can also do this to someone else. If you and a partner do this to each other this is known as mutual masturbation.

Masturbation is often seen as a taboo subject and is not often talked about in families or in RSE. As a result young people can feel that there is something wrong with them if they masturbate. The activities in this section are designed to prompt discussion about this subject and clarify that masturbation is a healthy, normal and enjoyable practice.

Key messages about masturbation to explore in RSE

- Masturbation is completely normal and ok for anyone to do or not do at any point in their life.
- Masturbation can help people learn about their bodies, what feels good and what turns them on.
- People of all genders and all ages masturbate.
- People masturbate for lots of different reasons – when they're in a relationship, on their own and with their partner – even when the sex they are having is totally satisfying.
- There is more stigma around female masturbation than male masturbation and this needs addressing so that everyone feels comfortable to masturbate should they so wish.
- There may be religious or cultural attitudes to masturbation that mean people from these religions/cultures may associate masturbation with feelings of shame.
- If you masturbate with someone else (touching each other's genitals), there may be a small risk of getting or passing on a sexually transmitted infection if you, or they, already have an infection. This is because infections can be spread by transferring infected semen or vaginal fluid on the fingers or genital area even if vaginal, anal or oral sex doesn't take place.

Useful resources include:
1. Bishuk.com has a range of useful articles and handouts on masturbation including a guide for parents and information for young people.
2. Masturbation: A hands on guide by RFSU: www.rfsu.se/globalassets/pdf/masturbation-a-hands-on-guide.pdf
3. https://dodsonandross.com/A-feminist-based – sex education site.
4. OMG Yes: www.omgyes.com/. This is a website for adults aged 18+ that uses research with women to educate women and their partners about female pleasure and masturbation. This site has a pay wall, with some open access. It would only be useful for the sex and relationship educators and older young people.

Masturbation for the nation

This activity is adapted from materials from the FPA Jiwsi resource and shared with permission. See *Jiwsi: A pick 'n' mix of sex and relationships education* activities by Mel Gadd and Jo Hinchliffe.[9]

 A discussion-based activity that uses an agree/disagree continuum to explore attitudes and values about masturbation. The activity works well as an introduction to the topic of masturbation. 20–30 minutes

 Flipchart paper, pens, Agree/Disagree title cards, discussion cards each containing one of the statements on the following page. 12+

To set up the activity place the 'Agree' and 'Disagree' title cards at opposite sides of the room or at each end of a table. Place the discussion cards face down in the middle of the participants.

Start by explaining or clarifying what masturbation is using the definition on page 227 at the start of section 3. To facilitate the activity ask participants, one at a time, to pick up a card, read out the statement and place it at some point along the agree/disagree continuum that reflects how strongly they agree or disagree with the statement. They then state their reasons why they placed it at this point. Once the participant has had the opportunity to give their reasons, the rest of the group can discuss and move the card if agreed. Alternatively you can read out the statements and ask participants to stand along the continuum. Use the 'Points to consider' (on p. 261) to guide your discussion. The aim of the activity is to create a safe space for discussion about a topic that for some (not all!) people is taboo and to emphasise that masturbation is a healthy, normal, enjoyable and harmless practice.

To conclude the activity discuss the following questions:

- Was it difficult or easy to do this activity?
- How easy or difficult is it to talk about masturbation?
- Where would it be appropriate and inappropriate to masturbate?
- Why do you think masturbation is a taboo issue/rarely discussed publicly?
- What messages do adults/society send to children about masturbation?

Extension: Campaign Ideas

As an extension activity ask the group to design a poster, meme or other campaign material that busts myths about masturbation. For example, selling masturbation as the safest form of sex/celebrating the health and wellbeing benefits of masturbation. Discuss whether such materials could be displayed and the challenges of doing so today and in the past.

Masturbation discussion card statements

Most people are happy to talk about masturbation.	People only masturbate when they haven't got a sexual partner.
Masturbation is a private activity.	It is embarrassing to talk about masturbating with a partner.
Women don't masturbate.	Masturbation is normal.
Masturbation means you get to learn what turns you on.	You can't catch sexually transmitted infections if you masturbate on your own.
Masturbation is harmless.	You can catch a sexually transmitted infection if you masturbate a partner and/or they masturbate you. This is called mutual masturbation.
Your first sexual partner should be with yourself – masturbation!	Only teenage boys masturbate.
It is ok to masturbate in front of your sexual partner.	People should be free to make their own decisions about masturbation.
Everybody masturbates.	Parents should tell off their teenage daughter if they find them masturbating.
Masturbation can help you learn about your body.	Parents should tell off their teenage son if they find them masturbating.
It's normal not to masturbate.	Your partner should be the only one who gives you pleasure.

The anti-masturbation device: a historical perspective

This activity is a based on a lesson plan created by the *Sex and History* project team at the University of Exeter. It has been edited and shared with permission. The full lesson and resources required can be accessed free online.[10]

 This activity uses an image of a late 19th century/early 20th century anti-masturbation device and information about its historical use to prompt discussion about masturbation taboos and the control of sexuality today and in the past. This activity works as an introduction to the topic of masturbation using a novel method of engaging young people in debates about social norms and taboos relating to sexuality. 20–30 minutes

 Image of an anti-masturbation device available for free online.[11] 11+

Without explaining what it is show the group a picture of the anti-masturbation device using the slides and/or printouts of the image provided (Figure 6.4) in the free online resource.

For more images of historical anti-masturbation devices use the Wellcome Collection search tool: https://wellcomecollection.org/works.

Ask the group:

- What is this?
- What was it used for?
- When might it have been made?

Give the group a minute to discuss in pairs and then take group feedback about their thoughts. See if anyone can guess the correct answer!

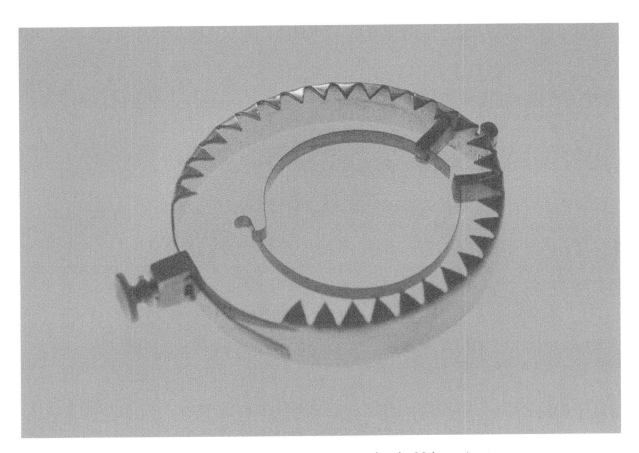

FIGURE 6.4 Anti-masturbation device, late 19th century/early 20th century

Credit: Wellcome Collection. CC BY

Explain to the group that the object is an anti-masturbation device created in the late 18th century. Ask participants to discuss in pairs:

- How would it work?
- Who would wear it and why?
- How would someone feel wearing this?

Take feedback and explain to the group that since the late 18th century special garments made out of cloth or metal have been created to prevent masturbation. This particular device was designed to fit over a penis at night to stop someone from having involuntary 'nocturnal emissions' or what we now call 'wet dreams'! The metal teeth would have made any swelling very painful.

Ask participants to discuss in their pairs:

- Why might someone want to control sexual urges in boys?
- Do you think anyone actually wore these?

Take feedback and explain that from the 18th century to the early 20th century there was much discussion of the possible medical and moral dangers of masturbation. Masturbation was linked (erroneously) with a range of problems including impotence, depression and muscle-wasting. Other preventions for masturbation discussed at the time were mountain walks, cold baths and medicines. This kind of device was sold by specialised surgical suppliers and was expensive. It is not clear whether they were actually that widely used. They may have been used in hospitals and mental wards, or simply displayed in popular museums.

Finally ask the group:

- If devices like this were not made to be worn by the general population, why might they have been created?
- Why do you think there weren't similar products designed for vulvas?
- Are there any attempts to prevent young people masturbating today (perhaps in more subtle ways)?
- What message do young people today learn about masturbation? Is the message the same for girls and for boys?

Gender and masturbation

 In this activity participants work in small groups to look at a series of quotes from research about experiences of masturbation. Their task is to try and guess the gender of the research participant. In doing so participants reflect and think critically about gendered myths and assumptions about masturbation.

 20–30 minutes

 Quotes printed and cut up on individual pieces of paper. One set per four–six participants to allow for small group working.

 11+

Divide participants into small groups and give each group a set of quotes about masturbation (see Table 6.2). Explain that these quotes are taken two studies – one with adults and one with young people. Ask each group to sort the quotes into piles according to whether they think the person speaking identifies as male or female (none of the participants in these studies identified as non-binary). You may also want to ask participants to identify which of these quotes were spoken by an adult, and which by a young person. Make sure you give each group a mix of quotes from each of the three groups (young women, young men, adult women).

Take feedback from groups and reveal the answers.

Note: the quote about masturbation causing a person with a penis to lose zinc/get it back from a vagina is incorrect – be sure to correct this myth!

Discussion questions

- Did any of the quotes surprise you? Why?
- What myths and assumptions have you heard about women and masturbation?
- What myths and assumptions have you heard about men and masturbation?
- Do any of these stories confirm or debunk the myths you have heard about?
- Do any of these stories contain a message you would like others to head?

Quotes

These quotes are taken from two studies, one of young men and women in England aged 16–22[12] and one of adult women in the US[13]. None of the participants in either study identified as transgender or gender non-binary and no men participated in the adult study. We have provided the gender of the research participants (and indicated whether they were an adult or young person) above the quotes but obviously do not provide this information to participants! Keep a note for yourself of the gender/age of participants so that you can reveal the correct answers.

TABLE 6.2 Quotes about masturbation taken from research with adult women, young women and young men

Young woman

--✂

Some of my friends say they do it, but I don't know if I will try it. It seems a bit like naughty! I am curious to know what it is like, but I then I'm like…no! Cos it's sort of taboo so I think, no. I don't want to do that.

--✂

I think it's quite like a negative thing.

--✂

Every time I think about it I think about something that was said when I went to my church youth group. They were saying that if you like masturbate and stuff like that it is like a sin. If you masturbate by the time you get married and you have sex, you won't know what pleasure is because you have been pleasuring yourself kind of thing. It was something like that, it always seems to stick in my mind.

--✂

The most pleasure I've had is from masturbation. I went to Ann Summer's and bought myself a toy and I use that. I tried using it with a partner but I didn't feel comfortable and my partner didn't either.

--✂

Young man

--✂

When I was 11 I took one of my cousin's films for myself and had a little look. I started experiencing masturbation and it was just like amazing.

--✂

Masturbation aint good at all. Don't do it. You loose zinc and that's what you need to be a man bruv. Like, you loose zinc everytime you buss yeah. But like the female's vagina yeah it gives you your zinc back. I heard about this. Plus like. If you wank yeah your dick won't be as hard.

I talk about it a lot. My friends talk to me about it when they do it. I talk to them about it when I do it.

Of course I masturbate! To be honest I can't find one person who doesn't.

At boarding school there was lots of masturbation, you know in dormitories and stuff. I'm sure it went on in other boarding houses as well, it's amazing how much experimentation goes on.

My cousins and I found out on the internet about wanking and tried it.

I masturbate about five times out of a week to maybe seven times a week, almost every day.

Adult woman

I masturbate about five times out of a week to maybe seven times a week, almost every day.

It's only pleasurable when absolutely private, no one bothering you, and there's a nice sound atmosphere, like nice music on the radio.

I like masturbating in the autumn or winter every day because it warms up your body.

It relieves stress, helps me to feel comfortable with where I am right now in my life.

A mass debate

 Participants work in teams to debate statements about masturbation. This activity helps to develop moral reasoning and communication skills as well as helping participants to clarify and explain their own beliefs about masturbation.

 30–60 minutes

 Flipchart paper, pens.

 13+

Divide participants into two groups – 'Agree' and 'Disagree' – and explain that they are going to debate a series of statements about masturbation. Explain or clarify what masturbation is if you have not done an introductory activity to the topic. You may also need to discuss why this is an important topic to cover in RSE (see 'Points to consider' on p. 261).

Choose one of the following statements for the group to debate. Before starting the debate, task each group with coming up with reasons for or against the statement (depending on whether they are in group 'agree' or 'disagree') and preparing a two-minute speech. Groups can make notes that can be used during the debate. If participants disagree with the side they have been allocated (agree/disagree), remind them that the point of the exercise is to develop their reasoning and debating skills and to practise seeing issues from different points of view. This helps us to clarify what we believe and why we believe it.

Statements:

- Masturbation is a good way to learn about your body and what turns you on.
- Children shouldn't masturbate.
- It is wrong for women to masturbate.
- Masturbation is more socially acceptable if you have a penis rather than a clitoris.
- An orgasm should be the only goal of masturbation.
- Your first sexual experiences should be with yourself.
- You should only masturbate in bed.

Once each group has finished preparing they should select a team leader and four debaters to participate in the debate. The rest of the group will act as audience members. Start the debate by giving each team leader two minutes to set out their argument. Debaters and audience members can note down any questions or challenges that they have. Next open up the debate to all ten debaters, before moving on to take questions and comments from the audience.

At the end of the activity audience members can vote who wins the debate. You can repeat the activity for multiple statements. Reflect on the activity using the following questions:

- What have you learnt from doing this activity?
- Has this activity helped you to clarify what you think and believe?
- What did you enjoy about this activity?

Section 4: Pleasure and sensuality

Hand massage

 Participants give each other hand massages in pairs as a way of practising communication about touch, pleasure, consent and body boundaries.

 20–30 minutes

 Baby oil or hypoallergenic equivalent. Printouts of the hand massage exercises (optional).

 11+

Explain the task to participants which is to work in pairs to give a hand massage to your partner and receive one in return. Pairs will need to negotiate with each other the kind of touch they enjoy and feel comfortable with. As an alternative you can ask participants to give head and shoulder massages over clothes. In this instance, no oil is required.

This should always be an optional activity in which participants are able to work with a partner that they feel comfortable with. It may work better in youth work settings where participation is voluntary and where there are alternative activities to take part in.

Before you start check whether participants have any allergies to the oil being used and ask participants to wash their hands.

The task is for the masseur to give their partner an enjoyable hand massage. You may want to hand out copies of the hand massage tips (see the following list) but emphasise that participants will need to experiment with different forms of pressure and touch and find out what feels good for their partner. Before participants start, reinforce that it is really important that the masseur checks in with their hand massage partner throughout the activity and does not do anything that makes their partner feel uncomfortable.

Give partners five minutes to complete the massage and then ask them to reflect on the experience:

- What kinds of touch felt good?
- How did you communicate with each other about what did and did not feel good?
- Did you mainly talk ('that feels good'), make noises ('mmmmm'/'ouch!') or use movements (pulling away) to indicate what you did and did not enjoy? Which of these were most effective?
- How easy was it to communicate with each other?
- What kinds of things made it hard to communicate well?

Hand massage tips for participants (one set of tips per pair)

Hand massage tips:

- Pinch the tips of your partner's fingers, holding each pinch for two–three seconds.

- Use your thumb to massage your partner's palm starting in the middle and working your way outwards. Start with gentle pressure and increase as you go.

- Take the hand, palm facing upwards, and massage the whole hand and forearm with gentle pressure movements. Then turn over the hand and repeat on the other side.

- Take the whole hand in your own hand with interlocking fingers (as if you are playing mercy!). Carefully turn the wrist from left to right and repeat from right to left.

--✂

Hand massage tips:

- Pinch the tips of your partner's fingers, holding each pinch for two–three seconds.

- Use your thumb to massage your partner's palm starting in the middle and working your way outwards. Start with gentle pressure and increase as you go.

- Take the hand, palm facing upwards, and massage the whole hand and forearm with gentle pressure movements. Then turn over the hand and repeat on the other side.

- Take the whole hand in your own hand with interlocking fingers (as if you are playing mercy!). Carefully turn the wrist from left to right and repeat from right to left.

Swap over partners and reflect on the experience again. You may want to repeat the exercise and reflect on whether partner communication improves with practice and reflection.

At the end of the activity, use the following questions to reflect:

- Who took responsibility for the negotiation? Was it mainly the masseur asking questions ('is this ok?') or the person being massaged ('touch me here')? Whose responsibility should it be?
- What needs to be in place before, during and after for a massage to feel safe? (*Answers may include: knowing and trusting the massage partner; the location and room setup, e.g. lighting; the communication before, during and after by the masseuse.*)
- How easy was it to refuse unwanted or uncomfortable touch? What kinds of things prevent us from refusing touch that we don't want or enjoy? (*Answers may include: not wanting to offend someone; not wanting to make things awkward; not knowing the person very well; feeling pressured, coerced or threatened. Research suggestions that women find it harder to say no in social situations than men. This could be because women and girls are socialised to be more accommodating and 'nice' and are less likely to be encouraged to be assertive, direct and powerful.*)

My photo album

Adapted from an activity created by Susy Langsdale. Used with permission.

 A visualisation activity that asks participants to imagine and remember positive and pleasurable experiences. 20 minutes

 Copy of the script for educator. 13+

Ask participants to lie down somewhere comfortable with their eyes closed. Instruct them to start relaxing their bodies – starting at their feet and feeling them go heavy and flop out to the side and then working their way up to relax their knees, hips, stomach, shoulders, neck, head and face.

Once you've given participants time to relax read the script on the next page.

Once you have finished the exercise ask the group to sit round a big piece of paper and draw some of the experiences they had. They can write key words and describe or represent different experiences. Follow this with a discussion about the differences between experiences of pleasure and sexual pleasure – you can explore this in terms of sexual expectations rather than experiences, especially with younger groups. Do we expect the same positive sensations and feelings from sex as we do from other pleasurable experiences we have had throughout our lives?

Emphasise that it is important to keep your expectations around sexual pleasure rooted in who you are and what you enjoy in your everyday life.

My Photo album: Script for educator

Imagine yourself in a room where you feel completely relaxed and safe. Think about the colours of the wall, the light, the temperature. Are there any smells you can smell? Is there any music? In the centre of the room is a photograph album. You go over to it and pick it up. Think about how it feels, what it weighs and what it's like to open it. As you open it you see a photo of you as a toddler. Think about yourself at this age – do you remember something that gave you pleasure when you were that age? Think about that experience and what you enjoyed. What did it feel like in your body when that experience happened? Do you remember any of the noises or colours around you? Do you remember any of your emotions?

Now turn back to the photo album and turn the page. On the next page is a photo of you at primary school. Think back to this time, and think about something that gave you pleasure when you were that age. Sit with the memory, and remember all the sensations that you felt in your body. Was there music perhaps? Or smells in the background? Was anyone with you? Smile as you remember this pleasurable experience.

Now turn back to the book and turn over. You see a photo of yourself in the first few years of secondary school. Do you remember something you did at this age that gave you pleasure? What did it feel like? What emotions were you feeling? Why did it feel so pleasurable?

And now turn to the next page where there is a photo of you in the last year of secondary school. What do you look like? Can you remember a pleasurable experience at that time in your life? Where were you? Were you alone? With others? What were you doing? How did you feel? Can you think of one word to describe how you felt?

[After a pause] Ok, now start to focus on the feeling of the floor on your back, and noises in the room. Come back into the room slowly and open your eyes. Well done.

Sensuality star

This activity is adapted from the Jo Adams *RU Ready* pack (unpublished training manual) and shared with permission.

 An activity that uses object-based learning as a stimulus for discussions around sensuality. Enables conversations about relaxation and wellbeing for younger participants and sexual pleasure and sensuality for older participants. 20–30 minutes

 Handout for each participant with a blank sensuality star, range of objects designed to stimulate the senses (see Figure 6.5). 11+

Set out a wide range of objects that can be used to stimulate the five senses: touch, taste, sight, sound and smell. Objects can include perfumes, oils, scented candles or orange peel for smell; pictures and colourful objects for sight; sound bowl and musical instruments for sound; chocolate, coffee and fruits for taste; smooth and rough textured objects such as soft scarves and rope for touch.

Ask participants to spend some time exploring the objects and experiencing the ways in which they stimulate different senses. It's a good idea to check for allergies before any tasting begins.

Give each participant a sensuality star handout or ask them to draw their own star on a blank piece of paper. The task is for participants to draw or write what they think is the best object for stimulating each of the five senses. It can either be one of the objects provided or something else (e.g. smell of freshly cut grass).

If you are working with young people aged 11–14 ask them to think about how stimulating each of the five senses can make you feel. They can write their answers in and thoughts around their sensuality star. Answers may include: relaxed, calm, hungry, sleepy, excited. Have a discussion about things participants could do in their everyday lives to stimulate their five senses and how this might help to relax them if they feel stressed or anxious.

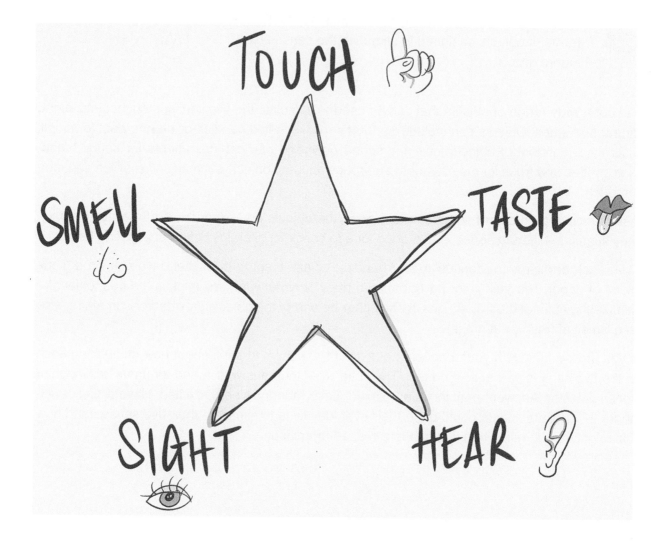

FIGURE 6.5 Sensuality star

Illustration by: Chrissy Baxter

If using this activity with young people aged 14+ you can also talk about the importance of the five senses in sexual situations, emphasising that how and where you have sex can make a difference to how you feel about the experience. You can extend the activity with some groups using the following prompts:

- How important are each of the five senses when it comes to sex?
- What are some of the ways in which you could stimulate the five senses when having sex? (*Answers may include: playing music; using flavoured condoms; massage; having the lights on/off; wearing/not wearing clothes; having sex in a comfy bed, etc.*)
- What might stop someone from experimenting with the senses in this way? How can these barriers or difficulties be overcome? (*e.g. young people may not have access to private space to have sex such as their own room which can make sex more rushed or less sensual and intimate; if someone doesn't feel comfortable and relaxed with the person they are having sex with they might not want to explore different senses; if someone doesn't feel confident asking for what they want when it comes to sex; if someone doesn't know what they want and enjoy when it comes to sex.*)

In your discussion emphasise the importance of good communication and consent when negotiating and having sex. This is important if you want to explore sexually and try out new sensual experiences with a partner. It is also ok to not want to experiment.

Mind, body and heart

A version of this activity is available from the *Brook Learn* e-learning platform, Pleasure course, module 3.[14]

Using scenarios, participants work in small groups to explore how it feels in the mind, body and heart when you are ready or not ready to have sex. This activity enables participants to learn about the body and how it changes during arousal, while also learning about consent and bodily autonomy.

 35 minutes

Scenarios (can be downloaded for free from the *Brook Learn* platform[15], Pleasure course, module 3), large sheets of paper and pens.

 13+

Note: With younger age groups this activity can be used to explore questions about sexual readiness. With older groups it can form part of sessions on pleasure and consent.

Divide participants into small groups and give each group one of the scenarios on the following page:

Scenarios for Mind, Body, Heart

---✂

ANNA: She is about to have sex with her partner but she doesn't really want to. She likes her partner and feels close to him. They have had sex lots of times before but today she doesn't really feel turned on. She doesn't know why.

---✂

ALI: He is about to have sex with someone but he doesn't really want to. He likes his partner and feels close to him but he doesn't feel turned on.

---✂

ZAHRAH: She is about to have sex with her partner. They have had sex lots of time before and Zahrah really enjoys the sex that they have. Usually it is Zahrah's partner who initiates sex but today it is Zahrah – she's feeling really turned on.

---✂

GEORGE: They are about to have sex with someone they met recently. This will be the first time they have sex. George is a bit nervous but they feel really turned on and want to have sex.

Ask each group to consider:

1. how the person in their scenario is feeling in their body,
2. what this person is thinking in their head,
3. what this person is feeling in their heart.

Participants can either write down their ideas or draw an outline of a body and annotate it with words and images to show their responses.

Ask participants with scenarios Anna and Ali to present their drawings and describe what their characters might have been thinking and feeling. Draw out examples of how it can feel to have unwanted, non-consensual or pressured sex. It may be helpful to write these on the board/flipchart.

Answers may include: not wanting to be touched; feeling repulsed or uncomfortable with the other person's touch; feeling scared, disempowered, out of control; feeling hot; having a red face; heart pounding; fluttering in their stomach; the vulva/penis is not swollen and is dry. (Remember a person can feel physically aroused and erect but not want to have sex. Physical changes should never be taken as a sign that someone does or does not want to have sex.)

Next ask participants with scenarios George and Zahrah to present their drawings and describe what their characters might have been thinking and feeling. Draw out examples of how it can feel to have sex when you are turned on, relaxed and happy. It may be helpful to write these on the board/flipchart.

Answers may include: longing to be touched; feeling excited, empowered, in control; wanting to be close to the other person; their vulva/penis is swollen and wet; their heart is pounding; they feel hot; they are red in the face as blood flow has increased; they are thinking 'This is great', 'just what I wanted' 'Yeeessss!'

The key learning from this activity is that one way of knowing if you are ready to have sex (the first time and every other time you have sex) is to think about how you are feeling in your mind, body and heart. If you don't feel happy and mentally and physically turned on, you do not have to have sex. Also, if you are having sex with a partner you need to check in with them to find out if they are feeling ready in their mind, body and heart. When you both are feeling this way sex can feel enjoyable for everyone involved.

Research and create: understanding pleasure and sexual response

 This is a creative activity that asks participants to work on their own or in small groups to research sexual response, orgasm, arousal and/or pleasure and provide a creative response. We provide some research and discussion questions to help you facilitate this activity and support participants to unpick some of the norms, assumptions and beliefs about sexual response.

 One hour (minimum)

 Creative materials such as paints, coloured pens, modelling materials, coloured paper and card, modelling clay, scissors, etc. Online access or printed materials (see links in the following).

 16+

Each individual, pair or group is expected to choose one question from the following options. They will need to research the answer and think creatively about how they would like to present their response. Educators will need to provide participants with access to the resources outlined to support the development of their own resources and a range of creative materials so that they can choose to create paintings, sketches, collages, models, etc.

1. **How does the body change during arousal (the sexual response cycle)? How does it feel to be ready to have sex?**

    Suggested research resources:

    *   Brook Learn. An elearning programme on pleasure. See module entitled: *The anatomy of pleasure*.
    *   Scarleteen. Website. See article entitled: *With Pleasure: A View of Whole Sexual Anatomy for EveryBody*.
    *   RFSU (the Swedish Association for Sexuality Education) Free publications *Pussypedia* and *Dicktionary*.
    *   Masters and Johnson's human sexual response cycle – a four phase model of physiological responses to sexual stimulation based on research in the 1960s.

2. **What are some of the ways that the orgasm has been described and/or represented in science, media, literature and art? Does everyone experience orgasms equally? Why might there be differences according to sex, gender or sexual orientation?**

Suggested research resources:

- Scarleteen. Website. See article entitled: *Sexual Response & Orgasm: A Users Guide*;
- The YouTube clip from *Friends* 'Orgasm by Numbers' where Monica explains to Chandler how to hit the seven erogenous zones; Meg Ryan's fake orgasm from *When Harry Met Sally*; *American Pie*, *Inbetweeners*, *Big Bang Theory* clips referencing masturbation;
- The surrealist image of the female orgasm entitled *1940s Illustration of the female orgasm*;
- Journalist Mona Chalabi's graphical depictions of the orgasm gap found within *The Guardian* article entitled '"Golden trio" of moves boosts chances of female orgasm, say researchers' published 23 February 2017[16];
- *The Vagina Dispatches*, Episode 3 The Orgasm gap. Created for *The Guardian*.

Encourage participants to be as innovative as possible. If participants get stuck, here are some of our creative ideas:

- A volcano graph or model based on the sexual response cycle with a stick person climbing the desire and excitement peaks until orgasmic eruption and then resolution. (See Mona Chalabi's data visualisations of the orgasm gap – available online.[17])
- Create body map covered with drawings and writing around the body what changes during arousal.
- 'Mind the Gap' London tube sign illustrating information about the orgasm gap (the fact that more males than females will orgasm during sexual activity, and/or more lesbian women report orgasm during sex compared to straight women). See Frederick, D,A, John, H,K,S, Garcia, J,R, & Lloyd, E,A, (2018) 'Differences in orgasm frequency among gay, lesbian, bisexual, and heterosexual men and women in a U.S. national sample' Archives of Sexual Behavior, 47(1), pp. 273–288. https://doi.org/10.1007/s10508-017-0939-z.
- A poster showing the three factors that increase the chance of a woman having an orgasm during sex: deep kissing, manual genital stimulation and/or oral sex in addition to vaginal intercourse (see Frederick et al. 2018).
- An artwork that represents the orgasm or different kinds of orgasm. (For example, see the image of the 1940s surrealist representation of a female orgasm by 'Tina' widely available online which describes orgasm as an 'all consuming nervous explosion which permeates the entire being…both physically and mentally', and is 'unique and unmatched in all other human experiences'.)

When participants have finished their creation ask them to present it to the rest of the group. Use the following questions to unpick participants' ideas around desire, pleasure, gender and sexual responses:

- When thinking about the anatomy of pleasure why do we focus on the genitals? What organs do we forget about that are just (if not more) important?
- Does everyone experience the sexual response cycle in the same way? If not, why might there be differences?
- Why is there an orgasm gap between men and women and between straight, gay and bisexual people? Can orgasm equality ever be achieved? Can we have pleasure equality without orgasm equality?
- Is orgasm the only goal of sex? What does sex without a goal look like?
- Why might people fake orgasms?

As a group decide how you want to display or disseminate your projects.

Yes, no, maybe so

 An activity that participants can complete at home or on their own that encourages them to think about their own sexual desires and boundaries. 20–30 minutes

 Paper and pens. Internet access. 14+

Ask participants to write a list of the different ways they can think of being intimate or sexual with another person. They will need to work on their own for this activity and it may be best to set this as an individual activity to do alone.

Participants should go through their list and consider whether this is something that they would like to try (Yes), wouldn't like to try (No) or would maybe like to try (Maybe). Participants may want to look at the blogpost by Justin Hancock at BISH called 'OMG Yes, No, Hmm: work out what kind of sex you like' for further discussion of this activity.[18] Justin has included a list of sexual activities that participants can refer to if they have struggled to come up with their own. For older participants you may want to share the blogpost and sexual inventory stocklist from Scarleteen 'Yes, No, Maybe So: A Sexual Inventory Stocklist'.[19]

Ask participants to reflect on the activity using the following questions. You may want to discuss these as a whole group if you feel this is safe.

- How did it feel to do this activity?
- Have you learned anything about yourself from doing it?
- Would you share this list with a partner? How would it feel if they shared their list with you?

Emphasise that the idea behind this activity is that it helps us to think about what we like and enjoy when it comes to sex – rather than focussing on what others think we *should* be doing. Sharing a list like this with a partner can help you to start conversations about what you both want from sex, what you enjoy and what you are worried about. Finding this out about each other is key to enjoying the sex you have together.

Section 5: Sexual ethics and consent

Meet and greet

Based on an activity created by Justin Hancock and Meg John Barker and adapted by Elsie Whittington and young volunteers at *Brook*. Digital versions of this activity are available through the *Brook Learn* platform[20], Consent course, module 4 and *DO…RSE for schools*.[21]

 This activity aims to create a safe space for participants to practise asking for and giving consent. This interactive activity opens up critical discussion about how social norms influence how we 'do' consent and acknowledges that asking for and giving consent can sometimes be awkward and confusing.

 20 minutes

 A room with space to move around.

 14+

Ask participants to walk around the room. Each time they pass someone ask them to greet each other with a handshake and say hello. After a few minutes ask participants to stop moving and ask them to reflect on the handshakes they have received so far. You may want to ask:

- How did your last handshake feel?
- What would have made it better? Would you have liked it firmer or softer?
- Do you normally shake hands with each other?
- Why did you shake hands with each other? Would you do whatever I told you to?

Next ask participants to start moving and again greet each other and say hello. This time, ask participants to take the time to have a conversation first about how they want to greet each other. For example, they may want to say:

- Do you want a hug? Fist pump? Handshake? Nod? What kind of a hug? Gentle? Quick? A slap on the back?

After a few greetings ask participants to stop and reflect. Ask how they greeted each other and how it felt doing it this way. Some participants may say that it was better because they got the kind of touch that they wanted and were more comfortable with. Others may say that they felt awkward, weird or uncomfortable because we don't normally stop and ask people how they want to be greeted/touched. Acknowledge this awkwardness and the fact that it is unusual to stop and negotiate verbally what kind of greeting you want.

Finally, ask participants to try meeting and greeting each other for a third and final time. This time ask them to try and find a balance between the first and second greetings. Can they pause and check out how their partner wants to be greeted without it being awkward? For example, through making eye contact or gesturing to each other.

After a few minutes ask participants to stop and share examples of when this worked and did not work and discuss how this activity relates to negotiating sexual consent. You may want to ask:

- Why do you think that as a society we don't ask people directly how they want to be touched or kissed?
- What would it be like if we did?
- What are some of the ways that we can ask for sexual consent?
- What are some of the ways that we can say yes and no to sex?

The consent continuum

This activity was developed by Elsie Whittington as part of her doctoral research project on the grey areas of consent. Shared with permission. For more information and to access free online training on how to use the consent continuum with young people please access the *Brook Learn* platform: Consent. Module 3.[22]

 This activity provides a framework for exploring the grey areas around consent that are not easily understood using a legal framework. Using scenarios, participants work in small groups to explore real life situations that young people have described to researchers and consider the challenges and complexities of negotiating consent.

 30 minutes

 Scenarios printed onto card.

 14+

Tip: Make sure you have done an activity that introduces the topic of consent before starting this activity.

Divide participants into small groups. Give each group the same consent scenario and ask them to discuss and decide whether or not consent has been agreed. Ask groups to feedback to the whole group one at a time and discuss the difficulties of deciding if consent has been agreed or not.

Draw the consent continuum on the board by writing the following concepts in this order:

Rape	*Non-consent*	*Passive consent*	*Active consent*
Sex is unwanted and consent is not given. There is an explicit use of force, violence or coercion.	Sex is unwanted and consent is not given. Participants may not identify their experience as rape but the sex was not consensual.	Accepting or allowing what happens or what others do, without active response or resistance.	Participating, engaged or ready to engage.

Explain that in the law there is just rape and consensual sex but that many people describe sexual experiences that don't seem to fit easily into one of these categories. This is because many people see rape as violent, forceful and enacted by strangers, which does not reflect the majority of people's experiences. This continuum is based on research with young people and has been created to represent the grey areas of consent where it is unclear to those involved whether or not consent has been given and/or whether or not rape has taken place.

Scenarios for Consent Continuum

Sam and Chris

Sam and Chris have been married for nine years and have sex every night before they fall asleep. It's very routine and they never talk about it. Sex is over as soon as Chris comes and Sam never has an orgasm. Sam would rather read but decides having sex is worth it, as it makes the relationship smoother.

Do you think Sam is giving consent?

Kerry and Stu

Kerry's 14 years old and has been told by her friends that anal sex is best (even if it hurts). She's keen to try it, but very nervous. Her new 19-year-old boyfriend Stu suggests it's time that they try it. Kerry says yes, even though she is unsure whether she wants to do it.

Do you think Kerry is giving consent?

Harrison and Adnan

Harrison and Adnan have been in a relationship for three years but things are pretty rocky. Whilst on holiday, they decide the relationship will be over at the end of their trip. Adnan doesn't want to have any more sex as this will make things complicated between them. Harrison says this makes him feel undesirable, ugly and worse about the whole thing.

One morning, Adnan wakes up to Harrison stroking and caressing him. He gets hard and Harrison takes this as a sign to carry on. Adnan feels awkward and doesn't have the energy to stop it and lets Harrison continue.

Do you think Adnan is giving consent?

Kirsty and Pete

Kirsty meets Pete in a club and after kissing, goes back to his. He fingers her in the taxi but once back at his house, she tells him she's changed her mind and doesn't want to have sex now. He tells her that she's a 'tease' and could at least give him a blowjob. She feels really guilty, so does it.

Do you think Kirsty is giving consent?

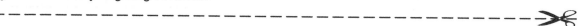

Taylor and Alex

Taylor and Alex have been together for 12 months. They have an active sex life but one night, Taylor asks Alex to stop because it hurts. Alex is just about to come, so carries on for about another 20 seconds. He comes and then stops.

Do you think Taylor is giving consent?

Ask the group where they would put the scenario already discussed. There is no right or wrong answer but participants should be encouraged to explore why they think the scenario belongs where it does. Give out the remaining scenarios and ask participants to place them on the continuum working in small groups or as a whole group.

Finish with a discussion using the following prompts:

- By law, sex without consent is always rape. This means that in legal terms each of these experiences could be considered as 'rape' as consent was not clearly sought or given. How might it help or not help the people involved in these scenarios to understand the experience as rape? (*Answers may include: a sense of relief in understanding this as rape; a desire to pursue justice; may stop similar experiences from happening; may be too extreme/uncomfortable; may be upsetting; the criminal justice system has often failed rape victims and has more work to do to support victims to obtain justice.*)
- What could the people in these scenarios have done differently to ensure that consent was actively requested and given? (*Answer may include: talked to each other before having sex about what they wanted; shared fears and anxieties; checked in with partner throughout the experience (verbally or reading body language); stopped as soon as partner requested; masturbated to have an orgasm rather than apply pressure to partner; accepted partner's decisions and didn't apply pressure; suggested an alternative non-sexual activity to do rather than have sex when one person didn't want to.*) **Note:** Ensure that this conversation does not lead to participants blaming the victim. Remind participants that it is always your responsibility to *seek* consent for other people, not to wait for consent to be given to you.

Play pause stop

 This activity explores how you know if you give (and how you know you have got) consent to have sex. Participants brainstorm verbal and non-verbal signs of enthusiastic consent (play), signs that consent has not been given (stop) and signs that you need to take a break and negotiate consent (pause).

 25 minutes

 Internet access to the 'Play pause stop' website.[23] Individual sets of red, green and yellow pieces of paper or card printed with the Play (green), Pause (yellow), Stop (red) symbols.

 13+ (Can be done with younger age groups if the focus is on non-sexual consent)

Show participants an image of a traffic light and ask: If you are getting intimate with someone what three options do you have? (The traffic light is a clue!) The answer is that you can:

1. STOP being intimate.
2. PAUSE. Take a break from the intimacy and either carry on later. This could be in two minutes, two hours or two weeks or perhaps you might decide to stop altogether.
3. PLAY. Carry on with the intimacy and enjoy being with your partner(s).

Ask the group to brainstorm all the ways that you can signal that you want to STOP being intimate with someone. Prompt the group to consider verbal (things you might say) and non-verbal (things you might do) signals.

Next brainstorm all the ways that you can signal that you want to PAUSE an intimate or sexual experience. And finally brainstorm all the ways that you can signal that you want to PLAY. Each time consider verbal and non-verbal signals.

You can do these brainstorms as a whole group or divide into three groups and work round in a carousel.

As a whole group use the *Play Pause Stop* website to check your answers.[24]

You can also use the website to emphasise the key message which is that it is really important that you make sure you get and give consent before having any kind of sex. You don't necessarily need to have to have a sit-down chat about it, but consent should always be clear. If you are ever in doubt about whether you have someone's consent, you should stop and ask.

You may want to use the following discussion prompts to explore this further:

- Whose responsibility is it to make sure that consent is in place? (*Possible answer: Everyone involved in the sexual experience. Remember it is not just your responsibility to GIVE consent but to actively SEEK consent from the person or people you are having sex with.*)
- Is it ok to carry on with an experience if negotiating consent feels a bit awkward? (*Possible answer: Yes! Negotiating sexual consent can be awkward sometimes but if you feel comfortable with the person you are with and both of you are up for playing then it's ok.*)
- Why might it feel uncomfortable to ask for consent verbally? (*Possible answer: Sometimes it feels awkward to talk about sex; as a society we don't always talk openly about consent or see it modelled in films – for example, people don't often ask to kiss or touch someone.*)
- What are some of the challenges of asking for consent non-verbally? (*Possible answer: You might misinterpret someone's signals, particularly if you don't know them very well.*)

To apply their understanding of Play Pause Stop in action you could do the following short activity:

Watch *The Havens Centre* 'Where is Your Line?' film on YouTube[25] which shows two people who meet on a night out and end up having sex.

Give each participant a set of coloured cards in green/yellow/red with play/pause/stop corresponding to the traffic lights. Ask participants to hold up their signs when they think the situation is play, pause or stop. (If the film is not suitable for your group you can also do this by writing short made up scenarios and asking participants to hold up cards as they listen.) Across the group there may be variations in understandings of consent so the green cards being held up may change to amber and then red at slightly different times (or not at all). Finish off by reflecting on the diversity or similarity of cards that were held up at different points and highlight that individuals may interpret situations differently but the only way to truly know is to regularly check in with your partner.

Nude strategies

A discussion-based activity in which participants work in small groups to explore strategies for responding to the circulation of 'nudes' (sexually explicit, naked or semi-naked images) in different scenarios. The aim is for participants to develop strategies for saying no in situations when they feel coerced or uncomfortable whilst also exploring fun ways of engaging in online conversation or play that feels safe and consensual.

 20 minutes

Zipit app. Flipchart, paper and pens.

 13+

Divide participants into small groups and allocate each group one of the following scenarios:

- Someone you know asks you for a nude.
- Someone you know sends you a nude (of themself).
- Someone sends or shows you a nude of someone you know.

Ask each group to brainstorm as many strategies (good and bad) that they can think of for responding to this situation. Encourage groups to think as creatively as possible.

Prompt participants to first consider how they might respond if they feel comfortable and relaxed with the person they are in contact with and then with someone they feel uncomfortable and pressured by.

If you have time, ask groups to swap their brainstorms with another group that had a different scenario and add any additional strategies that they can think of. Repeat this so that each group has considered each scenario.

Ask groups to get their own brainstorm back and to go through and underline all those strategies that they think would be effective in real life. Take feedback and discuss the feasibility and risks of the strategy as follows:

- Is it realistic? (Would you actually do/say that?)
- Is it consensual? (Whose consent is required? How could you obtain/give consent?)
- What are the risks and/or harms to yourself? What are the risks and/or harms to others?

Ask groups to feedback their ideas for realistic strategies. In your discussion try to move beyond the 'correct' response (say no/block them/report them) as research suggests that the exchange of nudes usually takes place within peer groups and young people do not want to report or block their friends and peers. Instead, explore ways of saying no, or fun ways of engaging in conversation or play that feels safe and consensual. If not already discussed share with the group the Zipit app produced by Childline which offers some funny images and gifs that help provide young people with tools for responding to requests for nudes. For further activities on ethical relationships, consent and saying no, see Chapter 3: *Relationships*.

You may want to clarify in the discussion that in the UK it is illegal to send sexually explicit images of someone under 18. This means that for 16- and 17-year-olds it is *legal* to consent to sex but *illegal* to consent to sending sexually explicit content. One risk of sending a nude is that you may get into trouble with the police, although the law is designed to protect children and young people from harm, not criminalise them.

Finally ask participants whether they were imagining that the people involved have a particular gender (e.g. was it a boy asking a girl for a nude) and use the following questions to unpick why this makes a difference:

- What difference does someone's gender make in these scenarios?
- Do we react differently to pictures of penises (dick-pics) compared to pictures of breasts or vulvas? What about differences in how we react to people who send pictures of penises vs. boobs?
- What's the difference between asking and pressuring?
- What can we do to combat the slut-shaming of girls?

We know from research that girls and young women are more likely to be asked to send nudes, they are more likely to feel pressured to send a nude and more likely to have their nudes circulated without their consent. We also know that non-binary gender young people send and receive more nudes than cisgender young people and also experience more pressure to send nudes. Further, we know that young women are often shamed and bullied for being associated with nude images or sexual stories, whereas young men more often are not (see *Digital Romance*[26] for more information). It is important, therefore, that we don't see the requesting, refusing and sending of nudes as a gender neutral practice. This activity is designed to help young people navigate this unequal territory and develop realistic strategies for engaging in online conversations that are enjoyable and fun, rather than coercive and/or exploitative.

Extension: New strategies for nudes

As a creative extension ask participants to create new images or gifs that could also be used as responses in the scenarios given on p. 257 or in other situations when they are asked to send or respond to something that they are not comfortable with. As part of this activity encourage participants to think about ways of challenging some of the unequal gender norms that shame and pressure people in different ways.

Ethical decision making

 This activity asks participants to consider what makes a behaviour ethical or unethical. Working with a series of behaviour statements about sexual harassment, participants work in small groups to come up with the questions that need to be considered in ethical decision making. The creative extension to this activity encourages participants to share and showcase their ideas to raise awareness of sexual ethics and consent. 20–30 minutes

 Ethical decision making statements, large sheets of paper and pens. 14+

Note: Before facilitating this activity you may want do the 'Is this sexual harassment?' activity in Chapter 4: *Gender and sexual equality* (see p. 111). This activity uses the following statements as part of an interactive continuum activity in which participants have to consider whether the different behaviours can be categorised as sexual harassment or not.

To facilitate this activity divide participants into small groups and give each group three or four of the following statements. Each of these is a description of a behaviour that could be considered to be sexual harassment.

Ethical decision making statements

Commenting on someone's body shape or size.

Commenting on someone's dress sense or personal appearance.

Making jokes about sex.

Making jokes about rape.

Sharing a short film of two people from the year above having sex.

Discussing someone else's sex life.

Calling someone a slapper/slag/whore.

Saying 'that's gay!'

Looking at topless photos of women in the newspaper.

Staring at someone's body for a long time.

Pinging someone's bra strap.

Asking someone what their genitals are like.

Writing graffiti about someone's sex life in the toilets.

Upskirting (taking a photo up someone's skirt).

Repeating rumours or gossip about someone's sex life or sexual identity.

Touching someone's body.

Posting images of someone's naked body on a social network site.

Making graphic remarks about sex (e.g. she would look good naked on my bed) within earshot of others.

Wolf-whistling and cat-calling.

The task for each group is to make a decision about whether or not the behaviours they have been allocated are ethical. To do this, they should generate a list of questions that they would need answered in order to make their decision. In doing so participants will need to consider and explore what makes a behaviour ethical or unethical. For example:

Behaviour statement: Touching someone's body.

- Do you have active, enthusiastic consent to touch the other person?
- Are they able to tell you that they don't want to be touched?
- Are you able to listen if/when they say no?

Behaviour statement: Commenting on someone's body shape or size.

- Is the comment designed to hurt someone and make them feel bad about themselves?
- Does the comment contain a word that puts a group of people down? (e.g. women, men, gay people, trans people)

Behaviour statement: Posting images of someone's naked body on a social network site.

- Do you have the consent of everyone in the image/film to view the footage, have the footage on your phone and/or forward the footage to others?
- Is this legal?

Once participants have generated a list of questions ask them to create a flowchart for one or more statements that details the sequence of questions needed to make an ethical decision about whether or not a behaviour is ok. Use large sheets of paper and encourage participants to be imaginative and creative about how to visualise the flow of ethical decision making. As a group decide how and where to display these flowcharts to raise aware of the importance of sexual ethics and consent and to help normalise ethical behaviours and questioning. Take photos of the flowcharts and share them online with an agreed hashtag.

Notes

1 World Health Orgnaization (2006) Defining Sexual Health www.who.int/reproductivehealth/publications/sexual_health/defining_sexual_health.pdf
2 www.natsal.ac.uk/media/2102/natsal-infographic.pdf
3 www.natsal.ac.uk/media/2102/natsal-infographic.pdf
4 https://learn.brook.org.uk/
5 https://learn.brook.org.uk/
6 www.tes.com/teaching-resource/sex-and-history-version-2-sre-pshe-key-stage-4-and-5-11162331
7 http://bishtraining.com/planet-porn/
8 https://goodsexproject.wordpress.com/esters-phd-thesis/
9 www.fpa.org.uk/sites/default/files/jiwsi-sre-activities-english.pdf
10 www.tes.com/teaching-resource/sex-and-history-version-2-sre-pshe-key-stage-4-and-5-11162331
11 https://wellcomecollection.org/works/ynqgdv4g
12 McGeeney, E, (2013) What is Good Sex? Young People, Sexual Pleasure and Sexual Health Services. Unpublished doctoral thesis available at: https://goodsexproject.wordpress.com/esters-phd-thesis/

13 Fahs, B, and Frank, E, (2014) 'Notes from the back room: Gender, power, and (in)visibility in women's experiences of masturbation'. Journal of Sex Research, 51(3), pp. 241–252.

14 https://learn.brook.org.uk

15 https://learn.brook.org.uk

16 www.theguardian.com/lifeandstyle/2017/feb/23/golden-trio-of-moves-boosts-chances-of-female-orgasm-say-researchers

17 www.theguardian.com/lifeandstyle/2017/feb/23/golden-trio-of-moves-boosts-chances-of-female-orgasm-say-researchers

18 www.bishuk.com/sex/omg-yes-not-for-me-hmmm-working-out-what-sex-you-want-to-have-2/

19 www.scarleteen.com/article/advice/yes_no_maybe_so_a_sexual_inventory_stocklist

20 www.learn.brook.org.uk

21 www.dosreforschools.com/media/1183/lesson-plan-4.pdf

22 https://learn.brook.org.uk

23 http://pauseplaystop.org.uk/

24 http://pauseplaystop.org.uk

25 www.youtube.com/watch?v=j3TT0TfQHKM

26 McGeeney, E, & Hanson, E, (2017) Digital Romance: A Research Project Exploring Young People's Use of Technology in Their Romantic Relationships and Love Lives. London: National Crime Agency and Brook. Available for free online.

CHAPTER 7

Sexual health

Often sexual health becomes the sole focus of an RSE programme and sessions are concentrated on information giving and driving home key messages about the health risks of sexual activity. We would argue that sexual health is one of many important elements in a holistic programme of RSE. This chapter is full of interactive and engaging ways to facilitate learning around sexual health across the school curriculum or as part of an interdisciplinary informal education programme. Rather than focussing on giving young people information about sexual health we include activities that encourage young people to engage in research and think critically about the attitudes, values and ethics that shape how they will use this information and make decisions in the future.

There are activities in this chapter that would fit into a science lesson, drama class, craft workshop or activism project, although the nature of the chapter means there may be more 'science' type activities than provided in other chapters. However, you do not need to have in-depth medical knowledge in order to confidently facilitate the activities in this chapter. We recommend that you choose activities within this chapter best suited to your skillset and the interests and abilities of your groups. When facilitating sessions on sexual health the priority is to raise young people's awareness of their rights and the services that are available to support them. You can also help by encouraging open conversations about a range of sexual health issues, from contraception to STIs, pregnancy, parenting and abortion.

All the information that you and the young people that you work with need is available online. We have provided links to useful and reliable resources that you can use. Remember that none of this information is useful for young people on its own. They also need to learn about their own bodies and how they work and explore how to negotiate safe and enjoyable sexual experiences with others. We touch on these topics here, but they are more closely covered in Chapter 5: *Bodies* and Chapter 6: *Sex.*

Chapter summary

Section 1: Starting out with sexual health: sex, risk and health. Fun and interactive activities that open up conversations about sex, risk and sexual health and that explore ethical debates about sexual health and safer sex. These are good starter activities for a programme of work around sexual health to help develop confidence in talking about key issues.

Section 2: Using sexual health services. Activities that explore young people's rights to access sexual health services, their hopes and expectations around services and the impact of stigma on service use.

Section 3: Fertility and conception. Activities on fertility and conception, including assisted conception.

Section 4: Contraception. Activities exploring contraceptive choices and decision making. Includes activities on how sex differences and gender norms shape our contraceptive choices and how contraception can impact experiences of sex and pleasure.

Section 5: Condoms. Fun and interactive activities on using condoms (internal and external).

Section 6: Pregnancy choices. Activities exploring pregnancy choices, pregnancy testing and experiences of parenting and abortion.

Section 7: Sexually Transmitted Infections (STIs). Activities on STIs and STI transmission and an activity exploring people's experiences of living with HIV.

Points to consider

- Young people in the UK have the right to access free confidential sexual health services and contraception under the age of 16 without parental consent. In England, Scotland and Wales this includes the right to an abortion but abortion remains illegal in Northern Ireland for people of all ages. If young people only take away one message from a health focussed RSE lesson let it be that they have a right to free, confidential sexual health services regardless of their gender or sexual orientation. For more information see the Gillick test and Fraser Guidelines.[1]
- Sessions on contraception can often become heteronormative because the focus is on reproduction and reproductive (penis-in-vagina) sex. If you are talking about penis-in-vagina sex say so and don't assume that everyone will know what you mean by 'sex'. Be sure to mention the health needs of gay women as these are often left out of RSE.
- Remember to always talk about different kinds of sexual activity (and not just penis-in-vagina sex) and be clear about which types of sex carry the risk of infection and pregnancy (and which don't). There are activities in this chapter such as 'The risk thermometer' on p. 269 to help you do this.
- Similarly be mindful not to let lessons on sexual health become too negative about sex. Emphasise that sex should be enjoyable for all parties involved and be open about how negotiating and using contraception can enhance or decrease feelings of comfort and pleasure.

- We have found that some educators show graphic pictures of badly infected genitals or aborted fetuses when educating young people about STIs or abortion. It is important NOT to do this. Scare tactics have been shown not to work in RSE and can add to the shame and stigma around sexual health which impedes young people's capacity to make informed decisions about their health and their bodies.

- It is important to say Sexually Transmitted Infection (STI) and not Sexually Transmitted Disease (STD) because it is possible to be infected without showing any symptoms of disease. This is also why showing images of infected genitalia are unhelpful as they show extreme examples of infection that most people will never experience. A more helpful message is to always get tested if you have unprotected sex, as many STIs have NO SYMPTOMS at all.

- It's a really good idea to ask someone from your local sexual health clinic to come in and talk to the young people that you work with and even better if you can take participants to the clinic so that they know exactly where it is and what it's like. This is an important part of reducing the stigma around sexual health clinics and emphasising that attending one and getting tested is part of being a responsible sexual citizen and healthy sexual being.

LGBT+ inclusive sexual health guides

These guides are useful for educators to support the development and delivery of LGBT+ inclusive sexual health sessions. We also recommend making sure participants are aware of these guides in case they are interested in finding out more and to have copies available where possible.

- *Lesbian Sexual Health Guide - Beating About the Bush.*[2]
- *Good Sex Is...For Gay and Bi Men: An Inclusive and Positive Guide to Sex and Relationships for Gay and Bisexual Men.*[3]
- *Good Sex Is...An Inclusive Guide for Trans People.*[4]

Section 1: Starting out with sexual health: sex, risk and health

Sexual health balloon busting misconceptions

 A fun and interactive way to bust some common misconceptions about sex and sexual health and find out what participants do and do not already know.

 20–30 minutes

 Pack of balloons, marker pen, set of statements.

 13+

Note: Often in RSE, myth busting activities are set up as myth vs. facts or true vs. false games or quizzes. We think it's best to avoid doing this as there is a real risk of reinforcing the myth or falsehood simply by mentioning it (some young people may have never heard of the myth until you brought it up!) Instead we advocate starting with asking young people what they know and think and then giving them accurate information. This will bust any misconceptions or myths that they have heard. This activity is a fun, interactive way of doing this.

To set up this activity

Print off the list of statements of fact in Table 7.1 and cut them up so that each statement is on a slip of paper. Insert one of your chosen statements into a balloon, blow the balloon up and tie a knot in the end. Write the corresponding question on the outside of the balloon in marker pen. Repeat this for all of the statements you want to cover. Depending on the size and type of the group you may want to select the most relevant questions for your group. You can add your own statements but do take the time to make sure any facts and statistics are verifiable.

To deliver the activity

Throw one balloon around the room; participants can either stand in a circle for this or be sat where they would usually. The first young person to catch a balloon reads the question on the outside of the balloon and gives what they think is the correct answer. Encourage participants to guess if they do not know the answer but they can pass the balloon on if they prefer. Keep throwing the balloon to give multiple participants the opportunity to answer the question. If the correct answer is given, don't stop the balloon throwing straight away but make a mental note of who got it correct (most won't).

Once answers have been exhausted, ask someone to pop the balloon to reveal the correct answer. Acknowledge those that did guess the correct answer and discuss what people think and feel about the answers. Some answers they may find surprising.

Repeat this for the rest of the prepared balloons.

TABLE 7.1 Sexual health balloon busting: questions and statements

Question for writing on outside of balloon	Statement for printing on inside of balloon
What percentage of people have sex under the age of 16?	One quarter to one third of young people have sex under the age of 16. This means that the majority don't. Most young people will have had sex at least once by age 19.[1]
How common is masturbation?	Masturbation is a common sexual practice with significant variations in reporting between men and women. In 16–44-year-olds, 62% of men and 27% of women reported masturbating in the last seven days.[2]
What percentage of the population identify as Lesbian, Gay or Bisexual (LGB)?	Around 2.5% of the population (PHE, 2017), however it has also been suggested that one in two young people describe themselves as something other than heterosexual (YouGov, 2015). Stats vary because people may not always be comfortable putting their sexual orientation down on data gathering forms.[3]
What percentage of the population identify as trans or gender non-binary?	Increasing numbers of people are identifying as trans or gender non-binary partly due to increasing knowledge and acceptance of diverse gender identities. It is often estimated that the trans population is around 1% of the population and that less than 0.2% will go on to seek hormone therapy or gender confirmation surgeries.[4] Statistics vary because the questions around sex and gender on data gathering forms are often poorly worded so accurate information is not gathered.
Can you get an STI from oral sex?	Yes. Generally, the risk of infection is lower when you receive oral sex than when you give someone oral sex. STIs that are commonly caught through oral sex are: gonorrhoea, genital herpes, syphilis. Infections that are less frequently passed on through oral sex include: chlamydia, HIV, hepatitis A, hepatitis B and hepatitis C, genital warts, pubic lice.[5]
How common is chlamydia in young people?	One in ten sexually active young people aged 16–25 have chlamydia. There are often no signs or symptoms and left untreated can affect fertility in men and women. Tests usually involve giving a urine sample or taking a swab. It is a bacterial infection that is treated with antibiotics.[6]

Question for writing on outside of balloon	Statement for printing on inside of balloon
Who can get an STI and how are they transmitted?	Anyone who has anal, vaginal or oral sex without using a condom, femidom or dam. STIs can also be passed on through sharing sex toys. It doesn't matter if you are gay, straight or bisexual or whether you have had sex once or 100 times. And it's not just young people who get STIs either – rates are rising among older populations. STIs are transmitted in body fluids including semen, vaginal fluid, blood or contact with infected skin or mucous membranes.[7]
What do you know about HIV and AIDS?	**HIV** (human immunodeficiency virus) is a virus that attacks the human immune system, the natural defense system of the body. Without a strong immune system, the body struggles to fight off infections. **AIDS** (acquired immune deficiency syndrome) is the name used to describe a number of potentially life-threatening infections and illnesses that happen when your immune system has been severely damaged by the HIV virus. There is currently no cure, however there are effective drug treatments that can enable people to live for a long time. Worldwide an estimated 36.7 million people are living with HIV and an estimated 35 million people have died from AIDS.[8]
How many different types of contraception are there?	15 1. Condom 2. Femindom 3. Vasectomy (sterilisation by cutting and tying or blocking the tubes (vas deferens) that carries sperm from the testicles to the penis) 4. Tubal ligation (sterilisation by cutting and tying or blocking the fallopian tubes) 5. Combined pill 6. Progesterone only pill 7. Contraceptive patch 8. Contraceptive injection 9. Emergency contraception 10. Diaphragm 11. IUD 12. IUS 13. Contraceptive implant 14. Contraceptive vaginal ring 15. Natural family planning (including charting, apps and urine testing machines)[9]

Question for writing on outside of balloon	Statement for printing on inside of balloon
How common is abortion?	One in three women will have an abortion in their lifetime (NHS Choices). Over half of women who have an abortion have already had a child.[10]
What is the average penis size when it is not erect (flaccid)?	There are no average length figures for teenagers because people grow at different rates. In adults the average size is approximately 9–10cm long. Length of the flaccid penis does not necessarily correspond to length of the erect penis; some smaller flaccid penises grow much longer, while some larger flaccid penises grow comparatively less.
What is the average penis size when it is erect?	There are no average length figures for teenagers because people grow at different rates. In adults the average erect penis length is around 13cm. People often think the average penis size is much larger due to the tendency of pornography to display large penises.
What is the average length of a vagina? Unaroused and aroused.	There are no average length figures for teenagers because people grow at different rates. The vagina is a very stretchy organ that can range in length from 7cm–15cm unaroused to aroused. It basically doubles in length, increases in width and produces lubrication when aroused. So vaginas become erect just like penises!
What size is the clitoris?	There are no average length figures for teenagers because people grow at different rates. The clitoris is much, much larger than people think. The tip of the clitoris is roughly the size and shape of a pea, but the rest of the clitoris extends under the skin in bulbs in a wishbone shape that can be up to 10cm long. The clitoris is estimated to have more than 8,000 sensory nerve endings compared to the head of the penis which has around 4,000.
What is FGM?	FGM is Female Genital Mutilation. This refers to all procedures that involve the partial or total removal of the external female genitalia, or other injury to the female genital organs for non-medical reasons. FGM can cause severe pain, bleeding, problems urinating, cysts, infections, infertility, complications in childbirth, and even death. There are 200 million women and girls who are thought to be affected by FGM worldwide and FGM is mostly carried out on girls between infancy and age 15.[11]

Question for writing on outside of balloon	Statement for printing on inside of balloon
Which parts of the human body are important for experiencing pleasure?	This answer is entirely individual as people experience pleasure in different ways, although what we identify as an important body part for pleasure is shaped by cultural ideas about sex, gender and the body. Parts of the body relating to pleasure can include: brain, skin, nipples, head of penis, clitoris, inner labia, neck, lips, anus, but basically every part of the body can feel pleasurable if touched in the right way!

1 NATSAL-3 (2012) 'Sexual attitudes and lifestyles in Britain: Highlights from Natsal-3': www.natsal.ac.uk/media/2102/natsal-infographic.pdf

2 NATSAL-3 (2012) 'The National Survey of Sexual Attitudes and Lifestyles (Natsal-3) Reference tables': www.natsal.ac.uk/media/3935/natsal-3-reference-tables.pdf, Table 19.

3 PHE (2017) 'Producing modelled estimates of the size of the lesbian, gay and bisexual (LGB) population of England. Final Report': www.gov.uk/government/uploads/system/uploads/attachment_data/file/585349/PHE_Final_report_FINAL_DRAFT_14.12.2016NB230117v2.pdf and YouGov (2015) '1 in 2 young people say they are not 100% heterosexual': https://yougov.co.uk/news/2015/08/16/half-young-not-heterosexual/

4 GIRES (2015) 'Monitoring gender nonconformity – a quick guide': www.gires.org.uk/wp-content/uploads/2014/09/Monitoring-Gender-Nonconformity.pdf

5 NHS (2018) 'Sex activities and risk: sexual health': www.nhs.uk/Livewell/STIs/Pages/Sexualactivitiesandrisk.aspx

6 Brook (n.d.) 'Chlamydia': www.brook.org.uk/your-life/chlamydia

7 NHS (2018) 'Sexual health: STI symptoms that need checking': www.nhs.uk/Livewell/STIs/Pages/STIs.aspx

8 NHS (2018) 'Overview: HIV and AIDS': www.nhs.uk/conditions/hiv-and-aids/ and Avert (2018) 'Global HIV and AIDS statistics': www.avert.org/global-hiv-and-aids-statistics

9 Sexwise (n.d.) 'Which method of contraception is right for me?': www.fpa.org.uk/contraception-help/your-guide-contraception

10 NHS (2016) 'Overview: abortion': www.nhs.uk/conditions/abortion/ and Stone, N, & Ingham, R, (2011) 'Who presents more than once? Repeat abortion among women in Britain' *J Fam Plann Reprod Health Care*: http://srh.bmj.com/content/familyplanning/early/2011/06/30/jfprhc-2011-0063.full.pdf

11 WHO (2018) 'Female genital mutilation': www.who.int/mediacentre/factsheets/fs241/en/

Keyword Jenga

A fun activity to use at the start or end of a programme to explore what participants have learned or know already about a range of topics relating to sexual health.

10–15 minutes per game

Jenga set with pre-prepared key words written on (you can often pick up sets in charity shops). You may want to ask some volunteers to help you with this. (If you want to do this with a large group (more than 16 participants) you may need more than one set.)

11+

To set up the activity

Using a standard Jenga set write a key word from the list on pp. 268–9 on each block. There are 53 blocks so a full list of 53 words is available. Place the blocks in a tower.

To facilitate the activity

Divide the group into two teams of a maximum of eight participants each. A participant from one team should draw out a block from the tower and say a definition or a fact they have learned about that key word. All participants within their team should take it in turns to contribute as much information on that particular key word until the information dries up. The participant then places the block on the top of the tower. If no-one on the team knows anything about the word, they have to return the block and take out a new one.

A participant in the other team then gets to remove the next block and their team gets to respond with definitions and facts. Continue playing until the tower is so unstable it collapses. The educator decides the winning team based on who gave the most accurate information and thoughtful comments, balanced with which group managed not to destroy the tower.

The activity can take a really long time if you try and do all 53 words in one session! We suggest playing until the tower topples. The activity can be repeated at the start and end of a sequence of sessions to see what has changed in participants' knowledge and understanding. In this case encourage the group to reflect at the end of the activity on any changes in their knowledge, understanding, confidence and values. You can also differentiate this activity dependent on the age range of your group, for example by including more words relating to puberty and body parts for 11-year-olds.

List of key words:

1. vulva
2. vagina
3. fallopian tube
4. uterus
5. ovary
6. egg
7. cervix
8. clitoris
9. urethra
10. anus

11. penis
12. testicles
13. sperm duct
14. sperm
15. scrotum
16. foreskin
17. glans
18. breasts
19. oestrogen
20. vaginal fluid

21. pre-cum
22. semen
23. menstruation
24. yeast infection (thrush)
25. trichomoniasis
26. bacterial vaginosis
27. testosterone
28. progesterone
29. oxytocin
30. serotonin

31. dopamine	39. pubic lice	47. natural family planning
32. chlamydia	40. condoms/femidom	48. IUD/IUS
33. HIV	41. contraceptive pill	49. implant
34. gonorrhea	42. contraceptive patch	50. contraceptive
35. syphilis	43. contraceptive injection	vaginal ring
36. Hepatitis A, B or C	44. emergency contraception	51. sex
37. genital warts (HPV)	45. diaphragm	52. gender
38. genital herpes	46. sterilisation	53. sexuality

If you don't have access to a Jenga set there are two alternative activities that you can use to explore some of these words. See 'Taboo' and 'Call my bluff' activities, which can be found in Chapter 8: *Concluding the learning* on pp. 335 and 334.

The risk thermometer

This activity has been developed from content provided by Heather Corinna, founder and director of award winning sexual health organisation Scarleteen in the article: 'Can I get pregnant or pass on an STI from that?'[5] Shared with permission.

 An interactive activity that explores the relative risks of different sexual activities. This activity helps to check participants' knowledge about sex and challenge any assumptions that all sex is heterosexual, penetrative, penis-in-vagina sex. This is important for making sure that your RSE programme is LGBT+ inclusive and for making sure that young people understand what sex is before they are told about its risks and dangers! 20–30 minutes

 Large thermometer printed on A3 (see Figure 7.1 for an example that can be photocopied and enlarged), post-it notes, pens. (Optional sets of sexual activity cards.) 14+

Divide participants into groups of five–eight and give them post-it notes and pens. Ask groups to brainstorm all the different ways they can think of being sexual or intimate with someone. Ask participants to write one sexual activity on each post-it note. Prompt participants to think holistically and challenge the idea that sex is all about genitals. See Table 7.2 for ideas and if participants are struggling share some of the answers to help keep the conversation flowing.

Give each group a printed thermometer. Ask each group to decide what level of risk there is for each sexual activity. They should consider the risk of pregnancy and STIs. If they think an activity is high risk the post-it note should be placed at the top of the thermometer, if medium risk in the middle, if low or no risk then at the bottom.

Ask groups to feedback their answers and give the correct responses using Table 7.2. You do not need to give participants details of each STI that can be transmitted as this will be too much information to absorb! This is for your information only and to refer to if you or the participants are interested.

Where there is a risk of infection or pregnancy ask participants to clarify what the risks are and how infection is transmitted/pregnancy can occur. This will help to ensure that everyone understands what each sexual activity is and to increase knowledge and confidence around talking about bodies and the exchange of body fluids.

Questions:

- How can someone reduce risks of STI/pregnancy? (*STI risk is reduced through using a condom, dam, finger gloves or engaging in a no/low risk activity. Pregnancy risk is reduced through using a form of contraception.*)
- If someone has engaged in any of these activities without protection, what can they do? (*Visit a sexual health clinic for STI and pregnancy testing; if sex was in the past five days and carries pregnancy risk, visit a clinic or pharmacy for emergency contraception; if sex was within last 72 hours and carries risk of HIV transmission visit a clinic or A&E for Post-exposure prophylaxis (PEP) – a powerful one month course of HIV prevention medication.*)
- Is it possible to rank the activities on the thermometer in terms of pleasure? What would it look like? (*What counts as pleasurable is different for everyone, it will vary depending on whether partners have two vulvas/a penis and a vulva, etc., personal preference and many other factors; research suggests that the majority of women who have sex with men don't orgasm from penis-in-vagina sex although orgasm is not the only pleasurable sensation to be enjoyed during sex.*)
- What are some of the reasons why people might have unprotected sex? (*Answers might include: getting carried away in heat of the moment; lack of education; being drunk; thinking they aren't fertile; trying for a baby or don't mind if they have a baby.*)
- What are some scenarios in which someone may WANT to have protected sex but it turns out differently? (*Answers might include: condom might slip off or break; sickness or vomiting reduces effectiveness of pill; one partner lies to other about condom use – stealthing.*)
- What are some scenarios in which someone may not care about whether they have unprotected sex or not? (*Answers might include: low self esteem; high or drunk at the time and feeling uninhibited; confident about access to PrEP (Pre-exposure prophylaxis) or emergency contraception after the event.*)
- If someone does have unprotected sex what can they do AFTER sex to protect themselves against infection? (*PrEP if available (not yet widely available on NHS); getting tested; getting treatment; informing partners.*)
- If someone does have unprotected sex what can they do AFTER sex to protect themselves against unwanted pregnancy? (*Emergency contraception – pill/IUS or IUD; abortion.*)
- What other kinds of risks could there be? (*Answers could include: emotional risks (vulnerability, regret, etc.) and physical risks (violence, physical discomfort).*)
- Can sex ever be risk free? (*Answers might include: all activities (not just sexual) carry some level of risk but there are ways to assess risks and minimise those risks. Strong trust and feeling very comfortable with a partner can help to talk about risks and minimise potential harms.*)

A Safer Sex card sort which has similar learning aims to this activity can be found in *DO…RSE for Schools lesson plan 5 activity 2* written by Justin Hancock and Alice Hoyle: www.dosreforschools. com/media/1184/lesson-plan-5.pdf.

TABLE 7.2 The risk thermometer

Sex activity	Level of STI risk	Level of pregnancy risk
TALKING. Talking about sex, including cybersex, phone sex, or sexy texting; 'talking dirty'	**No risk**	**No risk**
KISSING	**No risk to low risk.** Possible risk of: Oral herpes (HSV-1), and common illnesses like colds, flu.	**No risk**
TOUCHING, PETTING OR MASSAGE. Stroking bodies or body parts without any naked genital contact, direct genital touching or fluid sharing; can include touching someone's genitals over their clothes; 'feeling up'	**No risk to low risk.** Low risk for broken or abraded skin with possibility of skin infections.	**No risk**
SENSATION PLAY. Exploring different sensations of the body, like with hot or cold items, objects like feathers or fabric, or using things like clamps, hands or other items for activities like spanking or suction; does not account for any direct genital contact or fluid sharing.	**No risk to low risk** Low risk for broken or abraded skin with possibility of skin infections.	**No risk**
MUTUAL MASTURBATION. Masturbating together, but only touching one's own genitals, not a partner's genitals.	**No risk to low risk** Low risk of bacterial vaginosis (BV) and urinary tract infections (UTIs) if hands are not clean or covered.	**No risk**
USING SEX TOYS. Use of something like a vibrator, dildo, butt plug, masturbation sleeve or other toy.	**No risk to low risk** Low risk for dirty and/or shared toys without barriers, like condoms or finger cots. Risk of bacterial vaginosis (BV) and urinary tract infections (UTIs) if toys are not clean or covered.	**No risk**[1]
MANUAL SEX. Engaging a partner's genitals with the hands or fingers; 'fingering', or 'handjob'.	**Low risk** Low risk of HPV, genital warts, chlamydia, herpes simplex virus (HSV) 1 and/or 2, syphilis	**No risk**[2]

Sex activity	Level of STI risk	Level of pregnancy risk
'DRY HUMPING', FROTTAGE OR DRY SEX. Rubbing your genitals together while clothed, in this case, without direct genital-to-genital intercourse or any possible fluid sharing because of clothing.	**Low risk** **Low risk** of pubic lice and trichomoniasis from direct skin to skin contact.	**No risk**, so long as at least one partner is wearing clothing that covers their genitals. If genitals are not completely covered – for example, only one partner is wearing a narrow thong – that may allow fluid sharing, and there may be low risk.
ORAL SEX – CUNNILINGUS. Stimulating someone's vulva externally (the mons, outer or inner labia, clitoris, vaginal opening or perineum) and/or internally (the vagina) with the mouth, tongue or lips.	**Moderate risk** Infections can be passed from vulva to mouth. This can include (not complete list): chlamydia, gonorrhoea, hepatitis B virus (HBV), hepatitis A virus (HAV), HSV type 1 and/or type 2, HIV (rare), HPV, syphilis.	**No risk**
ORAL SEX – FELLATIO. Stimulating someone's penis or testes with the mouth, tongue or lips.	**High risk** Infections can be passed from penis or semen to mouth. This can include: chlamydia, gonorrhoea, hepatitis B virus (HBV), hepatitis A virus (HAV), HSV type 1 and/or type 2, HIV (rare), HPV, syphilis.	**No risk**
RUBBING, FROTTAGE OR TRIBBING (when people are NOT wearing any clothing). Rubbing genitals directly together.	**Moderate to high risk** Risks are much higher with the presence of body fluids, like ejaculate. Without fluids risk is lower.	**Moderate risk** (higher if one partner ejaculates onto the other's genitals)[3]
SEMEN OR VAGINAL FLUID SHARING. Tasting or ingesting pre-ejaculate, semen and/or vaginal fluids; direct genital or oral contact with fluids.	**High risk** Infections at possible risk of: chancroid, chlamydia, gonorrhoea, HSV type 1 and/or type 2, HIV, HPV, hepatitis B virus (HBV), hepatitis A virus (HAV), hepatitis C virus (HCV).	**No risk** if sharing is only oral, high risk if sharing is genital and involves contact between semen and the vulva.

Sex activity	Level of STI risk	Level of pregnancy risk
ORAL SEX – ANALINGUS. Stimulating the anus or rectum with the lips and/or tongue.	**High risk** Infections at possible risk of: yeast/thrush (from trace fecal bacteria in mouth), chlamydia, gonorrhoea, hepatitis B virus (HBV), hepatitis A virus (HAV), HIV (rare), HSV type 1 and/or type 2, HPV, genital warts, syphilis.	**No risk**
ANAL INTERCOURSE. Entering the anus or rectum with a penis or sex toy.	**High risk** Infections at possible risk of: chlamydia, gonorrhoea, hepatitis B virus (HBV), hepatitis A virus (HAV), hepatitis C, HSV-2, HIV, HPV, NGU, pubic lice, syphilis.	**Low risk** **Note:** Low risk of pregnancy here as semen can dribble out of anus after sex and come into contact with vulva.
VAGINAL INTERCOURSE. Interlocking the penis with the vagina or vaginal intercourse using dildos with harnesses (AKA, strap-on sex).	**High risk** (only when penis-in-vagina, not for strap-on intercourse). Infections at possible risk of: chlamydia, gonorrhoea, hepatitis B virus (HBV), HCV, HSV-2, HIV, HPV, NGU, pelvic inflammatory disease (PID), pubic lice, syphilis, trichomoniasis.	**High risk** for penis-in-vagina sex but not for strap-on intercourse.

1   An important note: If toys are shared, but not covered with a latex/polyurethane barrier or sanitised in between, or you don't clean toys every time before and after use, there are possible risks of BV, UTIs and chlamydia. If toys are used for activities where there is some genital contact, like a strap-on used for intercourse, some STI risks, namely HPV or herpes, can exist due to there still being direct genital contact.

2   If engaging in deeper manual sex, where more fingers or a whole hand are inside the vagina or anus – some people call this fisting – infection risks increase. Also, if after or during unprotected manual sex someone puts their fingers in their mouths or a partner's mouth, infection risks also are increased, especially if manual sex involves the anus.

3   Naked rubbing like this can be something people turn into intercourse, or something people consider they're doing instead of intercourse with ideas like 'just the tip', or 'just for a few seconds'. If any vaginal entry at all is involved, that is vaginal intercourse, not this activity. If any genital entry into the anus is involved, that is anal intercourse, not this activity.

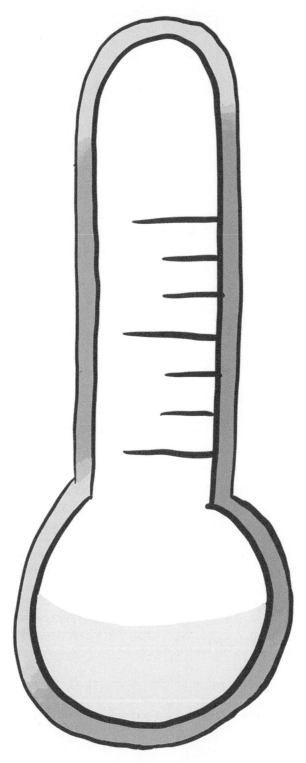

FIGURE 7.1 The Risk thermometer
Illustration by: Chrissy Baxter

Safer sex auction

This session is adapted from an activity in Hedgepeth, E M, & Helmich, J (1996) *Teaching about Sexuality and HIV: Principles and Methods for Effective Education* New York University Press. Shared with permission.

  This is a whole group activity that encourages participants to explore and reflect on their values, attitudes and assumptions relating to safer sex.

30 minutes

  Safer sex auction sheets – one per participant.

14+

Pass out the worksheet 'Safer sex auction'. Read the instructions (see p. 275) and give participants five minutes to decide how they would like to bid.

Begin bidding. Move quickly to determine who gets each item. Bids should increase in increments of £50.

Remind participants that if they do not get an item, they can put their money towards another item not yet auctioned. After bidding is complete facilitate a discussion using the following questions:

- What do your selections show about what is important to you?
- Did you bid to protect yourself or to protect others?
- If you won the item you most valued what would the outcome be?
- Did you learn anything from the exercise? If so what?

Safer sex auction worksheet

You have £1,000 to spend at an auction. Put the amount you intend to bid next to the line of the item.

As the auction proceeds and you spend or lose money on items you hoped to purchase revise your plan in the second and third columns.

Item	Planned bids	Revised bids	Revised bids
An inoculation that will make you immune to any STI including HIV.			
An un-infected, loyal, trustworthy partner.			
The ability to change unsafe sexual behaviour of all teenagers.			
Invent a cure for herpes.			
High quality relationships and sex education in all primary, secondary schools and colleges. Includes a compulsory one session a week delivered by well trained educators.			
End prejudice and discrimination against those who are Lesbian, Gay, Bisexual, Trans (LGBT) and/ or other gender or sexual minorities.			

Turn over to see more items up for auction

Item	Planned bids	Revised bids	Revised bids
Write a book that would make you famous for describing healthy sexual development through the lifespan.			
Make £20 billion inventing and marketing the 'pleasure condom' that makes sex more comfortable and enjoyable.			
Be certain that no-one you know will die of AIDS.			
Workshops for all young people on how to feel good about their sexuality.			
A magic ring that tells you if someone is infected with an STI.			
An endless supply of free condoms for you and your friends.			
Outlaw all sexual intercourse without marriage.			
A chance to talk honestly with adults you respect about sex.			
Require that everyone carry a card informing of their STI status.			
Free and easy access to PrEP for anyone wishing to take it. (Pre-exposure prophylaxis is HIV prevention medication taken before sex to reduce the risk of getting HIV.)			

Section 2: Using sexual health services

The story of Gillick – your rights vs. parental rights

 This activity involves examining a key historical legal case that shapes how young people's sexual health services are delivered today. The aim is to encourage discussion and debate about consent and children vs. parental rights and clarify that young people have the right to access free confidential sexual health services without parental consent.

 30 minutes

 Copies of *The Story of Gillick* printed with discussion questions. Copies of the short 1983 news article, *Mother loses contraception test case*, available from the BBC *On This Day 1950–2005*.

 13+

Open the activity with a quick three question quiz:

- What is the legal age of sexual consent in the UK? (*Answer = 16*).
- Can under 16s go to sexual health clinics without their parents knowing? (*Answer = yes*)
- Which of the following can they get without parental consent: contraception, STI testing, and referrals for an abortion? (*Answer = all three*).

Give the answers and explain that the right of young people under 16 to access *confidential* sexual health services is enshrined in law in the UK. The focus of this activity will be on exploring how these rights *became* enshrined in law and what the group think about the ethics of the current legal situation.

Divide into pairs or small groups. Give each pair a copy of *The Story of Gillick* and ask them to read it through together, underlining any words or concepts that they don't understand. It is a complicated story so make time to explain the technicalities to your participants.

Ask pairs to feedback and facilitate a group debate. Ensure that whatever views are discussed you emphasise that young people under 16 have the legal right to access confidential sexual health services.

The Story of Gillick

In the 1980s there was a woman called Victoria Gillick who was a Roman Catholic mother of ten children, living in England. In 1982 she took her local health authority and the Department of Health and Social Security to court to attempt to stop doctors from giving contraceptive advice or treatment to young people under 16-year-olds, without parental consent.

At the time of the case, the authorities had previously stated that the age at which children could consent to medical treatment was 16. This included sexual health and contraceptive testing and advice. But doctors and nurses were sometimes faced with under 16s presenting for sexual health advice and treatment and found themselves in a grey legal area as they knew that if they demanded parental consent young people would be unlikely to access their services. This led to the Department of Health issuing a circular stating that in strictly limited circumstances, staff could treat under 16s. This is what Mrs Gillick objected to.

The case went to the High Court. The judge – Mr Justice Woolf – had to consider the following:

- Could someone under 16 have sufficient mental maturity to consent to sexual health advice and treatment?
- If a healthcare professional provided contraception to a person under 16 were they aiding and abetting unlawful sexual intercourse? (Remember – sex under 16 is illegal.)

The Judge decided that under 16s could have the maturity and capacity to consent to healthcare treatment without parental consent and Mrs Gillick lost the case. Here is part of Mr Justice Woolf's judgment:

> ...whether or not a child is capable of giving the necessary consent will depend on the child's maturity and understanding and the nature of the consent required. The child must be capable of making a reasonable assessment of the advantages and disadvantages of the treatment proposed, so the consent, if given, can be properly and fairly described as true consent.
>
> (Gillick v West Norfolk, 1984)[6]

Mrs Gillick took the case to the court of Appeal who reversed the decision (meaning that Mrs Gillick had won the case). But in 1985 the case went to the House of Lords and the Law Lords who looked at the case (Lord Scarman, Lord Fraser and Lord Bridge) ruled in favour of the original judgment by Mr Justice Woolf. This was a landmark ruling that shapes how health services are delivered today.

In his judgment at the House of Lords, Lord Fraser set out a series of guidelines, which apply specifically to contraceptive advice. These are called the Fraser guidelines and are still used today.

Lord Fraser stated that a doctor could proceed to give advice and treatment 'provided he is satisfied in the following criteria:

- that the girl (although under the age of 16 years of age) will understand his advice;
- that he cannot persuade her to inform her parents or to allow him to inform the parents that she is seeking contraceptive advice;
- that she is very likely to continue having sexual intercourse with or without contraceptive treatment;
- that unless she receives contraceptive advice or treatment her physical or mental health or both are likely to suffer;
- that her best interests require him to give her contraceptive advice, treatment or both without the parental consent.'

The Fraser Guidelines are the basis on which young people under 16 in the UK are given sexual health advice and treatment today. Young people have the legal right to a confidential service, providing the healthcare professional views that they can understand the advice being given. This applies to people of all genders – not just girls.

In pairs ask participants to consider the following questions and complete the task. You may want them to write down their answers or to discuss and make notes.

Questions

1. At what age do you think children have the maturity to consent to medical advice and treatment? Think about getting antibiotics for an ear infection, asking for the contraceptive pill, having a heart operation, having an abortion.
2. Should parents have to be informed if their child is receiving any of these types of treatment? What if the parent and the child have a different view on what treatment they would like to receive?
3. Currently parents do not need to be informed if a young person under 16 receives sexual health advice. What do you think would happen if they were informed? What might be the benefits to this? What would be the negatives?
4. The legal age at which people can consent to sex in the UK is 16. Do you think that a healthcare professional is encouraging unlawful sex by giving a 14- or 15-year-old contraception or offering them STI testing? What do you think would happen if the law was changed and this became illegal?
5. Currently parents have the right to withdraw their child from RSE sessions in schools but they do not have the right to prevent their child from receiving sexual health advice or treatment. Should parents have the right to withdraw their child from RSE sessions in schools?

Visualising your local services

This activity is inspired by an exercise originally developed by Health Initiatives for Youth (HIFY-UK), a charity set up by Clint Walters who tested HIV positive at 17 years of age and died aged 31 in 2010. The exercise was reproduced in Blake, S & Power, P (2003) *Teaching and Learning About HIV: A Resource for Key Stages 1 to 4*. Published by NCB and JKP. Used with permission from NCB.

 A visualisation activity that enables participants to become familiar with local support services and explore their thoughts and feelings about accessing them. 30 minutes (minimum). Can be extended into longer project.

 Local posters/flyers and information about local and national sexual health services. 14+

Ask participants to close their eyes and take part in a visualisation. Read the script see page 282.

In small groups ask participants to draw on their experiences to complete the following task:

Create a resource for young people in your school/youth club to support them to access your local sexual health services. To do this you will need to research details of your local sexual health services and think about what information young people need to make it possible for them to visit the service and get the tests and treatment they may need.

Reflect on your feelings and concerns during the visualisation to help you do this. What were you worried about and what information, support or reassurance would have helped you feel comfortable and confident about accessing your local services? This may include knowing where the clinic is or whether you need an appointment or can just turn up; knowing whether or not the service is LGBT+ friendly; knowing whether the service is accessible to disabled young people; understanding what is involved when you go for an STI or pregnancy test; worrying about the service contacting your parents.

If you don't know the answers to these questions, look online and contact your local sexual health services and ask for clarification. Decide what information or advice is most important and choose how to represent this to other young people.

Note: If there is time available we recommend that you organise a trip to a sexual health clinic, alternatively you could invite a local sexual health practitioner into a session to help facilitate this activity.

Visualising your local services: script for educators

Start by closing your eyes to block out distractions and help focus your thoughts. I will be reading you a visualisation that takes a few minutes. As I read try to be aware of how you are feeling, what you are thinking and what images come up for you.

As you sit in your chair make sure both your feet are flat on the floor. Place your hands in a comfortable position. Now take a deep breath, hold it and then slowly release it (pause). Do that again… (pause).

Imagine that you have just had sex without using a condom and no other method of contraception. You don't know if you have been exposed to an STI or not. If you had penis-in-vagina sex you may also be worried about possible pregnancy.

What do you do now and where do you go? (Pause) Do you know how and where to get a pregnancy test or if you even need one? What about STI tests? Where should you go to get help and what do you think will happen when you get there? (Pause) What are your worries and concerns about accessing the help you need?

Imagine you have somehow found your local sexual health clinic and have made an appointment. How do you feel now?

How do you think you would access the clinic? What do you think the waiting area might be like?

As you think about attending the clinic, what you are feeling? What emotions are you experiencing? (Pause)

What about going into the consultation room? How comfortable are you sitting and talking to a stranger about your behaviours and possible exposure to STIs or risks of pregnancy? What questions are you afraid to ask or answer? If after talking to a health adviser you decide to have the tests, what are you thinking as the test is done? What do you want to have happen next? (pause)

You wait for your test results. What will you do if the result tests positive for an STI or pregnancy? How will you feel? What about if your test results come back negative? How will you feel? Would your results make any difference to your sexual decision making in the future?

Keeping these thoughts and feelings in mind, I'd like you to take several deep breaths… and bring your attention back here to this room.

Exploring stigma

 A whole group activity that helps participants to understand how stigma can affect mental and physical health and access to services. 30 minutes

 A range of coloured stickers (blue, green, red, white). 14+

This activity refers to HIV and AIDS stigma. It may be helpful to have already covered basic knowledge about HIV and AIDS before facilitating this activity but this is not essential. You can cover the basics of HIV transmission within the activity or adapt to explore other forms of stigma such as mental health stigma.

Stick a coloured sticker on the forehead of each participant in the room so that it is visible to others but not to the participant. We suggest sticking to the temples and to avoid sticking the sticker in the centre of the forehead to avoid cultural appropriation of the bindi. Allocate colours at random. Ensure the participant does not know what their own colour sticker is and ask participants not to tell each other what colour their stickers are.

Inform the group that people with certain stickers have the following characteristics. It may be useful to write or display this information in the room.

- Reds – have an infectious disease that can kill.
- Blues – are people who appear nice but there is something different about them. This affects how other people interact with them.
- Greens – are the wealthiest in the community and will help people they think are worthy of help.
- Whites – did something in their past that is not against the law but that society deems unacceptable.

Ask participants to walk around the room and greet each other, they can say hello, shake hands, fist pump, hug, etc.

After five minutes, tell participants to stop and without looking at the dots on their foreheads, get into four groups: greens, reds, whites, blues. Participants will have to guess where to stand based on how others have responded to them. Make sure participants do NOT tell each other where to stand – they may need to practise using their poker faces so as not to reveal the correct answers!

Once everyone has positioned themselves, have participants look at their stickers one group at a time. If people have aligned themselves to the wrong group ask them to stand in the group corresponding to their colour.

Explore why participants decided which coloured group they were in. Explain that this exercise is an exercise exploring stigma and discrimination and facilitate a discussion using some of the following questions. You can do this as a whole group or ask participants to stay in their coloured groups and appoint a spokesperson to feedback.

All groups:

- How did people respond to you during the game? How did you treat others?
- How did you feel during the game? Were you surprised by your feelings?
- Greens only: What did it feel like to be the privileged ones? How did this affect your behaviour?
- Who felt victimised? What did this feel like? How did you feel towards those who were privileged?
- What kinds of diseases might the reds have? (*Answers may include: ebola, tuberculosis, flu, HIV.*)
- Does it makes a difference how the disease is transmitted? (*Remind participants that HIV is not an airborne pathogen and is actually only transmitted via bodily fluids.*)
- If the red group were the living-with-HIV group instead how would this have affected interactions during the exercise? How should we treat people living with HIV?
- What sorts of issues and differences might the white group have that this community deems unacceptable? (*Answers could include: been a teenage parent; had an abortion; had an affair; had a lot of sex; being LGBT. Make sure to unpick that not all communities will respond in the same way to these groups.*)
- What sort of differences might the blue group have that affects how they are treated? (*Answers could include: disabilities, disfigurements, specific health conditions.*)
- How can we make sure that everyone is included and treated with dignity and respect regardless of difference? (*Answers could include: challenging stereotyping; ensuring equal and equitable access (boosted access to marginalised groups) to resources; celebrating and welcoming difference.*)

Section 3: Fertility and conception

Story of sperm: the fertilisation journey

 This is a creative activity in which participants consider and document the journey of sperm in fertilisation. This can help increase understanding of the sexual and reproductive system and fertility.

 20 minutes (minimum). Can be extended to a longer project.

 Networked computers or tablets, YouTube, search engines, paper, colouring pens, crafting materials.

 11+

Show the group one of the many YouTube videos on the journey of sperm. We particularly like *Genesis* by Ramos David available on YouTube[7] which has no audio description but is a five-minute video set to music. If you had more time you could look at Channel 4's the *Great Sperm Race* which is a one-hour documentary using human sized sperm racing through difficult conditions.

The task is for the group to retell the journey of the sperm for someone a few years younger than them. They could document it as a cartoon, performance, storyboard, a poem, a map, a model, a story. Remember that the journey does not always start with penis-in-vagina sex since conception can occur as a result of fertility treatments such as intrauterine insemination (IUI) and in vitro fertilisation (IVF), possibly using donor eggs, sperm and surrogates. Encourage some participants to cover these journeys if they choose to.

Often fertilisation journeys show a series of aggressive sperm competing to penetrate the passively waiting egg. This depiction can reinforce ideas about aggressive masculinity (represented as fast moving, competing, enthusiastic sperm) and passive femininity (a still, silently waiting egg). Ask participants to think about ways of challenging these stereotypes in their retelling of the journey. For example, show what the egg does, its journey and how it moves; show how the vagina changes during arousal (see Chapter 5: *Bodies* for more on this) and consider the vagina's capacity to more than double in size during childbirth; show how the vagina tries to create a hostile environment for sperm; clarify that body parts such as the vagina, egg or sperm are not gendered – a trans woman can have sperm for example. Exploring this with participants challenges ideas about scientific objectivity and 'truth'.

Who owns sperm?

 This discussion-based activity explores the question: 'Who owns sperm?' as a way of exploring rights and responsibilities in relation to pregnancy and pregnancy choices.

 15–20 minutes

 None.

 11+

Tell the group: We are going to explore 'Who owns the sperm'. Lead a discussion with the group about parental and fertility rights using the following questions:

- Who owns the sperm when in the testicles?
- Who owns the sperm as it travels out of the penis during ejaculation?

- Who owns the sperm once it has been ejaculated into someone else's body?
- Who owns the sperm once it has swum past a cervix? (if partner has one)
- Who owns the sperm once it has swum down a fallopian tube? (if partner has one)
- Who owns the sperm once it has fertilised an egg? (if partner has one)
- Who owns the sperm implanted in a uterus? (if partner has one)
- Who owns sperm that has been donated to a sperm bank?
- Who owns sperm that has been purchased from a sperm bank?
- Who owns sperm that has been donated for medical tests or research?

As you facilitate the discussion prompt participants to consider physical, moral and legal arguments. You may find the following points useful to guide your facilitation:

- The sperm's DNA can be tested to reveal who produced the sperm.
- Sperm cannot also be retrieved easily once in someone else's body.
- When someone becomes a father they potentially:
  - Have a moral and legal obligation to any child born,
  - Have rights over how the child will be brought up,
  - Could be asked to support the child financially,
  - Could be named on the birth certificate.
- Legally a partner has no rights over a pregnancy should a woman choose not to continue with it.
- Sperm donors through licensed donation sites are legally exempt from being legal parents but unlicensed donations could result in the donor becoming the legal father with associated responsibilities.

The key learning message is that people can't get their sperm back once they have ejaculated. This means that they need to ejaculate responsibly and safely if they don't want the consequences! People whose sperm does lead to a conception will be equally responsible for any subsequent pregnancy and birth but with very limited rights in any pregnancy decision. This is due to a woman's right to bodily autonomy. You could discuss how someone might feel about their partner making a pregnancy choice that they don't agree with, and what help and support they could get in that situation.

Fertility crossword

 A simple activity that asks participants to create crosswords to facilitate learning about fertility. Can also be used as an assessment activity for any area of learning about sexual health. 30 minutes

 Plain paper, rulers and pencils or computer access for online crossword generators and research. 13+

Working individually or in pairs, the task is to create a fertility crossword. Participants will need to:

- Research information about fertility and fertility choices.
- Choose key words to include in their crossword based on their research.

- For each key word they will need to write a question or clue. For example:
  - Clue: Acronym for one of the techniques used to help people with fertility problems have a baby. Answer: IVF
  - Question: What is the term used for a fertilised egg? Answer: Embryo.

Websites such as NHS choices, the British Fertility Society and the Human Fertilisation and Embryology authority are all useful resources for participants to use.

Participants should aim for at least 20 clues and answers and will need to create a blank and completed version of their crossword. Once each individual/pair has completed their crossword, photocopy the blank versions so that the pairs can try out each other's quizzes. You can set this up as a contest and award prizes to the quickest crossword completers!

Depending on the group you could choose to focus the activity on fertility as a broad topic or on a specific subtopic of interest such as surrogacy, infertility, miscarriage, egg donation, etc. This technique also works well with other sexual health topics.

Section 4: Contraception

Contraceptive toolkit

 A simple activity that uses objects and visual images to facilitate learning and prompt discussion about different types of contraception.

 30 minutes

 A contraceptive display kit and model or diagram of a penis, a vagina and a uterus. FPA leaflets summarising methods of contraception.[8]

 13+

You can buy contraceptive display kits from *Health Education*[9] or you can make your own. To do this you will need the following items which you can either buy or ask for from your local sexual health service. It's worth asking as it's a good idea to build a relationship with your local service anyway! Condoms, lubricants, femidoms, dental dams, IUD/IUS, model contraceptive ring (**note:** the ring in a femidom can double up as a contraceptive ring), model implant (**note:** a single matchstick or a very thin bendy plastic rod the length of a matchstick can demo this), empty contraceptive pill boxes, a diaphragm, empty emergency contraception box or image.

Health and safety note: It is not advisable to have any actual hormonal methods of contraception including emergency contraception in your kit due to the possibility of them being consumed.

Lay out all the objects and visual aids. Pass round each method of contraception one at a time and answer questions from participants about the method. Ask participants to demonstrate how each method is used on diagrams or models of the sexual organs that you have provided. Make sure you discuss the following information for each method:

- How it works.
- How it is used.
- How effective it is.
- What are the advantages/disadvantages.
- Whether it is long acting (e.g. implant) or short acting (e.g. pill), reversible (most methods)/ permanent (sterilisation – unless reversed with variable chance of fertility returning).
- How fertility resumes after ceasing the methods.
- Any impact on pleasure, mood or general wellbeing.

Make sure you clarify the different emergency contraception options including the emergency contraceptive pill (Levonelle up to 72 hours (three days) after unprotected sex/EllaOne up to 120 hours (five days) after unprotected sex) AND the IUD/IUS (Copper coil or Hormonal coil Mirena up to five days after unprotected sex).

Use the FPA and Brook websites to find the information that you need. The *Brook Learn* platform has short (one-minute) animations of most methods which may be useful.

Alternatively divide participants into small groups and give each group one or more methods of contraception plus information leaflets and ask them to research and present the previous information to the rest of the group.

The key learning is that there are lots of different methods of contraception that participants can try. If one method doesn't work, go back to the clinic or your GP and discuss an alternative. Don't put up with a method that doesn't work and don't give up on contraception just because the method you are using isn't working for you.

Soap star contraception

 This discussion-based activity asks participants to apply their knowledge of contraception to fictional characters and practice making contraceptive decisions. It is a good follow on from any activities that are focussed on information giving and knowledge acquisition around contraceptive methods.

 20–30 minutes

 None but it may be a good idea to research some examples of soaps/box sets ahead of time.

 13+

This activity is useful to do as an assessment activity following teaching about different methods of contraception to see how much participants have understood and identify any gaps in their learning. Ask the group to choose a tv soap, drama or box set that they are all familiar with that includes characters in a range of different relationships, e.g. long term married relationship, gay relationship, polyamorous relationships, one-night-stand, elderly couple, teenage relationship, etc. If this is hard to do, flag up the lack of relationship diversity in the programmes that participants are watching. Summarise each set of relationships on the board or as a handout (you may need to do this on a previous session).

Divide participants into small groups and ask them to decide on the best method of contraception for each character based on their circumstances and think about the reasons why. Participants will need to consider the advantages and disadvantages of different methods of contraception and think about the suitability for different characters, e.g. X and Y could use condoms. They are in a monogamous long term relationship so may not need protection against STIs so other options are available. X lives a chaotic lifestyle and travels a lot so might not always remember to take the contraceptive pill so a LARC method such as the coil or the injection might work better for her.

Feedback and discuss the findings as a whole group. Focus on asking participants to make their rationale explicit for choosing a particular method, and where different groups made different choices unpick why.

It would be helpful to include some emergency contraception options for discussion. You may also wish to explore scenarios where the characters need to access the following: PrEP, STI tests, abortion. Make sure you allow opportunities to talk about what each character might be thinking or feeling as well as discussing their choices.

Contraception and pleasure

This activity is based on research conducted by Higgins, Jenny A, & Hirsch, Jennifer S (2008) 'Pleasure, power, and inequality: incorporating sexuality into research on contraceptive use'. American Journal of Public Health, 98(10).[10]

 A research and present activity that explores how different methods of contraception can affect sexual enjoyment and pleasure. This is a good extension activity to the 'Contraceptive toolkit' activity on p. 288 and allows for honest and frank conversations about contraceptive choices and decision making.

 30 minutes

 FPA contraception guides.[11]

 14+

Divide participants into five groups and allocate each one of the following categories: external condoms, hormonal contraception, the ring, IUD, no contraception.

Explain the task which is to brainstorm advantages and disadvantages for the allocated method when it comes to making sex a positive and enjoyable experience for all partners.

- Think about the benefits for people of all genders and in different kinds of relationships.
- Think about new and long term relationships.
- Think about how the method may affect the body, libido and the sensation of sex.
- Think about the health benefits and level of protection against STIs and pregnancy.

Participants may find contraception guides such as the FPA contraception guide[12] useful for the information about the *health* advantages and disadvantages of different methods of contraception, but lacking in information about how each method may affect sexual enjoyment or pleasure. Prompt participants to explore this further, using information from Table 7.3.

Each group should either prepare a three-minute presentation on their method, addressing the points mentioned previously or think of a role play scenario in which to share and disseminate their learning (e.g. one person plays the unhappy contraceptive user, one the helpful friend/partner or sexual health advisor). Ask participants to write or perform their role plays for the rest of the group. Recap key points at the end of each role play.

TABLE 7.3 Contraception and pleasure: advantages and disadvantages of different methods of contraception

Advantages	Disadvantages	How to overcome/respond to possible barriers/disadvantage
External condom (see box on condoms (p. 296) for definition		
Protects against pregnancy which can help to feel more relaxed, safe and protected during sex.	For some people this method interrupts the 'flow' of sex.	Sex isn't always a seamless 'flow'. It can often be messy or a bit tricky. Stopping to talk about condom use or to put one on can be an important part of negotiating consent, checking in with your partner and taking a moment to look at your partner and take in the moment. If it's awkward for a few moments then don't worry – it's worth it for safe, enjoyable sex.
Protects against HIV and STIs which can help people to feel more relaxed, safe and protected during sex.	For some people this method takes away sensation and exacerbates vaginal dryness.	Try using different makes and types of condoms – there are hundreds and many are designed to enhance pleasure and sensation. The website www.theyfit.co.uk/ enables condoms to be found to suit any size. Use lube to combat any dryness and increase pleasure. People with penises can practice masturbating whilst wearing a condom to become familiar with the sensation or to try out different brands/types.

Advantages	Disadvantages	How to overcome/respond to possible barriers/disadvantage
External condom (see box on condoms (p. 296) for definition		
Some people enjoy the sensation of ribbed ones, and the taste of flavoured ones.	Some people dislike the smell and taste.	Try using different makes and types of condoms – there are hundreds and many are designed to enhance pleasure and sensation.
Some women find that having to take responsibility for using these makes them feel more confident and in control.	Some women find it difficult to have the sexual skills and confidence to negotiate using this method with a partner, whilst also managing social norms about female sexual respectability.	Practice putting a condom on a banana at home. Practice or think about how to bring up the topic of contraception and condom use with a partner. Try talking about it when you are not being intimate. Remember that contraception is both partners responsibility. Be assertive and proud. You are taking responsibility for your own body and health, as well as that of your partner. Don't slut shame or judge others for carrying condoms. Be respectful of their choices.
	Some people worry about losing an erection when using these.	Practice losing and regaining an erection at home on your own. Practice putting a condom on and masturbating with one on.

Advantages	Disadvantages	How to overcome/respond to possible barriers/disadvantage
Hormonal contraception methods (pill, implant, injection, IUS)		
No need to interrupt the flow of sex.	Side effects such as weight gain, breast tenderness, loss of libido or nausea could detract from women's sexual experiences and make sex less appealing.	Listen to your body. How you feel about your body and your sexuality is important so talk to a sexual health advisor if you notice adverse effects from hormonal contraception. Try a different method all together.
Protects against pregnancy.	Doesn't protect against HIV or STIs.	You can be creative about engaging in sexual activities where there is no risk of HIV/STI transmission such as mutual masturbation. You and your partner can get tested for STIs and if you are both STI-free and committed to a monogamous sexual relationship.
No physical barrier between partners.		

Advantages	Disadvantages	How to overcome/respond to possible barriers/disadvantage
The IUD (the 'coil')		
No need to interrupt the flow of sex.	Can cause longer, heavier and more painful periods which can detract from some of the enjoyment of sex.	If a change in your periods is uncomfortable for you or having a negative effect on your sex life talk to a sexual health advisor. Try a different hormonal method (there are lots of different contraceptive pills for example) or try a different method all together.
No physical barrier between partners.	Doesn't prevent against HIV or STIs.	As above.

Advantages	Disadvantages	How to overcome/respond to possible barriers/disadvantage
The vaginal ring		
Causes increased lubrication in the vagina. Does not interrupt the flow of sex.	Causes increased lubrication in the vagina and makes sex 'too wet'.	Some people enjoy the wetness! Experiment and see how it feels. Talk to your sexual health advisor if you feel this is having a negative impact on your sex life and try an alternative method.
No physical barrier between partners.	Can be felt during sex and sometimes pops out.	Sex can be funny, awkward and not always go to plan. Laugh about things if you can and enjoy those odd moments.

Advantages	Disadvantages	How to overcome/respond to possible barriers/disadvantage
No contraception		
No need to interrupt the flow of sex.	No protection against pregnancy.	You can be creative about engaging in sexual activities where there is no risk of pregnancy such as mutual masturbation, oral sex, anal sex (although there are risks of STI with some of these). You can learn and practice the natural fertility method.
No physical barrier during sex.	No protection against STIs or HIV.	As above.
No physical changes as a result of using hormonal contraception (although there may be natural fluctuations in hormones).	Less able to relax and enjoy sex.	As above. If you do want to have penis-in-vagina sex it is only a good idea to do this if you and your partner have been tested and confirmed to be STI-free and in a monogamous relationship and want to have a baby.

Advantages	Disadvantages	How to overcome/respond to possible barriers/disadvantage
No contraception		
A reason to explore different ways of having sex that don't involve the risk of pregnancy or STI or HIV transmissions.		

Note: Inform participants that this activity is based on research with heterosexual women and is focussed mainly on heterosexual experiences of having penis-in-vagina sex. Emphasise that experiences of contraception may vary from person to person.

Contraception and gender

With thanks to Andrew Pembrooke at *Teach SRE* for his help with the development of this idea.

 Explore how gender and sexual norms can impact on attitudes towards contraceptive choices. 20–30 minutes

 Large labels stating: agree; disagree; unsure. 13+

Create an agree/unsure/disagree continuum using the agree, unsure and disagree labels. Explain to participants that you will read out a series of statements about contraception and gender (see below) one at a time. Participants should stand along the continuum to reflect what they think about each statement. After participants have moved take feedback from participants standing by each label as to why they have decided to stand there. As conversations progress encourage participants to shift positions if they change their opinion.

Often conversation about gender inequalities can create passionate and sometimes heated discussions. Remember to refer to your ground rules to help you facilitate the discussion and encourage participants to use 'I feel...'/'I think...' statements. Use the discussion prompts on p. 294 to help you generate discussion and debate.

Contraception and gender discussion statements

- Vasalgel is a contraceptive that uses polymer gel to block the sperm duct and stop sperm being released during sex. It can be flushed out to restore fertility years later. Making this product available on the market would make contraceptive use more fair and equal between genders.
- Although there are side effects from hormonal contraception, this is better than using a condom because condoms can make sex less pleasurable.
- The reason we don't have any 'male' contraceptives (such as Vasalgel) is because men wouldn't put up with the contraceptive side effects
- It's easier to negotiate safer sex in LGBT+ relationships because they are more equal.
- There is too much focus on the external 'male' condom in sex education – the internal 'female' condoms should be covered just as much.

- There is more stigma for girls and women who carry condoms than for boys and men.
- It is a men's rights issue that to date there is only one non-permanent method of contraception for men (the condom) whereas women have access to many, many more options.
- LGBT+ people don't need to worry about contraception in the same way that straight people do.
- The responsibility for carrying and using condoms lies solely with the person who will wear them.
- It's ok to take the contraceptive pill every day without a gap as this means no periods and you can have sex whenever you want.

Discussion prompts

- **Whose responsibility is contraception?** All partners involved in an encounter need to take responsibility for contraception. Even if you are not the one who is going to take or use the contraception (e.g. your partner is going to take the pill/wear the condom) it is still your responsibility to take part in the decision making about contraception, support your partner in accessing the contraception and check that the method works ok for them. Remember that contraception can be used to protect against STIs as well as pregnancy so even if there is no risk of pregnancy (e.g. if you are in a same sex relationship) you will still need to use a barrier method such as a condom or dental dam to protect against STIs.
- **Is there a power imbalance in negotiating contraception in heterosexual relationships?** Ideals of masculinity as active and femininity as passive can shape how heterosexual couples negotiate sex, consent and contraception. To be feminine may mean to be unknowing or un-wanting when it comes to sex which makes it harder to be confident, assertive and prepared when it comes to contraception. (For example, if you're not 'meant' to want it why would you carry a condom?)
- **Are there similar power imbalances in LGBT+ relationships?** In LGBT+ relationships while there might not be a need for pregnancy prevention, there will still be negotiations around safer sex to reduce risk of STI transmission that need to take place. There will also need to be negotiations around consent and pleasure. Although there may not be the same heterosexual power inequalities in LGBT+ relationships this does not mean that all LGBT+ relationships are equal!
- **Is there shame and stigma associated with certain types of contraception?** Yes there can be. There may be particular shame and stigma for women since ideals about femininity suggest that women should not be interested in sex and/or sexually available. These norms and stereotypes are changing – discuss with participants whether they think there is stigma in their communities and how this varies by gender.
- **Who has more contraceptive choice? What impact does this have?** There are a wide range of contraceptive choices available for women but not for men (there is only the condom)*. Having more choices can offer women a greater chance of finding a suitable option that makes them feel safe, in control and able to enjoy sex. However, this can mean that women end up taking responsibility for contraception and suffer the burden of contraceptive side effects.

  * This statement does not apply to trans men who may have other contraceptive options.

- **If a range of 'male' contraceptives were widely available what might the impact be?** There have been attempts to develop contraception for people with penises but this has proved difficult as there are issues with biological factors such as sheer numbers of sperm compared to a single egg. Also as society is used to women having most responsibility for contraception there are concerns about how easy it would be to make the shift towards a people of all genders taking equal responsibility.

To conclude the activity ask participants to imagine what the perfect contraceptive would be regardless of sex and gender – one that could work for everyone regardless of body parts and protects against both STIs and unintended pregnancy? What sorts of things would make a perfect contraceptive? Ask participants to think about ease of use (both in everyday life and during sexual activity) side effects, whether it is long term or short term and how easily reversible it is. If such a contraceptive became available what impact do you think it would have on sex/gender equality? STI rates? Unintended pregnancy rates?

Alternative version: If you are in a room where space is limited you could use traffic light cards (Red – disagree, Amber – unsure, Green – agree) or *Sperm Keyrings* offer sets of Traffic lights of sperm keyrings to use in RSE sessions which can make the activity lively and fun.[13] Participants will still need to give feedback on their responses.

Section 5: Condoms

Condoms get their own special section in this chapter as the only method of contraception to protect against STIs (and pregnancy if needed).

Condoms and lubricants: points to consider

- Condoms are the ONLY method to protect from most STIs and unintended pregnancy. Other methods of contraception help prevent pregnancy, but do not offer a barrier against STIs and HIV.
- There are two types of condom. The external condom which is inserted over the penis and the internal condom which is inserted inside the vagina. External condoms tend to be more available and are much more widely used.
- There is also a barrier method called a dental dam which is a soft plastic latex or polyurethane square (about 15cm in size), which is used to cover the vulva or anus during oral sex to prevent the transmission of STIs. These are not widely available after the main manufacturer ceased making them but they can also be made by cutting the tip off an extra large condom and unrolling it and cutting lengthwise down the condom to provide a latex sheet. Some people also choose to use latex gloves for manual stimulation of the genitals and/or anus for hygiene reasons and to reduce risks of transmitting infections.
- Condoms can be obtained from a local family planning clinic for free. Most areas now have a condom scheme (often referred to as C-card). Make sure you inform young people about the local scheme in your area and let them know how to register and get free condoms if they need them. Where possible invite someone from your local scheme to meet your group and offer possibilities to register during or after the session.
- Remember that condoms are only used by people who have a penis or have sex with someone with a penis. Pointing this out and ensuring you talk about the risks and possibilities of other kinds of sex and sexual relationships is key to delivering inclusive RSE.
- Penises and condoms come in all different shapes and sizes. The website www.theyfit.co.uk/ enables condoms to be found to suit any size.
- Remember that knowing what a condom is and how to put one on is not enough to ensure that young people are able to use them effectively. There are many barriers other than ignorance, including feeling too embarrassed to get/carry condoms (especially for girls and women), not feeling able to talk to a partner about using them, perceiving that condoms are a barrier to pleasure and/or intimacy. Good RSE needs to address these barriers and challenges.
- Always do a condom demonstration and give young people opportunities to practice putting external condoms on. If you are unsure how to do this have a look at some of the short films that are available online. Try 'condom demo video'[14] by Brook which shows how easy it is to put on a condom, even if you only have use of one hand due to disability. We also like 'NHS Highland – Condom demo'.[15] Always show internal condoms and dental dams as well as external condoms You can use diagrams or models to show how to use these.
- Make sure you give young people information about lubrication:
  - Lubrication is needed during penetrative sex to reduce friction and discomfort.
  - Naturally the walls of the vagina produce a certain amount of liquid when someone is aroused, the penis also produces a certain amount of liquid called pre-cum. The anus does not produce any natural lubricant.

- ○ Sometimes the body doesn't produce enough lubricant (or one at all in the case of anal sex) so you will need to use artificial lubricant to make sex comfortable and pleasurable.
- ○ Condoms will form a barrier between any natural lubrication produced by the body and while they do contain a small amount of lubricant sometimes additional lubrication is needed. Always make condoms available for participants to touch so that they can feel the amount of wetness/lubrication.
- ○ Oil-based lubricants such as Vaseline or baby oil will damage a condom causing it to tear. Always use water-based lubricants such as KY jelly. These can be bought online or in shops or obtained for free from sexual health clinics. See the 'Exploding condoms' demonstration on p. 298 as a fun way of exploring this with participants.

Condom Olympics

A high energy circuit of activities that aims to get participants familiar with touching and using condoms whilst also learning about their safety limits. These activities help to reduce the stigma around condoms and sexual health more widely.

 40–50 minutes

Internal and external condoms, oil- and water-based lubricants, paper clips, tins of baked beans, ping pong balls, jugs of water, pre-prepared condom demo box with condom demonstrator. If available, also include artificial semen and blacklight[16] and 'drunk goggles'. (These are goggles with special lenses that alter vision, perception and balance; they can be purchased from suppliers such as Health Edco.) Cardboard box with lid.

 14+

Set up a carousel of activities around the room. You can include all, or a selection of, the following activities. Divide participants into groups and ask them to work their way round each activity. At each station the educator should quickly demo the activity or provide brief instructions so that groups know what they need to do.

- **Paper clip challenge:** Challenge participants to pick up as many paper clips as they can with a condom over their hand before the condom splits. This shows how much you can feel through a condom as well as emphasising their fragility if fingernails and other sharp objects tear them. Usually between 10–20 can be picked up before the condom splits.
- **Baked bean tin challenge:** Challenge participants to see how many stacked tins of baked bean they can fit in an internal/external condom before it splits. This reinforces how strong condoms are and that it is a myth that someone could have a penis that is too big for a condom! Almost all condoms will cover one tin easily. Some larger, stronger condoms will cover three–four tins without splitting. Although penises of slightly longer lengths than two tins of baked beans have been recorded, no penis the 'girth' of a tin of baked beans has ever been recorded!
- **Dental dam catapults** How far can a ping pong ball travel when a dental dam is used as a catapult? This will take two people, one to stretch the dental dam between hands, and the other to pull back the dam with a ping pong in it and release.
- **Water challenge:** How much water can an external condom hold before bursting? This shows how strong they are. After 500ml water external condoms will often start to fail. Remind

participants that average volume of ejaculate is 3–5ml! You can't really do this activity with internal condoms as they don't stretch in the same way so the potential for flooding and mess is much higher!

- **Spin challenge:** Test how fast participants can put a condom on a condom demonstrator after being spun around. This shows how you need to be sober to use a condom effectively. If you have access to 'drunk goggles' then you can also ask participants to put a condom on the demonstrator whilst wearing them.

- **Condom in a box:** Get a cardboard box with a lid (A4 photocopying paper boxes are perfect for this). Cut out two hand holes in one side of the box. If desired you could also cut a tv sized hole on the opposite side of the box to the hand holes so the group can see what is happening. Ask for a volunteer to try and put a condom on a demonstrator in the box when they can't see what they are doing and their movement is restricted. If there is a 'tv hole' the other side the rest of the group could support with directions! This shows that it is helpful to be able to see what you are doing when putting on a condom!

- **CSI condoms:** Do a condom demonstration using an ejaculating condom demonstrator and UV sensitive artificial semen (or hand soap works as well). Use a blacklight to identify where the semen is (on hands, demonstrator, etc.). Reinforces the need to wash before cuddling!

- **Exploding condoms:** Ask two volunteers to blow up two condoms. Volunteer one should rub vigorously on the blown up condom with an oil-based lubricant such as petroleum jelly (Vaseline) or baby oil. Volunteer two should rub vigorously on the blown up condom with a water- or silicone-based lubricant such as KY jelly or Durex play. The condom with oil-based lubricant will burst after a minute or two of rubbing, the condom with water-based lubricant should not. This activity makes the point that only water-based lubricants should be used with external condoms. If you have time experiment with a range of different water-, oil- and silicone-based lubricants or moisturisers/lipsalves, etc. to see what effect they have on condoms. (**Note:** not all condoms will burst immediately with some oil-based moisturisers taking time to degrade the latex (possibly bursting after the session has finished) so be careful this doesn't change your learning message that oil-based lubricants will damage latex condoms.) Internal condoms are made from polyurethane and therefore oil-based lubricants can be used with them; they are also not as inflatable as condoms so don't use for this activity.

At the end of the activity, bring the group together and ask participants to share what they have learnt from doing the activities. Remind participants how safe condoms (internal and external) are if used properly and that they are the only method of contraception that protects against STIs, as well as pregnancy (if having penis-in-vagina sex). Testing the limits of the effectiveness of condoms should definitely NOT be used to reinforce the idea that they are ineffective.

Extension: Excuses, excuses

To extend the activity and conclude this session ask the group to think of all the excuses that people might come up with for not using a condom or dental dam and list these on the board. For each excuse ask the group to think of a range of possible responses to the excuses and role play them. The aim is to support young people to practise negotiating their use. As part of your discussion flag issues that can prevent young people (and adults) from being able to negotiate condom use. This includes unequal power dynamics, abusive or controlling relationships, poor relationship communication, lack of confidence in talking about condoms with a partner. Discuss what people can do in these circumstances.

The internal condom conundrum

With thanks to Laura Hurley for the development of this activity.

 A creative project that focuses on the positives of the internal condom (sometimes known as the 'femidom'). This method of contraception is not widely used and tends to get bad press. This activity encourages young people to think about the positives of the method and address issues of gender stereotyping and contraception stigma.

 One hour

 Computer and online access, poster materials.

 14+

The task is to create, design and lead a campaign that promotes the internal condom to young people in the UK. Participants need to work in small groups and present their campaigns to each other. Start by explaining what the internal condom is and how it works. It may be helpful to explain that the internal condom is often referred to as the 'femidom'. It can be inserted into the vagina or the anus to protect against STI transmission (and pregnancy if relevant) by anyone, regardless of their sex or gender identity. To extend the learning you could challenge participants to create this campaign without talking about pregnancy or STI risk, i.e. frame it in around debates about pleasure, control and gender identity

Points to consider and discuss as a group:

- What kinds of sex can internal condoms be used for? (*Answers: penetrative vaginal sex with a penis or a sex toy – some people use them for penetrative anal sex although there are no studies yet to show whether this is a reliable method*.)
- What are the selling points of the method? What are the advantages for women? What about for men? Think about issues of safety, ownership and control, pleasure, gender identity. (*Answers can include: period sex may be less messy with an internal rather than external condom; women have greater control when using an internal condom; you can insert an internal condom before you have sex when the penis isn't erect so you don't have to worry about losing an erection; they prevent STIs and unwanted pregnancy; they offer slightly more protection for STIs passed skin-to-skin as they cover a wider area than the more widely used external condom; they can be latex free if someone is allergic to latex; they are less restrictive on the penis so the sex may feel better.*)
- What assumptions do people make about people who carry condoms or other barrier methods? (*Answers might include: good at looking after their own health or 'sluts looking for sex'.*) Is this different for men/women? (*Answers might include: men are expected to carry condoms but women are stigmatised if they do same.*) How can issues such as slutshaming towards girls and women who carry condoms be addressed in a campaign? (*Answers might include: celebrating ownership of sexual healthcare needs; positive images of women with condoms.*)
- How can young people be encouraged to carry the barrier method of their choice as and when they want to? (*Answers might include: peer education and social norming of barrier methods; positive advertising; sex education.*)

Extension: Contraception campaigns

You can also try this activity for the other latex methods (e.g. external condom, the dental dam, diaphragm) or for the contraceptive ring which is a newer method of contraception that is not yet widely used or available. Participants could focus their campaign on increasing supply thereby reducing the cost of the ring.

Condom demo quiz

 When learning about condoms it is always a good idea to lead a condom demonstration and give participants the opportunity to have a go at putting a condom on a demonstrator. If you are not able to do this, or want to consolidate the learning from a condom demo, you can use this quiz. The information in the quiz is also useful to include as part of your demonstration.

 20 minutes

 Printed copies of quiz.

 14+

Use the following quiz to either check and consolidate learning at the end of a condom demonstration or embed the questions throughout to expand on each step of the demonstration. These questions are all about the external condom.

a. When might you need to use a condom? (*Answer: if you are having penis-in-vagina, penis-in-anus or penis-in-mouth sex.*)

b. What are the three things you need to check before you take a condom out of its packet? (*Answer: expiry date; British safety kite mark; that packet isn't damaged – it should puff up like a little pillow.*)

c. What way round should the condom go on? (*Answer: the condom should look like a 'sombrero' from the top, with a point in the middle and a brim round the edge. If it looks like 'Gandalf's hat' with a point and no brim then you've got it inside out.*)

d. If you make a mistake and put a condom on the penis the wrong way round, what should you do? (*Answer: throw it away and use a new one. When a penis is erect a small amount of liquid is produced that may contain sperm. This is sometimes called pre-cum. This can transmit infections (and lead to pregnancy if having penis-in-vagina sex). If the condom touches the end of the penis it is likely to come into contact with pre-cum and so cannot simply be turned round the other way and used.*)

e. The penis needs to be erect before you can put a condom on. What should you do if you go to put a condom on and the erection goes? (*Answers: take a short break and talk; relax or try another sexual activity that might turn you or your partner on (e.g. kissing, stroking, masturbating, etc.) and see if the erection returns. If it doesn't this can be frustrating but don't give up on using condoms! It just takes practice and patience.*)

f. What is a foreskin and where should it be when you put a condom on? (*Answer: the foreskin is the fold of skin that covers the end of the penis that can be moved up and down when a penis is erect. Many people find this very pleasurable. Most penises have a foreskin but some have it removed for cultural, health or religious reasons. This is called circumcision. Before putting on a condom, the foreskin needs to be pulled back to expose the head of the penis.*)

g. As you unroll the condom all the way to the base of the model you need to squeeze the tip of the condom and make sure there are minimal air bubbles. Why is this important? (*Answer: because air bubbles can cause the condom to break during sex. It is important to make sure that the condom fits well, stays on and is intact throughout sexual intercourse.*)

h. Each time a penis ejaculates, how much sperm is released on average? (*Answer: 2–5 ml for a healthy person. Pause to think about how little this is. This can be an important counter to information gleaned from pornography where large volumes of semen can be produced.*)

i. When should you take a condom off and how do you dispose of them? (*Answer: condoms should be removed shortly after sex whilst the penis is still erect. It is important to hold onto the base of the condom as the penis is withdrawn. This will help prevent the semen from leaking out. Point out that this is one of the ways for condoms to fail (or the user to fail!) – if the person doesn't hold onto the condom as they withdraw, then the condom and the semen are left inside the partner. After use condoms should have a knot tied in. Condoms should never be flushed down the toilet. They should be wrapped in a tissue and placed in the bin.*)

j. What is lubricant and why do you need to use it if you use condoms? (*Answer: lubricant is a substance designed to reduce friction. It is needed during penetrative sex to reduce friction and discomfort. Naturally the walls of the vagina produce a certain amount of liquid when someone is aroused, the penis also produces a certain amount of liquid called pre-cum. The anus does not produce any natural lubricant so lubricant is always needed for anal sex. Condoms will form a barrier between any lubrication produced by the body and while they do contain a small amount of lubricant sometimes additional lubrication is needed. See 'Exploding condoms' demonstration on p. 298 for more information and do this with participants where possible – it only takes five minutes and is good fun!*)

Condom quiz

1. When might you need to use a condom?

2. What are the three things you need to check before you take a condom out of its packet?

3. What way round should the condom go on?

4. If you make a mistake and put a condom on the penis the wrong way round, what should you do?

5. The penis needs to be erect before you can put a condom on. What should you do if you go to put a condom on and the erection goes?

6. What is a foreskin and where should it be when you put a condom on?

7. As you unroll the condom all the way to the base of the model you need to squeeze the tip of the condom and make sure there are minimal air bubbles. Why is this important?

8. Each time a penis ejaculates, how much sperm is released on average?

9. When should you take a condom off and how do you dispose of them?

10. What is lubricant and why do you need to use it if you use condoms?

Section 6: Pregnancy choices

Pregnancy tests role play

This activity is developed from *Abortion: decisions and dilemmas: An educational resource for those working with young people aged 13 to 18.* The full resource is free to use as a Brook online learning module.[17] Shared with permission.

 This is a role play activity that gives participants the opportunity to get a sense of what it might feel like to take a pregnancy test and have to make a decision about a positive test result.

 20–30 minutes

 Pregnancy tests pre-prepared with a result drawn on in coloured pen and envelopes. You will need enough tests and envelopes for one per pair of participants.

 14+

This activity enables participants to learn about pregnancy testing and explore what it might feel like to take a test. The activity works by asking participants to role play scenarios in pairs where they are about to take a pregnancy test, before receiving a randomly allocated test result from the educator. Participants need to role play their thoughts and feelings before, during and after 'taking' the test.

Note: You can do this activity with people of all genders and sexual orientations including all male groups and LGBT+ groups. Anyone who has penis-in-vagina sex could become pregnant or make somebody else pregnant regardless of their sexual or gender identity.

You will need to prepare for the activity by buying enough pregnancy tests so that there is enough for one per pair (they can be bought cheaply online or in a pound shop or you can print out photographs of tests or draw outlines of tests on cards). Before the activity prepare the tests by marking them as 'positive' or 'negative'. Use the packet instructions to show you what a positive and negative test result looks like and mark the tests with a permanent marker pen of the correct colour. Prepare a selection of positive and negative test results.

Conclude the activity with a discussion, using the following prompts:

- How did you feel when you received your result? Did your feelings surprise you?
- What should you do next and who will you talk to?
- For those that received a positive result, how did you and your partner make a decision about what to do next?
- For those that received a negative result, did you make any decisions about next steps in terms of trying to conceive or not conceive in the future?
- How did you manage any differences or conflict between you?

Ensure that participants understand where to get free pregnancy tests from in your local area and know that they have the right to free confidential support if they become pregnant.

Researching parenting

 This is a group research project to find out about why people become parents and what experiences of parenting can be like.

 Session one: 5–10 minutes.
Session two: 20–30 minutes.

 None.

 11+

The task for the group is to conduct a research project with the aim of exploring why people become parents and what it is like to be a parent. To do this, participants will need to each conduct one or more short interviews with a parent or carer in their family or personal network. They will need to record or write down the interviewee's responses (with the interviewee's consent) and share them with the rest of the group the following week. This can be done anonymously.

Session one: In session one, explain the activity and task participants with coming up with interview questions that will help them meet the research question (why people become parents and what it is like to be a parent). Here are some example questions:

- Did you decide to become a parent or did it just happen?
- How did you decide to become a parent/carer?
- What are the best things about being a parent/carer?
- What has been the hardest thing about being a parent/carer?
- Is there anything you wish you knew before you became a parent/carer?
- What support did you need to be a parent/carer?

Session two: In the next session ask participants to work together in small groups to share the findings from their research. Depending on what has been agreed when negotiating consent, participants may need to change the names of their interviewees to protect their anonymity and work out how to describe their relationship (e.g. say a friend's mum rather than my mum to keep it anonymous). The task is to create a two-minute presentation to the larger group that summarises their findings as a small group. They will need to decide what key findings and messages they want to share and whether they want to include key messages or quotes.

After each group has presented, explore any themes and patterns in the research conducted by the group as a whole. In your discussion unpick the difference between actively choosing and not actively choosing to become a parent and whether or not it matters. Here it is important to challenge any assumptions that only young people have unplanned pregnancies.

At the end ask participants to close their eyes for a few minutes and think about:

- Would you like to be a parent?
- If yes, what would be the ideal situation for you to be a parent? How old would you be? Would you have a partner? Would your partner become pregnant or you? What would your life be like before the baby? What would it be like after?
- What do you need to do to put this preferred situation into practice? Whether this is to never be a parent, to become a parent in the next few years or to have a baby in ten years after travelling the world, having a successful career or running five marathons…What action can you take to make this happen? How would you feel if this didn't happen?

Points to consider: abortion

- Whatever your personal feelings about abortion it is important to represent a factual, impartial view of pregnancy choices to participants. One in three women have an abortion in their lifetime and 50% of under 18 conceptions end in abortion. It is therefore important to provide young people with information about the options available should they (or their partner or friend) face an unplanned pregnancy or need an abortion for any reason.

- Views about abortion are often polarised and it gets discussed as a moral argument, rather than a health decision or choice (such as deciding which form of contraception to use). To avoid this do not set up sessions in a 'pro-choice/pro-life' debate or invite one 'pro-life' and one 'pro-choice' speaker to meet your group. Such debates unhelpfully polarise the discussion into positions such as 'pro-life' vs. 'anti-life/pro-abortion' or 'pro-choice' vs. 'anti-choice'. These are unhelpfully blunt terms for what is a complicated issue. The reality is for most individuals they will have a mixture of personal values, opinions, feelings and viewpoints about abortion that may change throughout their lives depending on the situations in which they find themselves. What young people need is a safe space to explore and to develop the attitudes, skills and knowledge they need to be able to make their own, informed choices in the event of unplanned pregnancy.

- Graphic images or videos of abortion should also never be shown in a session on pregnancy choices. Doing so would not be in line with best practice in RSE, which should never aim to shock participants or induce shame about sex, bodies, relationships or sexual health decision making.

Abortion brainstorm

This activity is developed from *Abortion: decisions and dilemmas: An educational resource for those working with young people aged 13 to 18.* The full resource is free to use as a Brook online learning module.[18] Shared with permission.

 This short brainstorm activity aims to elicit what participants think and know about abortion, including religious perspectives on abortion. It is a good way to draw out participants' thoughts and ideas about abortion at the start of a session and to clarify essential facts about abortion.   10 minutes

 Whiteboard/flipchart and pens.   13+

Write 'abortion' on the board and ask participants to call out any words they can think of relating to abortion. Write down every word with a question mark after it. The question mark indicates that none of these words have authority as a fact and all need to be explored and discussed. Usually a wide range of words – positive, negative, factually accurate and incorrect – appear on the board, reflecting the diverse views people hold about abortion.

When you have elicited all the words the participants can think of, ask them to consider which of the words have factual answers and which are more subjective. Circle the words that can be checked against facts such as 'dangerous', 'expensive', 'common', 'time limits', etc. As you are doing this encourage participants to think about why some words can't be checked against facts, e.g. 'right', 'wrong', 'murder' (e.g. because these are subjective words/opinions about abortion and not facts – you may believe that abortion is murder but this is not supported by law as abortion is legal in the UK). Some words may be true in some instances and not in others, e.g. 'fear', 'secrecy', etc.

The key learning is for young people to understand that there are a wide range of opinions about abortion and to be able to distinguish between facts and opinions.

Whilst discussing the brainstorm give participants the following key factual information about abortion:

- Abortion in the UK is very safe, safer than continuing a pregnancy and giving birth.
- Abortion does not lead to infertility.
- Abortion in the UK is very common – one in three women will have an abortion.
- Abortion is legal in England, Scotland and Wales (and is available for free on the NHS) but remains illegal in Northern Ireland. The Irish Republic has recently changed its laws to permit abortion. In other countries abortion laws vary but where abortion is illegal, abortions still happen at similar rates but they are often unsafe.

Figure 7.2 shows an example of what an abortion brainstorm might look like.

FIGURE 7.2 Abortion brainstorm
Illustration by: Chrissy Baxter

Exploring abortion stories

 The aim of this activity is for participants to explore real life experiences of abortion and to learn about the reasons behind unplanned pregnancies and abortions. The stories are drawn from a project called *My Body, My Life* that aims to combat the stigma surrounding abortion by speaking openly about women's real life abortion experiences. It is based on research with women who have experienced abortion. For more information about the project go to: http://mybody-mylife.org/the-exhibition/

 20–30 minutes

 Flipchart paper and pens, stories from the *My Body, My Life* project either printed out or available online, post-it notes in two colours and pens.

 14+

It is a good idea to do an activity that introduces the topic of abortion, such as the 'Abortion brainstorm', before facilitating this activity.

To set up the activity

Write each of the following questions on a piece of flipchart paper (one question per sheet) and stick up around the room:

- Why might someone get pregnant when they don't want to be?
- Why might someone choose to have an abortion?
- How do people describe the experience of making the decision to have an abortion?
- How do people feel after having an abortion?
- How can partners support someone having an abortion?

To facilitate the activity

Give participants some post-it notes (all of the same colour) and ask them to brainstorm their initial thoughts to the questions and stick them around the room. This can be done individually or in pairs. Only allow a few minutes per question at this stage.

Next, divide participants into small groups of two or three. Give each group one of the stories from the *My Body, My Life* project and inform participants that this is a real story from someone who decided to have an abortion. These are available from http://mybody-mylife.org/stories/. Select stories that cover a range of different themes and reasons for having an abortion including poor mental and physical health, abortion stigma, failed contraception, religion, having children already.

Ask participants to read the story and discuss their initial reactions. They may want to draw or write these around the story.

- How do you feel after reading the story?
- Does anything about the story surprise you?
- What questions would you like to ask this person if you could meet them?

Ask participants to read the story again and this time use it to answer the questions on the flipcharts (e.g. how did the person in the story end up pregnant when they didn't want to be? Why did they want an abortion? Etc.). Answers should be recorded on post-it notes (all in the same colour but a different colour from the beginning of the session) and placed on the flipcharts.

Once this has been completed, gather around one piece of flipchart at a time and look at the responses together. The aim is to explore the diversity of experiences of abortion. Facilitate a discussion that highlights this and that draws out any differences between participants' initial thoughts about abortion (recorded on the first set of post-its) and the reality of women's experiences, based on the *My Body, My Life* research (recorded on the second set of post-its). You may want to point out:

- It is often assumed that most people who have abortions are young, single and childless, but actually 54% of women who had abortions in 2015 had already had at least one pregnancy resulting in a live birth or a stillbirth.
- Women of all ages have abortions but the largest number of abortions are provided to women between the age of 20 and 24.
- Most people who ask for abortions were using contraception when they became pregnant.
- Abortion is common. Women are fertile for over 25 years of their lives and no method of contraception is 100% effective. It is perhaps then not so surprising that one in three women will have an abortion at some point in their lives.

Section 7: Sexually Transmitted Infections (STIs)

Points to consider: Sexually Transmitted Infections (STIs)

- Sexually Transmitted Infections (STIs) can be transmitted through different kinds of sex including oral sex and penetrative vaginal and anal intercourse. Try to avoid talking about STIs being transmitted by having 'sex' and to be specific about what types of sex you mean. This can feel strange but it increases confidence in talking about different sexual practices and raises awareness of their relative risks/possibilities. It also helps you to be inclusive of all types of sexual relationships and avoid heteronormativity (by assuming that sex always takes place between a man and woman and that men and women always have penis-in-vagina sex. This excludes LGBT+ people and ignores the wide range of ways two or more people can be sexual together).

- Condoms (internal and external) are the ONLY method to protect from *most* STIs. We say most because there is no method of contraception that can protect against genital warts, herpes and pubic lice. Other methods of contraception help prevent pregnancy, but do not offer a barrier against STIs and HIV.

- It is not appropriate to show images of infected genitals. The images are usually extreme examples of symptoms that most people will never experience. This is an unhelpful message to give since some STIs have no symptoms at all. A more helpful message is to always get tested for STIs if you have unprotected sex, even if you have no symptoms at all. The images also add to the shame and stigma surrounding STIs rather than combating it. Usually the only thing that young people remember about them is that they were 'disgusting' rather than any useful information about how to protect themselves and others or how and where to get tested.

STI party!

 This is a practical activity that models the spread of infections through asking participants to mix cups of clear fluid. Each person has a cup of liquid but only one person has an 'infected' cup at the start. At the end of the activity the educator tests the cups to see if the infection has spread. 30–40 minutes

 Plastic cups, pipettes or teaspoons (enough for one per participant). Bottle or jug of tap water, blue litmus paper, citric acid solution – this is easily made up from citric acid powder (which is available online or from some chemists). A small teaspoon of powder dissolved in approximately 100ml of water should give the right strength solution. Audio music player. 11+

Note: This activity is often carried out using milk, starch and iodine because milk is a similar colour to semen! However, we find that this can sometimes give ambiguous test results (colour change is brown (negative result) or blue black (positive result) that can be hard to tell in milk). We have provided an alternative method developed by Alice Hoyle (qualified science teacher) that can be safely facilitated by educators without any science background. However, it is a very good idea to practice this with colleagues or peer educators before you do it with the group and make sure everything works – it causes a headache if it doesn't work in front of the class!

A health and safety note: Citric acid is the same chemical that is found in lemon juice. It is relatively harmless but care should be taken not to get it in eyes. If it does, flush with water. If it gets onto skin just wash off.

To prepare for the activity

Fill each cup with approximately 50–100ml of water, except for one which is to be filled with citric acid solution (the 'infection'). You will need enough cups for one per participant.

To facilitate the activity

Give each participant a clear plastic cup full of liquid and a plastic pipette or teaspoon. Tell participants not to drink the liquid!

Inform the group that they are going to pretend they are at a party where they will get to know lots of new people. Play party music to set the scene. Tell the group that as they get to know people at the party they can choose if they want to share the contents of their cup. This can be done using a teaspoon or pipette or by tipping liquid from one cup into another and back again. Let participants know that they can choose who they want to mix with and how many people they want to mix with. Reinforce that participants must ask permission before they 'mix cups' with someone and that anyone who doesn't is guilty of 'an assault' and will be removed from the activity.

Once the participants have had sufficient opportunity to mix their cups, stop the music and inform them that someone at the party had an STI. Inform them that the STI could have been spread among party-goers and that the only way to find out who is infected is to have an STI test.

Next the educator will test each cup for 'infection' with blue litmus paper. If a participant has been infected with an 'STI' the indicator paper will turn pink.

Once each cup has been tested discuss the following:

- Do you know who you got the infection from? Does it matter?
- In real life, how are infections passed from one person to another? (*Answer: through the exchange of bodily fluids that happens through some sexual activities (anal/vaginal sex, oral sex, etc.), or through skin to skin contact (genital lice/warts).*)
- Which STI could this activity be about? (*Answer: technically this STI could be about any infection passed through body fluid (chlamydia, gonorrhea, syphilis, hepatitis or HIV). However, it is worth pointing out that with HIV if the infected person is on treatment then their viral load reduces to undetectable levels and they cannot pass on HIV.*)
- In real life, if someone finds out they are infected do they have an ethical responsibility to tell anyone else or is this private information for their ears only? (*Answer: this is an ethical debate with different possible views to explore. We would argue that you have an ethical responsibility to inform people you may have passed the infection to. STIs are a public health as well as a personal issue.*)
- How could we have prevented the infection from passing to others? (*Answer: used an internal or external condom; not had sex; got tested/treated and waited to have sex until the infection had cleared; had sex with one person only.*)

For further discussion questions see those at the end of 'The STI learning toolkit' activity on p. 311, which could be used to generate critical discussion at the end of the STI party!

Note: Participants will often be very interested in the original source of the infection. Remind them this is often difficult to tell and not important in this session. The key learning is about what steps we need to take to protect ourselves from getting an STI and to think about our ethical responsibilities towards others. STIs are a public health issue!

The STI learning toolkit

 A creative group task that requires participants to research information about STIs and think creatively about how best to represent this information and educate others.

 One hour (minimum). Can be extended to a longer project.

 Online access/leaflets about STIs, a range of craft materials, playdoh, etc.

 13+

Divide participants into small groups. Task each group with creating a resource (a poster, PowerPoint, meme, advert, etc.) that can be used to educate other young people about a specific STI. Allocate each group a different STI so that the group collectively creates an STI toolkit.

Remind the young people that they don't need to memorise all the facts about STIs to keep themselves safe. The key message when delivering work around STIs is that STIs exist and can be transmitted via most (but not all) sexual activities. Many have no symptoms which means that it is ALWAYS a good idea to get tested after sexual contact with a new partner.

Explain that each resource will need to include:

- Visual prompts or objects (e.g. STI models fashioned from playdoh or a set of the STI cuddle toys to prompt discussion).
- Relevant information including: possible symptoms of that STI, how it is tested for, what its treatment is, any consequences if left untreated.
- Points for young people specifically to consider.

Participants will need to conduct their own research using online information for reliable websites (Brook, FPA and NHS choices are all good resources) and think about what information is relevant and useful to other young people.

Ask all groups to present their finished resource to the rest of the group. Where possible you could also arrange for groups to use the toolkits to facilitate a session with younger peers. This should only be done as part of a wider RSE programme and with appropriate support from staff. To assess the learning based on this activity you can use the STI quiz. You could also use the self and peer assessment tables in on p. 330 in Chapter 8: *Concluding the learning* to assess the learning from this activity.

Use the following questions to conclude the activity:

- How might it feel to find out you have an STI? (*Answers may include: feeling embarrassed, exposed, worried about their health or how people might respond when they find out.*)
- Is there an idea that some STIs are worse to have than others? (*Answers may include: knowledge about whether or not an STI can be treated/cured; the potential severity of an infection; the 'gross factor' (pubic lice for example can be seen as more 'gross' than other infections).*)

- Why is there shame and stigma surrounding STIs compared to other infections? (Compare STI viruses with the herpes virus that causes cold sores.) (*Answers may include: taboos around sex; shame associated with having multiple sexual partners; fears around disease and contagion.*)

- What are the key messages about STIs that all young people (and adults) need to know? (*Answers may include: that STIs exist and can be transmitted via most sexual activities, particularly vaginal, anal or oral intercourse; that some STIs have symptoms but some have none; that you should always get tested if you have had sex with a new partner; that tests are quick, easy, free and virtually pain free.*)

- Are STIs a private or public issue? (*Answers may include: STIs are often transmitted through private and intimate acts but they are a public health issue. In seeking testing and ensuring we finish our course of treatment we are protecting not only ourselves and our partners but the wider population. We can only stamp out STIs if everyone does the same.*)

STI quiz

With thanks to Dr Rosie Vincent for her help with this activity.

 A quiz that assesses participants' knowledge about STIs. It can be used to find out what young people already know and to give information about STIs or to assess learning at the end of a programme of learning.   10–15 minutes

 Quiz sheet.   13+

You could facilitate this activity in different ways, as a written activity or a team game with prizes.

Answers:

1) **Which STIs can be passed on to another person by penis in vagina sex?** (*Answer: all of them!*)

2) **Which STIs can be passed on to another person by oral sex?** (*Answer: most of them! Infections commonly caught through oral sex include gonorrhea, genital herpes, syphilis and chlamydia. Less likely to be orally transmitted but technically possible are hepatitis A, hepatitis B and hepatitis C, genital warts, HIV and pubic lice – pubic lice can end up in facial hair and occasionally eyelashes and eyebrows but not hair on the scalp. Trichomoniasis is not thought to be transmitted orally.*)

3) **Which STIs can be passed on to another person by anal sex?** (*Answer: most of them! Infections caught through anal sex include gonorrhea, genital herpes, syphilis and chlamydia. HIV, hepatitis A, hepatitis B, hepatitis C, genital warts and pubic lice can also all be transmitted anally. Trichomoniasis is not thought to be transmitted anally.*)

4) **Which STIs can be passed by skin to skin contact and are therefore not fully protected against by condoms?** (*Answer: genital herpes, HPV, pubic lice, syphilis.*)

5) **Which STIs are caused by a bacteria and therefore able to be treated with antibiotics?** (*Answer: syphilis, gonorrhea, chlamydia. It's important to note that antibiotic resistance is on the rise. Also trichomoniasis is a parasitic not bacterial infection but it can be treated with antibiotics.*)

6) **Which STIs are caused by a virus and therefore not easily curable?** (*Answer: hepatitis B, HPV, HIV, genital herpes.* Note: *in some cases there are vaccines abaovale for Hep B and some strains of HPV and anti-viral medication can suppress the effects of HIV and herpes.*)

7) **Which STIs are caused by a parasite?** (*Answer: trichomoniasis and pubic lice. Trichomoniasis is cured by antibiotic treatment and pubic lice are cured by lotions and shampoos.*)

8) **What are some of the possible symptoms of STIs?** (*Answers: sores bumps lesions (e.g. HPV, syphilis, genital herpes), unusual discharge (e.g. chlamydia, gonorrhea, trichomoniasis,) pain or discomfort around genitals, during urination or intercourse (e.g. chlamydia, gonorrhea). Symptoms can vary hugely and can be very non-specific (e.g. with symptoms of HIV seroconversion symptoms might include generalised rash, fever, muscle pain, sore throat etc.).*)

9) ***What does it mean if someone is sexually active but has no symptoms of an STI?*** (*Answer: it is important to note that all of the STIs can have no symptoms at all, therefore it is important that EVERYONE who is sexually active should go and get checked regularly.*)

10) **Which STIs are vaccine preventable?** (*Answer: HPV, hepatitis B, hepatitis A.*)

11) **Which STIs can cause infertility?** (*Answer: chlamydia and gonorrhea.*)

12) **Which STIs can be tested for free at a local sexual health clinic?** (*Answer: all of them!*)

STI Quiz

1. Which STIs can be passed on to another person by penis-in-vagina sex?

2. Which STIs can be passed on to another person by oral sex?

3. Which STIs can be passed on to another person by anal sex?

4. Which STIs can be passed by skin to skin contact and are therefore not fully protected against by condoms?

5. Which STIs are caused by a bacteria and therefore able to be treated with antibiotics?

6. Which STIs are caused by a virus and therefore not easily curable?

7. Which STIs are caused by a parasite?

8. What are some of the possible symptoms of STIs?

9. What does it mean if someone is sexually active but has no symptoms of an STI?

10. Which STIs are vaccine preventable?

11. Which STIs can cause infertility?

12. Which STIs can be tested for free at a local sexual health clinic?

Living with HIV

With thanks to Rosalie Hayes from National AIDS trust for her help with the development of this activity. This activity compliments the lessons within the *National AIDS Trust HIV in Schools* pack which is freely available to schools.[19]

 A creative activity that aims to increase participants' understanding of what it may be like to live with HIV.

 One hour (minimum). Can be developed as an extended creative project.

 Internet access or access to case studies.

 11+

Participants' task is to research people's experiences of living with HIV. This can be done online using the three stories included in lesson 2 of the National AIDS Trust's *HIV in Schools* pack (pages 35–42), the National AIDS Trust's *Real Life Stories of People Living with HIV*[20] or stories from the *Life in My Shoes* website.[21] You could also invite in a speaker with HIV who has been trained and supported to talk about their experiences of living with HIV in educational settings. Contact the Terrance Higgins Trust's Positive Voices project[22] to find out more.

Based on what they find out about people's experiences of living with HIV, participants need to write a short story, drama/TV script or poem. This could either be a creative response to the stories that they have read or a creative project that uses the stories as the basis for developing a drama or short story. Once projects have been completed create a forum (assembly, exhibition, online space, etc.) for sharing participants' work and showcasing the range of experiences of living with HIV. Choose a hashtag or exhibition title that will help raise awareness of HIV and tackle HIV stigma.

Notes

1 www.nspcc.org.uk/preventing-abuse/child-protection-system/legal-definition-child-rights-law/gillick-competency-fraser-guidelines/

2 https://lgbt.foundation/downloads/FinalBeatingAboutTheBush

3 www.lgbtyouth.org.uk/media/1471/good-sex-is-health-resource-for-gay-and-bisexual-men.pdf

4 www.lgbtyouth.org.uk/media/1469/good-sex-is-guide-for-trans-young-people.pdf

5 www.scarleteen.com/article/bodies/can_i_get_pregnant_or_get_or_pass_on_an_sti_from_that

6 Great Britain, 1984. Gillick v West Norfolk and Wisbech Area Health Authority. *The all England law reports, 1985*(1), p. 533.

7 www.youtube.com/watch?v=I7E10BFoTE8

8 If the FPA 'Your guide to contraception leaflet' is no longer available on their website due to FPA going into administration (www.fpa.org.uk/sites/default/files/your-guide-to-contraception.pdf) please search for it via other NHS providers who often host this leaflet. Or use any online guides that list the pros and cons of the different methods of contraception.

9 http://healtheducationuk.com/store/index.php?id_product=1831&controller=product

10 www.ncbi.nlm.nih.gov/pmc/articles/PMC2636476/

11 If the FPA 'Your guide to contraception leaflet' is no longer available on their website due to FPA going into administration (www.fpa.org.uk/sites/default/files/your-guide-to-contraception.pdf) please search for it via other NHS providers who often host this leaflet. Or use any online guides that list the pros and cons of the different methods of contraception.

12 www.fpa.org.uk/sites/default/files/your-guide-to-contraception.pdf

13 https://microplasmouldings.com/mpm-brands/sperm-keyrings/

14 www.youtube.com/watch?v=9jRhPFVTYLU

15 www.youtube.com/watch?v=Rr2bahvJuOo

16 You can buy a condom demonstrator model penis and testicles from Health Edco that enables artificial semen to be used when demonstrating correct ways to put on and remove a condom. This can be used alongside a UV blacklight and artificial semen: www.anatomystuff.co.uk/condom-training-model.html

17 https://learn.brook.org.uk/

18 https://learn.brook.org.uk/

19 www.nat.org.uk/publication/hiv-schools-pack

20 www.nat.org.uk/real-life-stories

21 http://lifeinmyshoes.org

22 www.tht.org.uk/our-charity/Resources/Community-projects/positive-voices

CHAPTER 8
Concluding the learning

This chapter contains tools and techniques for safely bringing your RSE programme to a close. It includes ideas for reflecting on learning, assessing learning and evaluating learning.

Every RSE session should include an activity that enables participants to reflect on their learning and experience of participating in the session and working as a group. This is an important part of the learning cycle and essential for ensuring that you close a session safely and check that the content and style of the programme is meeting your participants' needs.

Chapter summary

Section 1: Closing activities. Activities that will help you to safely close the space you have created and enable participants to reflect on the work that you have all done together. These activities are particularly useful if you have been tackling sensitive topics or working with a group intensively for a period of time.

Section 2: Assessment activities. Activities to assess the learning that has taken place, looking first at ideas for in-depth assessment and then quick fire activities that you can use if you are short of time or wanting to keep the pace and energy high.

Section 3: Evaluation activities. This section contains activities to help you and your participants evaluate your RSE programme and plan for future work. We include fun, high energy, quick fire evaluation activities for shorter sessions as well as in-depth evaluation activities to be used to help you reflect and evaluate longer programmes of work.

Points to consider

- Remember that not all young people's thoughts, values or behaviours will be influenced or changed by your sessions. Although this may be what we would like to achieve, it will not always be the case. Be open to this when evaluating your work and try to unpick what (if any) value the sessions have had for the young people that you work with.
- Your RSE sessions should be subject to the same quality assurance processes and procedures as other areas of your work. If you are in a school make sure that RSE has the same level of scrutiny and support as other subjects as this helps give it equal status and value.
- Involve young people in scrutiny and quality assurance. Make sure you consult and get feedback from young people as well as getting them to help design and assess activities, sessions and programmes. Where possible go back to participants and explain how you have used their feedback to make changes.
- Don't leave all evaluation and reflection to the end of the programme. You need to know as you go along whether participants are learning and how they are feeling in the space you have created.
- Where possible, embed evaluation and reflection activities in the programme itself. For example, through asking reflective and evaluative questions as part of your discussions. Or through asking participants to produce creative or reflective materials that you can use for evaluation and/or assessment.
- If you need to collect materials or data for evaluation/assessment make sure you are clear about this and explain what you will do with the information you collect and who will see it. Be clear about what is anonymous and what isn't. This is an important part of modelling consent. Always remember that participants have the right to pass and opt out of any activities that you set up.

Section 1: Closing activities

Burn it

A closing activity to help participants leave behind issues that have arisen in the session that they have found difficult and don't want to take away with them.

5–10 minutes (more if with a large group).

None.

11+

At the end of a session, sit the group in a circle or semicircle and explain the task as follows:

> We have talked about some difficult issues today. You may want to take some of our discussions away with you to think about further but there may be feelings, comments or issues that you want to leave in this room. Before we go I would like you all to imagine there is a fire in the middle of the room. We are going to go round the circle and each of you has the chance to say what you would like to throw on to the fire and leave here to burn.

Go round the circle giving each participant a chance to share anything they want to leave behind. Remind participants of the group agreement and the right to pass.

The gift of a compliment

Based on an activity created by *Brook*. Shared with permission.

This is an activity for the final session in a group work programme that helps participants to reflect on the relationships they have built over the course of the programme and to recognise the contributions that each person has made to the group. It involves each person giving and receiving compliments to/from others in the group.

10 minutes

One pack of compliment cards.

11+

Preparation: Create one pack of compliment cards by printing the compliments (see instructions in the following paragraphs) – one per card. Laminate if you can so that they last longer!

This activity is conducted in silence. Each participant stands up one at a time and walks over to a pack of cards that you have placed face down in a pile on a table. Each card contains a written compliment that the participant must give to another member of the group. You will need to make these cards ahead of the session.

The participant takes the top card from the pack, reads it to themselves and decides which group member to give it to. The person who receives the card can read it, but they do not have to share it with others if they don't want to. After giving out the card, the participant sits down and the next person stands up and repeats the exercise. This is repeated, in silence, until there are no more cards.

If a participant picks up a card and doesn't understand it, or can't think who to give it to then they can put it back in the middle of the pack. Try to discourage this and support participants to understand the card so that some participants don't just pick the easier cards.

It is a good idea for the educator(s) to take part in the activity as well. Before you start decide what order people will go to pick up a card as this helps the activity run smoothly.

After the activity has finished lead a discussion with the group using the following questions:

- What did it feel like to receive a compliment?
- What did it feel like to give a compliment?
- How did it feel doing the exercise in silence? Why do you think we do this?
- Did anyone find it uncomfortable to give or receive a compliment?
- Do we often give and receive compliments in everyday life?
- Are there any recurring themes in the compliments that people have received? Does that tell you something about yourself that surprises you?

Figure 8.1 shows some suggested compliments, feel free to add your own.

You make everyone laugh

You are a good listener

You have great ideas

You are someone I feel I can trust

You are someone I can talk to

You make interesting and thoughtful comments in discussions

You cheer everyone up

You are someone who is going places

You are good at helping and encouraging others

You are kind to everyone

You are confident in a group situation

You have creative ideas

You are someone who speaks up for others

You are very reliable

I would call you in an emergency

You are a very considerate person

I think you have
tried hard
in the group

You are the
person
who is the
most intelligent

You have a really
good sense
of humour

You are the
most helpful
person in the
group

You are a really
organised person

You are a really
good
team player

You have made
a massive
effort in the group

I like the way you
always
think about other
people's feelings

You are the
person
I would call
a mate

You are the
person I would
like to get to
know better

You don't say
a lot in the group
but what you
say is very
meaningful

I really think you
will succeed in life

I have found you
great to get
on with in this
group

I think you are
really honest
and open about
your opinions
and feelings

FIGURE 8.1 Compliment cards

Imagine an alien

 This closing activity asks participants to imagine they are describing a key concept from your RSE curriculum to an alien as a way of pulling together and checking their knowledge, understanding and critical thinking skills.

 10–20 minutes

 Paper and pens.

 11+

Choose a topic or concept you wish to assess participants' understandings of [Concept X]. For example, consent, contraception, gender.

Explain the task as follows:

Imagine an alien has just landed on planet earth. This alien knows absolutely nothing about [Concept X].

- What questions would the alien have?
- How would you explain [Concept X] to them and what underlying concepts would you also need to explain or get them to understand?
- How you would answer their questions?

See 'Alien understanding (sex and gender)' activity on p. 332 for an example of how this activity can work as an extended assessment activity for the topic of gender.

Check out

 A reflective activity that closes a session by asking participants to identify take home messages.

 5–10 minutes

 A phone/voice recorder to record evidence if needed.

 11+

Go round the circle and ask young people to say one thing that they are going to take away from the session. If you need evidence of learning/impact you can record these comments by passing round a phone/recorder and asking young people to speak into the recorder. This activity is also a good way of closing a session safely.

Section 2: Assessment activities

Extended assessment activities

An excellent way of assessing and/or reflecting on learning in RSE is by asking participants to advise someone else on a particular issue. There are a number of ways that you can do this. This section is filled with examples of activities that assess learning through tasking participants with passing on their knowledge and raising awareness of key issues from the RSE programme that are important to them.

Write it on a postcard

 This activity assesses participants' learning through asking them to identify and pass on their learning to others. This includes reflecting on what they have learnt and thinking critically about how useful or relevant this learning is for themselves and for others.

 20–50 minutes depending on task

 Blank postcards, pens. Optional – stamps, display boards, camera, online access.

 11+

Give participants the following task:

> Write a postcard to someone you know telling them about what you have been doing as part of this programme and what you have learnt. Think about who to send the postcard to, what you would want to say and what image you would have on the front.

Participants may want to cut up materials or work they have created and use this as the central image. If appropriate send the postcards! If not, create a display in your place of work to raise awareness of the work you have been doing and the issues you have been discussing. You can take photos of the postcards, participants' messages and your display for assessment perhaps, and to share online with participants' consent.

RSE core messaging

With thanks to *Brighton and Hove PSHE Education service* for the development of this idea.

 An activity that invites participants to identify key themes and core messages relating to RSE that they would like to pass on to other young people or raise awareness of in their local community.

 60 minutes (can be extended to longer project)

 Internet access, paper, pens.

 11+

Once you have completed your RSE programme ask participants you have been working with to list the main overarching themes of RSE they feel are important or that they have covered in sessions.

Once these have been agreed and established as a group, divide participants into smaller groups of three or four. Ask each group to come up with two or three core messages under each heading that they think their peers should know about. If participants are struggling with this look at the examples in the box below relating to sex, which were developed by Brighton and Hove PSHE Education service who regularly review and update their core messages with young people.

Come back together as a group and look at the core messages for each area. Work together to create a strong set of messages about RSE for young people in your area. Agree how best to disseminate these messages. For example, mock up a design using a free graphic design app like Canva to create a poster that can be displayed online and around the local community. Identify a hashtag and the target audience. Where possible use the school/youth club/organisation's social media account and make these entries go live.

Brighton and Hove RSE core messages

The core stuff – key messages for secondary and college age young people about sex (updated June 2018)

In the right time

- Wait until the time is right. Most under 16s in Brighton & Hove haven't had sex so there's no need to feel that everyone has done it.
- There is no pressure to rush to have sex, not everyone is doing it all the time – even if they say they are!

Trust gut instincts

- It's important to always feel safe when having sex, trust gut instincts to help manage safety and decide if ready or not.
- Remember a person's body is theirs only.

Get consent

- If someone can't/won't consent to sex, don't have sex with them!
- Sex needs to be consensual and even though it can be a good/pleasurable experience, but that does not mean that everybody wants/needs to have it. It is also important to be able to talk openly about it with a partner so that boundaries can be set up that both feel comfortable and happy with.
- If someone forces or pressures another person in to sexual behaviour or having sex, this is sexual assault/rape.

It's OK for someone to be themselves

- Sex is whatever someone wants it to be. It doesn't have to be penetrative.
- How someone feels about their sexually, their sexual thoughts, desires and sexual health are all important parts of being them – it's ok to explore these as long as it doesn't harm anyone.
- Gender identity and the gender(s) people find attractive may change over time.
- Some people are not interested in sex at certain stages in their life and/or are never interested in sex.

Enjoy it

- Friendships and relationships should be fun, equal, respectful and healthy.
- Sex should be enjoyable, should feel good, and have the potential for pleasure (and orgasm).
- It's important for someone to know and explore their body; people can't expect a partner to know how to pleasure them if they don't know themselves.
- Just because someone has had sex does not mean they have to keep doing it.

Stay protected, get tested

- Using condoms, dental dams and other contraceptives keep people protected from STIs and mean that they can choose if and when they want to have children.
- Getting regularly tested for STIs is what all sexually active people should do.

Show feelings

- Think about the many different ways someone can show care and love. There are other ways than penetrative sex (intercourse) – some are sexual (e.g. kissing, cuddling, touching/ playing with each other, massage, etc.).

Stay in control

- If someone has been drinking/taking drugs a partner should rethink if now is a good time to have sex. It is illegal to have sex with someone who is too drunk or high to give their consent.
- Never put pressure on someone to have sex.
- Having sex when drunk can also make sex less good and can make them feel sick.
- Use technology wisely.

Keep talking

- It's important for someone to talk to the person they're thinking of having sex with (or are already having sex with) about what they want out of the relationship and find out what the other person wants out of the relationship too.

Stay connected

- Remember there are people around (parents, carers, youth workers and other support workers) who can give help and advice if faced with tricky decisions or situations.

It's a right

- All young people have a right to top quality, professional information, advice and guidance about relationships and sex in a way that suits them.

These statements were developed by young people in Brighton and Hove in collaboration with the Brighton and Hove PSHE service.

Problem pages

 A fun activity designed to consolidate and assess learning by asking participants to respond to real life sex and relationship situations and dilemmas.

 20–30 minutes

 Pre-prepared problems or scenarios. You can find some online in *DO…RSE*, Lesson 6[1], or Brook Learn Pleasure course, module 2 – Having Sex For the First Time. Navigate to the extension activity in the *Teach It* section.

 13+

Divide into small groups and give each group one or more 'problems' or scenarios that they have to respond to. You can use examples from existing resources (such as those listed in the 'Resources' for this activity) or ask participants to create their own, based on the situations and problems they see people experiencing in their friendship and peer groups.

This activity can be used to focus on a particular area of RSE, such as first sex or gender identity, or it can be used as a general recap at the end of a comprehensive programme covering a range of topics. For example, scenarios could be based around the following:

- A condom splits during sex
- Having sex whilst drunk and is unsure if consent was given
- Fancying a friend and don't know how to tell them
- Being in a controlling relationship
- Missing a contraceptive pill
- Having unprotected sex
- Fancying someone of the same sex
- Going through a difficult break up
- A positive pregnancy test
- Having unusual discharge
- Having a nude image going around school that everyone thinks is you (even though it's not)
- A partner threatens to share your nude images
- A partner is exerting pressure for sex
- A friend has bad body odour
- Feeling confused about your gender identity
- Curious about masturbation

Explain the task which is for participants to imagine they are experts working for an online youth advice platform. They have to create an advice column or blog that responds to the scenario or problem using text and/or animation. Alternatively they can design and perform a role play phone in or live TV talk show based around the scenario. To extend the learning you could have them apply an ethical framework to solving the problem as shown in 'Ethical relationships' on p. 94 of Chapter 3: *Relationships*.

Research, present and assess

 A group work activity in which participants research a particular topic or issue and present the information to their peers.

 30 minutes+ for preparation and 30 minutes+ for presentations.

 Paper, pens, internet access.

 11+

Divide participants into small groups and ask each group to choose a topic or issue from the RSE programme that they are interested in. The task is to research the topic, drawing on the learning from the RSE programme and elsewhere and work out how best to present a reflective summary of the learning to the rest of the group. This could include a presentation, poster, leaflet, blog, radio interview, etc.

On p. 329 are some suggestions of topics/issues and points for participants to consider.

It may be helpful to instruct participants to assign specific roles to each group member to encourage participation. This also works to support individual participants either to strengthen or develop a particular skill or to differentiate by ability where some roles may be too challenging for some lower ability or Special Educational Needs (SEN) students.

- Group leader – in charge of ensuring everyone carries out their tasks and meets the deadlines – does bulk of presentation.
- Researchers – in charge of finding accurate sources of research.
- Writers – in charge of translating the research into an accessible format.
- Designers – in charge of making the research visually appealing.
- Creatives – in charge of inventing new ways of imparting information.
- Executive assistants – in charge of helping the smooth running of the whole group by supporting individual team members or completing key tasks.

Once complete, each group presents their project. Ask the rest of the group to assess their peers by either completing a peer assessment sheet OR considering the following questions and providing verbal feedback:

- Did the presentation contain accurate and relevant information?
- Was the information presented in an interesting and engaging way?
- Did the presentation include well articulated personal reflections and ideas?
- Did the presentation help you to think critically about the issue or topic? Or inspire you to do something different?
- Were questions fully considered and addressed?

Topic/issue	Points to consider
Abortion and pregnancy choices	• Types of abortion and when they can be carried out. • How many women have abortions and who has abortions. • Abortion rights and the law in the UK and worldwide. • Reasons for needing to access abortion. • Life experiences of women who have had abortions.
Equality	• Case study of a specific example of inequality (e.g. Violence Against Women and Girls (VAWG), LGBT+ discrimination, racism). • Key statistics relating to case study. • Impact on wellbeing, ethical relationships and/or sexual health. • Analysis of factors creating and sustaining the inequality. • Relevant national and international legislation. • Personal reflections and ideas for social change.
Contraception	• When and why contraception is needed. • Overview of methods of contraception OR case study of one or more methods. • How they are used. • Advantages/disadvantage for young people. • Considerations for LGBTQ young people. • Barriers to using contraception and how to tackle them .
Digital technology and relationships	• Current technology used by young people including key statistics. • How technology can help young people develop positive relationships. • How technology can aid harmful/abusive relationships. • How tech can enhance or reproduce inequalities. • Young people's views and experiences of using tech in relationships. • How teachers/youth workers/parents/young people can assist others in using tech to have positive relationships with others.

Assessment criteria for an RSE resource

The following tables enable participants to rate their own performance and that of their peers. This works as follows:

- Peers should assess first, with the participant conducting their own self assessment at the end.
- Participants can choose an overall verdict of basic, better or best based on whichever category they have used most for the assessment criteria.
- For the final level, the educator, in conjunction with the participant, can then use their own judgement based on the presentation, self and peer assessment grades to determine the overall grade.

Self and Peer Assessment

Name:		Final Level	
Self Assessment Level Awarded		Peer Assessment Level Awarded	
Peer Comments:		My response to comments:	

	Peer Assessment Level	*Peer Assessment Level*	*Peer Assessment Level*	*Self Assessment Level*	*Final Level*
Verdict on resource overall					

	Basic	*Better*	*Best*
Information selection	Contains little or none of the required information.	Contains most of the required information.	Contains all or almost all of the required information.
Information interpretation	Shows weak understanding in selecting and interpreting appropriate information.	Shows fair understanding in selecting and interpreting appropriate information.	Shows clear understanding in selecting and interpreting appropriate information.
Critical thinking	Contains little or no critical thinking.	Contains some critical thinking.	Contains high levels of critical thinking.
Reflection on personal values	Contains little or few reflections on personal and social values.	Contains some reflections on personal and social values.	Contains well thought through and well articulated reflections on personal and social values.
Design	Information is presented but not in a logical or visually attractive or clear way.	Information is clearly laid out with mostly suitable design/presentation to enhance presentation.	Information is well supported with suitable visually appealing design/presentation. Appropriate pictures that complement the text/ narrative are used where appropriate.
Key word explanation	Some key words are incorrectly explained.	Most key words are explained.	All key words are explained.
Signposting for further help	Incomplete information about where to go for further help is provided.	Some information about where to go for further help is provided.	All the necessary information about where to go for further help is provided.
Referencing	Some inappropriate or inaccurate sources of information used.	Recommended websites used.	Recommended websites used as well as additional appropriate sources of information which are clearly explained.

Flashcard story

Based on an activity in *AGENDA: A young people's guide to making positive relationships matter* (see *Useful resources* at the end of this book). Used with permission.

 A creative assessment activity that enables participants to research and explore one issue or topic and present to their peers and wider audiences.

 One hour

 Paper and pens, phones/tablets/computers to research online and make short films, A3 card and marker pens, a quiet space.

 11+

Ask participants to work on their own, in pairs or small groups and choose a topic or issue relating to relationships and sexuality that interests them. Their task is to research the issue and make a flashcard story that can be uploaded online.

A flashcard story is a short film of a person that is usually posted on YouTube where the person silently holds up a series of flashcards each containing a sentence. The words tell the person's story, without them uttering a word. If participants don't know what a flashcard story is ask one of the group to explain and have a look at an example from YouTube.

To create the flashcard story participants will need to research their topic and write down ten things they have learnt from their research that they didn't know previously. These sentences can be structured start 'I didn't know that…but now I know….' Alternatively participants can focus on beliefs and values and write: 'Before I thought…now I think…' The idea is to raise awareness of an important issue and to highlight the gaps in young people's learning about debates and topics that are important to them.

Using A3 card – divide each card in half. On the left write the 'I didn't know' that statement and on the right write 'I now know…'. Illustrate with drawings, emojis, photos.

Choose a quiet place to film the flashcard story. Avoid including faces, voices or any identifiable features. For example, by filming people holding the flashcards over their faces. Upload onto a school or youth group vimeo or YouTube account. Create a hashtag and share the video with your school council, local council or anyone else that you and your school/youth group think need to hear your story.

Alien understanding (sex and gender)

 A research activity that asks participants how they would explain specific questions relating to sex, gender and relationships to an alien race.

 40–60 minutes

 Flipchart paper and pens.

 11+

Explain to the group that aliens have landed and they have no concept of how things work on Earth around sex and gender. They are trying to understand so they have some questions for us.

Divide participants into small groups and allocate each group a question or series of related questions that they need to address. You can adjust the questions to suit your group and differentiate the questions according to the needs of participants in the group.

- How many sexes are there? How many genders are there?
- What is the difference between sex and gender?
- Why do Earthlings group by gender and have separate spaces?
- Can you tell somebody's sex/gender just by looking at them?
- What assumptions are made about someone based on their sex/gender?
- What is a gender stereotype? How is it maintained? What are the costs of not maintaining a gender stereotype? What are the benefits?
- Are gender stereotypes true?
- What makes a female a female? What makes a male a male?
- Does one group hold more power in your society than the others? Why?
- How do humans reproduce and control reproduction?
- Why do humans have sex?

Groups should use the learning from your RSE programme and their own research to work out how best to answer the questions. If using online search engines to research these questions participants may find inaccurate, contentious, contradictory or polarised answers. Therefore, participants should be encouraged to think about the following when doing the research:

- Is the information **relevant** to answer the alien's question?
- How they can prove their information is **reliable, accurate and verifiable**?
- Is their information **objective/subjective**? Is there any **bias or particular perspective presented?**

Each group should present their findings to their question to the whole group including information about their sources and the reliability of the info.

To finish, you can imagine and discuss as a group how the alien would feel when they returned home. Ask the following questions:

- What elements of our society might they adopt to improve their own?
- What elements might they reject for not being possible/suitable for their own?
- What would a sex/gender utopia look like?
- What would a gender neutral world look like?
- What other questions do you think the aliens should ask of us?
- What other questions should we ask of ourselves?

Educate, agitate, organise

 This is an open activity in which participants pursue their interests in any area of the RSE curriculum. Their task is to research an issue and design a campaign that aims to 'educate, agitate and organise'. One hour (minimum)

 Internet access, paper, pens. 11+

Explain to the group that 'Educate, Agitate, Organise' is a widely used phrase in social justice campaigns taken from a speech made from Indian politician and social reformer D. B. R. Ambedkar in 1971:

> My final words of advice to you are educate, agitate and organize; have faith in yourself. With justice on our side, I do not see how we can lose our battle. For ours is a battle, not for wealth or for power. It is a battle for freedom.

Share this quote and the following definitions of the three key terms:

1. Educate: To raise awareness, knowledge and understanding of a particular issue.
2. Agitate: To call attention to an issue; to disturb or excite emotionally.
3. Organise: To make plans, arrangements or preparations for change.

Working individually, or in small groups, participants need to research the issue that they are interested in that relates to your RSE curriculum. Their task is to plan how they want to educate others about this issue, raise awareness of its importance and make plans for how to bring about change. Where possible support participants to put their plans into action.

Quick fire assessment activities

These are all fun, interactive activities that can be used to assess learning at any point during an RSE programme – to conduct baseline assessments and kick start the learning, to check in midway to review learning or at the end of the programme as part of a final assessment. You could also adapt a version of the 'Keyword Jenga' activity on p. 268 of Chapter 7: *Sexual health* to use as an assessment activity.

Call my bluff

 A game that tests participants' knowledge and familiarity with key terms and concepts covered in your RSE programme. This activity enables you to check learning so far and flag up any gaps in knowledge and understanding.   20 minutes

 Pens and paper.   11+

Divide participants into two teams and give each team a list of terms or concepts that you have covered in your RSE programme. Each group has to come up with three definitions of each word – only one of which must be correct. For example:

- **Vulva:** A) the external genitals of most girls and women (and some trans/non-binary people), B) another word for the vagina, C) a sexually transmitted infection. (*The correct answer is A.*)
- **Heterosexual:** A) a person who is attracted to people of the same gender, B) a person who has sexual relationships with only one person at a time, C) a person who is attracted to people of a different gender. (*The correct answer is C.*)

Once the definitions are prepared teams play against each other by presenting one word and set of definitions at a time and giving the other team one minute to decide which is the correct answer. The team with the most correct guesses wins.

Taboo

 A quick, fun game that tests participants' knowledge and understanding of key words and concepts relating to relationships and sexuality. It can be used at the beginning of a session as an energiser and way of checking participants' levels of knowledge, or as a reflection and assessment activity to check learning at the end of a session or programme. 10 minutes

 Bag of key words (choose a selection of terms and concepts that you have covered in your RSE programme). 11+

Divide the group into two teams. Teams take it in turns. A participant from the first team chooses a key word from a bag and describes it to the other members of the group without using the word itself. For example, if the word is *contraception*, you might say: '*what some people use so that they can have sex without getting pregnant*'. The person who guesses correctly gets to be the next person to draw out a word and describe it. Each team has one minute to see how many words they can guess correctly. Switch teams until there are no more words left.

Game rules:

1. You are not allowed to use any slang words as this makes it too easy (e.g. saying 'rubber' for condom, 'boobs' for breasts or 'shag' for sex).
2. You are not allowed to use any part of the word or a derivative of the word, e.g. pregnancy if the word is pregnant.
3. You are not allowed to use gestures or mimes.
4. You are not allowed to use 'sounds like' or 'rhymes with'. Instead you must *describe* the word.
5. If you don't know what a word means you can pass and return the word to the bag. The team will lose one point for each returned word.

Playdoh pictionary

 A fun game that tests participants' familiarity with key words and concepts covered in the RSE programme. Good for visual learners and for breaking down some of the taboos surrounding RSE. 10–30 minutes

 Bag of key words (choose a selection of terms and concepts that you have covered in your RSE programme), tubs of playdoh. 11+

Divide the group into teams that take it in turns. One person from each team draws out a key word from the bag which they have to make using the playdoh. All teams and players can try and guess the word and the first team to guess gets a point. The winning team is the team with the most points.

The activity works particularly well for key words relating to anatomy and contraception. It's a good idea to time each player limiting them to one–two minutes to ensure that the game stays lively and engaging. If you don't have any playdoh available you can do this activity using pens and paper.

Quizzes: points to consider

- Quizzes are a quick and popular way to check learning in RSE. They work as baseline assessment tools or as ways of checking learning midway, or at the end of a programme of learning. There are quizzes on contraception, STIs, pleasure, sex and the law, abortion, gender and sexuality and much more. We have included specific examples in Chapter 7: *Sexual health*, including the 'Condom demo quiz' on p. 300 and the 'STI quiz' on p. 312.
- Although quick and good fun, quizzes do tend to focus on checking knowledge, leaving little room for exploring attitudes, values and beliefs or critical thinking skills. Use them but be aware of their limitations.
- Avoid using True or False/Fact or Myth quizzes as they can introduce myths or falsehoods and myths that participants were not already aware of or unwittingly reinforce them.

Here are some suggested activities that are suitable for young people of all ages:

- **Quiz Rounds.** Participants create their own quizzes in small groups based on the learning in the RSE programme. Each group is allocated a different theme or task. For example, one group has to create a picture round, another a music round and another has to create a question that involves making something from foil/cardboard/playdoh.
- **Multiple Choice Quiz.** Provide a question with three possible answers where only one is correct.
- **What's the Question?** Show an answer to the group and ask them to think about what the question is. This generates discussion. Where there is dissent take a vote on the best question.
- **Balloon Busting Game:** Play the balloon busting activity that can be found in Chapter 7: *Sexual health* on p. 263 in which participants read out quiz questions written on balloons and guess the answers before popping the balloon to find the answer inside. Make up alternative questions and answers for any topic or area of learning.
- **Twenty Questions?** Write a key word relating to your RSE programme on a post-it note and stick it to one participant's forehead (you may want to use the list of key words in 'Keyword Jenga' on p. 268). The participant can ask up to 20 questions with a yes or no answer to the rest group until they guess correctly what the key word on their forehead is.

Here are some suggested resources that you and your participants can use to create your own quizzes:

- Findings from The National Survey of Sexual Attitudes and Lifestyles (NATSAL), conducted every ten years.
- Stonewall's *School Report*[2]: The experiences of lesbian, gay, bi and trans pupils in Britain's schools. Conducted every year.
- Research conducted by national charities such as NSPCC.
- The Sex Education Forum's webpage on evidence, data and statistics.[3]

Section 3: Evaluation activities

Evaluation is a key part of the learning cycle. It provides opportunities for participants and educators to step back and reflect on the *value* of an RSE programme for participants. It also helps you to identify what participants have learned and what else they would like to know, to reflect on what has changed and to create opportunities for participants to participate in developing future programmes by thinking about what should be done differently next time or in the future.

When planning which evaluation activities to use it's important to first establish:

- What is it that you are trying to find out?
- Who is the information that you are collecting for? Is the information for you? Your funder? Your organisation? Or for participants themselves?
- What will you do with the information you collect? What are you collecting it for? Who will see it? Will it be anonymous?

Be explicit about all of these points with participants when doing evaluation activities.

In-depth evaluation of learning

A body of reflection

 This activity helps participants reflect on how they felt in the learning environment and provide feedback to the group and the educator. 15–20 minutes

 Blank paper/paper with body outline, pens, camera (for educator). 11+

Give each participant a handout with the outline of a body or ask them to draw one on a blank piece of A4 or A3 paper. Inform participants that this is their space to capture their experience of the programme (so far). They can draw, write, annotate their thoughts, feelings, learning, reflections or questions in and around the body.

Encourage participants to think about how they felt during the activities in their bodies and their minds and to get creative about how they represent this on paper. This is useful information for you as an educator as it helps you understand whether participants felt safe, comfortable and included in the learning environment created.

At the end, ask participants if they are willing to share their body with you and let you take a photograph of it. Let participants know that the images will be anonymous and that their reflections will be used to inform your planning for future sessions/programmes. If you also need the images for reports to others, be honest and clear about this with participants.

To look at what has changed over the course of a programme, ask participants to draw two body outlines and annotate one body to represent how they felt at the beginning of the programme and one to represent how they felt at the end. This can help participants to reflect on personal changes and learning and can also be used as evidence of impact if required.

Photo choice

 To enable participants to reflect creatively and visually on their learning experience using photo cards. This activity can create powerful evaluation data and provide opportunities for rich discussion.

 20–30 minutes, depending on the size of the group

 Sets of photo cards – one per participant if possible or one per small group. Post-it notes and pens OR paper, glue and pens. Camera (for educator).

 11+

Give participants a set of photo cards either individually or one set per small group. The cards should contain a range of strong emotive images such as a rocket going off, fireworks, stormy seas, a crowd, grey skies, a carnival scene, someone on their own, etc. (Pictures from Instagram or Pinterest, greetings cards, old photos and magazine adverts work well.)

Ask participants to choose the images that most represent how they feel about the session/programme and their experience so far. Then ask participants to share with the group the image(s) they have chosen and why they have chosen that image.

If you need to collect more detailed evaluation data, ask participants to write down why they chose that image on a post-it note and take photographs of these next to the selected image. Alternatively you can ask participants to stick the image of their choice on a piece of paper and write their thoughts and feelings about the session/programme around it. Paper, pens and glue will be required. Give time to this task to allow participants time to reflect.

Sentence stem sticks

 A quick way of enabling participants to reflect and evaluate their learning and experience of the group space. Participants' feedback can be shared anonymously to create a powerful group reflection.

 5–15 minutes

 Pens and paper, list of sentence stems (for educator) written on lollipop sticks or printed on card. Cardboard box or plastic tub.

 11+

Sentence stems are an alternative to questions that can be used to encourage participant reflection and collect evaluation data if you need it. Write each sentence stem on coloured lollipop sticks and create as many sentence stems as there are participants in your group (sentences can be repeated in the set). Place the sticks in a box.

Ask each participant to draw out a sentence stem and write it and their answer on a post-it note which should be gathered in by the educator. Participants can take and respond to one or more sticks.

Depending on the topic or sentence stem you can then read out participants' responses anonymously without revealing the identity of the participant. This can make for a powerful collective response and group reflection. If some of the responses suggest that there are issues within the group that need to be addressed make time in the next session to discuss and address these. Remember to revisit and possibly update your group agreement where participants feel this is necessary. Keep the sentence stem sticks for reuse at the end of further learning cycles.

Example sentence stems (or make up your own):

- The best thing about this programme/ session was…
- The worst thing about this programme/ session was…
- Whilst taking part in the programme I felt…
- The thing I will never forget is…
- One thing that surprised me is…
- The key message that I will take away is…
- I learned that…
- I now appreciate that…
- One thing that made me feel safe in today's session is…
- One thing that made me feel unsafe today was…

- I now want too…
- I can now…
- I now feel…
- I now think…
- I now know…
- I feel comfortable that…
- I feel uncomfortable about…

An alternative version of this activity would be to write the sentence stems on a Jenga set for some 'Evaluation Jenga'. This would only work in groups where participants are happy to share their reflections with the rest of the group. To do this follow the instructions in 'Feel good Jenga' in Chapter 2: *Creating safer spaces* on p. 35.

If some of the sentence stems feel difficult to respond to in the group environment discuss what makes a question/statement safe or unsafe to answer in a group and what group members can do to make people feel safe to share. Link this discussion back to your group agreement and encourage participants to be mindful of how they ask questions of each other (and you).

Draw and write

 This is a quick activity that asks participants to reflect on their experiences during the session through drawing or writing down their thoughts, feelings and ideas. Resources can be collected at the end and used as evaluation data if required.

 5–10 minutes

 Large piece of paper (A1+) and flipchart pens. If you are working with a large group you will need multiple pieces of paper.

 11+

Place an A1 piece of paper in the middle of the table. Draw a large rectangle in the middle. Inside the rectangle write 'draw' and on the outside write 'write'. Ask participants to sit around the piece of paper. You may need to work in small groups.

Ask participants to individually either draw or write their responses to the session. This can be their thoughts or feelings, knowledge they have learnt or beliefs that have changed or been clarified for them during the session. You may want to use the following questions as prompts, or you may want to leave the task open ended.

Encourage students to be creative and make it clear that the aim of the activity is for them to reflect on the session and their learning experience.

- What did you think of today's session? Brainstorm five key words.
- How did you feel during the session? How do you feel about what you have learnt today?
- What do you know now that you didn't know before?
- What have you learnt about how you work as a group?
- Write or draw a belief that has become clear to you in this session.
- How would you represent the session visually?
- What else would you like to discuss or learn about in future sessions?

Before and after

This activity has been adapted from 'Before and After' from Blake, S, Muttock, S, Beal, S, & Handy, L, (2012) *Assessment, Evaluation and Sex and Relationships Education: A Practical Toolkit for Education, Health and Community Settings*. NCB and Jessica Kingsley Publishers; and 'Then and Now', a technique used by the PSHE Association to assess against lesson objectives. Used with permission.

 An evaluation form that can be used at the start and finish of a programme of learning to capture participants' reflections on how well session outcomes have been met, and how participants think, feel and respond to the content of the session.

 5 minutes before and after a session or programme of learning.

 Blank Before and After evaluation (one per participant).

 11+

At the start of the session or programme of learning

Hand each participant a copy of the "Before and After" assessment sheet. Ask them to fill in the title of the session or programme as well as the intended session outcomes for each programme in the spaces provided. For example, learning objectives to use in sessions see UNESCO (2018) *International Technical Guidance on Sexuality Education* (see *Useful resources* at the end of this book).

Either ask participants to feedback their responses or hand their sheets in so that you can review their initial assessments (each sheet will need to be named). If the majority of the class have rated their existing knowledge understanding and skills in the chosen outcomes as High you may need to adjust your session outcomes accordingly to ensure that the programme meets participants needs. If this is the case use the results from the evaluation to prompt discussion with the group about what they already know and what else they would like to know.

At the end of the session or programme of learning

Revisit the sheet at the end of the programme. Ask participants to rate each outcome again in the '*after*' section.

	Before and After evaluation sheet.

Your name_____

Session title_____

Before you start the session please record your answers in the BEFORE half of this sheet. Once you have completed the session(s) you should fill in the AFTER section of this sheet.

	BEFORE Low ----------------------------High					**AFTER** Low----------------------------High				
Outcome 1:	1	2	3	4	5	1	2	3	4	5
Outcome 2:	1	2	3	4	5	1	2	3	4	5
Outcome 3:	1	2	3	4	5	1	2	3	4	5

Please complete the following sentences:
When it comes to RSE and the topics covered in this programme…

I think…		
I feel…		
I want…		
I am most interested in…		

Quick fire evaluation activities

Graffiti it

 A creative way of collecting participants' thoughts, views and opinions about a session or programme. 10 minutes+

 Large wall or flipchart paper labelled 'Graffiti wall', pens for each participant. 11+

Create a graffiti wall for participants to write or draw their thoughts and views about a session or programme. Some question prompts are provided here to help you:

- What did you think, know and believe about the topics and issues we have covered, before taking part in this programme? What about now?
- Is what you think, feel and believe about this session/topic different from other people in the same session? Did the discussions help you to clarify your own thoughts/feelings and beliefs?
- What are some of the comments made by others that you found particularly interesting or useful?
- Do you think you will do anything differently as a result of taking part in the programme, either now or in the future?
- What is the key message that you are going to take away from this programme?
- What else would you like to learn about?

Give participants five minutes or more to write down or visualise their thoughts and then gather round the wall to discuss the feedback. Encourage participants to read each other's responses and comment on them – as you would on a graffiti wall – and to add further comments during the discussion as and when they arise.

If you want to ask specific questions you can write these on the wall in advance, or leave it blank for participants to tell you what they think you need to hear.

Remember to take a photo of the wall if you need to collect evidence.

Move it!

 A interactive way of asking participants to respond to simple evaluation questions. Good for non-verbal learners. 5 minutes

 Evaluation questions and space to move around. 11+

Ask participants to respond to simple evaluation questions using their bodies. For example, hands up/hands down; thumbs up/thumbs down; stand up/sit down; stand in different corners of the room with each corner representing a different response (e.g. great/good/ok/not very good).

Try using questions such as:

- What did you think of today's session? (Good, ok, not so good)
- Did you learn anything new in this session? (Yes, No)

- Would you recommend this session to a friend? (Yes, No)
- On a scale of 1–10 to what extent do you think this programme will help you now or in the future? (1–10)
- Which session did you find most useful? (list of sessions)

If you need evidence of learning/impact you can nominate someone to count and write down numbers of responses

Shout it!

 A simple way of generating verbal feedback on RSE sessions. Good for low literacy learners or time pressured educators! Five minutes

 Evaluation questions, flipchart/board and pens. 11+

Ask questions and encourage participants to call out their answers. You can write responses on flipchart/the board.

Vote for it

 A simple way of generating anonymous feedback on a session. Works with low-literacy and non-verbal learners. 5 minutes

 Counters or tokens, labelled boxes, evaluation questions, post-it notes and pens. 11+

Ask participants a series of questions and ask them to respond by voting. To do this give participants counters or tokens (pound store domino counters or tiddlywinks work well). Set up a series of boxes (old shoe boxes or ice cream tubs work well) and ask participants to place their counter in the box that best represents their answer. This activity can be extended by asking participants to explain why they voted the way that they did and writing down their response on a post-it note that they stick to the box of their choice.

Exit tickets

 A way of collecting anonymous written feedback from participants about a session or programme. 5 minutes

 Pre-prepared exit tickets OR blank A5 paper/post-it notes, pens for each participant, box or tray to collect tickets. 11+

When finishing a session and before participants leave the room issue them with small exit tickets to fill in and place in a box or tray as they leave the room.

The exit ticket could include the following:

- How I feel about the session (can provide a range of emojis to circle).
- Something I will take away from this session.
- Something I might need to find out more about/need help with.
- Any other comments.

Alternatively you can give participants a blank A5 sheet of paper or post-it note and ask them to record whatever thoughts, ideas and feelings they have about the session.

Thinking ahead

 A reflective activity that encourages participants to think about the impact of the session on their lives and relationships.

 5 minutes

 (Optional) post-it notes and pens.

 11+

Ask the group if any of them think they are going to do anything differently as a result of taking part in the session. This could either be something they are going to do differently now or in the future.

Ask for a show of hands to indicate yes/no before asking participants what they are going to do differently or carry on doing. They can call these out or write anonymously on slips of paper depending on the nature of the group and sensitivity of the topic. Remember the right to pass.

Rate it

 A simple way of asking participants to rate their experience of a programme visually. This can be used to generate reflection and discussion.

 5 minutes

 Different coloured stickers and a pre-prepared rating sheet.

 11+

Create a diagram or poster of a target or thermometer that represents a scale from 1–10. Ask participants to rate their experience of a session or programme by placing different coloured stickers on the scale. For example, red for how comfortable they felt in the space, green for how confident they now feel around the issue covered, or a different colour for how well each learning outcome has been met.

It is possible to do this activity at the start of a programme by asking participants to rate how knowledgeable, confident and comfortable they feel about RSE/a particular area of learning and then repeating it at the end of the programme. This can be used to generate discussion with participants on whether anything has changed for them as a result of their participation in the programme.

Curate it

 A creative way of capturing the learning from the session or longer RSE programme. 5 minutes+

 Phones with cameras, access to social media platforms, course materials, pens and paper. 11+

Ask participants to take one or more photos that sum up their learning during a session or programme that can be shared on social media. They may want to take a photo of some of the materials they have created or used during the session or create new images.

This activity can work well at the end of a programme if you get out all the materials that you have used and/or recap on the activities and topics covered over several weeks. This helps jog participants' (and your) memory and sparks reflective conversations in the group.

To extend the activity ask participants to think about who they would want to share their images with and what hashtag they want to use. In larger groups, ask participants to work in small groups and verify each other's images before uploading them to social media.

Emoji evaluation

 To enable participants to reflect creatively and visually on their learning experience using emojis. 5 minutes

 Interactive whiteboard displaying full range of emojis. 11+

Display a range of emojis on the whiteboard. Ask participants to come up and circle the emoji that they feel most describes how they feel about a session. Ask them to give reasons for their answer. Alternatively if facilities are available and the setting policy permits this, you could ask participants to email, tweet, text their emojis and a single sentence about why they have chosen that emoji.

Notes

1   www.dosreforschools.com/media/1185/lesson-plan-6.pdf

2   www.stonewall.org.uk/school-report-2017

3   www.sexeducationforum.org.uk

Useful resources

In this final section we provide a list of resources that are recommended for educators working with young people in the UK to create and deliver RSE. We have included:

- Useful websites for young people to access, but which are also great sources of information for educators too.
- Free online training resources for educators.
- Relevant guidance documents for educators.
- Educational resources, including session plans and activities.
- Glossaries to help educators and young people identify and understand key terms used in RSE.

We have only included resources that we have used in our own work and that fit with the key principles that guide our approach to RSE (as set out in Chapter 1 of this book). Our list is not exhaustive and we recognise that there will be many other fantastic resources missing. We encourage all educators to also use their personal and professional networks to find out from other RSE educators what resources they are using as new resources are created all the time in order to respond to changes in young people's lives and the world around them. With any resource (including those listed here) it is important that you assess its suitability for the participants that you work with. We recommend using the Sex Education Forum's resources check-list to help you do this: www.sexeducationforum.org.uk/resources/frequently-asked-questions/6-can-you-recommend-good-rse-resources.

Useful websites for young people

Recommended websites for young people to use to access up to date, inclusive and positive information, stories and resources about relationships, sexual health and sexuality. (These are all great sites for educators too!)

- **Amaze:** An American website containing sex education resources for children aged 4–14. Lots of short video clips for young people, as well as resources for educators and parents. https://amaze.org/
- **BISH UK:** This is a UK-based website with lots of information for 14+ young people on sex, sexual health, relationships and much more. It is positive, critical and informative. The site uses great graphics and short films, as well as blogs and information, making it very accessible and user friendly for young people. www.bishuk.com/
- **Brook:** This is a young people friendly website that offers information on all aspects of sex, relationships, bodies and sexual health for young people of all ages. It has lots of detailed text that may not be suitable for low literacy users or young people with additional learning needs. www.brook.org.uk/
- **Scarleteen:** This is a US website packed with extended essays on sex, sexual health, relationships, bodies and much more. This is a positive, critical and informative site that uses lots of text so may not be suitable for low literacy and younger users. www.scarleteen.com/
- **Sexgenlab:** A website that aims to build and disseminate knowledge about sexuality to the general public. Aimed at a US audience but lots of relevant information and articles. This website is not aimed at young people and is only suitable for older young people and those with good English language literacy. https://sexgenlab.org/

Recommended online training for educators

- **Brook Learn** is a free e-learning platform for RSE educators created by Brook. Includes modules on pleasure, consent, relationships and contraception. Also includes some activities to use with young people. https://learn.brook.org.uk
- **DO...RSE for schools**. Whatever your level of experience in delivering RSE it is a good idea to do some self-reflection exercises. *DO...RSE for schools* has activities that provide you with an opportunity to unpack your own personal feelings about things like sex, relationships, education and society before you start planning or delivering an RSE programme. Also includes session plans for KS4 and policy-based resources. www.dosreforschools.com

Guidance documents for educators

- **Best practice toolkit: Abortion education.** Free guidance for practitioners to help develop your abortion education provision from Education for Choice and Brook. www.brook.org.uk/images/brook/professionals/documents/page_content/EFC/efcabortioneducationtoolkit.pdf
- **Facilitation Toolkit; Tips and tricks for participatory and empowering facilitation.** Useful guidance for facilitating inclusive and empowering workshops produced by Transgender Europe. https://tgeu.org/wp-content/uploads/2018/11/FacilitationToolkit_TGEU2018.pdf

- **Guidance on teaching about consent in PSHE education (key stages 3 & 4).** General advice for schools on teaching about consent accompanied by eight lesson plans. Created by the PSHE Association and available for free download. www.pshe-association.org.uk/ curriculum-and-resources/resources/guidance-teaching-about-consent-pshe-education-key

- **Renold, E, & McGeeney, E, (2017)** *Informing the Future of the Sex and Relationships Education Curriculum in Wales*. A summary of recent evidence relating to RSE which is used to inform a set of core principles and key themes for RSE. There is a focus on Wales but this is relevant to educators working in England and all the devolved nations. www.cardiff.ac.uk/ __data/assets/pdf_file/0016/1030606/informing-the-future-of-the-sex-and-relationships-education-curriculum-in-wales-web.pdf

- **RFSU.** The Swedish Association for Sexuality education has a number of free publications to download that may be useful to educators and some older young people. In particular the guides on the penis (Dicktionary), vulva (Pussypedia), vaginal corona and masturbation. www.rfsu.se/om-rfsu/om-oss/in-english/about-rfsu/publications/

- **UNESCO (2018)** *International technical guidance on sexuality education: An evidence-informed approach*. (Revised edition). A summary of international evidence underpinning RSE as well as an example curriculum with eight concepts and corresponding topics and learning objectives. This is an invaluable resource for educators building a new RSE curriculum. www.unaids.org/sites/default/files/media_asset/ITGSE_en.pdf

- **Walsh, J, Mitchell, A & Hudson, M, (2017)** *The Practical Guide to Love, Sex and Relationships* from the Australian Research Centre in Sex, Health and Society, La Trobe University, Melbourne, Australia and based on the original work of Moira Carmody. www.lovesexrelationships.edu.au/

Recommended educational resources and session plans

- **Abortion decisions and dilemmas:** An educational resource for those working with young people aged 13 to 18. Created by Education for choice at Brook. www.brook.org.uk/shop/ product/abortion-decisions-and-dilemmas1

- *AGENDA: A young people's guide to making positive relationships matter.* A set of creative and participatory activities developed with and for young people that are particularly useful for working with young people to find out what is important to them and ensure they are involved in developing the RSE curriculum. Founded by Professor Emma Renold and free to download and use. http://agendaonline.co.uk/ Also see *Primary AGENDA: Supporting Children in making positive relationships matter.* Although aimed at primary aged children (7–11) some of the activities and ideas are useful for RSE with people of all ages. www.egino. cymru/resources/agenda_0319/primary_agenda_en.pdf

- **Assessment, Evaluation and Sex and Relationships Education**. A practical toolkit for education, health and community settings by Simon Blake and Stella Muttock, revised by Sam Beal and Lisa Handy (2012) NCB/JKP. This is an easy to use guide that includes baseline assessment activities, formative and summative assessment ideas as well as evaluation activities.

- **Brook Learn**. This is an e-learning platform with training for educators on relationships, consent, pleasure and other areas of RSE. It also contains activity ideas that can be used directly with young people. It is created by Brook and is free to use. https://learn.brook.org.uk

- **Carmody, M, (2015)** *Sex, Ethics, and Young People*. Springer. This book brings together research and practice on sexuality and violence prevention education offering educators both theory, research and guidance as well as a practical toolkit.

- **DO...RSE for schools**. Free training and resources for educators. Includes session plans on love, communication and consent, safer sex and problem solving. www.dosreforschools.com/how-do-can-help/do-for-educators/lesson-plans-and-stimulus/
- **Expect Respect Education toolkit**. A resource produced by Womankind consisting of a session for each year group from reception to year 13 based on themes that have been found to be effective in tackling domestic abuse. www.womensaid.org.uk/what-we-do/safer-futures/expect-respect-educational-toolkit/
- **Gadd, M, & Hinchliffe, J, (2007)** *Jiwsi: A pick 'n' mix of sex and relationships education activities*. An education resource for educators working with vulnerable young people, including young people with disabilities. www.fpa.org.uk/sites/default/files/jiwsi-sre-activities-english.pdf
- **Health Education UK.** This website offers a wide range of purchasable resources to do with sexual health education. https://healtheducationuk.com/
- **HIV Schools Pack.** Three session plans, a quiz and useful guidance on teaching HIV in Schools in the UK. Created by the National AIDS Trust and free to download. www.nat.org.uk/publication/hiv-schools-pack
- **LGBTI rights activity pack.** An educational resource that enables educators to explore the human rights of sexual and gender minority groups with children and young people. Created by Amnesty International and free to download. www.amnesty.org.uk/resources/lgbti-rights-activity-pack
- **Low Cost, No Cost Youth Work – 101 Positive Activities for Young People.** An online collection of youth work activities created by Vanessa Rogers for the National Youthwork Agency (NYA). Contact the NYA for information about how to access this resource, which is free to members. www.nya.org.uk/resource/low-cost-cost-youth-work-101-positive-activities-young-people/
- **Primary AGENDA: Supporting Children in making positive relationships matter.** A resource containing starter activities and case studies to support educators to work with children aged 7–11 to make positive relationships matter. Although aimed at primary aged children, some of the activities and ideas are useful for RSE with people of all ages. Founded by Professor Emma Renold and free to download and use. www.egino.cymru/resources/agenda_0319/primary_agenda_en.pdf
- **Sex and History.** Session plans and activity ideas that all use a historical object as the starting place for conversation and learning about a number of topics in RSE, such as the body, gender, power, sex, masturbation, etc. Created by researchers and educators at the University of Exeter these resources are free to download and available from a range of online platforms. See http://sexandhistory.exeter.ac.uk/sex-and-relationships-education/; www.tes.com/teaching-resource/sex-and-history-version-2-sre-pshe-key-stage-4-and-5-11162331 and http://lgbthistory.exeter.ac.uk/
- **Sexual Ethics for a Caring Society Curriculum (SECS-C).** Created by Sharon Lamb. A curriculum that is designed to help students develop their own ethical standpoint about sex and sexual behavior. Can be purchased for a small fee or donation. http://sexualethics.org/
- **Sexuality aGender 2: An inclusive Sexual health toolkit.** A set of education resources that can be purchased from The Proud Trust and used to deliver inclusive RSE and sexual health education (ages 13+). www.theproudtrust.org/resources/education-resources/sexuality-agender-inclusive-sexual-health-toolkit-ages-13/
- **Sexuality Education Matters: Preparing pre-service teachers to teach sexuality education** by Debbie Ollis, Lyn Harrison and Claire Maharaj. April 2013. A free training resource aimed at trainee teachers. Some of the activities can be adapted for use with young people.

www.deakin.edu.au/__data/assets/pdf_file/0004/252661/sexuality-education-matters-april-2013-online.pdf

- **The Practical Guide to Love, Sex and Relationships.** A teaching resource for years 7 to 10. Created by the Australian Research Centre in Sex, Health and Society (ARCSHS) at La Trobe University, Australia. www.lovesexrelationships.edu.au/

Glossaries

- **Planned Parenthood Glossary of Sexual Health Terms.** American site but most terms relevant and useful. www.plannedparenthood.org/learn/glossary
- **Scarleteen Glossary.** Useful for young people. www.scarleteen.com/glossary
- **Stonewall LGBT+.** Glossary of terms. www.stonewall.org.uk/help-advice/glossary-terms
- **The Proud Trust.** Glossary of LGBT+ terminology. www.theproudtrust.org/resources/resource-downloads/glossary/